CW01081820

Andrew Lang

Andrew Lang

Writer, Folklorist, Democratic Intellect

JOHN SLOAN

OXFORD
UNIVERSITY PRESS

Great Clarendon Street, Oxford, OX2 6DP,
United Kingdom

Oxford University Press is a department of the University of Oxford.
It furthers the University's objective of excellence in research, scholarship,
and education by publishing worldwide. Oxford is a registered trade mark of
Oxford University Press in the UK and in certain other countries

Published in the United States of America by Oxford University Press
198 Madison Avenue, New York, NY 10016, United States of America

British Library Cataloguing in Publication Data
Data available

Library of Congress Control Number: 2023908030

ISBN 978-0-19-286687-5

DOI: 10.1093/oso/9780192866875.001.0001

Printed and bound in the UK
by Clays Ltd, Elcograf S.p.A.

Links to third party websites are provided by Oxford in good faith and
for information only. Oxford disclaims any responsibility for the materials
contained in any third party website referenced in this work.

Preface

When Andrew Lang died in 1912, his contemporaries were at a loss to do justice to his astonishing range and diversity. He bridged, like no other, scholarship and journalism. He overturned accepted theories in comparative mythology about the linguistic origins of myth. His analysis of household tales, or *märchen*, in the related field of folklore study, was equally ground-breaking, and his enormously successful coloured Fairy Books, edited in partnership with his wife, did much to shift taste in children's literature from tales of real life to fairy stories and fantasy. He was an important influence too in the early phase of the Aesthetic movement in England, with his verse translation of the French Parnassian poets, and as a poet in his own right. As a classical scholar, he single-handedly turned academic opinion in England against the then dominant German theory of Homer's epics as the work of many hands over several centuries, in favour of the unity of the epics, a view generally accepted by the majority of Homeric scholars today. Late in his career, he achieved recognition as a combative, corrective historian. In addition to all these scholarly activities, he revolutionized the high-brow section of the daily newspaper; wrote novels and short stories, some anonymously, and produced numerous articles, reviews, and introductions to other people's books. There seemed something almost uncanny in the speed and variety that book after book, article after article, appeared in his name. It became the joke in literary and academic circles that 'Andrew Lang' was a syndicate of writers, a brand name, not a real person. On Lang's death, Edward Clodd, a fellow member of the Folklore Society, declared that a 'syndicate of assessors' was needed to do bare justice to his 'marvellous versatility'. G. K. Chesterton compared Lang to a 'kind of Indian god with a hundred hands'.

Ever narrowing specialization, and the growing separation of literature and science into the 'two cultures', prevented a full understanding and appreciation of Lang's multidisciplinary approach to learning and writing. Among his contemporaries, many of his fellow writers regarded him primarily as a literary man, a poet and critic, who dabbled as an amateur in other fields. The more informed acknowledged his many-sidedness but stuck to their own areas of expertise. Lang criticism continued along these lines. The first book about

Lang, which appeared thirty years after his death, Roger Lancelyn Green's *Andrew Lang: A Critical Biography* (1946), was essentially an act of homage to Lang as the champion of romance and 'master of fairyland', whose contributions to other fields were of secondary interest, and left for others to judge. The annual Andrew Lang Lecture established by the University of St Andrews in the 1920s and given by specialists in the many diverse fields Lang wrote about, was intended to further Lang's reputation, but by the 1950s, as Lang's contribution to individual disciplines became a subject mainly of historical interest, his reputation faded. From being recognized as one of the most influential men of letters of the late-Victorian and Edwardian periods, Lang became a largely forgotten figure, remembered, if at all, as the compiler of fairy books for children.

There have been recent healthy signs of a revival of critical interest. Andrew Teverson, Alexandra Warwick, and Leigh Wilson, editors of *The Selected Writings of Andrew Lang*, the first scholarly compilation of Lang's varied writings, argue that Lang's privileging of facts over theories, and his practice of making connections across apparently distinct disciplines and genres, were an original and effective way of opening new areas of human enquiry. Nathan K. Hensley, in Penny Fielding and Andrew Taylor's *Nineteenth-Century Literature in Transition: The 1880s*, advocates Lang's method of mediation between fields of knowledge as a model for the practices which modern-day scholarship demands.

It is in the context of this critical revival that the present biography appears. An important key to understanding Lang is the distinctive culture and tradition of generalism in education which retained a strong hold on the Scottish mind. The tradition was one which encouraged a broad range of subjects and taught the value of communication and connection between scholarship and society, between what one learned and the shared ethos and concerns of the whole community. Hence the term 'democratic intellectualism' sometimes given to it. That generalist, egalitarian spirit of enquiry found expression, in Lang's case, in the emerging human and social sciences—anthropology, comparative mythology and religion, evolutionary psychology—in a period of rapidly advancing literacy and education. In the field of Scottish historiography, Catriona Macdonald has suggested that Lang's challenge to the accepted narratives of Scottish national history casts doubt on the supposed decline in the nineteenth century of that intellectual tradition. Lang won a Snell scholarship to Balliol College, Oxford. At the time, the idea of a specialist, English-style model of education was gaining some support in Scotland, but there remained strong opposition, and for the bright and ambitious, Oxbridge was still considered the way to academic and social advancement. As A. D. Lindsay, the Scottish-born Master of Balliol observed, the Snell Exhibition awards were a typical example of Oxford 'training and anglicising young Scots intellectuals'. A striking feature of Lang's character and writing practice was that alongside his specialist academic success at Oxford, first as an undergraduate at Balliol College, then as a classics fellow of Merton College, he never lost his generalist instincts and habits of mind. Though socially conservative, he was, throughout his life, resolutely non-political.

Lang's history is fascinating not just for his unique consilience of interests, but for the light it sheds on changes in social and cultural life in the last quarter of the Victorian era. His fellowship at Merton College coincided with reforms that transformed university life—a reduction in the number of fellows in Holy Orders; the admission of married dons; and an extension of the range of study to include 'all branches of useful learning'. After he resigned his Oxford fellowship, he enjoyed a highly successful career in literary journalism, but by keeping up his connections with Oxford and St Andrews and by continuing to contribute to scholarship, he highlights the sometimes uneasy, but reciprocally beneficial interchange between the university and the literary world, between the proverbial 'Grub Street and the ivory tower'. More controversially, Lang's life also raises uncomfortable questions about the reluctance of his generation to confront the darker aspects of the previous Age of Improvement to which he and his generation owed their material and cultural advantages. The brutal part Lang's maternal grandfather had played as factor to the Duchess of Sutherland, in the eviction of Highland crofters to make way for sheep farming, left a stain on the family name. The effect of that legacy on Lang's life and work has until now been almost entirely overlooked. The sins of the past touched many in the Victorian age. Lang's Bristol-born wife, Leonora Blanche Alleyne, was the daughter of Charles Thomas Alleyne, a former slave plantation owner in Barbados, who received generous financial compensation from the British government following the Slavery Abolition Act of 1833 and returned to England.

This critical biography is the first frank and fully documented account of Lang's personal life and professional career. I have adopted a chronological approach, convinced that far from making it difficult to follow all the byways of Lang's thought, as Roger Lancelyn Green supposed, a chronological approach provides greater understanding of their origins and of the interconnections between Lang's life and work. Green's life of Lang was, by his own admission, not a biography 'in the ordinary sense of the word'. He thought it probable there never would be one, owing to what he claimed was 'the complete absence of all biographical materials of a personal and intimate nature'. Lang, the most guarded and private of men, certainly put obstacles in the way of biographers. He burned most letters he received as soon as read and instructed his wife to destroy his personal papers on his death. His widow, helped by her niece, dutifully carried out his wishes and reportedly complained that 'her wrists ached for weeks' after tearing up his papers. But many thousands of Lang's personal as well as business letters have survived. Marysa Demoor's excellent editions of Lang's correspondence with his American friends, and with Robert Louis Stevenson, are valuable for the light they shed on literary and cultural life in the late-Victorian and Edwardian period. These are only a tiny proportion of his surviving unpublished correspondence. The largest collection of his personal papers is held at St Andrews University and includes numerous letters to his family and close friends. There are also significant collections in other British institutions, and holdings of manuscripts and correspondence in the United States. More letters have come to light during the preparation of this book: Lang's personal and business correspondence with Charles Longman, his publisher; his widow Leonora Lang's papers and private correspondence; and previously unknown collections of letters to Charles Longman's sister, Mrs Emmeline Puller; to John Addington Symonds, a neighbour and close friend of Lang's wife in Clifton, Bristol; to Anne Thackeray Ritchie, the novelist's daughter; to his Scottish friends, Ella Christie and her sister, Mrs Alice King Stewart; to Professor Gilbert Murray; to Edward Clodd; and to Sir Oliver Lodge and Sir William Barrett of the Society for Psychical Research. The first challenge for Lang's biographer is not the absence of correspondence, but Lang's almost indecipherable handwriting, which, in Lang's forties, deteriorated into a series of spidery dashes and strokes. Fortunately, with patience and familiarity, the handwriting becomes decipherable.

I am grateful to the following for the help I received during the writing of the book: St Andrews University; the Master and Fellows, Balliol College, Oxford; the National Library of Scotland; Bodleian Library, Oxford; Pitt Rivers Museum, Oxford; Merton College, Oxford; St Edmund Hall, Oxford; the Old Library of the Oxford Union; Cambridge University Library, which holds the archives of the Society for Psychical Research; Trinity College, Cambridge; the University of Bristol Library; Edinburgh University Library; the Brotherton Library, University of Leeds; the University of London; the University of Reading; Columbia University, New York; Eton College Library; Bristol Archives; the British Library; Cheshire Archives and Local Studies;

Dundee Central Library; Heritage Hub, Hawick; Hertfordshire Record Office; Hove Central Library; Norwich Public Libraries.

I am grateful to my sister Sheila Boyle for her assistance with the illustrations, and to my wife, Elizabeth who helped me copy and transcribe archive material at the National Library of Scotland and Hove Central Library.

Contents

List of Illustrations xii
Abbreviations xiv

1. A Curious Boy 1

2. Looking South 15

3. Under Jowett's Wing 27

4. 'Young Oxford' 40

5. The New 'Pen' 62

6. Holding Course 87

7. Captaining 'The Ship' 110

8. A Double Existence 130

9. Turning Historian 158

10. Unexpected Honours 182

11. The Last Cast 201

Epilogue 225

Notes 229
Select Bibliography 265
Index 271

List of Illustrations

Figure 1.1. Patrick Sellar, Lang's grandfather, in 1851. From a painting by Sir Daniel Macnee, reproduced in Eleanor M. Sellar's *Recollections and Impressions*. W. Blackwood, 1907. Reproduced courtesy of the Trustees of the National Library of Scotland. 3

Figure 2.1. St Leonard's Hall group, 1861–2. Lang, *back row second from left*, resting his arm on the shoulder of Henry Brown. Others, *back row from left to right*: Mr Rhoades, S. Deas, R. Pringle, A.E. Henderson, R. Cox. *Front row*: J. Patterson, D. Younger, W. Gordon. Reproduced courtesy of the University of St Andrews Libraries and Museums, ID: ms38243. 16

Figure 3.1. Lang, *on right*, in 1866, age 22, during his second long vacation from Balliol College, with his brothers, John, 17, Craig, 14, and seated, Thomas William (T.W.), 12. Reproduced courtesy of the University of St Andrews Libraries and Museums, ID: ms38243. 31

Figure 5.1. Lang in the 1880s. Reproduced courtesy of the University of St Andrews Libraries and Museums, ID: ms38243. 74

Figure 5.2. Leonora Blanche (Nora) Lang. Reproduced courtesy of the National Library of Scotland. 75

Figure 5.3. Frontispiece for *The Library*. Drawn by Walter Crane. Public domain. 80

Figure 6.1. 'Andrew Lang'. From a painting by Sir William Blake Richmond. Photograph by Frederick Hollyer. © National Portrait Gallery, London. 103

Figure 7.1. Drawing by Ernest Haskell. Reproduced courtesy of the University of St Andrews Libraries and Museums, ID: msPR4867.C7 (ms922). 116

Figure 8.1. 'The Turtle Outwitted'. Illustration by H.J. Ford for *The Brown Fairy Book*. Public domain. 138

Figure 8.2. Nora as Mrs Malaprop in Sheridan's *The Rivals*, 1893. Nora's hand embroidered dress was made in the 1770s, the decade in which *The Rivals* was first performed. Reproduced courtesy of the National Library of Scotland. 146

Figure 8.3. Lang delivering his Presidential Address at the opening of the International Folklore Congress at Burlington House on 1 October 1891. *The Daily Graphic*, Friday 2 October 1891. Public domain. 149

Figure 9.1. 'La Pucelle Blessée'. Drawn by Selwyn Image for *A Monk of Fife*.
Public domain.   161

Figure 9.2. Lang in 1895. From Herbert Maxwell's *Evening Memories*.
Alexander Maclehose & Co., 1932. Public domain.   166

Figure 10.1. Lang, about 1902, by Walter L. Colls. From the frontispiece of
Lang's *Poetical Works*, volume III. Public domain.   192

Abbreviations

Balliol	Historic Collections Centre, Balliol College, Oxford.
BL	Manuscript Collections, British Library.
Bodleian	Bodleian Library, Oxford.
Bristol	University of Bristol Library.
Brotherton	Brotherton Library, University of Leeds.
Cheshire	Cheshire Archives and Local Studies.
Columbia	Frederick Coykendall Collection, Columbia University.
Eton	Eton College Collections.
Hawick	The Heritage Hub, Hawick.
Hertford	Hertfordshire Record Office.
Hove	The Wolseley Collection, Hove Central Library.
London	University of London Library, Senate House.
NLS	National Library of Scotland, Edinburgh.
Norfolk	Norwich Public Library Manuscript Collection, Norfolk Record Office.
Pitt Rivers	Manuscript Collection, Pitt Rivers Museum, Oxford.
Reading	University of Reading Library.
St Andrews	The Andrew Lang Collection, University of St Andrews Special Collections.
SPR, Cambridge	Society for Psychical Research, University of Cambridge.
Trinity	Special Collections, Trinity College, Cambridge.

1

A Curious Boy

A statue of Sir Walter Scott, erected in 1839, overlooks to this day the wide, sloping market place of Selkirk, the town in the Scottish Borders where Andrew Lang was born. Scott stands guard before the courthouse where Lang's grandfather and namesake, as Sheriff-clerk of Selkirk, sat at Scott's right hand when Sir Walter—then plain Mr Scott—was sheriff of the county. The Lang family had maintained positions of influence in the town's affairs since the sixteenth century, when John Lang had risen from the ranks of the guild of tailors to become Dean of the Five Trades.[1] Some of the women who married into the Lang family came from more illustrious stock. Lang's grandmother, Margaret, the daughter of Thomas Suter, Sheriff-clerk of Ross-shire, claimed descent on her mother's side from a great historic family, the Scotts of Harden. Her uncle, Gideon Scott, left the small private landholding of Overwells, at Jedburgh, to Lang's father, John, who, as 'John Lang of Overwells', was the first in the family with the status of property owner. He succeeded to the offices of sheriff-clerk and agent of the British Linen Bank on the death of Lang's grandfather. The Langs of Selkirk were essentially dutiful, local men, whose existence went largely unnoticed in the wider society.

This was not so with the Sellars, Lang's mother's side. The part played by his maternal grandfather, Patrick Sellar, in the Highland Clearances earlier in the century was a matter of historical record and widespread controversy. The son of Thomas Sellar of Westfield, an Elgin lawyer, Lang's grandfather studied law before taking up the post of factor or land agent on the Duke and Duchess of Sutherland's estate, responsible for the removal of crofters to make way for sheep farming. The plan was to resettle them on coastal allotments and encourage them to better themselves through education and profitable industry. The motive was also to make money on a grand scale. Patrick Sellar regarded the Gaelic-speaking Highland people as little more than primitive aborigines. The speed and rough handling of his evictions, often accompanied by taunts and jokes, met with resistance and violent confrontations. Cottages were burnt to prevent reoccupation. Matters reached a head with his arrest and trial for 'culpable homicide, oppression and real injury', when an old, bed-ridden, 90-year-old woman died following a chaotic and rancorous

Andrew Lang. John Sloan, Oxford University Press. © John Sloan (2023). DOI: 10.1093/oso/9780192866875.003.0001

removal at Strathnaver, in north Sutherland. Despite the weight of eyewitness testimony that the cottage was set alight before the old woman was carried out, the jury, made up principally of local landowners, acquitted him of all charges.[2] The case outraged land agitators and defenders of crofters' rights. A Gaelic 'aoir'—a verse satire—written by Domhnall Bàillidh shortly after the trial described Patrick Sellar in bitter, mocking terms, as a devouring wolf, with a nose like an iron plough share—he had, as a photograph shows, a large nose (see Figure 1.1). The poem was preserved in Prince Edward Island, Canada, where many of the evicted emigrated.[3]

Sellar, unrepentant, prospered as a sheep farmer at Morvich on the lands in Sutherland where he had carried out the evictions. He married Ann Craig, the daughter of an Elgin farmer, and they had nine children—seven sons and two daughters. His oldest daughter, Jane, was Andrew Lang's mother. She discovered while growing up that the pretty girl with the same name as herself who was 'always in the kitchen', was her father's 'accidental daughter' by his housekeeper before his marriage.[4] Sellar, called 'the Governor' by his children, was known to have driven his sons hard to be top of their class at school, as the way to getting ahead in the world and making money. Tom, the eldest, enjoyed success as a trader with the Merchant Banking Company of Dennistoun, working in Liverpool and New Orleans. Pat also joined the company but went home to Sutherland to help his father manage the Morvich estate. Willie, who remained top of his class at school and university, was elected a fellow at Oriel College, Oxford. Lang, as a small boy, found his grandfather an intimidating figure. Asked in later years by a compiler of Sutherland folklore if there had ever been reports of ghosts at Morvich Lodge, the Sellar family home, he responded wryly, 'Spooks in a body would have given my grandfather a wide berth'.[5]

Lang's mother and father were married at Morvich on 13 April 1843. He was 30; she, 21. They made the two-hundred-mile journey south to begin married life at Viewfield, a single-story, bay-fronted house on elevated grounds off Scott Place, a short walk to the centre of Selkirk. It was here, on 31 March 1844, that Andrew Lang was born, the first of eight children. Gideon Scott, the third child, named after their father's great-uncle and benefactor, died at just a year old, when Lang was 4. According to local memory, few in Selkirk at that time received the title of 'Mister' when spoken of or spoken to, and just two got 'Mistress'. Lang's mother was one; the other was the Minister's wife at the Manse.[6]

Lang recalled learning to read at about the age of 4, by picking out the letters of the elegy of Cock Robin, which he already knew by heart.[7] Victorian

Figure 1.1 Patrick Sellar, Lang's grandfather, in 1851. From a painting by Sir Daniel Macnee, reproduced in Eleanor M. Sellar's *Recollections and Impressions*. W. Blackwood, 1907.

chapbooks for small children often combined popular fairy stories and tales of legendary heroes with the alphabet or a spelling primer. Fairy books were his favourite reading. He wrote, 'a boy of five is more at home in Fairyland than in his own country'. He recorded that early joy in his 'Ballade of a Bookworm':

> The number of his years is IV,
> And yet in letters hath he skill,
> How deep he dives in fairy-lore![8]

Selkirkshire enjoyed a rich tradition of folklore and oral storytelling. Walter Scott, whose writings gave literary form to local tales and legends, had a special place in the Lang house. Lang said of Scott that he was 'not an author like another, but our earliest known friend in letters ... Scott peopled for us the rivers and burnsides with his reivers; the Fairy Queen came out of Eildon Hill and haunted Carterhaugh'.[9] Such tales caused him night fears as a child. Later in life, he paid tribute in verse to an older girl cousin, who 'exorcised the Ghostly Fears/That flocked about my Bed in dozens'.[10] He thought it odd that he had never experienced the same terror of the Devil and hell fire which seemed to have blighted the childhood of many of his friends and fellow writers. At Viewfield, as in other Scottish homes, only the Bible was permitted reading on Sunday, and, like other Scottish children, he learned obediently to recite the Shorter Catechism, but in his case the words had no meaning or actuality, and nobody at home 'was so unkind as to interpret the significance of the questions and answers'.[11] Robert Louis Stevenson, who grew up in a strict Presbyterian household, wrote harrowingly of his childhood terror of sin and eternal punishment on the Day of Judgement. Lang recalled that for himself as a child, 'the last Day seemed a long way off'.[12]

Lang's family, according to a descendent, were 'High Church Episcopalians who did not find it easy living in a Presbyterian community'. As a young boy, he 'attended a local Presbyterian church, but travelled to Edinburgh two or three times a year to take communion at St Paul's Episcopal Church'.[13] Lang's Episcopalian childhood throws light on some key aspects of his later life and work: his emotional and imaginative attachment to the House of Stuart, for example, and his disputes with Presbyterian historians on their account of the Reformation. It perhaps also accounts in part for his general guardedness about his private life. Religious persecution and restriction were things of the past in the Victorian period, but some in the Presbyterian Church of Scotland, the nation's dominant church, continued to regard the 'English Kirk', as they called it, and the Romanist tendencies of High Church Anglicanism, with a degree of suspicion.

Lang was 6 when his mother took the family to 'the south of England' for a year for her own and her children's health. They stayed, in fact, in Clifton, where her brother Tom had been sent ten years before to recover from illness.[14] Clifton Hotwells had begun to regain some of the popularity it had once enjoyed as a fashionable watering-place in the eighteenth century. A new pump room had been built, with adjacent reading rooms, and the dome-lit swimming pool restored.[15] A feature article in the *Illustrated London News* during their stay praised its beautiful walks on the heights of Clifton Downs 'made interesting by the constant passing and repassing of steamboats and other vessels'.[16]

Lang's memory of their stay was of finding a 'paradise, a circulating library with brown, greasy, ill-printed, odd volumes of Shakespeare and the Arabian Nights'.[17] His mother's sister Helen joined them at Clifton. She was engaged to Alexander Whishaw, a young vicar at Chipping Norton in Oxfordshire, and they were to be married that September at Clifton Church. The Sellar family began to arrive in the days before the wedding. Four carriages conveyed the wedding party to what his mother called light-heartedly 'Helen's execution'. A letter to her friend Helen Brown at Elgin gave a lively account of the wedding: the bride in a pink bonnet and velvet dress with a white lace shawl; their 'Mamma' looking 'beautiful in a grey velvet gown, and honiton lace cap'; and the children 'at church, and very much delighted'. She wrote, 'After signing in the vestry we all returned here to luncheon. It was very handsome, & the champagne flowed largely'. The whole party went the next day on an excursion to Tintern Abbey, which meant crossing the Severn Estuary to Chepstow by steamer and taking the Wye Valley turnpike road to the famous ruins, a popular destination for romantic sightseers. The flirtatiousness of 15-year-old Miss Tibby Cross earned his mother's disapproval: 'The gentlemen all admire Miss Tibby immensely. *I* did not. A forward thing, I call her ... I daresay she is pretty, but the adulation she has met with since she came here is enough to turn a steadier head'.[18] Lang liked the 'forward' Tibby, who later published a collection of poems.[19] When he was older, she encouraged him to read Robert Browning's *Men and Women*, and to add Browning to his pantheon of poets.[20]

The excitements of the wedding over, they began packing for their return to Scotland. Lang's grandparents and Uncle Willie were the first to leave. Willie was Lang's favourite uncle. He loved his uncle's composure and lack of self-importance. Growing up, he tried to be like him. It was known in the family that Willie was deeply unhappy with life as an Oxford Don. His former tutor at Balliol College, and now his close friend, Benjamin Jowett had found him in the vacation depressed and secretly self-medicating at the spa town of Malvern.[21] Oriel College was sensitive. It was agreed that Willie could retain his Oxford fellowship but be allowed to transfer to Glasgow University to assist his old teacher, Professor William Ramsay, who was ill. Lang's grandfather was heard to say that he had lain awake through the night blaming himself for his son's illness and regretting having driven Willie so hard when he was young. This surprised Jowett, coming as it did from a man who seemed always to believe he was right.[22]

Lang's grandfather fell ill on his return from Clifton and died, aged 70, the following October. In a codicil to his will, made twelve days before his death, he instructed that, after provision for his wife, the remainder of his estate should be divided equally between his sons 'share and share alike'—an alteration made at the insistence of the eldest, Tom, who had stood to have it all. He also left instructions for payment of the marriage settlements of £3000 to his daughter Jane's husband John Lang, and his daughter Helen's husband Alexander Whishaw, to be made payable from the estate. He was buried in Elgin Cathedral churchyard, with the whole family present, Helen and Alexander Whishaw having made a rapid journey north from Chipping Norton to attend the funeral. Four months later, Helen too was dead, from sepsis following the birth of a baby boy.[23]

Lang started school when he was 7, a usual age at that time. Selkirk was in process of transformation from declining, old-fashioned market town into a more populous and prosperous mill town. Large woollen mills were springing up along the river Ettrick. There were about two hundred boys at Selkirk Parochial and Grammar School, which taught the three 'Rs' and gave lessons on geography, history, and the Shorter Catechism, and, for the more able boys, the rudiments of Latin. The newly appointed rector, Alexander Scott, also inspired pupils with his love of botany and science.[24] Dickens's *Hard Times*, published when Lang was 10, satirized the educational emphasis on 'Facts, facts, facts'. Dickens feared the rise of industry and manufacture would destroy the child's moral and imaginative world of fancy. In fact, traditional tales, beliefs, and practices were still part of the lingering fabric of social life and experience in Victorian manufacturing towns and cities.[25] Lang, growing up, combined a retentive and prodigious memory for facts and out-of-the-way information with a continuing love of fairy tales and romance. His Aunt Eleanor, after her marriage to his Uncle Willie, was astonished on her first visit to Viewfield to see him, age 8, reading six books at once, laid out on chairs. She could not at first believe he understood them, but Lang's mother assured her he knew what was in all of them.[26] Lang believed he derived his love of books from forebears on both sides of the family—on his mother's side from his grandmother, a great reader; on his father's from his grandfather, whose library of over 500 books remained in the family at Viewfield. Lang tried them all in turn.[27] Two of his favourites were Kenny Meadows' illustrated volumes of Shakespeare and the antiquarian Robert Pitcairn's *Ancient Criminal Trials of Scotland*, which no one else in the family had read.[28] Fact and fiction, the real and imagined world, united and interested him. He carried into adult life an awareness that ordinary people could be more widely read than academics in their study, and that learning was not solely the province of an intellectual elite.

Previous accounts generally suppose that Lang passed his first ten years 'in his pleasant Selkirk home, broken only by the one long visit to England'.[29] In fact, Lang travelled much in Scotland as a child and came to know the history and traditions of different places. It was an age when people travelled by slow train, and remoter places could still only be reached by coach. One of his earliest memories, at about the age of 4, was hearing the watchman in Aberdeen wake the sleeping city with his cry, 'Four o'clock on a misty morning!'[30] He was again in the north-east, this time in Elgin, when he was 7, for his grandfather's funeral. A great-aunt on his mother's side Margaret Craig, told him of the heroism of Jacobite forebears in the rising of 1745, most notably Nelly McWilliam, from Gauldwell, who was engaged to Lord John Roy Stewart, an officer of Prince Charles's army, who was wounded at Culloden. She hid him in a cave the day after the battle, while she entertained the Duke of Cumberland's English officer and troops who were searching for him. She nursed him to recovery and helped him to get to the coast, where he took a ship to France, never to return. She never married, and on her instructions the bloody handkerchief which she had taken from his wound was placed over her face when she was buried.[31] From his great-aunt Margaret he also heard the fairy tales 'Rashin Coatie' and 'Nicht Nought Nothing', the first a Scottish version of 'Cinderella', the second of the Jason story, which he enjoyed so much that she wrote them down for him in broad Scots.[32] He was, he said, 'a born folklorist'.[33]

From Elgin they travelled further north to Morvich Lodge, his mother's childhood home in Sutherland. This meant travel by coach to the coast, and a ferry voyage, hugging the dangerous rocky coastline. Their landing point, Dunrobin Castle—the seat of the Duke and Duchess of Sutherland—looked like a palace in a fairy tale, with its towering, flag-topped turrets, and gardens extending down to the sea, but inland the gloomy hills and straths of that corner of south-east Sutherland, where his grandfather had carried out evictions, looked desolate and empty except for grazing, Cheviot sheep. The great gathering place for the Sellar family was not Morvich, but the house and estate of Ardtornish, in Argyllshire, his grandfather's home in his later years. The whole family gathered at Ardtornish in summer, 1853, when Lang was 9, Lang's uncles with their young wives and new-born babies. Though geographically dispersed, the Sellar family remained close and clannish, in a resolutely Scottish way. Ardtornish was reachable by steamer from Oban. The ship had to anchor out on the Sound of Mull, and passengers, on embarking and disembarking in an open boat, were hoisted up and down the towering black hull, with babies, luggage, and, if it was dark, dimly burning lanterns.[34] The house stood on a wooded hillside, beyond the seaward ruin of Ardtornish Castle, the seat centuries earlier to the chiefs of Clan Donald, Lord of the Isles. Ardtornish was a place of adventure for Lang as a boy, with coastal cliff walks, excursions to a cascading waterfall in the high woods, and fishing in the small, salt-water Loch Aline. There were lighthouses, built by the Stevenson family, at Eilean Musdile on the west tip of Lismore and further north-west at Ardnamurchan Point, but his grandmother always lit a lamp high up in the house as a beacon to be seen out at sea at night by the fishing boats and other vessels passing up and down the Sound of Mull.[35] Lang, on learning that the Poet Laureate, Alfred Lord Tennyson, had visited earlier that summer, caused laughter by asking if Tennyson was 'a real poet, like Sir Walter Scott'.[36]

The gathering that summer was not entirely joyful. The family was concerned about renewed publicity regarding the Sutherland Clearances and the threat to the family's reputation. That spring the Duchess of Sutherland had hosted an anti-slavery petition at Stafford House, her London residence, with Harriet Beecher Stowe, an abolitionist and the best-selling author of *Uncle Tom's Cabin*, as guest of honour. This angered the defenders of American Southern institutions, enemies of abolitionism, and resulted in the reprinting of Donald MacLeod's *Gloomy Memories of the Highlands*, which had first appeared as a series of letters to the *Edinburgh Evening News* when Lang's grandfather was still alive. MacLeod, who claimed to have been an eyewitness to the events in Sutherland as a boy, described in shocking detail the ruthlessness of the evictions and the suffering of the Gaelic Highland population. Most damaging of all to the family, MacLeod quoted another present at the Strathnaver evictions who said that when he told Patrick Sellar of the poor old woman trapped in a burning cottage and unable to move, Sellar retorted, 'Damn her, the old witch, she has lived too long; let her burn'.[37] Harriet Beecher Stowe proved a friend to the family. She published a spirited defence of the Sutherland estate, pointing out that Patrick Sellar had been awarded heavy damages in his action against the sheriff-substitute who had brought the charges against him.[38] Lang was given a copy of her *Uncle Tom's Cabin* to read—the first book, he recalled, that 'ever made me cry'.[39] Though it might seem fanciful to imagine that Lang, as a boy of 9, would have taken notice of the concerns of the grown-ups, he displayed in his later life and writings a noticeable urge to defend those whose doubtful actions left a stain on their memory.

Lang's awareness of the world was widened by family contacts in the colonies. Opportunities in Selkirk were limited, and three of his father's brothers had emigrated to Australia, where they became pastoral pioneers and made peace with the Aborigines. The youngest, Gideon Scott Lang, published two books describing their experiences and their dealings with the indigenous tribes.[40] Lang played as a boy with 'lots of spears and boomerangs from Australia', and though he could 'never do very much with a boomerang', he learned to 'throw a spear to a hair's breadth'. The poultry, he remembered, 'used to have a hard time of it'.[41] Those original artefacts marked the beginning of an interest in Aboriginal folklore and customs that stayed with him all his life and formed an important strand of his writings on mythology, folklore, and the primitive origins of religion.

Lang's life changed decisively when he was sent, age 10, to Edinburgh Academy. The ill-effects on his Uncle Willie's health of social isolation and over-concentration on study as a boy did not deter the family from setting him on the same path. Admittedly, times had changed, and schooling was not the 'dull and plodding course of study', or 'incessant strain', it had been for his Uncle Willie.[42] The new emphasis in education was as much on character formation as on acquiring knowledge. Thomas Hughes's novel of 1857, *Tom Brown's Schooldays*, gave popular expression to the importance of sport and physical games. Lang was able to indulge his love of games, especially cricket, which had been introduced to Selkirk when he was a small boy, by two Yorkshiremen, up north to fit new looms in the woollen mills.[43] Nevertheless, his life for the next two years was a miserable, 'rather lonely' existence, spent 'in the house of an aged relation'.[44] A letter from his mother to her sister-in-law at Morvich, Agnes Sellar, suggests that the 'aged relation' was his grandmother, Mrs Margaret Lang, who had moved to Edinburgh after the death of his grandfather.[45]

Edinburgh Academy had opened in 1824 with the aim of providing a school in Scotland to rival English public schools, particularly in the teaching of Classics. A Classics master was head of each year group as it progressed through the school. Lang was in Mr Trotter's year. Lang remembered 'Old Trot', a tall, spindly man who dragged them through the Latin grammar.[46] Classes ran from 9 o'clock in the morning until 3 o'clock in the afternoon, with two breaks of a quarter of an hour. Novel-reading filled Lang's lonely out-of-school hours. The song of Lucy Ashton, the shy, unworldly heroine of Walter Scott's novel *The Bride of Lammermoor*, ran in his head on his way to school. Looking back on this time he thought its life-denying message a strange 'motto in life' for a boy of 10:

> 'Look not thou on beauty's charming,
> Sit thou still when kings are arming,
> Taste not when the wine-cup glistens,
> Speak not when the people listens.
> Stop thine ear against the singer,
> From the red gold keep thy finger,
> Vacant heart, and hand, and eye,
> Easy live and quiet die'.[47]

His obsessive reading habit caused concern, and he was banned for a time from reading novels, until it simply resulted in him reading Byron's *Don Juan* instead. He came later to wish the ban had been kept in place longer and that he been older before reading Poe's 'The Black Cat', 'The Pit and the Pendulum', and 'The Murders in the Rue Morgue', stories which left him unable to sleep, terrified of 'being buried alive' and 'of waking up before breakfast to find myself in a coffin'.[48] Yet he never thought of literature or novel-reading in his boyhood as an unhealthy escape from, or avoidance of life. He recognized something of himself on reading the life of the poet and anthologist, Francis Palgrave, saying of Palgrave, 'Literature was to him, as Scott says it should be, a staff, not a crutch. For me too, long ago'.[49]

He was considered a curious boy. George Dundas, then Sheriff of Selkirk-shire, who had just given a talk to the school, wrote to John Lang, his sheriff-clerk, saying how impressed and entertained he had been by young Andrew:

> He is a clever and very curious little fellow, with more general information than I ever remember having met with in one of his age. One of his most startling facts was brought out on the occasion of my showing him and the other boys of the party a collar of the Order of St. George, and explaining how St. George, the Cappadocian, after being an Archbishop, had become

the Tutelar Saint of England. 'Oh, if it's him,' said Andrew, 'he was a mean fellow; I know very well about him. He was a bacon-contractor for the Roman army'. ... On coming home, and referring to Gibbon, I found that it was so, though I had quite forgotten the fact in the history of the saint. The boy has many things in his character and manner that require to be corrected and watched—as all boys of any character have; but on the whole he is a remarkably nice little man, and I venture to prophecy that he will 'make a spoon or spoil a horn' yet.[50]

What required to be corrected and watched is easily guessed: no one likes a know-all. In *Prince Prigio*, Lang's humorous fairy tale for children, the moral lesson learnt by the hero is that it is far cleverer 'to *seem* no *cleverer* than other people, so people will like him'.[51]

When he was 12, Lang exchanged his 'hermitage', as he called it, for the 'very different and very disagreeable world of a master's house'.[52] The school's founders had originally planned to build a boarding house along the lines of English public schools, but it remained unbuilt, and individual masters took boarders in their homes. Lang boarded first at Professor D'Arcy Wentworth Thompson's house in Bellevue Terrace, a short walk from the school, at a cost of £60 a year, with extra fees for private tuition, for his subscription to the cricket-field and 'Private Cricket-Club', and 15/- a quarter for his pew at Broughton Church, where he day-dreamed through many a dreary sermon.[53]

Lang was fond of his housemaster who 'kept a houseful of books', which he left 'within reach', showing him 'what struck him as being worth reading'.[54] The disagreeable side of the master's house was the bullying. It did not matter if your father was a solicitor, as Lang's was, or if you were the son of a duke. No one escaped. Lang said with his own experience clearly in mind, 'The life of small boys at school (before they get into long-tailed coats and the upper-fifth) is often a mere "laying-off"—a relapse into native savagery with its laws and customs'. He sometimes wondered whether there was something wrong with him, and he had been born civilized.[55]

Schooling at Edinburgh Academy, in conformity with the generalist tradition of Scottish education, included a broad range of learning. But in attempting to match the success of English public schools, the founders also made provision for 'a more extended instruction in Greek', than was usual in Scottish schools. The relative neglect of Greek in other Scottish schools until then was in part cultural. Scotland, like France, inclined more to Latinity than Hellenism. In the lower school, Greek, with its 'fantastically irregular'

verbs and near unintelligible 'middle voice', was for Lang a 'plague and torment' which he detested 'with a deadly and sickening hatred'.[56] That changed
in the upper classes when the Rector, James Stephen ('Goudie') Hodson, an
Englishman and Oxford graduate, took over the teaching of classics. Hodson
dressed in the style of an academic of distinction with velvet kid gloves, black
frock coat, and narrow trousers. He had a haughty and disdainful manner
and speech to match. No one was spared his sharp tongue: boys he disliked,
parents, even the long-suffering directors of the school, who tried unsuccess-
fully to remove him on more than one occasion.[57] Hodson encouraged literary
enjoyment rather than narrow grammatical instruction. He set the class long
passages of the *Iliad* or *Odyssey*, and, when the work was done, made them
read on adventurously for themselves, translating as best they could 'without
grammar or dictionary'.[58] At a turn, Lang began to love Homer—'the surge
and thunder of the hexameters'; the wonderfully imaginative mix of fantas-
tic story with reality and 'love of detail'. The recent excavations of Mycenae
had given historical reality to Homer's world. Lang remembered that he used
to 'stare wistfully' at a picture of the ancient ruins and 'Lion Gate' of Mycenae
and 'think of how Agamemnon had driven his chariot through the portal, with
all his spears behind him, on his way to besiege Troy'.[59]

The year Lang turned 15 was the Centenary of Robert Burns's birth. On
25 January, in towns and cities throughout the English-speaking world, commemorations were held in his honour—a popular tribute unimaginable for any
other poet, apart from Shakespeare. In Edinburgh, many of the shops closed
at two o'clock, and there were banquets and festivals throughout the day.[60] At
the Crystal Palace in Sydenham, outside London, 14,000 people attended a
grand afternoon concert, followed by the unveiling of Calder Marshall's bust
of Burns, and the recitation of the winning poem in the Burns Centenary
Competition.[61] To Lang's amazement, the runner-up for the fifty-guinea prize
was a 16-year-old schoolboy from Cheltenham College, called Frederic Myers,
with whom he later became friends. Myers' ode, which the judges considered
'nearly equal to the prize poem', addressed in passionate rhetoric the conflict of
'a great heart by low passions swayed'. Lang read the poem 'with a kind of
awe'.[62] He himself tried writing poems, which he showed to his mother, who
rather dampened his spirits by telling him 'to rhyme was one thing, and to be
a poet quite another'.[63] A short story, which he entered for a newspaper short
story prize competition, met with similar lack of success.[64]

He met his first real-life author, James Payn, at dinner at the Sellar family house in Edinburgh. Payn, a regular contributor to Dickens's *Good Words*,
was in Edinburgh to edit the popular literary *Chambers' Journal*. Lang was

dazzled by his 'black curly hair and handsome, laughing face'.[65] He became for him a model of the university man whose literary tastes and talk flew in the face of narrow academic pursuits. Payn knew all the great writers of the day—Dickens, Trollope, Wilkie Collins, Thackeray. Payn himself seemed to have stepped out of the pages of Thackeray's *Pendennis*. Payn moved to London shortly after, unable to bear the Edinburgh east wind and the grim restrictions of the Scottish Sabbath, which earned him a reprimand from his landlady simply for drawing up the window-blinds;[66] but he left in Lang's young mind an image of the successful literary man—versatile, good-humoured, and without pretentions.

Lang finished his schooling at Edinburgh Academy when he was 17. Ardtornish, the Sellar family estate in Argyllshire, had been sold the previous year, and for a second summer his uncle Willie leased Harehead, a beautiful house on the banks of the Yarrow, a few miles from Selkirk. He and his uncle went for long walks together, and he cherished nostalgic memories of his small cousins 'in their scarlet cloaks, running on the green beside the river'.[67] The two families saw much of each other, the Sellars generally lunching at the Langs' on Sundays, after going to church in Selkirk.[68] They discussed his future, and it was felt best that he should continue his studies at St Andrews University, where his Uncle Willie was now the Professor of Greek. He went along happily with this, although he had no ambition to excel as a student or to follow his uncle into academia. He had already decided what he wanted to do in life.

He spoke long after of this to Robert Louis Stevenson, who had attended Edinburgh Academy at the same time, though a younger pupil, and whose ambitions to be a writer also dated from boyhood. Lang told him:

> I always understood, from my nurse and others that Wellington was a good and brave man, and in rather early life I hoped to emulate his valour and eclipse his conquests. My genius rather promptly recoiled from the perils and fatigues of the martial life, and I determined to be like Sir Walter Scott, instead. Later reflection and reading produced a new model in *Pendennis*.[69]

Pendennis, Thackeray's semi-autobiographical novel of young Arthur Pendennis's exhilarating life as a London journalist, gave decisive shape to Lang's future hopes and ambitions. From that time on, he wanted to go to London and become a literary man. He wrote:

> The story of Pen made one wish to run away to literature, to the Temple, to streets where Brown, the famous reviewer, might be seen walking with his

wife and his umbrella. The writing of poems 'up to' pictures, the beer with Warrington in the mornings, the suppers in the back-kitchen, these were the alluring things.[70]

But first, he travelled along the North British Railway line and enrolled as a student at St Andrews University.

2

Looking South

'It was a case of love at first sight, as soon as I found myself under the grey sky and beheld the white flame of the breakers charging over the brown wet barrier of the pier':[1] so Andrew Lang recalled of the day he arrived at St Andrews, age 17, to begin his new life at Scotland's oldest university. Lang enrolled as an undergraduate at United College, a union of the old colleges of St Salvador and St Leonard, for those taking the general Arts degree. It had long been customary for students at St Andrews to find their own lodgings or 'bunks' in town. The professor of humanity (Latin), John Campbell Shairp, with a happy experience of undergraduate life at Oxford, proposed the establishment of a student hall of residence. James David Forbes, the recently appointed principal of United College, adopted the plan, and, in the face of opponents in the university who resented the attempt to 'Anglify' St Andrews, a vacant gothic dwelling which formed part of the old St Leonard's College was refurbished for the purpose.[2] Forbes hoped to turn the educational tide which for thirty years had taken the sons of the Scottish aristocracy southwards to Oxbridge. Lang was one of the cohort of student residents of the new St Leonard's Hall of residence which opened its doors for the first time in 1861. He shared a room with Alexander Henderson, like himself a former Edinburgh Academy boy. Lang described St Leonard's Hall as 'something between an Oxford Hall and a master's house at a public school, rather more like the latter than the former'.[3] They had 'more liberty than schoolboys, less than English undergraduates'.[4] They were the butt of constant mockery from students who enjoyed the freedom of town lodgings. The residents of St Leonard's Hall were strictly 'gated', the subject of a ribald verse-lampoon in the student magazine:

> Now, like good boys, be punctual to dine, -
> A little work, then prayers, then bed at nine,
> Perhaps you come to see some student life;
> But I will keep you boys, till boys, you take a wife.[5]

The college gates were shut at 9 o'clock. After an early breach of what Lang called 'studying human nature in St. Andrews after dark', three of their number were sent down.[6] A group photograph of the first cohort shows Lang

Andrew Lang. John Sloan, Oxford University Press. © John Sloan (2023). DOI: 10.1093/oso/9780192866875.003.0002

Figure 2.1 St Leonard's Hall group, 1861–2. Lang, *back row second from left*, resting his arm on the shoulder of Henry Brown. Others, *back row from left to right*: Mr Rhoades, S. Deas, R. Pringle, A.E. Henderson, R. Cox. *Front row*: J. Patterson, D. Younger, W. Gordon.
Reproduced courtesy of the University of St Andrews Libraries and Museums.

resting his arm on the shoulder of Henry Brown, his close friend in college. (see Figure 2.1)

After the expulsions, according to Lang, calm reigned and they 'settled down to work a little and play a great deal'. He liked the warden, Henry Rhoades, a former Rugby School pupil and Oxford graduate in his mid-twenties, who coached them in sports and won their trust, while at the same time satisfying the powers above. In December, Forbes appointed a housekeeper to keep the hall in good domestic order. They soon discovered why. That month, the Duke and Duchess of Argyll visited the university and were given a tour of the hall where they planned to send their two sons the following winter.[7]

Lang's joy was the College Library. He read the old books on magic and the occult. Students at university have dabbled in the dark arts since ancient times. Lang, with the curiosity of youth, decided that 'to raise the devil ... would be a singular triumph'. A prerequisite was Cornelius Agrippa, the Renaissance occult philosopher praised by Doctor Faustus in the opening conjuring scene of Christopher Marlowe's play. He also read Agrippa's disciple Johann Weyer, on witches, and the sixteenth-century Jesuit Petrus Thyraeus, on apparitions, demonic possession, and exorcism. His own magical experiments proved disappointing. He said of the books, 'It soon became evident enough that the devil was not to be raised by their prescriptions'. Though their spells and charms proved ineffectual, the books marked the starting point of his lifelong interest in the way that open-mindedness towards the abnormal, the despised, even the forbidden, could open to progressive knowledge and ways of seeing. Weyer, for instance, though he believed in the devil, condemned witch hunts, observing from his experience as a physician that most witches were suffering from delusions. The old librarian, seeing Lang so often in the College Library, told him he was 'the right sort of student'.[8] Lang felt guilty, as the books he read were not for use in examinations. In addition to occult literature, he borrowed twelve volumes of *Fraser's Magazine*, and made a study of London periodicals— *Temple Bar*, *Macmillan's Magazine*, the *Quarterly Review*, *Punch*—to train himself to write like the literary men in Thackeray's *Pendennis*.[9]

Although technically a first-year student, a 'bejant', from the French for a 'yellow beak' or young bird, he joined the second year for Latin and Greek, on account of the concentration on the Classics at Edinburgh Academy. Despite pressure from both inside and outside, Scottish universities continued to encourage breadth of learning over the specializing tendencies of education in England. Philosophy and mathematics remained compulsory components of the General Arts degree. Compulsory mathematics proved a stumbling-block for many, and Lang was one. He wrote, 'Nobody could teach me Euclid, still less Algebra. My brain and nervous system broke down; my eyes filled with childish tears. I sobbed hysterically. That way lay madness. Of Arithmetic I was equally incapable'.[10] The university magazine joked that a German band should be employed 'to play the "Dead March of Saul"' as the candidates on the General Arts course filed in for the mathematics examination.[11] Lang was surprised when he passed and suspected that the examiners must have allowed his Classics marks to compensate for his 'mathematical imbecility'.

His student experience was overshadowed that first year by the death of Henry Brown, his dearest friend. Lang generally avoided emotional self-exposure in his writings, but his grief was to surface in poems throughout his life, most movingly in his elegy 'Clevedon Church: In Memoriam, H. B', written twenty-three years later, after he spent Christmas at Cleveland Court, the manor house of Sir Edmund and Lady Agnes Elton, in Somerset. Its title recalls Tennyson's great elegy, *In Memoriam*, in which the poet mourns the death of the beloved Cambridge friend of his youth, Arthur Hallam, who was buried in the Elton family vault in St Andrew's Church close by Cleveland Court, on a hill overlooking the Bristol Channel. Lang thought the place 'very ancient and beautiful'.[12]

Lang takes for his epigraph lines from the Cavalier poet Richard Lovelace's 'To Lucinda, Going beyond the Seas', giving reassurance of the unaltered union of souls separated physically by time and space. 'Clevedon Church' explores the same divide. 'The little church upon the windy height', where Hallam is buried; the 'ashen light'; and the 'turbid Channel' which 'mourns through the winter day … its monotone of pain': these carry Lang in memory 'back to the winter rose of northern skies', and his own 'sleepless love'. The remembered scene of St Andrews is of the erosion and decay of ancient places of worship:

> ... the long waves of the ocean beat
>   Below the minster grey,
> Caverns and chapels worn of saintly feet,
>   And knees of them that pray.
> And I remember how we twain were one
>   Beside that ocean dim.

That momentary reconnection with the past vanishes again in the final lines in the speaker's more melancholy, modern recognition of the unbridgeable gulf between the living and the dead:

> And dreaming of the voice that, save in sleep,
> Shall greet me not again,
> Far, far below I hear the Channel sweep
> And all the waves complain.[13]

Over that first summer, the College Hall added four rooms, and in November student numbers rose to fifteen. The group photograph that year captures him fixing a bold and mischievous look at the camera. Among the newcomers were the Duke and Duchess of Argyll's two sons—John, the Marquis of Lorne, fresh from Eton, age 17, and his younger brother, Lord Archibald Campbell. Lang and they became lifelong friends. Together, they started a weekly college magazine called *St Leonard's Magazine*, a 'manuscript affair' containing stories, reviews, verses, and humorous illustrations. Lord Lorne contributed an account of a Chamois hunt in the Austrian Alps, and Lord Archibald a cartoon of medieval monks playing golf and cricket.[14] After the initial enthusiasm, as is often the case with student productions, Lang, as editor, was left to write most of it himself. Another student, Allan Menzies, remembered, 'When Friday night arrived, and no contributions had come in, we feared we should have no magazine that week. But it was there, nevertheless; the editor shut himself up on Friday night and had the twelve pages ready for us in the morning'.[15] Lang laid them out in the common room, while students 'fenced and boxed, and played cricket (with a golf ball and a poker)'.[16] The magazine afforded them 'great entertainment with its Socratic discussion of the student questions of the day, its rhymed chronicles of cricket matches, its verses after Browning'.[17]

Lang had been introduced to Browning's dramatic lyrics and monologues by Tibby Cross, his Aunt Eleanor's niece, now 26. She wrote a parody of Browning for inclusion in St Leonard's Magazine. Lang followed with more of his own.[18] In his satirical verse monologue, 'A Letter from Bird-of-Freedom Sawin', he adopted the character and accents of the rascally Yankee private of James Russell Lowell's The Biglow Papers. Lang wrote it in 1863, a turning point in the American Civil War in favour of the North. Lang has his 'Bird-of-Freedom Sawin' call on the South to renounce slavery and rejoin the Union, while doubting his own willingness to make peace:

> 'Twoud raise the dander of a skunk, 'twoud turn a dormouse yellar,
> When some one's shot your father for to shake hands with the fellar.[19]

In a different mood was his verse translation of the famous elegy by Catullus at the side of his brother's grave, a way for Lang's to give voice to the irrecoverable loss of his dearest friend:

> Brother, I come and stand beside thy tomb,
> To give thee the dead offering of the grave,
> ...
> Accept the sorrow that they cannot tell,
> And through the long eternity of years,
> Brother, farewell, for ever fare thee well![20]

That winter, he sent one of his poems to the popular London monthly Temple Bar—a verse rendering of Malory's account in Morte d'Arthur of Sir Lancelot's troubling dream and sense of sin in the chapel of waste. It was returned by the sub-editor, Edmund Yates, with a rejection slip that read unceremoniously, 'No. E. Y.'.[21] Lang published the poem, under the pseudonym

'J. P', in March 1863, in the second monthly number of the newly launched *St Andrews University Magazine*.[22] It was the first time he had the pleasure of seeing his work in print. His 'Flos Regum' (in English, 'Flower of Kings') appeared in the same number, a scholarly appreciation of Malory's *Morte d'Arthur*, recognizing the place of epic cycles in the making of national heroes. He followed this in April with an essay on 'Scottish Nursery Tales', and later that year with an article on 'Spiritualism Medieval and Modern'. We see in these essays the beginnings of his fascination with the diffusion and universality of myths and folklore around the world, and with the ghostly survival of primitive habits of mind in civilized culture—an important thread of enquiry in his later writings. In 'Flos Regum', he observes, 'All nations have their half mythic heroes, all with points of resemblance, in their origins and deaths, and fate'.[23] Although Lang dismissed his student productions as 'amazing trash',[24] they demonstrate remarkable energy and versatility over a wide range of subjects and styles, and show him to be already a knowledgeable critic, with an interest in French and English literature, and with a burgeoning talent for verse translation and parody in verse and prose.

A relaxing of the strict discipline of the hall in Lang's second year allowed him to attend evening meetings of the University Literary Society. He found the student essays comically wordy, and the debates tiresome and predictable. He decided to ruffle feathers with a paper arguing that William Wallace, Scotland's national hero, was a petty rebel against rightful authority, and that, contrary to Scottish belief, England's Edward I, the 'Hammer of the Scots', was really a benign and merciful ruler, and a far-sighted politician. He adopted a pseudonym—'Mr McGregor'—and arranged for a St Leonard's Hall friend, Robert Cox, to read the essay at the Society meeting on 10 January. The anger it caused went beyond anything he anticipated. Feelings ran so high that the usual vote of thanks was withheld, and over several heated meetings there were objections and amendments to the wording of the minutes, which recorded the Society's 'non-acceptance' of the essay's conclusions. Lang recalled that, when it became obvious to all who the author was, 'I conceived that my personal safety and dignity would be best consulted by withdrawing from the somewhat stormy debates of the Society'.[25] His humorous allusions to the incident have led some to assume that the views he put forward in the essay are not to be taken seriously. Yet he voiced a similar view of Wallace and Edward I in his corrective, ground-breaking history of the Wars of Scottish Independence nearly forty years later.[26] Behind the seemingly shy, amiable personality he showed to the world, Lang was also an intellectual contrarian, who believed a jarring and ruffling of received wisdom was necessary to advance knowledge.

A major row erupted in his second year when students defied Principal Forbes' ban on Kate Kennedy Day, the annual student carnival. Forbes
abhorred the event as merely an excuse for drunken rowdiness. The masked
procession, barred from entering the college building, marched round the
quadrangle, chanting and singing. Forbes arrived on the scene in a temper,
tore the mask off one of the revellers, struck him, and threatened expulsion.
Forbes's actions lost him the support of the college, and that afternoon a large
demonstration of students protested and booed outside his house.[27] Lang
recalled later with regret that he and the 'lordly youths of St Leonard's ... rather
looked on the Kate Kennedy affair as beneath our Olympian notice',[28] although
his remark masked the fact that Forbes came to St Leonard's Hall to plead for
support but was refused.

That year, he enjoyed James Frederick Ferrier's lectures on the history of
Greek philosophy. Philosophy remained a central part of Scottish university
education, with the educational aim of fostering an enlightened, logical understanding of the ordinary, common-sense principles and intuitions shared by
everyone in a society or community. Paradoxically, in his first year, Lang
found the densely worded and quasi-technical language of the school of Scottish common-sense philosophy an obstacle to the very civic education they
were supposed to promote. He admitted, 'Neither then, nor afterwards, could
I understand what it was about, and what the pupils of Sir William Hamilton
were driving at'.[29] Ferrier's lectures, by contrast, were notable for their clarity
and simplicity of style. Lang remembered them as 'the most interesting and
inspiriting' he ever attended.[30] The generalist nature of the degree meant that
Ferrier lectured on the Pre-Socratics without obliging students to read the texts
in the original Greek.[31] Ferrier had studied at both Edinburgh University and
Oxford and strongly resisted pressures inside and outside the university for
Scotland to adopt the specialist model of English education, as he feared that
Anglicization would dislodge moral philosophy from its central place in the
Scotland tradition. He objected to common-sense philosophy. For Ferrier, the
educational purpose of philosophy was not simply intellectual, but moral, its
aim not to legitimate the inadequacies of man's ordinary thinking, but, through
critical enquiry, to correct and refine it.[32]

Lang spoke of the 'mysterious reverence' they all had for Ferrier: 'There was
I know not what of dignity, of humour, and of wisdom in his face; there was
an air of the student, the vanquisher of difficulties, the discoverer of hidden
knowledge, in him, that I have seen in no other'.[33] He found Ferrier's lectures on the history of Greek philosophy 'so fair and persuasive, that, in each
new school, we thought we had discovered the secret. We were physicists with

Thales ... now Empedocleans, now believers in Heraclitus, now in Socrates, now in Plato, now in Aristotle. In each lecture our professor set up a new master and gently disintegrated him in the next'.[34] Giving Greek philosophy a prophetic, contemporary relevance, Ferrier, for example, made a compelling case that the Sophists' claim for 'nature' over accepted standards of morality was a revolt against society's man-made norms and conventions, only to make an equally compelling case for Socrates's reasoning in favour of virtue above personal happiness, since 'in sacrificing happiness to virtue ... we only cease to be *happy* men, but in sacrificing virtue we cease to be men, because virtue is the preservation and perfecting of our nature'.[35]

A photograph of the Moral Philosophy class taken at the door of the college in April 1863 at the end of the session, shows the white-haired Ferrier, surrounded by students, seated augustly on the top step with his lecture notes on his knee. The students are all wearing their black formal best, apart from Lang, sitting in light-coloured trousers and with a Kilmarnock bonnet in his hand, by the professor's side. Ferrier, William Sellar, and their wives and families were 'extremely intimate',[36] and Lang may have heard a little of the tragic failings that accompanied Ferrier's aura of urbanity and dignity—his heavy drinking; the syphilis he contracted during an academic delegation to London; the strains in his marriage. Ferrier died of 'congestion of the brain' the summer after the photograph was taken.[37] The greatest lesson Lang took from Ferrier's lectures, it would seem, was a lifelong scepticism about masters having the secret of life.

Lang left St Andrews at the end of his second year and transferred to Glasgow University in order to compete for a scholarship—called a Snell Exhibition—which would gain him a place at Balliol College, Oxford. He was encouraged by his Uncle Willie who had gained a Snell Exhibition to Balliol twenty years before. The Snell awards dated back two hundred years and enabled students at Glasgow to study at Oxford, with the aim of encouraging intellectual links between the two universities and, indeed, the two nations.[38] They also served to extend Balliol College influence. The Snell Exhibitions allowed Balliol to pick 'the classical flower of Glasgow University'.[39] Many Snell Exhibitioners already held key educational posts in Scottish schools and colleges. In Lang's day, the scholarship was worth £120 a year, enough to cover fees and basic living expenses. Classical education had advanced significantly in Scotland since the founding of Edinburgh Academy, but the path to higher classical learning still took the academically ambitious southwards to Oxford.[40] Indeed, at Edinburgh Academy, boys in the upper school were introduced to the English style of pronunciation of Latin and Greek. Lang enrolled at Glasgow for the winter session from November 1863 to April 1864. 'My sole and purely mercenary object', he said, 'was to get the Snell Exhibition'.[41] He knew that if he gained a place at Oxford, Jowett would be his tutor.

He had first seen Jowett at Ardtornish when he was 14, and in 1860 Jowett had been a summer guest at Harehead,[42] when controversy raged over the publication of *Essays and Reviews*, a collection of essays by liberal theologians on religion in an age of science. Jowett's contribution, the most contentious in the book, argued that the aim of scripture should be to understand the original intended meaning of its authors in their cultural and historical context, rather than to suppose the authority of divine revelation.[43] Published just four months after Darwin's *Origin of Species*, the book was regarded as an assault on Christianity. In conservative Oxford, Jowett was under sustained censure as a heretic, and an increase in his salary as Regius Professor of Greek was withheld. Lang walked and talked with him.[44] He remembered a 'face of peculiar sweetness and gentleness' under prematurely grey hair.[45] During his first weeks at Glasgow in November 1863, Lang wrote 'The Lay of the Bookselling Elder', a verse satire on religious hypocrisy in which the speaker, a Scottish Presbyterian bookseller, denounces the heretical Broad-Church authors of *Essays and Reviews*, while hypocritically feathering his nest by selling the book:

> If one is worse than all the rest
> I am prepared to show it
> To be that Heretic unblest,
> The Greek Professor Jowett.[46]

To Lang, for whom religion was never theological speculation or doctrinal dispute, Jowett's essay seemed only 'to speak organised common sense'.[47] Lang's poem 'Dei Otiosi' ('Inactive Gods'), published that month in the *St Andrews University Magazine*, took for its title the Epicurean doctrine that the gods, if they do exist, are 'careless, indolent deities',[48] indifferent to human suffering and sorrow:

> Why should we care for the gods
> who care so little for us?
> Far from the ways of man, sitting
> apart at their ease[49]

He signed the poem 'R.I.P.'—an ironic allusion to his departure from St Andrews.

Glasgow, for Lang, was 'undesirable exile'. He lodged with two 'kind old Highland ladies', sisters of Revd Dr Norman Macleod, minister of the Old Barony Church near the college, and editor of the popular monthly *Good Words*. They were his only social acquaintances. The Old College at that time was on the busy, industrialized High Street, two miles from where he lived. Lessons began at eight o'clock in the morning, which proved a torment, as Lang liked to lie late. Unpleasant, too, were the small, fetid, unventilated class-rooms, crowded on a winter morning with unwashed students. Outside, the old, seventeenth-century buildings were black with soot, and the gardens behind were 'black, bare, and squalid'. A perpetual smell from a tallow manu-factory near the college hung in the air. Life was 'all work and no play'. There was no rugby football, and there was no cricket club, as he was there during the winter session.[50] He laughed many years later when an astrologer sent him his horoscope claiming that, in 1863, he had suffered a disappointment in love. He responded that, at 19, he 'never was so precocious', being too busy studying for his scholarship.[51]

He continued to contribute articles, verses, drawings, and reviews to the *St Leonard's Magazine*, entertaining his old friends with tales of his 'Glesky' ordeals—the ungodly hour of morning lessons; his walk in the rush-hour crowds of 'Gobbling Merchant Men', going 'office wards'; and the 'great race' for the Blackstone Prize in Greek and Latin. He composed a spoof preliminary report of the rival candidates, which predicted that 'A. Lang would have a better chance over an extempore course, where a fine recklessness as to his tenses, and verbs in general, might pull him through. As it is, has little or no chance'.[52] He was shocked, nevertheless, when the result of the Blackstone was announced in December: he came 'absolutely last'.[53] It dealt a serious blow to his hopes for the Snell. One of his cartoon drawings in the first issue of *St Leonard's Magazine* after Christmas pictured 'The *Foolish* Student at 2 o'clock a.m.', studying at his desk by candlelight; another, 'The *Wise* Student at 2 o'clock a.m.', asleep in his bed.[54] Lang's real life had taken the direction of the first. He 'overworked deplorably'. As the Snell examination loomed, his poem 'A Prospective Farewell' made no secret of his longing for his Glasgow ordeal to be over:

> Smell, Gesky: To the gibbous Moon,
> Thy smoke and fog deliver,
> I'll cut your stenches very soon,
> For ever and for ever.[55]

He illustrated the poem with a drawing of a student about to step off a cliff edge. There were hours of written papers in the Snell Exhibition. He wrote, 'It was a blessed thing when the session ended, and we could boat on a part of the Clyde which was still beautiful'. He remembered nothing of the oral examination that followed, except that one of his rivals, who had already been interviewed, told him Kepler's Laws in the quad. The result: he was awarded an 'open Exhibition at Balliol'. From that day, he never saw anything of Glasgow, apart from the railway station.[56]

Lang passed the summer term before he went up to Balliol as a boarder at Loretto School, a small, private, fee-paying school, six miles east of Edinburgh. Pupils were mainly the sons of the professional, landed, and upper commercial classes. Lang's cousin from India, James Jasper Atkinson, had been a pupil there.[57] Numbers at Loretto had been low since the founding of the school in 1827, but after taking charge two years earlier, the new headmaster, Henry Hutchinson Almond, had doubled enrolment to about thirty boys,[58] with the addition of a handful of young men reading for Oxford. Almond himself was a former Snell Exhibitioner but made no bones about his dislike of Oxford,— 'the white chokers, the gowns, and long black coats'—and though grateful for Jowett's help, confessed he never took to a man 'who was both a Platonist and no sportsman'.[59] Parents and students arriving at the school were surprised to be met by a 'young active man … short and thick-set, clad in loose tweeds, without a hat and with a loose collar open at the neck', who introduced himself as the headmaster.[60] Almond was challenging conventional attitudes to education in Scotland in matters of dress, discipline, and learning. Individuality was encouraged; caps, ties, and waistcoats were discarded; and open windows and cold baths every morning were the order of the day; above all, sport and exercise were given a central place in the curriculum. The college anthem, 'The Old Red Coat', celebrated Almond's robust resistance to Victorian conventions:

> To the Old Red Coat, and the open throat,
> And the school where we can wear it,
> And we shall always bless the free jolly dress,
> And be glad we still can share it.[61]

Lang and the other senior boys studied Greek with the Classics master, George Beilby, fresh from Cambridge. M. de Flandre, son of a French émigré, came once or twice a week to give them French lessons. On Sunday afternoon, the whole school walked the four miles for a choral service conducted by

Mr Beilby at the Episcopal Church at Dalkeith, where they were urged by Almond to 'sing out'.[62] Lang played a good deal of cricket, and a game for which he invented the name 'puddex'[63]—a fun version of cricket, played with a wooden club and tennis ball by teams made up of boys from all age groups.

For all his enjoyment in outdoor sports, Loretto was not a happy time for Lang. He was 'nearly dead' after his winter at Glasgow University. He had, as he put it, been educated till he dropped.[64] When the school closed for the summer, the Head took him and 'a little boy called Campbell', on a fishing tour of the Highlands, first to Speyside, and then further north to Sutherland. Lang remembered:

> First we went to a cottage in Laggan, where I mainly lived on cherry gum and oat-cake ... The fishing was hopelessly bad, and we went to Inchnadampf ... in Assynt. There were 300 lochs in the parish, all good then, but I was so ill from overwork at Glasgow that I scarcely fished and was, in my opinion, most disagreeable company. How the Head put up with me where opportunities for drowning a languid, discontented person were so numerous and eligible, I cannot conceive.[65]

Overwork had taken him to the edge. His low spirits in the weeks before he went up to Balliol suggest fears, too, about the path he had chosen.

3

Under Jowett's Wing

By the mid-1840s, the rail link from London to Oxford had finally opened, after years of objection by Oxford University, worried about the moral danger to students of easy access to Ascot, Henley, and the London theatres. On Lang's arrival at the new passenger station in the 1860s, a cab carried him from Frideswide Square, up the gentle slope of George Street to the Broad, where Balliol tower rose on his left. Past the old gate, he was enchanted by the air of the antiquity of the front quad with its 'blackened and crumbling stone'. He was taken to the inner or garden quad by way of an alley and ancient arch, past the master's house and the large Italianate 'Fisher's Buildings' on his left, which contained the best rooms in college, to his 'one-windowed room under the pediment' of the building at right angles to Fisher's.[1] This was to be his new home.

As a fresher at St Andrews, he had given more attention to sports than to his historical surroundings. At Oxford, the history of the place was immediate. In Broad Street, 'a small stone cross' marked the place where the Protestant martyrs Nicholas Ridley and Hugh Latimer had been burned at the stake for heresy in the reign of 'Bloody Mary'. Walking through Oxford, he saw everywhere—in colleges, chapels, doorways, and windows—'the handwriting, as it were, of many generations'. He thought Oxford a 'more beautiful and fascinating town'.[2] For some reason, perhaps illness, or a postponed arrival in Oxford, he did not attend the matriculation ceremony with the other freshmen on Monday morning, 17 October, which meant that he was not formally sworn in as a member of the university until January. He thought the Oxford undergraduate gown a 'scanty rag' compared with the long scarlet gown he had worn at St Andrews.[3]

His first weeks as a freshman at Balliol were taken up with a great many invitations to breakfasts and to 'wines', as small, after-dinner gatherings in students' rooms were called. Their aim was to welcome freshmen into the wider Balliol community. In his light verse poem 'Freshman's Year', he conveys the exhilaration of those first weeks at Balliol:

> Return again, thou Freshman's year,
>   When bloom was on the rye,

Andrew Lang. John Sloan, Oxford University Press. © John Sloan (2023). DOI: 10.1093/oso/9780192866875.003.0003

> When breakfast came with bottled beer,
>   When Pleasure walked the High;
> ...
> When tick was in its early bloom
>   When Schools were far away,
> As vaguely distant as the tomb,
>   Nor more regarded—they![4]

Amidst the exhausting activities, freshers also received a summons to their tutor's room to receive advice on reading and assignments. The man Lang faced was no longer the young scholar who had been his uncle's tutor and friend in the 1840s. The 48-year-old Jowett was a silver-haired figure of authority. For Lang, there was always in Jowett's appearance 'something unexpectedly and almost discordantly cherubic'.[5] Jowett had been passed over for the master-ship ten years before, losing out to the more traditional Revd Robert Scott. But since then, his influence and supremacy among the fellows had grown.

Although the 'Homeric battles' fought over Jowett's income as Professor of Greek had been resolved in Jowett's favour earlier that year, theological tensions remained a feature of university and college life. Attendance at chapel every morning was still compulsory for undergraduates, a practice that was not abolished until after Jowett became Master five years later. Lang thought the chapel building ugly, its alternate layers of red and white stone resembling 'streaky bacon', but he admired the beautiful glass windows and the Jacobean panelling inside, which had been preserved from the old chapel. Aesthetic surroundings, however, were not enough to get him out of bed at the uncomfortable early hour of eight o'clock on cold winter mornings. He received a shy reprimand from Revd Mr Woollcombe, known as the 'Wolx', the Dean of Chapel. An undergraduate ignored this at his peril. At the end of term meeting, known as 'Collections', in the College Hall, the Dean of Chapel would make a point of reporting to the 'stiff and austere' Dr Scott, the master, that in the matter of chapel attendance', you had set 'for a *scholar*—a very bad example'.[6]

Teaching, then as now, was done mainly in college, with the university—the colleges collectively—responsible for setting and marking examinations. Lectures and classes began at nine or ten, after chapel service and breakfast. Generally, lessons were over by 1 o'clock, leaving afternoons free, but Jowett gave his Greek lecture between 1 and 2 o'clock, when stomachs were crying out for lunch.[7] Matthew Arnold, Oxford Professor of Poetry at the time, lectured in the afternoon, but Lang, contrary to recent claims,[8] never attended his talks, which clashed, as he put it, 'just at the hour when wickets were pitched on Cowley Marsh'.[9] At St Andrews, Ferrier had lectured on the pre-Socratic philosophers without the Greek texts. In the advanced, exclusively classical curriculum of Literae Humaniores, or 'Greats', at Oxford, Lang studied in the original Greek many of the thinkers covered in Ferrier's lectures. He had also to write a weekly essay, alternating between a Latin essay for Dr Scott one week, and an essay on classical or contemporary topics for Jowett the next. Much has been written about Jowett's guiding influence on the development of the Oxford tutorial and its aim to stimulate critical thinking through dialogue and debate. John Addington Symonds believed Jowett's tutorial method 'gave a sceptical and sophisticated direction to those who accepted his way of dealing with problems'.[10] The reality was that approval or disapproval from Jowett, after the student read aloud his essay, was often simply a look. Lang wrote, 'His look could express ... sympathy or disapproval, but when he seemed to disapprove, his fancy was really absent; he was not attending but thinking of other matters'.[11]

It might be imagined that the tutorial regime at Oxford matched to some extent the breadth and social relevance aimed at in the generalist tradition in Scottish education. Moral philosophy had a central place in the teaching of 'Greats'. In having undergraduates write tutorial essays on contemporary topics outside the curriculum—on economics, politics, or social questions, for example—Jowett sought to prepare Balliol men for the real world. Indeed, Jowett made it his mission to encourage closer contact between university men and the wider community. Paradoxically, these measures were a recognition of a divide between Oxford and the rest of society which needed to be bridged. Most Oxford students were from English public schools. The continuing dominance of the Classics reinforced their sense of superior social status and served as their passport to influential positions in the civil services, the higher professions, and the established Church. The matter and manner of Jowett's tutorial curriculum did not make generalists. Many found writing essays on contemporary topics a chore. Adolphus Liddell, Lang's contemporary, recalled,

> The work at Balliol consisted entirely of preparation for coming exams, with the exception of a weekly essay which we had to read every Saturday to the Master ... I found it uncomfortably difficult to put together four pages on "Casuistry" or the "National Debt" in one or two hours on Friday evening. Like others of our set, I occasionally had recourse to Andrew Lang, whose

good nature and extraordinary power of disquisition made him willing and able to knock off an essay on any subject in half an hour.[12]

Lang's own essays did not always meet with Jowett's approval. On one occasion, Jowett dropped his usual reserve, and told him bluntly, 'Don't write as if you were writing for a penny paper'.[13]

Lang faced Jowett's displeasure when he refused to take sides on the controversy surrounding the Morant Bay Rebellion in Jamaica at the beginning of his second year. Edward John Eyre, the island's governor, imposed martial law and ordered the execution of hundreds of black Jamaicans, following violent protest over social injustice and widespread poverty. Eyre's supporters, led by Thomas Carlyle, regarded him as a hero for his decisive response to the crisis. At Balliol, Thomas Hill Green, a young philosophy tutor and friend of Jowett's, led calls for Eyre to be tried for murder. Lang displeased Jowett by saying that if the choice was between whether Eyre was a saviour of the colony, or a despot who made the emperor Nero seem like an angel, it would be wrong to give an opinion without having weighed up the evidence.[14] A stubborn independence of mind and insistence on evidence were characteristic of his manner and outlook. It may also have not been far from his mind that his grandfather's actions caused a similarly troublesome, fiercely partisan division of accusers and defenders. In the closed, collegiate atmosphere of Oxford, where people knew everything about you, the scholar's mask could provide some form of concealment. He and Jowett also disagreed about miracles. Professor Baden Powell, one of Jowett's coauthors of *Essays and Reviews*, argued in his contribution to the volume that miracles, 'the supposed suspension of the laws of matter', were inconceivable, and of no value as evidence for the truth of Christianity.[15] Jowett appeared to share that view, choosing to regard the miraculous as contrary to the laws of nature and inconsistent with science and common sense. Lang, for his part, believed that abnormal occurrences, of the kind we call 'miracles', were 'only too common',[16] and deserved scientific attention and rational enquiry.

Lang kept up his connection with St Andrews. He continued to contribute occasional verses, drawings, and reviews to the *St Leonard's Magazine*. Alexander Henderson, his old roommate at St Leonard's Hall, visited him in Oxford, and they arranged a touring cricket side to play against teams in Edinburgh and the Borders during the long vacation. They named themselves the Eccentric Flamingos and designed a striking black and scarlet uniform. Lang included his younger brothers in the team, calling them 'Les Enfants Perdus' (see Figure 3.1). At Balliol, Lang played cricket for the second eleven, declaring in a

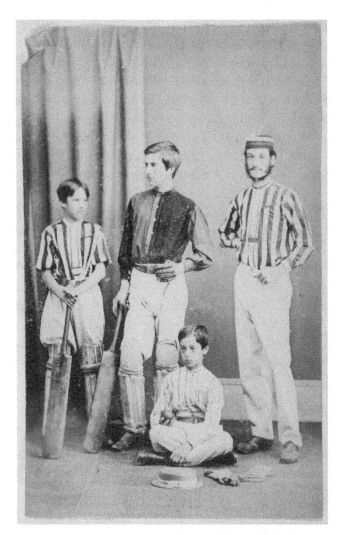

Figure 3.1 Lang, *on right*, in 1866, age 22, during his second long vacation from Balliol College, with his brothers, John, 17, Craig, 14, and seated, Thomas William (T.W.), 12.

Reproduced courtesy of the University of St Andrews Libraries and Museums.

letter to a friend that this was almost equal to 'the first eleven of most colleges'.[17] Curiously, he does not appear in any of the Balliol group photographs—and there are many—during all his undergraduate years. Though he was happy at Oxford, St Andrews, it seems, still had his heart.

He spent his first long vacation from Oxford in rural Perthshire, at Tullymet, a house 'charmingly situated among woods, above an old-fashioned garden', which his Uncle Willie had leased for the summer. William Sellar was now Professor of Humanity at Edinburgh. Lang remembered 'the happiest of all vacations, reading beneath the trees, where the squirrels chattered in the boughs, and the voices of the children ... called him to play from the distance'.[18] Jowett had chosen nearby Loch Tummel for his undergraduate reading party in the Highlands that summer, and Jowett and T. H. Green visited Tullymet. As Jowett positioned himself as the college's master-in-waiting, Green took on the mantle of the 'Prophet of the college', thought 'great and wise' and 'a leader of thought and young men'.[19] Undergraduates found Green's lectures difficult to follow, but despite, or perhaps because of this, they believed that to think and write like Green held the key to examination success. Lang's personality did not dispose him to the kind of 'tutor worship' common at Balliol.[20] Ferrier's lectures at St Andrews had made him sceptical about system-builders and masters of thought. He found more to admire in Green's 'simplicity' and good nature than in his Hegelian reading of Aristotle's 'common good' as illustrative of man's historical, evolutionary progress to an ideal future state of personal and social fulfilment. Aristotle's *Politics* made a deep impression on him, but, to his mind, its message was that there was no secret road to 'a happy life at all'—this and 'the impossibility of imposing ideal constitutions on mankind'.[21]

In his second year, Lang began to attract some notice in the competitive undergraduate community of Balliol Exhibitioners, scholars, and public-school boys. Undergraduates could sit their first public examination—Honours Moderation (known as 'Mods')—at Easter, or wait and take it in their seventh term, in November. Lang's friends all took theirs at Easter and got Seconds. Lang waited and gained a First. He was amused to hear his friends make up a story to explain this 'miracle'. They became convinced that one of the examiners had given his nephew a First, and everyone with better marks had to be awarded the same distinction.[22]

Four months after sitting Mods, in March 1867, Lang entered a poem for the prestigious Newdigate Prize, awarded annually for the best narrative poem on a chosen subject. The subject that year was 'Marie Antoinette'. His efforts to make a name for himself among Balliol's would-be poets were unlikely to have pleased Jowett, who seems to have felt there were already enough of them.[23] Lang was under the spell of the rhapsodic, musical metrical experimentation of Swinburne's debut volume of verse, *Atalanta in Calydon*.[24] With Swinburne as his model, he began his Newdigate poem with a rapt description of the Great Lisbon earthquake of 1 November 1755, the eve of Marie Antoinette's birth. Matthew Arnold, in his last year as Professor of Poetry, was one of the judges. There was much speculation at the time about who should succeed him. Lang failed to win the Newdigate but attracted notice when the *Oxford Undergraduate's Journal* published his humorous verse parodies of John Campbell Shairp, Robert Browning, and Swinburne, under the heading 'Why They Don't Stand for the Poetry Chair'.[25]

Shairp, Lang's old Latin professor at St Andrews, had ruled himself out. Lang, three years before, had written an irreverent review of Shairp's *Kilmahoe and Other Poems* for the *St Leonard's* Magazine, in which he had announced that 'Tennyson and Browning are still safe in their lofty thrones'. Browning was favoured by many to succeed Arnold, but a petition with many signatures requesting that an honorary degree be conferred on Browning to allow him to stand was turned down by Hebdomadal Council, the university's governing body. Swinburne, the poet most admired by the young, stood no chance of being elected by a convocation of current members and alumni, the majority parsons. The pagan sentiment, and sexual, sadomasochistic themes of Swinburne's recently published *Poems and Ballads* had scandalized readers and prompted the *Oxford Undergraduate's Journal* to say that 'English stomachs are not yet strong enough to relish such food as Théophile de Gautier and Alfred de Musset have supplied to an admiring French public'.[26]

In Lang's parody of Browning's 'The Grammarian's Funeral', the speaker questions, in the ironic, top-lofty style of Browning's original, the fitness of a poet-preacher of high-seriousness such as Browning to 'sit in the chair',

> Of one, whose laughter mingled with his teaching
>> Freshened the air.

'The author of Kilmahoe' declares his preference for the peaceful waters of the River Tweed to the screams of 'coxes and captains ... on the Isis'.[27] Lang's liveliest and most amusing piece parodied in galloping, anapaestic metre the besotted, sadomasochistic lover of Swinburne's sacrilegious monologue, 'Dolores, Our Lady of Pain':

> Oh frantic and festive Dolores,
>> Shall I leave thee, ferocious and fair
> For the sterile old Common Room stories,
>> For the chapels, the chaff and the chair;
> For the dwellings of dons and of doctors;
>> For the maids of the *Turl* and the *High*,
> For the wrath on the lips of the Proctors!
>> Our Lady, not I!

He sent a handwritten copy of 'Reasons Why They Don't Stand for the Poetry Professorship', accompanied by a finely detailed drawing of the three poets, for inclusion in the *St Leonard's Magazine*.[28] In the event, the choice facing Convocation on the day of the election was between Sir Francis Doyle, author of the patriotic ballad of British manliness and pluck, 'The Private of the Buffs', and two clergyman the undergraduates had never heard of. Doyle won by a majority of ninety-one votes of the 700 cast. The *Undergraduate's Journal* noted with a trace of irony that of hundreds in Oxford that day to vote, many 'returned to London by special train after 8 o'clock'.[29]

Lang lived out in his final year. He took rooms in Turl Street, just a stone's throw from the college gates. An ancient university statute requiring undergraduates to reside within the college walls had been gradually relaxed by the proctors, in response in part to Jowett's initiative to accept students from poorer backgrounds, unable to pay the college residential and tuition fees. Conveniently, the relaxation of the regulation also eased the temporary problem accommodating undergraduates at Balliol when work began on the demolition and rebuilding of the front quad.[30] Even the master, Dr Scott, had to vacate his lodgings and take a house for two years in the High Street.[31] Lang, with his love of old things, was sorry to see the gate-tower and ancient quod knocked down and replaced with pretentious 'yellowish stone and red roofs'.[32]

Living out for Lang meant no longer having to eat 'the worst and ... the most expensive dinners in Oxford'.[33] It also allowed greater freedom. It made him laugh when he read Arthur Conan Doyle's ghost story 'Lot No. 249', in which Oxford undergraduates stay out all night without being observed by the porter or sent up before the dean.[34] To live within the walls of an Oxford college in those days was to be closely watched. A group of Oxford contemporaries, calling themselves 'The Shooting Stars', used their freedom as out-students to stage operettas and burlesques, with the female roles performed in wigs, make-up, and magnificent dresses supplied by Nathan's of London.[35] The scandal caused when the photographs of the female impersonators became popular with male buyers landed the group in trouble with the proctors and led eventually to the banning by the vice-chancellor of all theatrical performances 'within the precincts of the University'.[36] Lang, writing twenty years later, described the character of Cecil Graham in Oscar Wilde's short story 'The Portrait of Mr W. H.' as 'one of the pretty undergraduates who used to act the girls' parts in College plays'—a 'class of young man ... not universally "respected in the parish"'.[37] One of the founding members of the 'Shooting Stars', Foster McGeachy Alleyne of Merton College, who played the male leads, later became Lang's brother-in-law.

The perceived divide at Oxford between athletes and aesthetes, which became a popular subject of press lampoons a decade later, was already beginning to be noticed. *The Oxford Spectator*, a 'humorous little periodical' enjoyed by Lang in his final year, poked regular fun at the difference between Oxford men, 'who came out intending to exercise themselves in some manly and healthy way, and those whose design it was to exhibit the elegance of their person and their dress'.[38] Lang was one of the first to fall under the spell of French avant-garde literature and poetry long before this became the badge of the English aesthete; before, as he put it,

> The first aesthetic lily
> > Broke through the sandy plain.[39]

At the same time, he counted himself among the cricketers and sportsmen he chose as his friends. His friend Arthur Godley (afterwards Lord Kilbracken), who captained the college cricket team, remembered Lang as 'an interesting and picturesque figure' among the Scottish Exhibitioners at Balliol at that time:

> He was brilliant in conversation, took a great interest in games (though he played them badly), and, as a writer, was already nearly, if not quite, as admirable as he was in later life, which is saying a good deal. I shall never forget listening to an essay of his on Rabelais, which he read to an audience of two or three at the meeting of a small Essay Club to which he and I as undergraduates belonged: it filled me with amazement, and from that moment I always anticipated for him real greatness as a writer.[40]

Lang's essay on 'Rabelais and the Renaissance' is likely to have drawn inspiration from Walter Pater, at that time a young college lecturer at Brasenose College, who was attracting attention in Oxford for advocating a subjective and sensuous cultivation of beauty. In Lang's final year, Pater concluded a review of William Morris's poetry by urging those who sought beauty in life to 'catch at any exquisite passion ... or any stirring of the senses'.[41] An *Oxford Spectator* lampoon of the 'Aesthetic Don' whose room was 'a bower of bliss, drawing room, boudoir, picture-gallery all in one' may have been targeted at Pater, who furnished his room with a Persian carpet, tapestry, cushions, blue chintz curtains, and engravings of Renaissance artists.[42] Jowett is known to have occasionally sent Balliol undergraduates to Pater for tuition, among them Gerard Manley Hopkins, in the year above Lang. Pater saw the devotion to art and beauty over conventional morality in the art and poetry of the French and Italian Renaissance as a model for his own restless generation. For Lang, the 'antagonism between culture and faith' in the sixteenth-century French Humanist Rabelais' satirical *Gargantua and Pantagruel* recalled similarly 'the breaking of old restraints', and 'intellectual eagerness' for new knowledge in the Victorian age.[43]

A recent study by Sebastian Lecourt places Lang with Arnold and Pater in the tradition of a Victorian liberal humanist view of religion as matter of cultural inheritance rather than of personal conscience or belief.[44] Absent, however, is any attention to Lang's actual religious background, or to his stated attitude to the Victorian crisis of faith. Lang, brought up as a Scottish Episcopalian in a majority Presbyterian community and culture, was all too aware of the near bewildering proliferation in Scotland of antagonistic Christian creeds. He recalled of his school days at Edinburgh Academy, 'We changed our creed with that of our housemaster. I have been many a Protestant complexion and was U.P. [United Presbyterian] or Free Kirk or Congregational, may be, or original Secession.'[45] His upbringing made him critical towards the Presbyterian militants of the Scottish Reformation who preached freedom of conscience but, as he believed the evidence of history showed, had persecuted those whose choice of worship differed from their own. Religious influences, rather than what Lecourt calls 'aesthetic secularisation', better explain Lang's many-sided respect for differing inherited faiths and cultures across time. He thought shallow the trend towards substitute faiths and experimental religion in his day:

> All ages are ages of transition; but, unluckily, we are conscious of the fact. Young men came up all folly from school, to find faiths and ideas in the melting-pot. Some waxed sad at night; some went over to Rome; some talked nonsense about paganism and Greek ideals. We cannot bring back the Mastadon, we cannot bring back Greek ideals ... or the Ages of Faith—or anything.[46]

Referring to Mrs Humphry Ward's solution of a secularized religion of humanity in her best-selling 'crisis of faith' novel, Lang said plainly, 'I never ... at all went in the way of Robert Elsmere.'[47] He saw a better example of 'how to live' in Jowett, who went about his business 'for others, for work, for duty, for friendship', and for whom our own existence was evidence enough for belief.

In Lang's reading, Rabelais' humanism served as a warning to those of his own day who offered aesthetic culture and heightened individual consciousness as an answer to the problems facing modern man. The Renaissance dream of the transformative force of culture and learning was flawed, because culture and learning remained the province of privileged scholars. Their interest was neither collective nor democratic—democratic, in the sense of being for everyone. Lang wrote, 'The claim of the educated man to enjoy the right of free search for beauty, pleasure and knowledge ... neglects the needs of the multitude which required, not the privilege of vague liberty of thought, but an answer to practical questions'.[48] For Lang, the voyage of Rabelais' Pantagruel and the 'needy, unprincipled scholar', Panurge, to 'seek through all the world the oracle of truth' was analogous to the restless quest for purpose and meaning he saw at Oxford. Rabelais' description of the Isle of Macraeones (literally 'isle of long-livers', that is, 'the old'), 'where in a dark and deserted forest lie the fanes of forgotten gods, and the shrines of creeds outworn; temples, obelisks, pyramids, and tombs', especially caught his imagination. 'Oxford', he wrote later, 'like the Isle of Macraeones, is a lumber-room of ruinous philosophies, decrepit religions, fatuous beliefs'.[49] The obvious lesson of Rabelais' burlesque denouement in which the mysterious oracle in the bottle whispers just one word, 'Trink', was that man's life, cut off from inherited belief, leaves 'an empty house to be occupied, perhaps by a coarse epicureanism'. This prompted Lang to conclude, 'Is it not here that so many of our new systems will fail, as the Renaissance failed, to satisfy the longings of the world?'[50]

These feelings were the inspiration of his poem-sequence 'Hesperothen', the best and most ambitious of his undergraduate verses. He recalled stolen minutes writing it during Jowett's lectures for finals on Plato, and while on his winter break in Scotland:

> A scholar was I, in the way to
>   Be idle with pencil and pen,
> And I rhymed—while the master read Plato—
>   Of Phæacian men.
>
> When the Ettrick was sullenly frozen
>   With snows on the hill and the plain,
> The tune of my singing was chosen
>   Of 'The Sirens Again'.[51]

His Phæacian poems and the song 'The Sirens' Music Heard Again' form parts of the sequence. The dream-like musicality and word-painting of 'Hesperothen' owes much to Tennyson. Like Tennyson's 'Ulysses', the poem takes as its theme the post-Homeric legend that Odysseus, after his safe return from

Troy, grew restless for adventure, and set out again on his final journey. Tennyson's 'Ulysses' gives expression to the poet's own 'need to go forward, and to brave the struggle of life'.[52] The final line, 'To strive, to seek, to find, and not to yield', sounds a heroic note of courage and endurance. In Lang's 'Hesperothen', by contrast, the voyage of the Greek mariners becomes a melancholy return to places that no longer satisfy or detain. Phæacia, a land of poetry and festivity, is no longer visited by the gods in human form; further west, the Sirens' song has lost its power to enchant, and Circe's isle of bodily delights holds only 'infinite regret'. The journey's end is a deserted, twilight shore, like Rabelais' Isle of Macreones, with 'the altars of old sacrifice', haunted by the faint voices of the dead.[53]

'The Sirens' Music Heard Again' appeared anonymously in the illustrated weekly *Once a Week* on 25 January 1868. It was Lang's first commercially published work. He used the guinea he was paid for it to buy the Catholic historian John Lingard's multi-volume *History of England*, which drew for the first time on Vatican archives and state papers of the major European powers. He was only months away from finals, but as is often the case with bright undergraduates, his reading took new, adventurous directions in his final year. He always disagreed with those who claimed disparagingly that Oxford men were mere crammers and 'only read what pays'. He insisted that, on the contrary, 'you could know nothing that might not "pay" in the schools and prove serviceable in examinations'.[54] His own wide reading paid off: it got him a First in finals. The question was: what next? He chose to treat as a joke Jowett's suggestion that he might become a solicitor.[55] Gaining Jowett's support, he decided to try for a college fellowship. At that time, most Oxford dons were still in Holy Orders, but gradual laicization of the university had led to the creation of fellowships open to anyone by special examination. Balliol had a history of sending its graduates to take up open fellowships at other colleges, while never electing an out-college man herself.[56] There was a vacancy for an open fellowship at Merton College that year, with examinations to be held in December.

Lang's jubilation at getting a First was overshadowed by events at home. His father was threatened with blindness. Even worse, if that were possible, his mother was diagnosed with breast cancer. On 19 September, she underwent a 'horrible operation' at home to have the breast removed to stop the spread of the cancer. A mastectomy at that time was a primitive, traumatic, and excruciatingly agonizing experience. Lang observed some years later, 'It is indeed curious ... how often the Oxford years of undergraduates are harassed ... by domestic sorrows'.[57] He abstained from novel-reading and poetry that summer to concentrate on preparing for the Merton examinations. He gave himself a headache with 'Latin and Greek History and Philosophy, Logic and Metaphysics, Politics and other extras' in preparation. As term approached, he wrote to his ten-year-old cousin, Adele Leonide ('Edie') Sellar, in London, making fun of the mystifying complexities of Hegelian metaphysics:

> My sister Helen is in *Metaphysics*, she says she understands Hegel, and how are we to prove she doesn't. You begin by thinking of *nothing* for a long time, till you're quite sure you grasp the situation, and then you think of *something*, only it must not be anything in particular, and gradually you see that something and nothing are both the same, and there you are![58]

He ended by assuring her his father and mother were 'pretty well'. He had good reason for trying to keep up a cheerful tone in writing to his young female cousin. Edie's American-born mother had died in July just two months earlier, leaving Lang's uncle, Thomas Sellar, a widower with eight children, the oldest just 15.

Candidates for the Merton Fellowship Elections had to call on the warden with their College Testimonials on 5 December. Examinations, consisting of papers on Classics, Law, and Modern History, began the next day. Lang left home for Oxford at the beginning of October, travelling by way of Edinburgh to visit his Uncle Willie, whose path from a First Class to an Oxford fellowship he hoped to follow.

4

'Young Oxford'

The first place for news of elections and examination results at Oxford was the notice board in the college porch. Lang was waiting in anticipation when the college messenger arrived at the porch on the appointed day. He never forgot his exhilaration: 'The most comforting words that the present writer ever heard in his life were merely his own name. "Who has got the Merton Fellowship?" "Mr Lang".[1] He took up residence after Christmas as a probationer at Merton. His rooms, in the fellows' quadrangle on the second floor, commanded a view over Christ Church meadow to the river beyond. After 'years of work and anxiety', his predominant sensation on his elevation to a fellowship at an Oxford college was one of 'benevolent repose'.[2]

Merton was ahead of Balliol in some respects in its response to the recommendations of the University Commission in the 1850s, calling upon colleges to modernize. Reform meant reducing the number of dons in Holy Orders and extending the range of study to include 'all branches of useful learning'.[3] At the time of Lang's appointment, already half of Merton's twenty fellows held ordinary 'non-clerical fellowships'. Of these, Robert Clifton was designing the first physics laboratory in Britain; another, William Esson, was advancing the new field of theoretical chemistry. The old guard were still a presence. Robert Bulloch Marsham, the rector for over forty years, had the 'temper and tastes of an old country gentleman' and seemed to belong to a different age.[4] He had gained minor notoriety for defending publicly the embargo on corn during the bitter winter of 1842–3, when he earned the unflattering nickname 'Potato Dick' for proclaiming that although British workers could not buy bread, they 'rejoiced in potatoes'. Lang found it 'almost incredible' too when George Hammond, an older fellow at the college, mentioned matter-of-factly having been at Eton with Shelley.[5] Although the old guard were nominally in charge, real power in the college had shifted to the younger, more liberal fellows, principal among them, George Brodrick, whom all saw as the rector-in-waiting. Brodrick, a star student of Jowett's from Balliol a decade earlier, should have been Lang's natural ally, but Brodrick's outspoken opinion that 'all persons of sense and decency took the liberal side in the Governor Eyre's case', would have put Lang on his guard.[6] Another prominent figure was 25-year-old Mandell

Andrew Lang. John Sloan, Oxford University Press. © John Sloan (2023). DOI: 10.1093/oso/9780192866875.003.0004

Creighton, promoted that year from Junior Dean to Principal of Postmasters. Originally, the Principal of Postmasters had charge of undergraduate scholars maintained at the college's expense, but he was now effectively Senior Tutor, responsible for the discipline and behaviour of all students.

Merton had a reputation at that time for rowdiness and high spirits rather than for academic achievement.[7] Its undergraduates, the majority from Eton and Malborough, gained greater distinction on the cricket and sports fields than on the university pass lists. Merton library was open to undergraduates for only one hour a week. Creighton, who had been nicknamed 'the Professor' or 'the P.' while still an undergraduate,[8] followed Jowett's example in encouraging student industry and discipline, and in trying to prepare the young men under his charge for an active and purposeful life. Lang found in Creighton a tall lean figure with a bushy auburn beard, a 'kind and constant friend'.[9]

Lang and Creighton were relatively untroubled by the supposedly conflicting truths of science and religion which shook the traditional faith of many of their generation. For Lang, as for Creighton, who was preparing to take Orders, it seemed simplistic to be certain that the revelations of science, wonderful though they were, 'exhausted all causes in nature'.[10] He and Creighton were also drawn to the aesthetic trend, which in 1860s Oxford meant a taste for Renaissance art, and a desire for beauty. Creighton, whose father owned an interior decoration business in Carlisle, wore silk neck ties and furnished his rooms at Merton with *objects d'art* and 'old oak'.[11] Lang's one decorative purchase was an old, coloured print of a pert young lady seated at her bedroom mirror while her scolding duenna retrieves a forbidden romance from under her pillow.[12] His scope for collecting was limited by his salary of £200 a year as a fellow, a modest sum for a gentleman to live on at Oxford. Unlike Creighton, he did not have the additional income that came with tutorial duties and college offices.

His joy in his new position was cut short by tragedy at home. His father suffered a series of strokes which left him paralysed, and his mother's recovery after her operation proved short-lived.[13] She was ravaged with hydrothorax, an accumulation of fluid in the lungs. Then the cancer spread to her liver, causing cirrhosis and renal failure. She died on Thursday 2 September. Two days later, at 9 o'clock at night, his father had another severe cerebral haemorrhage and died two hours later without recovering consciousness. When Robert Louis Stevenson's father passed away some years afterwards, Lang wrote bleakly, 'It is not much anybody can say in such a loss. I have been through it, my father and mother both lying dead in the house at the same time'.[14]

Lang, at 25, became head of the family. Of his brothers, Patrick, his junior by a year, and a graduate in law at Edinburgh, took over his father's duties as sheriff-clerk and Commissioner of Taxes. John, age 20, and in banking, was inconsolable; Craig, 17, was at Loretto School, and Thomas William (T.W.), 15, was a star batsman at Edinburgh Academy. Nancy Gray, the family's nurse for over twenty years, stayed on at Viewfield, while the future of the youngest—Helen, 14, and William Henry, 10—was decided.

Home and the surrounding countryside were for Lang haunted ever afterwards by ghosts. He gave voice to this in his elegiac 'Twilight on Tweed' in the year following his parents' deaths. The pictured landscape of the opening line—'Three crests against the saffron sky'—carries suggestions of heraldic allegiances and belonging. Hearing again 'the distant music' of the river, he is moved to 'quiet tears', conscious that,

> Where Scott, come home to die, has stood,
> My feet returning stand.

'A mist of memory'—'ballad notes' and 'old songs' that sang in his head as a boy—settles upon him in the gathering dusk. There is a caesura before the final stanza—a break or pause for feelings that lie too deep for words—then a shift back from memory to the twilight landscape which now only speaks to him of an absent presence:

> Twilight, and Tweed, and Eildon Hill,
> Fair and thrice fair you be;
> You tell me that the voice is still
> That should have welcomed me.[15]

On his return to Oxford at the start of the new academic year in October 1869, a month after his parents' burial, he was making his way from Oxford High Street through Oriel Lane when he saw John Conington, the university Professor of Latin, standing under the lamp post in the middle of the cobbled square, gazing intently towards Corpus Christi College.[16] Conington, with his greenish moon-face, was an unmistakable figure.[17] Lang turned the corner into Merton Street and thought no more about it. He was taken aback when he learned that Conington had not returned to Oxford but had died at his widowed mother's home in Lincolnshire about the time Lang saw him in Oriel Square. Lang from that time on collected records and reports of those who had similar uncanny experiences.

Lang was elected a full fellow of Merton—'*in perpetuam societatem*'—and swore the college's oath of obedience, fidelity, and secrecy.[18] As holder of an open fellowship, he was under no obligation to teach or perform administrative duties, but he was expected to undertake a course of higher study or research. Studying Greek and Latin mythology as an undergraduate, he had read the Professor of Philology at Oxford Max Müller's works on the subject 'with interest, but without conviction'. In his *Essays on the Science of Language*, Müller argued that the names of the gods in Vedic Sanskrit and Greek had their origin in the nature concepts of a common nature-worshipping Aryan ancestor. After taking up his fellowship, and with leisure to read more widely on the myths of other races, Lang's distrust increased. He kept finding myths very closely resembling those of Greece in all ages and countries, even among people who were not of Aryan origin. An added problem was how to account for the obscene, incongruous elements in the higher mythologies which puzzled the civilized mind—for example, when 'the beautiful Sun-god makes love in the shape of a dog'. Müller explained these 'blots' as instances of a metaphorical or poetical conception degenerating through linguistic corruption—in Müller's phrase, 'a disease of language'—into a literal or vulgar story. Lang, on the contrary, thought these 'ugly scars' might be remnants of the primitive, savage fancies—in short, that the origin of mythology, as in every phase of evolution, was from low to high, not the other way round. He imagined with the excitement of youth that he was the first to think of this but was delighted to discover anticipations of the idea in the works of the early Christian historian Eusebius, and the eighteenth-century French philosopher Bernard de Fontenelle's *De L'Origine des Fables*.[19]

Lang's idea of looking for the beginnings of human culture and civilization, not in conscious organization, but in barbarous social customs, was strengthened on reading John Ferguson McLennan. In *Primitive Marriage*, published when Lang was in his first year at Balliol, McLennan detected in Roman marriage contracts relics of collusive forms of bride abduction and, in turn, of a more primitive social rule of matrilinear descent which he called 'exogamy', forbidding marriage between those with the same clan or totem name. He followed this in 1869–70 with articles suggesting that religion may have evolved from the primitive totemic worship of animals and plants by tribal peoples.[20] McLennan, a Scottish lawyer, was in London in 1870 as parliamentary draughtsman for Scotland when Lang's uncle Alexander Craig Sellar, was serving as Legal Secretary at the Crown Office in Edinburgh. Lang thought McLennan 'the most acute and ingenious' person he ever met.[21] McLennan's 'writings on early marriage and early religion' opened his mind to a whole new chain of possibilities: 'The natural people, the folk, has supplied us, in its unconscious way, with the stuff of all our poetry, law, ritual; and genius has selected from the mass, has turned customs into codes, nursery tales into romance, myth into science, ballad into epic, magic mummery into gorgeous ritual'.[22]

Lang's difficulty was how to address this new field of enquiry. Anthropology was not recognized as mainstream academic discipline. The elements that comprised a science of man were subsumed within existing university disciplines: Philology; Historical Jurisprudence; Ethnology; and Natural Science. In compliance with the academic expectations of his fellowship, Lang proposed to write a series of introductory essays for students on Books, 1, 3 and 4 of Aristotle's *Politics*, a favoured set text for finals in Literae Humaniores. He also undertook a new prose translation of the *Odyssey* beginning with Book 6, describing Odysseus' shipwreck on the isle of the Phæacians, where he encounters the beautiful princess Nausicaa. Translation in today's Oxford is not ranked particularly highly by academic peers; but in Victorian Oxford, accurate and scholarly translations of Greek and Latin authors were regarded as valuable student aids to the originals.

Lang travelled to Europe for the first time during the long vacation to join his Uncle Willie and his family at Sankt Blasien in the Black Forest. William Young Sellar had succumbed to his periodic bout of depression, and Sankt Blasien had been recommended for its curative climate and scenic beauty. Fraulein Jason, the children's governess, was from Karlsruhe, the region's capital. The hotel where they stayed was a converted monastery. They made friends with Herr von Göler, Aide-de-camp to Grand Duke Frederick of Baden, who was staying at the hotel with his wife. On 16 July, Von Göler came to them in agitation with the news that he had been ordered back to Karlsruhe. He had received a wire from the duke which read, 'Krieg erklärt' ('War declared'). Almost overnight, all the men in the village, including the waiters at the hotel, went off to war. Louis Napoleon's French army had crossed into Prussia, and Bismark's German coalition forces retaliated swiftly.[23]

With news of fierce fighting on the German French border, they decided to take refuge in Switzerland. They stayed first in Zurich, then moved to Engelberg near Lucerne. Lang made trips on his own to Lausanne and stayed at the Hotel Gibbon, built on the site of 'La Grotte', the house where Edward Gibbon wrote his *The Decline and Fall of the Roman Empire*. On their way home in late August, they stopped at Karlsruhe, and Lang visited the town hospital where he witnessed the 'touching sight' of German and French soldiers 'playing cards, draughts, and other games'. A small army of surgeons and nurses from the newly formed National Society for Aid to the Sick and Wounded in War was there with medical supplies and equipment to treat the wounded. Lang was moved by the sight of young English nurses going about the sick and dying to write a sonnet, 'Two Homes [To a young English lady in the Hospital of the Wounded at Karlsruhe, September 1870]', in which he imagines the 'sweet eyes' and 'gold hair' of his 'young English lady' stirring in the final 'dim gaze' of a dying German soldier, a 'dream or memory' of the 'deep green valleys of the Fatherland' and 'girls with locks' and eyes like hers:

> —so past homes, or homes to be,
> He sees a moment, ere, a moment blind,
> He crosses death's inhospitable sea.[24]

Lang's 'Two Homes' anticipates the sensibility of early twentieth-century poets to the pathos and suffering, rather than the supposed glory and masculinity of war. As they sailed down the Rhine towards home, the signs of war gradually receded, although everywhere there were rumours of disastrous defeats suffered by Louis Napoleon's ill-prepared and poorly led army.

Back in Oxford, the spirit of reform was beginning to change the centuries-old nature of college life. The increase in 'ordinary fellowships', together with the decreasing number of fellows studying Theology or Canon Law, meant that the atmosphere in the colleges grew more secular and less restrictive. In July 1870, the University Tests Bill had had its third reading in the House of Commons. If passed, as seemed likely, the act would finally allow the election of Catholics, Nonconformists, Jews, other non-Anglicans to University posts. It was victory for the reformers and resulted in increased calls for the admission of women to the university. That year, Creighton for the first time admitted to his lectures women from the newly founded Ladies' Associations for the Advancement of Women's Education, although they were requested to sit in the gallery. During Lang's final year at Balliol, the *Oxford Spectator* had lamented in burlesque style that the 'unhappy Oxford Man' had to wait until the vacation before he could again 'regain the long-pined-for society of the unenfranchised sex'.[25] Women were now becoming a more noticeable presence in Oxford life.

Lang viewed the desire for change through the lens of literature as a return to the spirit of the Renaissance. An often-overlooked consequence of the exclusion of non-Anglicans from the university was that the bar was not only on British Catholics and religious dissenters but also on Catholic Europe and German Lutherans. The bar prevented in effect the beneficial interchange of a common European culture. In his article on the Italian renaissance philosopher and martyr of the Inquisition, 'Giordano Bruno', published in *Macmillan's* magazine, Lang invests Oxford with a symbolic place in the unity and transmission of European Humanist values, through his account of Bruno's visit to Oxford with Sir Philip Sidney in the summer of 1583. His opening description of Oxford in summer suggests, too, the civilizing presence of women, who make past and present-day Oxford for a moment in imagination like Rabelais' fictional Abbey of Thélème, where monks and nuns may marry:

> Her academic generations have been so many and so fleeting, that she is invested with an even greater charm than other towns of beauty and antiquity not less than her own. While her gardens, filled with summer visitors, seem to bring back for a little the lettered ease and liberty of the Abbey of Thélème, even the lightest hearted lounger may feel the permanence of the scene, the shifting of characters and costumes; may seem to see for a moment, in the alleys, the laces and velvets of Charles's court, may remember how short is summer and take to heart the lesson of the roses.[26]

Despite a 'feverish desire for change', college dinners and social events remained almost exclusively male, and there was little to attract seekers after culture to Oxford that was not better served at Cheltenham or Bath. That changed when John Ruskin, the newly appointed Slade Professor of Fine Art, began a series of lectures in February 1871 at the Sheldonian Theatre in Oxford, that were open to the public. Ruskin enjoyed a reputation as a charismatic thinker and speaker far beyond the university, and visitors flocked to the town to hear him, many of them young women.

Lang's romantic attachments during his first years at Merton, by his own account, were only with the ladies conjured in his verses:

> On ladies that never existed
>   (Or never in space and in time)
> I founded my fancies, and twisted
>   The strands of a rhyme.[27]

This was not the case with others in his circle of friends. At Ruskin's first lecture, on landscape in art, an attractive young woman in a yellow scarf in the crowded Sheldonian caught Mandell Creighton's eye. She was Louise von Glehn, who had just passed the first University of London examination for

women. She had come up to Oxford specifically to hear her idol and was staying with Benjamin Brodie, the Oxford Professor of Chemistry, and his wife
at Cowley Lodge (later St Hilda's College).[28] She also knew Humphry Ward,
a visitor to the von Glehn family, who planned to propose to her. Creighton
and Humphry Ward became rivals in love. The day before Louise von Glehn
left Oxford three weeks later, she and Creighton became engaged.[29] Humphry
Ward quickly transferred his love to Mary Arnold, daughter of his Brasenose
College colleague, Tom Arnold, Matthew Arnold's brother. The historian John
Richard Green, who knew everyone involved in this 'little Oxford Comedy',
was highly amused by how much 'Young Oxford', as he called it, had changed
from the days 'when no young maidens descended on our earthly sphere'.[30]

Creighton's engagement prompted Merton to reopen the contentious question of relaxing the rule against fellows marrying. The argument for retaining
the restriction was the same as the reason given by the Catholic Church for a
celibate clergy: a single man was considered better able to devote himself more
fully to his duties. At a meeting of the Governing Body on 30 May 1871, lasting
from 10 a.m. until 4.00 p.m., after much argument, a proposal to allow up to
four married fellowships was finally carried by fourteen votes to two. Three
more fellows immediately put in a request to marry under the new statute,
prompting Creighton to remark, 'Merton has always been regarded as the most
advanced and maddest College in Oxford; but the spectacle of all its Fellows
rushing headlong into matrimony at once will make everyone in Oxford die
with laughter'.[31]

Meanwhile, Lang contributed to the first number of a new Oxford monthly
magazine, *The Dark Blue*, founded and edited by John Christian Freund, a former undergraduate at Exeter College, who had left before taking his degree.
Lang's essay on 'Théophile Gautier' voiced reservations about the Aesthetic
movement that was attracting converts at Oxford. He praised Gautier as 'a poet
of the school of art' to whom 'the emotion is only the matter of the poem, the
art the form', but he noted too a 'real danger' that the excesses of 'art-for-art's-
sake' can become 'a cancer which devours the rest of the moral nature'.[32] He
followed this in the May issue with 'Three Poets of French Bohemia (François
Villon, Gérard de Nerval, Henri Murger)',[33] in which he sought to dispel the
fantasy of an English equivalent to Bohemian Paris in the tavern-haunting
coteries of literary and artistic London. He argued with insight that Bohemia,
the province of France's radical artistic intelligentsia, had its origin in the conditions of medieval Paris where the 'most luxurious and lawless court' existed
'side by side with the University overcrowded by poor students', resulting in
the natural opposition between a personal literature 'that envied and despised'

and the official allegorical and traditional forms of literature 'patronised by the court'. He concluded that such collective opposition did not exist in England where the university remained largely distant from everyday life: 'England has never combined the university and the capital, nor fixed so wide a gulf between the two classes of men of letters'. He discounted too the sentimental romance of garret life, given vogue in England by Henri Murger's *Scènes de la vie de Bohème*. The poets of French Bohemia, he wrote, shared a 'sorrowing sense of life's brief endurance', and in Murger's poems and stories, he found 'less of mirth, more of the pain and hopelessness of the Bohemian'.

The *Oxford Undergraduate's Journal*, reviewing the first issue of *Dark Blue*, singled out his article on Gautier as 'one of the best', although adding, 'If this writer would throw a little more of himself into his work, and seem to care less for saying a thing merely because it has not been said before, he would be second in promise to none of our younger writers'.[34] The magazine had only unqualified praise, however, for his translations of Villon, De Nerval and Murger as executions of 'rare grace and felicitousness'.[35] Lang's own 'Spent Golden Hair', inspired by Villon's affectionate '*les petites vielles*' ('old ladies'), whose eyes still have 'power to waken sad memories',[36] appeared in the June issue of the *Oxford Undergraduate's Journal*. His verse received even wider recognition on Commemoration Day, at the end of the academic year, a day of college balls and celebratory promenade following the conferring of degrees, when, according to the *Oxford Undergraduate's Journal*, Oxford prepared itself for an annual invading army of 'beautiful Vandals' with 'the silk parasol for the spear'.[37] In its widely distributed 'Commemorative Double Number', Lang's poem 'In College Gardens', evoking Oxford summers and its graceful lady visitors through the ages, was given central place. The poem reflects the mood of his description of Oxford in his essay on Giordano Bruno. The poet, sadly conscious of summer's transience, observes Oxford's female visitors, strolling in college gardens, their voices carrying him back in imagination to graceful ladies of earlier times, like Lady Dorothy Sidney (the 'Sacharissa' to whom the Cavalier poet Edmund Waller wrote his love poems):

> Listen, and look in gardens green
> The bright array, the floating curls,
> The voices of the English girls,
> Where Sacharissa's voice has been.[38]

Lang spent the long vacation with his Uncle Willie, Aunt Eleanor, and the Sellar family at Sorn on the northernmost tip of the Isle of Mull. The previous year, his Uncle Alexander had married Gertrude Smith, who had inherited Ardtornish on her father's death, bringing the estate back into the family. The party stayed there before crossing the Sound of Mull by boat to their small holiday house near Glen Gorm. The estate manager at Ardtornish, on hearing that they hoped for good air at Sorn, exclaimed, 'Air! Why, there's naething but air'.[39] Sorn proved indeed to be a wild, dreary, depopulated place. James Forsyth, a Jamaican slave plantation owner, had cleared crofters from the area in the 1850s in order to build an isolated Baronial-style Glengorm Castle. They dined there with his widow Maria Magdalena and her daughters but found the conversation wearisome. Lang joked many years later of that summer, 'Mull home of me youth—and a very dull island it is'.[40] His Aunt Eleanor's widowed cousin, Constance Hamilton, came on her yacht, the 'Diana', and took Lang's uncle, and cousins Nellie, 17, and Eppie, 12, to a livelier gathering at Dunvegan, the MacLeod estate on the Isle of Skye.[41] Florence, 15, stayed on Mull. She shared Lang's love of Scottish history and literature, and was devoted to arts and crafts, particularly woodcarving. People said of her that she was 'direct and confident' and showed 'what good talk could be'.[42] Lang had a playful relationship with all his young female cousins. He wrote plays for family performance and light-hearted verse sending up the foibles of the family circle. But with Florence, despite their difference in age, he began to develop a closer, more emotional tie, which did not go unnoticed.[43]

Lang planned a surprise for family and friends that Christmas. The house of Longmans was to publish his debut volume of verse, *Ballads and Lyrics of Old France*. He had made friends with the publisher's eldest son, Frederick, at Balliol. Tragically, a sporting accident forced Frederick to leave Oxford without taking his degree and left him a lifelong invalid. Frederick's younger brother, Charles James ('C. J.'), took Frederick's place in the family business after completing his degree. The official publication date for *Ballads and Lyrics* was 1 January, but copies were made available for him to give to family and friends as Christmas presents.[44] The collection included verse translations of Villon, Charles d'Orleans, and other old French poets; together with translations of nineteenth-century French Romantic poets, and a selection of his own original verse under the heading 'Ave' ('Hail'). Publication brought him his first taste of literary controversy. There had been a moral backlash in the press against indecency and the poisonous influences imported from France, following a rancorous attack the previous October by 'Thomas Maitland' (Robert Buchanan) on Rossetti and the 'Fleshly School of Poetry'.[45] Lang took a different view, praising Rossetti, in an unsigned review, for his success in uniting modern 'refinement' with the spirit of the ancients: 'Love in his poems ... has ... found its own image, with a difference, in the light desire of Greek antiquity, and the ecstasy of mystic medieval romance'.[46] He especially admired Rossetti's translations of Villon. His own translations of French poets came in for censure as 'indecently warm' by some reviewers, who singled out Victor Hugo's 'Since I have set my lips to your full cup, my sweet' as the most flagrant.[47]

Over Christmas Lang wrote three fairy tales for a small Oxford manuscript magazine, the *Miscellany Magazine*, edited and handwritten by Margaret Louisa ('Daisy') Bradley, daughter of George Granville Bradley, Head of House at University College, and her cousin Miriam Bradley. The magazine was very much an amateur family affair. Subscribers included among others Miriam's brother, Andrew Cecil, and W. H. Mallock, both undergraduates at Balliol; Thomas Arnold's son, William; and Selwyn Image, an art student studying under Ruskin. The magazine was circulated in strict order, allowing each subscriber five days to read it. Lang's stories—'In the Debatable Land', 'A Lady of White Heather, A Border Fairy Tale', and 'Poppy's Heart'—were coming of age tales of desire, suffering, and strength through sorrow.[48] The most dramatic, 'A Lady of White Heather', based on a dream Lang had as a boy,[49] was a version of the story found in all ballad traditions in which the hero is visited by a virgin goddess or spiritual lady and must choose between earthly love or a divine ideal of womanhood. In Lang's version, the young hero, disobeying the virgin goddess's injunction, plucks the white heather for a young girl, so losing 'the fairest fortune that ever man had'. His stories were illustrated in manuscript by 19-year-old Janet Mary Tylor, the daughter of a brass-founder in Surrey, Alfred Tylor, a follower and friend of Ruskin.

Lang's acquaintance with the Tylor family marked a significant turning point in his life. In March 1872 he met Alfred Tylor's brother, Edward Burnett Tylor, a pioneering thinker in the new field of anthropology. He had not read or heard of any of Edward Tylor's books, but their meeting 'sent him off to borrow Tylor's *Primitive Culture* from Merton College Library'.[50] He was exhilarated by Tylor's findings. He wrote later of Tylor, 'He had proved that man, in Byron's words, "is always and everywhere the same unhappy fellow", whatever the colour of his hair or skin, and the shape of his skull. Homo, in the earliest age at which we make his acquaintance, is already the philosopher, artist, and man'. Tylor's evidence for the continuing residual 'survival' of 'savage' or 'primitive' habits of mind in advanced, civilized society gave scientific foundation to his own dissatisfaction with Müller's theory of myths. He wondered whether Tylor's lack of a degree, and the fact that he was largely self-taught, explained why he refrained from 'throwing a stone into the adjacent garden of Mr. Max Müller'.[51] In June, following their meeting, Lang took it upon himself to throw the first stone in an article on the 'Kalevala, or the Finnish National Epic'. Compiled from oral ballads and folk songs in Finland's scattered rural communities, the 'Kalevala' provided him with evidence of an evolutionary link in poetic development from ballad (the unsophisticated songs of the people) to epic (the mythological verse of the chiefs and rulers). His argument that the higher forms of artistic poets developed out of the materials of primitive people offered a corrective to Müller's theory that the simpler forms of narrative were 'degradations of the inventions of a cultivated class'.[52] The stone he threw was to cause ripples for many years to come. Confident of his ground, he began a second essay on the eleventh-century French epic, *La Chanson de Roland*, showing that, contrary to the view of Müller's followers, who read the poem as an example of Aryan natural phenomena transformed through the corruption of language into imagined characters and story, *La Chanson de Roland* contained, like Homer's epics, 'traces and survivals of an earlier genre of story, the folk-song'.[53] In taking to the field, he hoped cultural anthropology would be taken seriously as a human science,[54] but challenging Müller was not a wise career move by a junior don at Oxford.

Social life at Merton changed that year. Two days before Christmas, the college's Governing Body granted the requests made by Creighton and three other fellows for permission to marry. After the meeting, Henry Musgrave Wilkins, a senior fellow, is reported to have said, 'There were four seats on the matrimonial coach, and they were all immediately taken'.[55] Social gatherings after that were no longer exclusively male affairs confined to the College Hall and Senior Common Room. Mandell and Louise Creighton married on 1 January and rented a house on St Giles Road East. They christened it 'Middlemarch', after George Eliot's novel about the march of human progress being serialized in *Macmillan's Magazine*. Lang 'made a great effort' to have George Eliot's works put in Merton Library, but George Eliot, who lived openly with George Henry Lewes, a married man, was still regarded by some with disapproval, and F. H. Bradley, who had come from Balliol to Merton on an open fellowship, managed to defeat his proposal.[56] The Creightons fostered a more mixed society at Oxford. Lang was a regular guest at their 'little dinners of six or eight'. Louise Creighton remembered him in those days 'constantly with us, in and out of the house when he was living in rooms at Merton, or sometimes staying with us'.[57] The Creightons' other bachelor friends were Walter Pater, who lived with his unmarried sisters, Hester and Clara, in Bardwell Road in North Oxford; Reginald Copleston, who as an undergraduate at Merton had produced with Humphry Ward the satirical *Oxford Spectator*; and George Henry Woods, of Trinity College. Humphry Ward and Mary Arnold, married three months after the Creightons, were also frequent guests. Humphry Ward had been obliged to give up his fellowship to marry, although he retained his position as college tutor. Other regulars were Arthur Johnson, chaplain of All Soul's, and his wife Bertha, and Lang's old tutor Thomas Hill Green, and his wife Charlotte, the sister of John Addington Symonds, Jowett's friend and former protégé.[58] Visitors from outside felt the group talked shop and lived too much in their own little world, but the Creighton circle also looked beyond Oxford in their advocacy of the extension of university education to women. Symonds's house in the affluent suburb of Clifton in Bristol was the meeting place for the Clifton Association for Higher Education of Women, one of the most active in the country, and starting in the spring of 1872, Creighton, Humphry Ward, and T. H. Green gave lectures and classes there to prepare women for the Higher Cambridge Examination. Sarah Frances (Fanny) Alleyne, co-secretary of the Clifton Association, was the older sister of Creighton's friend in their undergraduate days, Foster Alleyne, who had played the male leads for the 'Shooting Stars'.

Events drew Lang, too, to Clifton. Two years earlier, his brother T. W. had transferred from Loretto School to Clifton College, with its excellent reputation for cricket and sports, to complete his schooling before applying to Oxford. Jowett's friend, Evelyn Abbott, was Assistant Master there. In September 1872, Lang arranged for his youngest brother, William, 13, to join T. W. at the school. As the winter of 1872–3 began to close in, his own life at Oxford took an unhappy turn. His passing reference to this is enigmatic. He wrote, 'Unfortunately, life at Oxford is not all beauty and pleasure. Things go awry somehow. Life drops her happy mask.'[59] It is usually supposed that the cause of his sadness was disappointment in love. Evidence for this is found in Lang's poems of lost love—'Love and Wisdom', 'Good-bye', 'Summer's Ending'—in his *Ballads and Lyrics of Old France* of 1872. His verse 'The Singing Rose', with its evocation of college gardens and eternal separation, is also cited:

> Yes, unawares the unhappy grass
>   That leadeth steps astray
> We trod, and so it came to pass
> That never more we twain, alas,
>   Shall walk the self-same way.
> And each must deem, though neither knows,
> That *neither* found the Singing Rose.[60]

Lancelyn Green has suggested an unrequited love for Frederick Longman's sister, Sybil Augusta, seemingly unaware that Sybil in 1872 was just 11 years old.[61] Lang, who liked to amuse young female cousins, and his friends' younger sisters, was a frequent and welcome visitor to Ashlyns Hall, the Longman family estate in Hertfordshire, and had a drawing of Sybil as a child by her sister Ada Mary. In fact, it is more likely that the shadow that fell on him was criticism at Merton of the slow progress of his research, and disapproval of his attacks on Müller. Darker still, he was told that a worsening lung complaint could prove fatal. Before the end of Michaelmas Term 1872, he was ordered south to the Riviera for the winter in the hope of a cure. Before his departure, he left his essay on *La Chanson de Roland* with Pater. Pater wrote to John Chapman, editor of the *Westminster Review*, on 17 November, 'I send you by this post an article on *The Chanson de Roland* by my friend, Mr. Andrew Lang, Fellow of Merton College, the author of a volume of translations from French poets etc. which you may have seen. He is now in Cannes, and has entrusted the article to me, hoping you might be able to find a place for it'.[62] In Oxford, where succeeding generations of scholars and students are so fleeting, individuals are soon forgotten. Some of Lang's colleagues at Merton thought his departure probably marked the end of his academic career; some too, suspecting the worst, that his life might soon be over.

*

With the coming of the railway in the 1860s, Cannes on the French Riviera became a favoured destination for those with money enough, who needed to escape the cold, damp, foggy British winter. The climate of the town was thought ideally suited to people with lung complaints: the south-facing bay sheltered by hills and mountains, and the dry warm air which resulted in temperatures ten degrees higher on average than England. In the 1870s, the journey from Paris to Cannes by express train took twenty-two hours. The *Rapide* left the Gare du Nord at 7.15 in the evening and arrived at Cannes at 5.25 the following afternoon, passing on route through Dijon, Lyon, and Marseilles. A sleeper could be booked in advance at 1 Rue Scribe, Paris, for forty-six francs, in addition to the ordinary fare.[63]

Cannes was a largely British resort. More than half of its six thousand winter visitors—'des hivernants'—were from Britain. English was spoken everywhere. Lang could read and translate the most complex works of French literature, but he claimed that the only person who ever understood him when he spoke French was a Finn.[64] In the early 1870s, Cannes was a place with few amusements. Visitors relaxed on the beach, or went for a stroll on La Croisette, the boulevard that stretched along the bay. Lang's favourite walk was to the red rocks a little to the west, to watch the 'curving lines of creamy spray'.[65] At the harbour, you looked seawards to the Lérins Islands of Saint-Honorat and Sainte-Marguerite, where the mysterious 'man in the iron mask' was imprisoned during the reign of Louis XIV—a historical mystery Lang set out to solve in later life He enjoyed the peace. While there he wrote 'Mythology and Fairy Tales', his most sustained and powerful demolition of Müller's theory of the origin of myths, in which he argued that 'the supernatural element' in Märchen, or fairy tales, was 'more easily explained as a survival of animal-worship, and of magic' rather than as 'the last remains, the detritus ... of an ancient mythology', and that 'the religious imagination of the Indo-European race', with its adoration of 'bodiless forces', must have passed through an earlier stage of fetishism, animal worship, and savage customs.[66]

By March he longed for home. During a solitary drive along the winding coastal road out of Cannes, the Corniche de L'Esterel, he read the opening chapters of William Black's serial novel *The Princess of Thule* in *Macmillan's Magazine* and felt homesick for Scotland's wild seas and hills.[67] The winter season at Cannes stretched on until the end of May, but with the coming of spring and troublesome mosquitoes, many English visitors returned home.[68] On his arrival back at Merton, Lang moved to rooms above Lecture Room 'A', on the first floor of staircase 5 of the Fellows' Quadrangle.[69] He furnished them with an ornate door frame imported from the south of France. That month he met Swinburne for the first time, when the poet visited Jowett. He hoped to speak more fully to Swinburne at a dinner party at Jowett's house but was disappointed when Swinburne failed to turn up after lunching with John Churton Collins, a Balliol graduate, who shared his interest in Jacobean drama. Swinburne's chair at dinner remained empty.[70] Lang's meetings with his idols at Oxford often ended in disillusionment. When he was introduced to Robert Browning on Browning's election as an honorary fellow of Balliol, he was rather alarmed to see Browning's hands shaking like Swinburne's. During his absence abroad, Pater had published his *Studies in the History of the Renaissance*, which included a flattering note praising Lang's 'excellent' translations of French Renaissance poetry. Pater's book, however, had met with disquiet and disapproval at Oxford. Pater's declaration in his 'Conclusion' to *The Renaissance* that 'the only thing worth living for is momentary enjoyment' amounted, in the eyes of conservative Oxford, to a dangerous charter for youthful paganism.

Lang had begun to question his future at Oxford. His fellowship came without obligations, and in theory he was free to follow his own studies, but Oxford was, and still is, a place of hidden pressures and expectations. Lang found it 'a discouraging place', where everyone lived 'in an atmosphere of criticism'.[71]

His writings on anthropology and myth were disregarded as irrelevant to the curriculum, and his articles and reviews in the London periodical press discounted condescendingly as dilettantism or 'by-work'. There was disapproval too of his generalist habits of mind in an academic atmosphere of carefully guarded specialist interests, and a tendency to scorn those who strayed from literary scholarship into literary journalism. David Orme Masson, his Uncle Willie's colleague at Edinburgh University, and an influential figure in London and Edinburgh literary circles, arranged for his election to the recently founded Savile Club, fast becoming the hub of London literary circles, with many of the leading editors and writers of the day among its members. Masson introduced him to Charles Appleton, cofounder of the club and editor of the *Academy*, who offered to send him books to review. Family influence also helped get him on the books of the *Saturday Review*. The *Saturday*, founded in 1855 as a flagship of liberal conservatism, felt almost like a family magazine. His Uncle Willie was among its first contributors, while Charles Bowen, another leading contributor to the review from its earliest days, had been Alexander Craig Sellar's inseparable companion at Rugby and Balliol, and the two remained close friends.

His dangerous lung complaint again forced him to winter at Cannes. In February, he moved to Menton, sixty kilometres along the coast. Menton had grown in popularity as a winter retreat for lung sufferers, following an English doctor James Bennett's book on Menton's beneficial climate. Lang had also learned that Sidney Colvin, a fellow member of the Savile, was at Menton. Colvin had an enviable reach as a leading literary reviewer, with many friends and useful contacts in London literary and artistic circles. Lang, never slow to seize opportunities to his advantage, took rooms at the Hotel des Anglais and called on Colvin at the Hotel Mirabeau on 11 February. That day Colvin introduced him to Robert Louis Stevenson, who was convalescing at the Mirabeau after a serious illness. Lang had never heard of Stevenson, and his first impressions 'were not wholly favourable'. Stevenson was wearing a large, blue cloak with a flamboyant Tyrolese hat, and Lang at first thought him an aesthetic poser, 'though a very clever one'.[72] Stevenson, on his side, had heard about Lang from his mother's friend and regular visitor, Lang's Aunt Eleanor. At Menton that day, Stevenson was put off by Lang's comment that the French author and art critic, Paul Bins, was 'not a British sportsman', and discounted Lang as 'good-looking, delicate, boyish, Oxfordish'.[73] They grew to like each other after Colvin left for home, dining often together at Hotel des Anglais,[74]

Lang had been a senior boy of 17 at Edinburgh Academy when Stevenson, six years younger, was among the crowd of small boys in 'the lowest form'.[75]

They both knew the Ferrier family. Walter Ferrier, the son of Lang's former philosophy professor at St Andrews, was Stevenson's closest friend. Stevenson, who had served as an apprentice lighthouse engineer in his family's business, was familiar with Ardtornish and the western coast of Argyllshire, where he had witnessed tearful scenes of evicted families being taken on board vessels.[76] More than anything, their talk was of literature. Lang interested Stevenson in old French poetry and the verse forms of rondeau and ballade and introduced him to Tylor's theory of primitive 'survivals', and its evolutionary psychology, which shaped Stevenson's view of romance fiction. Stevenson, with just two paid articles to his name, felt a novice in the world of literature compared to Lang, who had published *Ballads and Lyrics of Old France* and was already writing two book reviews a month for the *Academy*. Lang, on his side, admired Stevenson's account of his illness, 'Ordered South', with its 'stoical acceptance of the likelihood of an early death'. He felt that Stevenson 'already knew so much more of life' than he did.[77] Stevenson made no secret of his current unrequited love for Mrs Fanny Sitwell, a woman almost ten years his senior, nor of his youthful sexual experiences with Edinburgh prostitutes.

Stevenson left Menton for Paris on 31 March. Lang returned briefly to Cannes, which turned disappointingly wet, before making his way back to England. During his absence, Gladstone's Liberal government had been swept away in a landslide victory in a General Election for Benjamin Disraeli and the Tories. The mood in England seemed to be polarizing into Tory nationalism and radical activism and unrest. Lang had little time for politics or politicians. His values were socially conservative, his sympathies, democratic. The scandal doing the rounds of London—'the most hideous story, bar none', he thought[78]—was that the painter Simeon Solomon had been arrested *in flagrante delicto* with a male prostitute in a public urinal near the Bourse de Valeurs in Paris and was awaiting trial for outraging public decency. Lang, who had added art reviewing to his list of 'can do's', attended the opening of the Summer Exhibition of the Royal Academy on 26 April and admired 'Guinevere's Ride to Almesbury' by William Hole, a friend of Stevenson.

His thoughts had turned to getting married. He was 30, the age his father had been on his marriage. He had made the acquaintance of the bright, strikingly pretty Leonora Blanche (Nora) Alleyne. Mandell Creighton is likely to have introduced them. Nora Alleyne had known Creighton since 1867, when she was 16, and he began to direct her studies while on a visit to her brother Foster at their home in Clifton. John Addington Symonds and his sister Charlotte, now Mrs Green, were Clifton neighbours and close family friends. Nora's father had profited from the uglier, hidden aspects of European progress and expansion, which Victorian England abhorred and repented. For generations, the Alleyne family had owned large slave plantations in Barbados. With the Slavery Abolition Act of 1833, Charles Alleyne received compensation from the British government for his 845 slaves and returned to England to settle at Litchfield Place in Clifton. He had died in 1872, aged 74; Nora's mother, Margaret, a long-term invalid, died a year later, aged 62. Nora's brothers went to Eton and Oxford. Her younger brother Percy had gone up to Merton in October 1873, just before Lang left for a second winter at Cannes. Nora's older sister Fanny was translating Eduard Zellar's *History of Greek Philosophy*, a task Jowett had originally given to John Addington Symonds. Nora, who had read every book in her father's library by the time she was 6, was a gifted linguist with wide-ranging interests in literature, history, geography, and the fine arts.[79] She was a devoted and knowledgeable admirer of Frederic Leighton, whose new unabashed nude painting, 'Antique Juggling Girl', was among the exhibits in the main gallery of the Royal Academy Exhibition that April. She later wrote an introduction to Leighton's life and work for the *Art Annual* and took a mordant view of English prudery.[80] In a light-hearted character sketch of Lang ('Versatilio'), written many years later, Nora described him as 'gifted with an innocent vanity which renders it impossible for him to conceive that any person can possess interests which he does not share'.[81]

Tradition has it that Lang proposed that year to his 16-year-old cousin, Florence, and was rejected, before asking Nora to be his wife. Although fiction is not proof, there is some evidence to support this story in Lang's and Nora's later writings. In Nora's semi-autobiographical novel, *Dissolving Views*, the heroine's would-be husband declares himself only after paying a visit to a young woman with whom he had first been in love; while in Lang's burlesque shilling-shocker, *The Mark of Cain*, the protagonist, Robert Maitland, feels bound by a 'tacit engagement' to his young ward, Margaret, while 'dimly aware of a new, rather painful, rather pleased, kind of interest in another lady'.[82] Whatever understanding there may have been in real life between Lang and Florence, whether spoken or unspoken, was resolved, with no hearts broken. Lang said of courtship, 'Love must begin with flirtation, with a tender dubious interest, with "friendship", lending books, and all the rest of it. You cannot say to a girl, when you first meet her, "Be mine!"—or not often. Approaches must be made'.[83] In 1874, he and Nora became engaged.

Lang knew that marriage probably meant having to resign his fellowship at Merton. A Merton friend and colleague, William Courtney, had resigned his fellowship after only a year to marry. Lang told Jowett of his decision. Jowett, on hearing of William Sellar's engagement twenty years earlier, had advised him not to get married without 'some permanent appointment', warning him that wives 'lament when they see their husbands with nothing to do'.[84] William Sellar at the time had the advantage of temporary university appointments; Lang, whom Jowett thought foolish, faced the prospect of leaving university with nothing but the unreliable business of literary work.

Finding employment became a priority. Lang accepted the invitation to contribute entries on 'Apparitions' and 'Ballads' for the ninth edition of *Encyclopaedia Britannica*, whose offices were in Edinburgh. Colvin's friendship also proved useful. Mrs Sitwell, Colvin's friend, had taken over the running of the College for Working Women at Queen's Square in Bloomsbury, which was about to turn coeducational, and Colvin suggested Lang give lectures on French literature there with Jules Andrieu, a French scholar and refugee from the Paris Commune. Lang, in return, seconded Colvin's nomination of Stevenson for membership of the Savile Club. In a review of John Addington Symonds' *Sketches of Italy and Greece* for the *Academy*, he made a point of contrasting Symonds' seductively aesthetic, idealized picture of the Mediterranean with Stevenson's poignantly realistic picture of the Riviera as 'the last harbour and shelter of waning life' for invalids, knowing this would be picked up by those that mattered at the Savile.[85] He wrote jokingly to Stevenson of the Savile, 'If your native genius, & the spirit of Sir W. W. [William Wallace] and the Commune and so on leads you to burn it down, I'll stand ... Petroleum. It is not a howff I fancy much,—a shebeen perhaps one should say'.[86]

He was at Oxford's Taylorian Library in early June, getting up his lectures on French literature. Anxious to not to lose face by leaving Oxford academically empty-handed, he devoted more time to his collaborative work on Aristotle's *Politics* with his Merton colleague, the Revd William Bolland. He also contributed academic pieces to the *Fortnightly Review*, among them a substantial essay on recent Homeric criticism, although, as he confided to Stevenson, the editor John Morley 'confines himself to *accepting* them, which is another pair of sleeves'.[87] William Courtney, on a visit to Oxford, remembered Lang on a garden bench in Merton College gardens, looking happier than he had been, and interrupting his work on Homer because 'a certain Miss Alleyne was coming to see him'.[88] Lang remained busy all through that summer reviewing for the *Academy* and the *Saturday Review*. He told Stevenson, 'I still can't get any employment, but I'm not quite the Blighted being I was'.[89]

Nora travelled to Scotland with him that summer to be introduced to the family. The women were 'greatly taken with her'. They thought her 'handsome, knowledgeable and impressively well-informed', and they were all a little in awe of her.[90] Before returning to Oxford in October, he contributed to

Miscellany Magazine 'The Loves of Pulvis and Umbra by Pulvis. London. For private Circulation, 1874', a spoof review of his own Rossetti-inspired verse. The magazine was now in printed format, costing the growing number of subscribers 4/- a year to cover production. Adopting a censorious, mocking tone, he ridiculed Pulvis's immaturity: 'His little work is as soporific as the murmur of bees in the lime blossoms, or conversation about Mr. Morris' wall papers'.[91] The jest was kept up in the next issue with an effusive defence of the young Pulvis, parodying the style of Pater's aesthetic prose. The review enthused, 'Between the truculent reviewer and the new poet Pulvis are interposed many a lost race, many a lost love. Look on the youth's face, and remember that the Pyramids are dumb, the Babylonian Temple of Baal is no more, the face of Athene a ruin, the Colosseum a desert. His eyes are a little weary, for they have seen a thousand civilizations pass away ... Arson, battery, mayhem, half-a-hundred crimes, some alas! long past away flit through our minds'.[92] Lang wrote to Stevenson, 'You should see Mallock's review à la Pater, of Pulvis & Umbra – it is a great joke, especially his lament over forgotten crimes'.[93] One of the Pulvis poems, 'From the Silent Shore' made its way into Lang's later *Poetical Works* under the title 'Rococo: The New Orpheus to his Euridice', with the self-mocking envoi, 'When first we heard Rossetti sing/We also wrote this kind of thing!'[94]

Lang was back in Oxford by the first weekend of October, before the beginning of the new academic year. The Creightons were pleased to see him looking so well. He dined in college with them on Saturday evening and joined them for lunch on Sunday.[95] They had moved from St Giles to Beam Hall, a small, medieval, college-owned house in Merton Street opposite the college gate. They now had two children and were facing a 'momentous decision'[96]— whether to stay on in Oxford or accept the attractive offer of the college living of Embleton Vicarage in Cumbria, which had become vacant. They had to let the college know their decision before the November meeting of the Governing Body. Most of their married friends advised them to go, whereas the single men, apart from Lang, advised them to stay. Lang had already made up his mind that to leave Oxford was the wisest course for a married man. He had a weekend visit from Stevenson before the term got under way. Stevenson was in melancholy mood. Lang claimed discreetly in later years that he remembered 'nothing of what we did or said, with one exception, which is not going to be published'.[97] That 'one exception' is likely to have been Stevenson's disappointed hope of winning Mrs Sitwell, who had moved house but was refusing to give him her new address.

Lang's decision to abandon his academic career has puzzled some. A married fellowship at Merton would soon have fallen vacant, and he might have applied successfully for college duties. Lang himself made perfectly clear his reasons for wanting to leave: 'If a resident in Oxford is to make an income that seems adequate, he must lecture, examine, and write manuals and primers, till he is grey, and till the energy that might have added something new and valuable to the acquisitions of the world has departed'. It concerned him that married fellowships were still experimental, and no one knew what life would be like in later years, perhaps with a family: 'It is easy enough to marry on a fellowship, a tutorship, and a few miscellaneous offices. But how will it be when you come to forty years, or even fifty?'[98] More than anything, perhaps, he was impatient with existing boundaries. His desire to bring the findings of anthropology to the centre of academic debate and to wider general notice is evident in his writings that year. In his scholarly survey of Homeric criticism for the *Fortnightly*, he positioned anthropology 'with comparative mythology and comparative philology' as a key to the 'real history of the *épopées* of early people preserved in the midst of romance and of supernatural incident', urging, 'We ought to recognise the tales of Homer … which exist in a coarser form among ruder races'.[99] On a humorous note, he made the coarser origins of higher mythology the plot of his comic fireside tale for the *Miscellany Magazine*, 'A Slipshod Story', in which farm animals and everyday country folk are transformed in a boy's nightmare into the monstrous figures of classical myth.[100] Learning, he felt, was not the property of the specialist, but of everyone.

He spent the Christmas vacation between Bagshot House, his Uncle Thomas Sellar's country residence in Surrey, where he skated a little, and London. His wedding was fixed to take place in April, but he still had not yet found a house.[101] He heard that John Addington Symonds was in town during the first week in January for the publication of the first volume of his planned multi-volume history, *The Renaissance in Italy*. Symonds' first chapter included a protest against Müller's theory of myth as a 'disease of language' and exclusive use of nature concepts as the origin of mythology. Lang saw him as a useful ally. Symonds was an encouraging model of what could be achieved by a man of letters outside the university.

Fellowships in Oxford colleges are renewed every seven years. Lang attended a meeting of the college's Governing Body on 15 January 1875, when his fellowship came up for renewal. In a generous gesture, the college agreed 'That a year of grace be granted to Mr. Lang in view of his approaching marriage, such a year to begin on 10 April.[102] His salary from the Merton fellowship provided a welcome lifeline while he stepped up his work for the London press. His willingness to work all hours got him a job writing leaders for the *Daily News*. He wrote to Stevenson on 7 March from the 'Daily News office, The Sabbath All Hours', warning him, 'Don't get married, if you want to write what you care for writing'. Stevenson, fishing for news of Mrs Sitwell, asked about the time and venue of M. Andrieu's evening lectures on French literature at the College for Men and Women. The first of the lectures had in fact taken place at Mrs Sitwell's flat in 2 Brunswick Row, behind the college. Lang, more cautious than truthful, replied that he had not seen Colvin 'for years' and did not remember 'where they were to come off'. He told Stevenson he planned to go to Oxford the next day 'much as one turns one's pillow when one can't sleep'.[103] The Creightons were packing to leave for their new life at Embleton Vicarage. Soon, Beam Hall would be empty.

A month later, on Tuesday 13 April, Lang and Nora were married at Christ Church, Clifton.[104] The witnesses, on her side, were her sister Fanny and her brother Foster; on his side, his brother, T. W., and uncle, Thomas Sellar. Nora's 71-year-old uncle, the Revd John Foster Alleyne, a former Balliol graduate, now Rector of Kentisbeare in Devon, conducted the wedding service. Lang was convinced that a man with ambition could 'best serve his University by coming out of her, by declining college work, and by devoting himself to original study in some less exhausted air, in some less critical society'.[105] Now he had to prove it.

5

The New 'Pen'

Lang, on leaving Oxford, had few illusions about the career he had chosen. As a youth, he had dreamed of the 'cakes and ale' of literary Bohemia after reading Thackeray's *Pendennis*. Experience so far showed him that the literary life in London was 'very like any other'.[1] He thought Henri Murger was right when he said that 'true Bohemia is only possible in Paris'.[2] The university in the heart of Paris, crowded with poor students, made the French capital a breeding-ground for Bohemian counterculture. England by contrast fixed a wide gulf between the university and the capital, and between the 'two classes of men of letters'—those who wrote for money, and the gentlemen-scholars of the university. Times were changing. With the rapid growth of the press in the 1870s, more and more university men were turning, as Lang had done, to journalism. Lang wanted to bridge the two worlds and to continue with his research while earning his living. But he knew that old attitudes died hard. The university disapproved of those who crossed the line, while Grub Street treated the new university 'types' with good-natured condescension.

He and Nora set up home at 1 Marloes Road, Kensington, an elegant three-storey town house with pillared entrance and basement, just over a half hour's walk from the city. He went to the offices of the *Daily News* in Bouverie Street three or four times a week. Frank Hill, the editor, gathered the staff at 4 o'clock to allot topics for leaders for the next day's morning edition. Hill liked to hear his own voice. According to Henry Lucy, the paper's parliamentary correspondent, Lang usually sat at the table with a book he was reviewing, 'quickly turning over the leaves', continuing to write, and 'occasionally contributing a pointed sentence', while Hill held forth.[3] Richard Whiteing, another on the paper, remembered that within an hour of being given a topic, Lang gathered up 'his slips from the floor' and sent them upstairs straightway to the printer.[4] Lang also called at the offices of the *Saturday Review* in Southampton Street, off the Strand. It was there that he ran into George Saintsbury, another of Mandell Creighton's friends from their undergraduate days at Merton, when Saintsbury and Creighton had shared rooms in the 'High' in their final year. Saintsbury had joined the staff of the paper after eight years as a

Andrew Lang. John Sloan, Oxford University Press. © John Sloan (2023). DOI: 10.1093/oso/9780192866875.003.0005

schoolmaster.[5] Lang sometimes walked part of the way home with him from the Strand to Kensington, where they both lived.[6]

That first September after their marriage, he and Nora stayed for a week with the Creightons at Embleton Vicarage, on route for Scotland. Their visit became an annual event. That year, it was something of an Oxford reunion, with Humphry and Mary Ward also guests.[7] The village was less than a mile from a lovely, golden beach at Embleton Bay. The party went sea-bathing before breakfast, enjoyed walks and expeditions, and played whist in the evening.[8] Mary had published articles on Spanish literature and history in *Macmillan's Magazine* and was at work on a children's novel, *Milly and Olly*; Nora, guided by Creighton, had begun writing *A Geography for Beginners* for the children's market. They also paid a visit to Nora's older sister Elizabeth and her husband Charles Grieve, a wealthy sheep farmer at Branxholme Park, just ten miles from Selkirk. The Grieves already had five children after five years of marriage. When Mandell Creighton, who had known Elizabeth very well in the 1860s, stayed at Branxholme Park with Louise after their marriage, Louise thought life dreary and cold as winter up in the hills even in summer, and Elizabeth 'reserved' and 'difficult to get on with'.[9] In contrast, Lang and Elizabeth became close. He was the one person she felt she could talk to about 'the things that matter'.[10] The final stop on Lang and Nora's tour of the north was Kenbank, his Uncle Willie's permanent holiday cottage in the Galloway Hills. Lang marked their get-together as he had always done with comic verse,[11] but having Nora by his side placed him in a changed relationship with Florence and his uncle William's family, with whom he had spent many summers. In his unvarnished way, he wrote to Hartley Coleridge who was about to marry, 'Marriage & Death & Division, these barren our lives'.[12]

Lang found Kensington squalid and dull, particularly after reading Stevenson's picturesque account of his carefree, Bohemian life in the artists' colony at Fontainebleau Forest.[13] He wrote to congratulate him, 'I wish I were in the same forest ... for the Mews opposite is ... more alive with the dances of Kensington maidens than a pure taste can admire'.[14] Although he had left Oxford, he found, as others have done, that 'Oxford takes a lot of forgetting'.[15] He was hard at work seeing his commentary on Aristotle's *Politics* through the press and trusted it would convince Oxford that the findings of anthropology could give fresh understanding to Greek texts. He claimed that Aristotle was at his most productive in his 'continual reference to history and to fact' and in applying his 'researches into the customs of barbarous tribes' to throw light on the institutions of early Greek society. Unlike Plato and other Greek philosophers, who regarded barbarian forms of government as 'absurd', Aristotle equated 'nature' not with 'primitive freedom' from conventional 'law, reason and custom', but with a realization of reason and order in the universe, which he saw mirrored in the Greek city-state. This suggested that primitive society was an earlier, partial realization of nature and reason. Lang's anthropological agenda was most explicit in his final essay, on 'The Origin of Society', in which he cited McLennan's evidence for matriarchy as the original form of kinship in prehistoric Greece. This challenged the assumption since Aristotle of the patriarchal family as the original unit of society, and races or peoples an aggregation of these. He also looked to field studies of tribal communities, among them his uncle Gideon Scott Lang's *The Aborigines of Australia*, for examples where children took after the mother's clan, and marriage was prohibited with women of the same clan. For Lang, the main lesson in this was that it gave support to the non-exclusive, non-homogeneous character of tribes, races, and peoples. The essays also marked the beginnings of a questioning of Enlightenment assumptions that primitive man was inferior and less complex than civilized man. His closing statement makes plain his rejection of racial prejudice and his awareness of the discomfort his study of family origins might cause: 'The origin of the family is a question that has its disagreeable side. The painfulness of the study may be compensated if it teaches us to throw away the absurd pride of race; which furnishes so-called Aryans with a semi-scientific excuse for despising the "lower races", on account of practices that have left their mark on Aryan institutions'.[16] Lang's essays give striking evidence that the range of subjects he would later make his own—primeval kinship ties, folklore, history and prehistory, the origins of religion—were central to his thought and writing from the beginning of his career. Reviewers recognized that the essays went beyond the needs of students for whom the book was primarily intended and were of practical and general interest. The *Saturday Review* wrote, 'Mr. Lang is learned, but his touch is as light as that of a French novelist; and the result, even when he is not dealing with his favourite subject of Primitive Society, is that he both tells truth and tells it well'.[17]

Lang was drawn that summer into the controversy stirring in Oxford about who should succeed Francis Doyle as the new Professor of Poetry. Pater and Symonds were prepared to throw their hats in the ring. Thomas Hill Green and his wife Charlotte formed a committee in support of Symonds' candidacy, with Lang representing literature; Foster Alleyne, Nora's brother, representing the law; and Ernest Myers representing general society. Two years earlier, Jowett had blocked Pater's appointment to the university proctorship after being shown letters which gave evidence of Pater's homosexual romance with a 20-year-old Balliol undergraduate. This time round, Jowett remained impartial, but W. H. Mallock's satirical portrait of Pater as the fluting, pagan aesthete, Mr Rose, in *The New Republic*, which began serializing in *Belgravia* that June, decided Pater to withdraw from the competition. Symonds conceded defeat and dropped out of the race under similar pressure, when Richard St John Tyrwhitt, Rector of St Mary Magdalene Church in Oxford, attacked his *Studies of the Greek Poets* for its corrupting, homoerotic influence. That left only John Campbell Shairp and William Courthope in the running, with Shairp the ultimate victor. Seeing the door close on Symonds in this way did nothing to change Lang's feeling that a literary man perhaps best served his university by 'coming out of her'.

Lang made new friends outside the university. Two days before Christmas he was introduced to Henry James by 'Robin' Benson at the Oxford and Cambridge Club. Benson had recently taken his degree at Balliol and become a junior banking partner with John Walter Cross, Lang's distant kinsman through his Aunt Eleanor. Benson introduced him to James as 'Andrew Lang, who writes in the Academy'. The James and Benson families were friends back in Boston, and Benson had evidently been tasked with introducing James to literary London. James, not yet famous, cut a lonely figure in London. Lang invited him to dinner at Marloes Road in January, and to lunch at the Savile the following month to meet Symonds. James wrote home to his mother, who was of Scottish descent, describing Lang as a 'young, Oxford & literary man, with a picturesque wife', and 'quite a delightful fellow' for a Scotsman.[18] James thought his industry extraordinary.[19] Lang at the time was turning out editorials for the *Daily News* and two 'small print' weekly leaders for the *Saturday Review*, besides working on his prose translation of Homer's *Odyssey*, and writing what he intended as a major anthropological study of the primitive origins of civilization. He and James shared a passion for French literature. James admired Lang's 'clever' article on the French novelist George Sand in the London *Quarterly Review*, and Lang puffed James with pride by declaring he thought James' article on the French critic Sainte-Beuve 'one of the best reviews he had ever read'.[20] They enjoyed many dinners and lunches together over the next few years. James wrote, 'I do like the quaint & homely *vie de province* of Kensington – where Mrs. Lang is the *Muse de département*.'[21]

Lang received an offer of work in February when Stevenson asked him to write a political leader for *London* magazine, a newly launched 'Conservative Weekly' which Stevenson was coediting for a former Edinburgh University law student and adventurer, Robert Glasgow Brown. The magazine had the endorsement of Benjamin Disraeli, the Conservative Prime Minister. Lang was determined to steer clear of politics. He found detestable Disraeli's reluctance to intervene in the Balkans, where reports through 1876 and 1877 were of terrible atrocities against Christians by Turkish forces. But he found almost as odious Gladstone's attempt to make political gain against the government. He turned down Stevenson's request: 'I *cannot* write a Tory article, and I don't think either party has shown well in this Eastern affair'.[22]

Lang discovered that saying what he thought about other people's work sometimes made lasting enemies of those who felt slighted by his reviews, but on other occasions it could lead to enduring friendships and associations. In his review of Edmund Gosse's debut volume of verse *On Viol and Flute*, he warned against 'borrowed rhymes' and 'tricks caught at second hand from Swinburne and Rossetti'.[23] Gosse took the advice to heart: his poetic manifesto 'A Plea for Certain Exotic Forms of Verse', in *Cornhill Magazine*, paid tribute to Swinburne, Morris, and Rossetti but advocated the introduction into English verse of the 'richness of rhyme' and 'strength of form' of the early French poets.[24] Gosse's recommended models were in effect the poets of Lang's *Ballads and Lyrics of Old France*. Lang was unreserved in his praise of Austin Dobson's *Proverbs in Porcelain*: 'Not the least interesting part of the volume', he wrote, 'is the imitation of the old French measures, roundels, triolets, and the like'.[25] Dobson and Gosse were friends. Lang invited them to dine at the Oxford and Cambridge Club, asking them 'to permit common tasks to take the place of an introduction'.[26] George Saintsbury joined them.

Gosse, always edgy and anxious to please those who might advance his ambitions, evidently felt they had not paid sufficient tribute over dinner to Lang's *Ballads and Lyrics of Old France*. He wrote to Dobson the morning after, 'I hope that in the excitement of last night I did not say or do anything rude— ruder than usual? This morning I am very tired and very humble. Saintsbury is very interesting, isn't he, but a little feverish and perfervid. Lang, I feel, we neither of us did justice to, but he seems very nice'.[27] Dobson remedied their neglect of Lang in 'A Note on Some Foreign Forms of Verse', in William Davenport Adams' anthology, *Latter-Day Lyrics, Poems of Sentiment and Reflection by Living Writers*, acknowledging that Lang's 'charming *Ballads and Lyrics of Old France* virtually led the van' in introducing the old French form of the ballade into English.[28]

Gerard Manley Hopkins, a keen and jealous watcher of poetic trends, christened Lang and the revivalists of old French verse forms, 'Rondeliers'.[29] Hopkins, Lang's contemporary at Balliol—and one of those who 'went over to Rome'—had since become a Jesuit priest. Hopkins supposed the 'Rondeliers' were a mutual admiration circle with Lang as their 'ringleader'.[30] In fact, Lang, in his characteristically honest way, managed to upset Gosse and Dobson with a cutting review of Davenport Adams' *Latter-Day Lyrics*, in which he questioned whether the fixed, 'old fashioned forms' of French poetry could be anything other than a vehicle for light, pleasantly ephemeral society verse. Pouring salt on the wound, he suggested that some of the poets owed their inclusion in *Latter-Day Lyrics* to favouritism, describing the editor's sentimental verse-dedication 'To My Wife' as 'intolerable', and quoting to withering effect Alfred Austin's rhyming of 'bury him' with 'worry him'. He commented, 'Here, to be sure, is a queer flower of what Mr. Adams calls "Britain's gold-branched poesy"'.[31]

Gosse tried to limit the damage with an unsigned review in the *Athenaeum* a week later, in which he praised highly Davenport Adams' 'unbiassed' selection and declared the section of 'Exotic forms of verse in English' the distinguishing feature of the book. A note from Lang inviting Dobson to Marloes Road suggests the consternation Lang's article had caused. It read, 'If you have nothing better to do tomorrow night at about 10, will you come and discuss Latter-day Lyrics, over a cigarette? I hope the article not too truculent—I'm sorry I said the Editor's Rondeau was insufferable, but it was'.[32]

What Lang found 'insufferable' in Davenport Adams' dedication to his wife was its sickly veneration of all-virtuous womanhood. The Lang-Gosse-Dobson circle, unlike many literary and artistic groups at the time, was not exclusively male. Gosse's wife Ellen, was an accomplished artist; Dobson's wife Mary, was a children's author; Nora was writing a novel while also at work on her geography for beginners and on a translation of the French historian Alfred Rambaud's *History of Russia*. It was with evident irony that Lang, in speaking to friends, referred to Nora as 'the Object'.[33] His double-sonnet 'The Nemesis of Art: To the Object of his Affections', sent to Dobson at this time, highlighted the sterility that attends man's worship of idealized goddesses and heroines of myth and art over the 'living laugh' and 'human tear' of real womanhood. He equated the sentimental lover of modern times to the hapless hero of Prosper Mérimée's tale of supernatural seduction, *The Venus of Ille*:

> We love like him that gave, long time ago
> To Venus's marble hand, his wedding ring.
> No more his lady's arm might round him cling!

The closing sestet warns that an attachment to 'ice-like' beauty sets a lethal barrier, between

> Our loves and us, to make us all forlorn.[34]

There is special irony in Lang's adoption of the Petrarchan love sonnet to spell out the threat of idealized love to natural, human connection. Lang reprinted the first of the sonnets over twenty years later, replacing its subtitle, 'To the Object of His Affections', with a note, 'Written after reading *The Tinted Venus*, by Mr. Anstey'.[35] He was being loose with the truth. Anstey's self-styled 'farcical romance', in which a statue of Venus comes to life, did not appear until 1885—that is, eight years after Lang sent a handwritten copy of 'The Nemesis of Art' privately to Dobson.

Although Lang doubted whether old French forms could be adapted to 'serious modern poetry', he valued their gaiety and ingenuity as a refreshing alternative to the trend towards platform or pulpit poetry.[36] He himself turned from translating old French ballades to composing original ballades of his own in English. The new *London Magazine* had already featured a series of ballades. Lang satisfied Dobson's curiosity about the identity of the anonymous balladeer: 'The *London* poet is one Henley: he came to town and I believe does not wish to hide his light under a bushel. R. L. Stevenson knows him'.[37] Lang began contributing ballades to *London* after Henley's arrival in London at the end of 1877 to take over as acting editor of the paper. Henley's younger brother, Joseph, an unpaid office boy, remembered Lang visiting the editorial office—a windowless garret with 'a high dingy skylight', at 281, The Strand:

> A rather tall, slim-built man of refined aspect came in and after an exchange of a few words asked for a piece of paper. I placed him in a chair, and he sat down at a table and wrote some words, pausing now and again as if to think of some phrase. When he had finished, he got up and handed the paper to the editor, who took it in almost at a glance and said, 'Most excellent; thank you; greatly obliged.' With what I thought was the most exquisite smile, the stranger left, and when he had gone I said, 'Who's that?'[38]

Henley liked to strike a stoical and elegiac note on universal themes in his ballades: the changing seasons; fate and circumstance; youth versus age. Lang preferred a light, good-humoured tone in the manner of his model, Théodore de Banville, and took his subjects from the newspapers and current affairs.

In November 1877, Lang led the call for the founding of a Folklore Society after reading Bishop Henry Callaway's appeal for contributions towards the printing of Zulu tales and traditions, collected when he was a missionary in Africa.[39] Lang's call was taken up by eager voices.[40] William Thoms, founder of *Notes and Queries*, where the idea had circulated for some time, put himself forward as 'promotor' of the Society, with an annual subscription at a guinea, open to 'any lady or gentleman'.[41] Other early members of the newly formed Folklore Society included Alfred Nutt, who had just succeeded to the family publishing firm; Edward Clodd, a banker and evolutionist; Charlotte Burne, who collected Shropshire folklore; and Joseph Jacobs, a student of Hebrew literature who made it his mission to counter anti-Semitism. Lang's article 'The Folklore of France' in the first issue of the Society's official periodical, *The Folklore Record*, restated with simple clarity the complex arguments of his earlier scholarly articles on the common threads linking fairy-tale and myth, folksong and epic: 'Folk-songs indeed are the "wild stock" whence the epic and the artistic lyric sprang. They are far older than the most ancient poetry of Greece, just as the wild white rose represents an earlier type of flowers than the complex blossoms of the garden'.[42]

Lang was equally tireless on behalf of friends who needed help. The precariousness of the writer's trade was brought home to him when Henley lost his position on *London* magazine and sank into depression. He urged Henley to get away for a fortnight and offered to take on his work, without payment, while he was away.[43] He sought Stevenson's help in persuading Henley to 'take a holiday'.[44] In the interim, he thought hard of openings for Henley. He suggested Henley try the *Pall Mall Gazette*, the *Saturday Review*, and the *Manchester Guardian* and advised him to send a good solid article or two to *Cornhill* and the *International Review*. Henley, who really wanted to write plays, pleaded his 'utter inability to write for magazines', but Lang was insistent, and made him write pieces on Robertsonian comedy and the drama for the *Magazine of Art*. Henley showed Stevenson some of Lang's letters, saying, 'They are the sort of thing one likes to keep, & not say anything about them, for good men don't like to have their weaknesses exposed'.[45] He asked Lang to return or destroy his letters, but Lang assured him it was his habit to burn all letters, as soon as read.[46] Lang admired Henley's courage—Henley had lost his left leg to tuberculosis—but he found Henley too vehement and pugnacious for his own good and had growing doubts about his suitability for journalistic work. He told Stevenson, 'I have moved heaven and earth, and the *Globe* to find somewhat for Henley to do, but it does not seem to come to anything. I suppose he is not quiet to ride or drive, as a literary hack should be,—or some such reason must be at the bottom of it'.[47]

He also consoled Gosse, who was smarting from adverse reviews of his first work of criticism, *Studies in the Literature of Northern Europe*. He had warned Gosse beforehand not to pay attention to reviews: 'I don't believe there are nine critics, on the press, whose opinion is worth sixpence, I seriously don't … The reviewers will give you the skimmed milk of yourself, diluted with the water of tasteless and careless incompetence'.[48] Gosse ignored the advice and suffered accordingly. The most hurtful comments, in the *Contemporary*, compared his translation of a Bjornstjerne Bjornson lyric unfavourably with Alexander Strachan's 'more musical and affecting' version, and with Robert Buchanan's 'London 1864', which expressed a similar sentiment. Strachan was the publisher of the *Contemporary*, and Buchanan its critical voice. Lang decided that encouraging Gosse to laugh would be the best course of action. He sent Gosse a spoof version of Buchanan's 'London 1864', making a mockery of its gushing description of the art of poetry as God's way of 'changing the flower of feeling,/To a poor dried flower that may keep!':

> If my Buchanan were a flower!
> I'd rush to seek him in the mire,
> I'd twist him round Rossetti's lyre,
> I'd plant him in the Laureate's tower,
> Where Tennyson, one rainy hour
> Beheld the new and old years meet,
> I'd rain the buds at Swinburne's feet,
> If my Buchanan were a flower![49]

When Gosse's *New Poems* came out later that year, Lang had again to rally him: 'What is success after all? ... Even selling well is not a real criticism, still less published criticism, and the opinion of friends ... lop-sided'.[50]

Lang took praise or blame in his stride. He expected criticism in trying to please both academic readers and the wider public. His long-awaited collaborative prose translation of Homer's *Odyssey* came out at the beginning of 1879. His and Henry Butcher's aim was to convey the archaic and composite spirit of Homer's Greek by drawing on the rich history of the English language, while avoiding 'nearly obsolete' words that readers might find unfamiliar.[51] In his introduction, Lang acknowledged that 'without the music of verse, only a half truth about Homer can be told' but justified the choice of prose by quoting Matthew Arnold's comment, 'In a verse translation no original work is any longer recognisable'.[52] He felt that the habits of each age had given different qualities to English verse translations of the *Odyssey* that were not Homeric—for example, the mannerisms of Chapman in the Elizabethan age, and the dignity of Pope's heroic couplets in the age of Queen Anne.[53] *London* magazine, where he had 'friends', was lavish in its praise, describing it as 'a real and abiding acquisition to English literature'.[54] Not everyone was convinced. Matthew Arnold closed the book after reading 'that man of many a shift' as a translation of 'ἄνδρά … πολύτροπον' (literally 'man of many turns') in the poem's first line,[55] deftly altered by Lang in later editions to 'that man, so ready at need', which better conveyed the implicit sense of Odysseus's legendary resourcefulness and reliability. The verdict of literary history favoured his friends at *London* magazine: the translation went through many editions and became the most popular version until well into the twentieth century.

In addition to the seemingly inexhaustible stream of editorials, signed and unsigned reviews, and scholarly articles, Lang worked on a translation of Theocritus, an entry on Molière for *Encyclopaedia Britannica*, and a study of the origins of religion. The strains of literary work and life in London began to tell on his health. He confessed to Stevenson, 'The cold, Theocritus, Molière, newspapers, early religions and dinner parties have brought me near the grave'.[56] He found that working at home meant he was at the mercy of domestic interruptions and disturbance from neighbours. He lamented to Dobson, 'The people next door are playing dance music … I hear every note as if I were in the room, I wonder how late the wretches will go on'.[57] He gave voice to his mood in his 'Ballade of Theocritus',

> Ah! leave the smoke, the wealth, the roar
> Of London, and the bustling street,
> For still, but the Sicilian shore,
> The murmur of the Muse is sweet.[58]

He almost envied his brother Pat, who had resigned as Sheriff-clerk of Selkirk, and had emigrated to Australia with his wife and small son. On receiving news that they had arrived safely to damp weather, he replied, 'You couldn't find it damper than it is in England where we have not seen the sun for eight months'.[59]

That summer, he and Nora went to Paris, where warm, bright, autumn skies made a welcome change to a depressingly rainy Britain. Nora saw 'plenty of plays'; Lang toured the *bouquinistes*. He thought Paris 'a capital place, especially if one has either a contented mind, or £400,000 per annum'.[60] They were joined in Paris by Henry James, who felt himself more 'European' than they were. James wrote to his mother:

> For many days I have been nursing mother to the Andrew Langs who have never been in Paris before and are as helpless and innocent as the Babes in the Wood. It is a 'great pull' to catch the English abroad—they lose all their advantages and are strangely insular and innocent … I have to see that the

Langs get their breakfast properly—put the right stamps on their letters etc. When I first arrived, they put on English stamps.[61]

James was also waiting attendance on another visitor to Paris, Lady Louisa Wolseley, the Irish-born wife of General Garnet Wolseley, who was then in Africa commanding the British Forces in Zululand. James introduced them. Lang shared Louisa Wolseley's taste for old books and antiquarian relics, Nora her love of theatre-going. On their return to London, they stayed friends. When Gilbert and Sullivan's *The Pirates of Penzance* premiered in New York in December, everyone was convinced that Louisa's husband, the meticulous, small-statured Garnet Wolseley, had served as W. S. Gilbert's model for his 'modern major-general'.

On their return from Paris, Lang resumed his attack on Müller, demonstrating in a review of Müller's *The Origin and Growth of Religion*, the illogicality of Müller's theory of fetishism—belief in the supernatural power of objects—as a 'parasitical growth', a 'corruption' of early man's religious sense of the Infinite. Lang's position was that fetishism was not a 'corruption' of something older and purer, but 'one of the most primitive steps towards the idea of the supernatural'.[62] He was surprised by Müller's response to the review and wrote to John McLennan, who was in the high mountain health resort of Davos in Switzerland for the winter, 'I have had an amusing letter from Max. Reviewed him in *Mind*, and fancied I had exploded every theory, and damaged the character of several very seedy witnesses in the shape of quotations. So he wrote to me to say we only disagreed on superficial points of no importance! It is impossible not to admire such splendid cheek'. Lang was busily active trying to gain acceptance of anthropology as a serious human science. John McLennan's brother, Donald, another keen anthropologist, had given him news of William Robertson Smith, a young Cambridge scholar and orientalist, working on a history of ancient Jewish religion. Lang shared Robertson Smith's view of the primacy of ritual and social action over mythology. He joked, 'Your brother says Robertson Smith has convicted the Israelites of gross Totemism, out of the mouth of the prophet Ezekiel. This is to be in the *Journal of Philosophy* where no one will see it, I fear'. He enclosed with the letter a 'Ballade of Primitive Man', humorously extolling the culture of the Cave Man:

> He worshipped the rain and the breeze,
> He worshipped the river that flows,
> And the Dawn, and the Storm, and the trees,
> He buried the dead with their toes

> Tucked up, a peculiar plan,
> Till their knees came right under their nose,
> 'Twas the manner of Primitive Man.

The poem's 'Envoi' took a parting dig at Müller:

> MAX, proud as your *Aryans* pose,
> It was thus their journey began
> And as every Darwinian knows,
> 'Twas the manner of Primitive Man.[63]

He included the ballade in his collection of poems, *XXII Ballades in Blue China*, then in preparation, with an additional three stanzas by Tylor. Lang's ambition to write his great myth book was matched by Tylor's ambition to try his hand at poetry.

As winter gripped, he and Nora escaped London and spent a month in the country in the village of Mickleworth, where they were frequently joined by George Meredith in their wanderings over Box Hill. Nora did not share 'in the worship' shown to Meredith by 'his neighbours'. She always felt on reading his books that she must have turned over two pages, which became irritating. She liked Meredith's French-born wife, Marie, whom she thought a heavenly beauty. They all went in a waggonette with other friends to the Silent Pool, a popular place for visitors in the Surrey Hills. Meredith enjoyed provoking women; not even their discomfort served to check him.[64] Sitting opposite Nora in the waggonette with their knees nearly touching, he began to discuss her in French with his wife, 'who looked dreadfully uncomfortable'. Nora chose not to respond, saying of the incident, 'As it was impossible to pretend I didn't hear, I put on an air of polite interest with which one listens to details of total strangers'.[65]

Lang had his first real taste of celebrity with the publication in 1880 of *XXII Ballades in Blue China*. The critics were especially taken with his skill in combining clarity and easiness of style with an undertone of seriousness that let itself be 'felt rather than heard'.[66] His verses seemed to catch the mood of his time—a mood that looked beyond the heroic earnestness of the mid-Victorian period to a more cheerful, extravagant style. His title conveyed an aesthetic disregard for critics who demanded that poetry be moral. In the 'Envoi' to 'Ballade of Blue China', the insouciant collector of old china challenges his shrewish, stiff-necked critics:

Figure 5.1 Lang in the 1880s.
Reproduced courtesy of the University of St Andrews Libraries and Museums.

> Come, snarl at my ecstasies, do!
> Kind critic, your 'tongue has a tang';
> But—a sage never heeded a shrew
> In the reign of the Emperor Hwang.[67]

George du Maurier's famous cartoon, 'The Six-Mark Tea-Pot', sending up the aesthetic pretentions of the blue china vogue, appeared in *Punch* later that

Figure 5.2 Leonora Blanche (Nora) Lang.
Reproduced courtesy of the National Library of Scotland.

year.[68] Lang's collection of ballades had the attraction of seeming to be part of a new group movement. Austin Dobson supplied the applause in the collection with 'Dizain' (a ten-line poem), comparing Lang's use of double rhymes to a smiling couple, joining and parting in an old-world dance:

> So, in these fair old tunes of France,
> Through all the maze of to-and-fro,
> The light-heeled numbers laughing go.[69]

One thing had not changed since Lang's Oxford days. Throughout the winter he was unwell, driven low by the fogs and smoke of London, and by overwork. He also suffered from insomnia. Lang made it the subject of his 'A Ballade of Sleep', one of the few poems in his *Ballades in Blue China* which carries a truly melancholy undertone:

Sleep! death's twin brother dread!
Why dost thou scorn me so?
The wind's voice overhead
Long wakeful here I know.[70]

He and Nora decided it would be best for his health to go abroad. Learning that Henry James planned to leave for Florence in March, he offered to keep him company, which James was happy to accept 'for part of the way'.[71] The two travelled to Menton, where Lang took rooms at the Grand Hotel National, while James continued his journey to Florence on his own, with Lang to follow later.

Gosse was eager for news of their movements. Lang wrote from Menton, 'The place is greatly gentrified, but there are still water courses, olives, hills, maiden hair and flowers worthy of the pen of Theocritus or the pencil of Mrs Gosse'. A drop in the temperature that day altered his mood: 'After a scorching morning, lo, we have snow on the hill-tops ... I could shoot myself, and still more the people in the hotel'. Gosse's report of London poetry reviews and literary score-settling did nothing to raise his 'spiritual barometer': 'What sweet things you bards say of each other. O'Shaughnessy will say I am a barrel organ man ... and Dobson will call me a pinch-neck Banville. See what cynicism a shower of snow can beget'. He meant to leave for Genoa that night, stopping off at San Remo, where he had arranged to visit John McLennan, but the 'head of Italy' was 'swarming with pilgrims flocking to Rome', and he stayed on in Menton for a few more days. Gosse's friend, John Middlemore, a collector of Pre-Raphaelite art, whom Lang knew from the Rabelais Club, was already on his way to Florence, and Lang dreaded being dragged around by him to look at early Italian artists. At San Remo, he and McLennan visited coastal caves where recent discoveries of prehistoric artefacts raised new questions about the spiritual life of savage man. McLennan showed him a photograph of a prehistoric skeleton of a youth with a crown of seashells and a piece of precious metal, which had been excavated at the site. He was bewitched by the artistry of Palaeolithic man. Questions of the centrality of art in man's social evolution simmered in his mind during his onward journey to Florence.

Middlemore, contrary to his fears, turned out to be a perfect companion, and made his stay 'very pleasant'. He also met Symonds, whom he found 'wonderfully well ... and floating luxuriously in a sea of proof-sheets',[72] but he did not see James who had left on a ten-day tour to Rome and Naples. He remembered James' moving description in *Atlantic Monthly* of his visit to the 'desolate little villa' where Shelley had spent his last months,[73] and on his way back to

Menton in mid-April, he 'paid a pilgrimage' to the house on the bay of Spezia. He memorialized his visit in a picturesque sonnet, 'San Terenzo', their boat 'like shadowy barks that bear the dead' rounding the 'curved shores of Spezian bay', and before them,

> The roof that covered Shelley's homeless head—
> His house, a place deserted, bleak and grey.[74]

The rugged, lonely little villa where Shelley spent his last days converged imaginatively in his mind with the photograph of the prehistoric skeleton McLennan had shown him to form the germ of his essay-fable, 'The Romance of the First Radical: A Prehistoric Apologue'. The tale is Lang at his most mis-chievous in its mix of fiction, science, and humour. From the 'hints supplied by geology, and by the study of contemporary savages', Lang sets out to recon-struct the life and martyrdom of a prehistoric youth, the first dissenter or rebel against the 'despotism of unintelligible fact'. He gives his First Radical the name 'Why-Why'. A born sceptic, basing his actions on experience rather than on inherited beliefs, Why-Why transgresses the law which forbids a brother from speaking to his sister; he kills and eats a sacred totem animal; and he disregards a tribal sexual curse by marrying Verva, a woman with the same clan name as himself. For his defiance of tribal taboos, Why-Why and Verva are hacked to death at the prompting of the village medicine-man, only for 'Why-Why' to be honoured by the people after death for having freed them from foolish customs and superstitions. Fact and fantasy are interwoven in the image of the prehistoric youth 'crowned with a crown of sea-shells', buried and undisturbed for 'many thousands of years' until 'the cave was opened when the railway to Genoa was constructed'. 'Last April', the narrator ends, 'I plucked a rose from a tree beside his cave and laid it with another that had blossomed at the last house which sheltered the homeless head of Shelley'.[75]

The cave was the link connecting the archaeological discoveries at San Remo with Shelley in Lang's mind. In Shelley's great choral poem, *Prometheus Unbound*, the Earth proclaims that truth and love arise 'out of the lampless caves of unimagined being'.[76] Earth and evolutionary science in the nineteenth century shared with romantic poetry a sense of wonder and the sublime in nature. In the new fields of geology and archaeology, rock layers, fossils, and human bones in cave excavations provided the facts for a story as strange and sensational as the myths, poems, and household tales of the cave as a place of monsters and of darker, hidden forces in man and nature.[77]

The intersection of literature and science in the period has attracted much recent critical attention. Ralph O'Connor, in a study of the 'poetics of popular science', argues that a distinction between 'literary' and 'scientific' texts 'does not do justice to the common literary culture of the nineteenth-century reading public'; nor sufficiently recognize the status of public science as a transformational and transactional field of knowledge, rather than 'a simple diffusion of facts from above'.[78] Julia Sparks' reading of 'Romance of the First Radical' points out, in similar terms, that as 'a work of fiction and a replica of 'straight' scientific writing, the tale 'demonstrates how similar the two genres were at this stage of history when anthropology was yet a very young science'.[79] Lang's 'Apologue'—his 'moral tale'—belongs, in this context, among those early scientific romances, such as Mary Shelley's *Frankenstein*, which made science a subject of wider public knowledge and moral and aesthetic debate. The story was also another rehearsal of his major myth book, in which he planned to show that savage customs left their trace in the higher mythologies and survive in scarcely recognized form in modern-day superstitions. Lang's use of humour in the tale served as his democratic connection with his readers, and 'in the absence of history', as an admission of the impossibility of certainty in the speculations and reconstructions of prehistoric science. His narrator injects a note of self-mockery in his anachronistic appeal to Romantic psychology and 'philosophers who believe in the force of early impressions', to account for the growth of the youthful Why-Why's 'invisible hatred of established institutions'. His comically eccentric list of 'our advances in liberty' at the story's end ('brothers, if they happen to be on speaking terms, may certainly speak to their sisters'), and of savage survivals still to be overcome ('young ladies are still forbidden to call young men at large by their Christian names'), encourages the reader to humorous acceptance rather than resistance to the idea of connection between primitive and civilized man.

Lang found Menton 'dark and damp and dreary' on his return from Spezia.[80] The season was at an end, and he joined '*le retour des hivernants*'. He arrived back to find a description by Francis Hueffer in *Macmillan's Magazine* of Gosse, Dobson, Arthur O'Shaughnessy, John Payne, and Theo Marzials, and himself as the 'Modern Troubadours'.[81] He was happy to promote the idea of a shared literary spirit or brotherhood and prefixed verses by Dobson and Gosse to his forthcoming prose translation of the Greek pastoral poets, *Theocritus, Bion, Moscus*, which sought to convey the natural, earthy tone of the original idylls. Nora was rehearsing her part as a slave girl in a production at the British Museum Lecture Theatre of Lewis Campbell's translation of Aeschylus's *Agamemnon* directed by Professor Fleeming Jenkin of Edinburgh University, and financed by Mrs Stephen Winkworth, a benefactor to the arts. Invitations were sent to everybody notable. Performances took place over a week in Queen Anne's Mansions, Westminster. Nora's role was to lay down the carpet for the returning Agamemnon (a piece of drapery from Damascus lent to her by Frederic Leighton). The production had already been seen by hundreds at the private theatre in Jenkin's home in Edinburgh, with Jenkin's wife Anne acting both Clytemnestra, Agamemnon's adulterous and murderous wife, and Cassandra, the Trojan prophetess murdered by Agamemnon. Nora could not understand how a person with any dramatic sense would want to act both parts and said afterwards, 'The Clytemnestra was as a whole very impressive, but when it came to poor Cassandra: with her scanty greyish locks & high squeaky voice (to differentiate) it became ludicrous'.[82]

There was a change in the air in the literary world. The founding of the Oxford University Dramatic Society in the 1880s effectively marked the end of the ban on theatrical performances which had been introduced when Lang was a student a decade earlier. In a separate revival, Frank Benson, a New College undergraduate, with Jowett's permission, staged the *Agamemnon of Aeschylus* in the original Greek on 3 June 1880 at Balliol Hall. Lang was in the audience, as were Tennyson and Browning. Benson, playing the role of Clytemnestra took Lang's breath away.[83] America was starting to notice the change of mood in England, a recognition encouraged by Gosse and Dobson's friendship with Edmund Clarence Stedman, the author of an influential survey of Victorian poetry. Dobson sent Stedman a copy of Lang's *XXII Ballades in Blue China*, with the following lines:

> 'Twas I, Dear Friend, of late you wrote
> That like De Banville, sang;
> But now you'll have to add a note
> And say that it was Lang![84]

Stedman's friend, Brander Matthews, a New York journalist and critic, arranged for Lang's title poem to appear in *Scribner's Monthly* prior to the collection's publication in America.

Lang was introduced to the two Americans when they were in London in 1881. He met Stedman at a 'little breakfast' given by Frederick Locker (later Locker-Lampton) to show off his 'Rowfant Library', a collection of rare books and manuscripts from Rowfant Hall in Sussex, acquired on his marriage. Lang was about to bring out *The Library*, a handsomely designed and illustrated volume on book-collecting (see Figure 5.3). This and his Oxford insouciance led Stedman to take Lang for an English aesthete. Stedman, on returning to America, described him to readers of *Harper's Magazine* as a son of 'the aesthetic

Figure 5.3 Frontispiece for *The Library*.
Drawn by Walter Crane.

decorative, fastidious late-Victorian age that already outvies Queen Anne's in eccentricity, love of finesse, and minute experiment in life and art'.[85] Matthews, whose own manner shifted between academic loftiness and the 'easy and anecdotal', depending on the company, saw that Lang's 'outer crust of Oxford aloofness' was 'intended for external use only'.[86] The two met at one of Gosse's Saturday afternoons 'At Home' and discovered they were both writing a life of Molière. Lang magnanimously lent Matthews books he had collected on the subject.[87] The two became friends, active on each other's behalf with editors and publishers—Lang in London; Matthews in New York. They signed up as members of Walter Besant's Rabelais Club, ostensibly founded for writers committed to 'virility', but really with the aim of bringing British and American writers together as 'English one and all'.

Writers on both sides of the Atlantic shared common cause in seeking fairer deals in their agreements with publishers, and in combating piracy. *Recreations of the Rabelais Club, 1882–1885* included Lang's contribution, 'The Plumber and the Publisher: A Ballad of the Trade', a verse satire on the underhand tricks devised by publishers to defraud the writer. He has his unscrupulous publisher boast:

> ... when he comes to claim his share—
> The chap that held the pen—
> I prove by elegant accounts,
> *He* owes *me* seven pounds ten.[88]

Lang's anger was real. He felt he had been cheated in his dealings with Charles Kegan Paul, the publisher of his *Ballades in Blue China*. Learning that an American firm, Kid, Paul Jones & Co, planned to pirate his translation of the *Odyssey* in America, he told Matthews, 'Kegan Paul Jones would be a good name for a pirate'.[89]

His dislike was shared by Stevenson, who felt similarly aggrieved that he was being fleeced by Kegan Paul. Stevenson passed through London that summer with his new American wife on his way to Scotland, after wintering at the Swiss Alpine resort of Davos. Lang was amused by Stevenson's choice of wife— a Bohemian divorcee, ten years his senior, who smoked roll-up cigarettes. He wrote in joking style to Stevenson afterwards, 'I hear of a strange entertainment by Kensington artists, where ladies are to smoke. "Can this be right?"'[90] A few years later, when James was living at De Vere Gardens, he invited Nora— and her only—to lunch to meet Stevenson's wife, Fanny. Nora 'liked her very much and thought her excellent company'.[91]

The new individualism clashed frequently with the proprieties of the old etiquette. Henley, with Colvin's help, had been appointed editor of Cassell and Company's *Magazine of Art* on a salary of £300 a year. When Lang received a formal letter from him addressed 'Dear Sir' on Cassell's notepaper inviting him to contribute an article on 'Savage Art', he replied mischievously, 'Damned Sir, … the art of savages principally consists of carving and gilding their behinds'. The letter was opened at the central office and caused outrage as it went from hand to hand until it got to Philip Gell, who knew Lang. His laughter dispelled the disapproving looks and ever after earned Lang the nickname 'Merry Andrew', when out of earshot.[92]

Raillery and irreverence, always a feature of literary life, became more noticeable with the vogue for literary celebrity and rapid expansion of the popular press. George du Maurier's 'Maudle' cartoons in *Punch*, and the lampoons in *Vanity Fair* and in Edmund Yates's scandalmongering *The World*, set the tone, which veered between the good-natured and the venomous. Lang thought critical mockery—'scarifying', as it was called—too easy to do, and generally avoided it, but he could be droll about literary self-importance in his correspondence. When Oscar Wilde, amid great fanfare, sailed for America for his first lecture tour, he wrote to Matthews, 'I suppose our Oscar will soon be in the States. Pray keep him, fatten him, and sacrifice him to Mr. Blaine whom I take to be the incarnation of Tlaleatrololotl'.[93] Wilde had achieved notoriety that year as the model for Bunthorne, the 'ultra-poetical, super-aesthetical' young dandy of Gilbert and Sullivan's comic operetta, *Patience, or Bunthorne's Bride*. To Lang, Wilde was an Oxford 'First', and a Newdigate prize-winner whose *Poems*, published that summer, were considered derivative and lacking in literary sincerity—in other words, a 'harmless young nobody'. To see him setting sail for a lecture tour of America to promote the New York production of *Patience*, dressed like the character of Bunthorne, was in his eyes the height of humbug. He opened the first of his satiric 'Idylls of the Dado' in the *Pall Mall Gazette* with a lampoon about Wilde's departure on his American tour:

> Oh, Sunflower, west turn thou they crest,
>   Thy singer is not here;
> Ye Roses bright, pale, pale to white,
>   For him that is so dear!
> For Boston waits at all her gates,
>   Impatient hour by hour,
> A Pilgrim man, no Puritan,
>   Not May Flower, but Sunflower![94]

He followed this a week later with 'The Disappointing Deep', in response to Wilde's reported witticism to the waiting press in New York, 'Mr. Wilde disappointed with the Atlantic':

> Yes, disappointed quite,
> ... I watch the wind and foam and climbing spray;
> For far, too far, has flown,
> That infinite unknown.[95]

On receiving American press reports of the tour from Matthews, Lang wrote, 'It is unpleasant to see questions of literature mixed up with O. W. and his advertisements. It is all bosh about his "school", and so forth, he is only an exhibition'.[96]

He himself was the subject of lampoon when Henley encouraged Stevenson to join him on a series of verse satires of literary members of the Savile Club. The series was never published—Stevenson thought better of it—but a copy of Stevenson's send-up made its way to Lang:

> My name is Andrew Lang,
>   Andrew Lang,
>   That's my name.
> And criticism and cricket is my game.
> With my eyeglass in my eye,
>   Am not I?
>   Am I not
> A lady-dady Oxford kind of Scot.
>   Am I not
> A lady-dady Oxford kind of Scot.[97]

Lang took the ridicule in good part, signing off in his next letter to Stevenson, 'Yours very truly, A Lang, A. Lang, I repeat'.[98]

Far more difficult to dismiss with a joke or take lightly was the renewed attack on his grandfather, Patrick Sellar. This was triggered that spring by a new wave of evictions, protests, and violence in the Scottish Highlands and Islands. Alexander Mackenzie, editor of the *Celtic Magazine*, and a relentless campaigner on behalf of crofters' rights, found a powerful ally in Alfred Russel Wallace, president of the newly formed Land Nationalisation Society. Wallace called on the government at Westminster to end the abuses in the Highlands, quoting Donald McLeod's harrowing, eye-witness account of the inhumanity of the Sutherland Clearances.[99] The family was angered and upset by the public airing in the press of old grievances. There was bad blood between William Young Sellar and his Edinburgh University colleague John Stuart Blackie over the matter. The two had never been friends, but feelings turned bitter when Blackie suggested in his *Altavona*, a collection of dialogues on Highland history and folklore, that Patrick Sellar had been guilty of the crime of culpable homicide for which he stood trial: 'The person charged with the crime was acquitted; but the crime remains.'[100] Lang's uncles hit back. Tom Sellar threatened Blackie's Edinburgh publisher David Douglas with libel action, forcing Douglas to suspend sales. William Sellar, for his part, sought a sympathetic ally in Sir Alexander Grant, the principal of the university, who told Blackie bluntly that his actions were 'an unnecessary and unfeeling outrage' against a university colleague.'[101] Blackie resigned his professorship, but was unrepentant, insisting that 'the best thing' for the family would be 'to confess honestly' their 'unhappy connection with a great social wrong.'[102]

Tom Sellar's response to the attack was to bring forward publication of a long-planned booklet that would clear Patrick Sellar's name. He hoped that the booklet, *The Sutherland Clearances of 1814: Former and Recent Statements Respecting Them*, would correct, once and for all, the misinformation and false witness against Patrick Sellar. He documented in detail the history of the removals and included a record of the trial and acquittal of Patrick Sellar of the charge of 'culpable homicide' and 'real injury and oppression'. He also argued that the old clan system of 'tacksmen' (middlemen who collected rents and exacted services) kept crofters in 'bondage almost equal to that of negroes of the West Indies', and that the policy of removing the population from the bleak and barren interior to the coast was benevolent, and beyond doubt the region and its people derived 'immense benefits from the changes affected'. The book was published by Charles Longman.

Lang felt under pressure to take sides. Blackie's *Altavona* received some favourable reviews in the London magazines, many approving his condemnation of the Clearances. The *Athenaeum* wrote, 'Much was urged, and still may be, on the ground of political economy, in favour of "the Clearances"; but ... the highest patriotism which prefers men to money was then, as now, outraged by the purely commercial spirit which prompted the desolation of the glens.'[103] An exception was the *Saturday Review*. Although there is no evidence of Lang's authorship, the reviewer has something of his manner and tone, preferring to direct his self-declared 'lambent, and we trust harmless and playful humour' against Blackie's 'literary big talk and laughable ignorance of Oxford life'. The dismissal of Blackie's 'painful slur' on Balliol College and correction of Blackie's misattribution of a Greek phrase to Homer adds to the suspicion of Lang's hand. As to Blackie's account of the Sutherland Clearances, the review was more circumspect, agreeing that 'to prevail on men to go away by burning them out of their homes is to go beyond the resources of civilisation', but conceding that there were probably overpopulated districts in Scotland which could 'not support the people in any better state than one of semi-savagery and semi-starvation'.[104] This final point was central to Thomas Sellar's part-economic, part-moral defence of the Duchess of Sutherland's relocation policy. Thomas Sellar was disappointed in his hope that his booklet would silence detractors. Lang's uncle, Alexander Craig Sellar, elected that year as Liberal MP for Haddington in East Lothian, thought it expedient for his political future to combine his middle name and surname and be known as Craig-Sellar. Lang's younger cousin, a third generation Patrick Sellar, disliked his first name because of its negative associations and chose to be known as Arthur.[105]

Lang shared the reluctance of many of his generation to confront the darker, sometimes brutal side of the Age of Improvement, to which he and his contemporaries owed much of their material and cultural opportunities. He did not feel responsible for the deeds of the distant past. Lang, at this stage in his life, largely accepted his family's view that the Highland Clearances had been practical, necessary, and ultimately beneficial, but as he began, in his anthropological writings, to question the generally accepted distinction between civilized and 'barbarous' people, so too he began to question the justification for improvement which had resulted in the depopulation of the Highlands and destruction of a traditional way of life.

In the summer of 1882, Lang completed a long narrative poem on the legendary Helen of Troy. The poem, originally titled 'The Romance of Helen', 'in Spenserian verse, bar the Alexandrins',[106] had been many years in the making. Only his close friends knew about it, and it was not until they gave their approval to the manuscript that he decided to find a publisher. Dobson, busy on his behalf, obtained favourable terms from George Bell, who was confident he could get an American publisher on board.[107] Eventually, it was Brander Matthews who succeeded in arranging with Charles Scribner for an American edition. *Helen of Troy* was scheduled for publication on 20 September, and there were telegrams to Scribner's to coordinate the release date and prevent any American publisher form pre-empting them with a pirate edition. Lang worried that Scribner's would 'lose their dollars over Helen', telling Matthews, 'They never did me any harm, so I cannot rejoice as I would if they were Kegan, or Mac[millan]'.[108]

He and T. W. holidayed together that autumn at Loch Awe. They went fishing and read for pleasure Dobson's anthology of *Eighteenth-Century Essays*.[109] The literary giants of the previous generation were all passing away. Dickens, Thackeray, and George Eliot were already dead, and among poets, Tennyson and Browning were past their best. The deaths of Longfellow and Rossetti that spring only heightened his feeling that 'All the great men are dying'.[110] As publication day approached, despite some nervousness and misgiving, he remained hopeful that *Helen of Troy* would gain him wider recognition as a poet.

6

Holding Course

Lang, in the autumn of 1882, had reason to feel optimistic. Charles Longman was about to launch *Longman's Magazine*, a new publishing house monthly, and Lang hoped to be offered the editorship. The magazine would also provide him with an opportunity to try his hand at the lucrative business of serial fiction. Inspired by Stevenson's 'Latter-Day Arabian Nights' serial in *London* magazine, he concocted a sensational story outline, with similar twists, and invited Stevenson to be his coauthor. The plot of 'Where is Rose?', his novel's title, involved a haunted house in Berkeley Square and a Russian Nihilist princess; the mysterious disappearance of its English heroine, Rose; and a battle of wits between a Russian detective and a master criminal, ending in the rescue of the heroine, as a 'revenant', from a Siberian nunnery.[1] Stevenson liked the idea and agreed.

The first blow to Lang's expectations was Charles Longman's decision to hold the reins at *Longman's Magazine*. Lang reported miserably to Stevenson, 'I wish he would make me an Editor, but his thoughts do not run in that channel.'[2] Annoyingly, he found he was still expected to fulfil some of the duties of editor, but without recognition or remuneration. He had to calm Gosse, indignant that he had not been asked for a contribution: 'I knew several Longmans when I was at College but have no kind of official connection with the periodical or them'. But to soothe Gosse's grievance, he added:

> If I were to conduct a magazine you would be the first contributor I would go for. But all I have done is speak to men whom the Editor of *Longman's* wanted out of those I suggested, and it is not my fault, but very much the reverse, if he has known so little of his own business as not to enlist you.[3]

A second disappointment was that he and Stevenson had to let their serial collaboration lapse when Hugh Conway's best-selling thriller, *Called Back*, anticipated their idea.

These disappointments were nothing to the 'cool response' of critics to his *Helen of Troy*. When Gosse complained about the bad reviews his *New Poems* was receiving, Lang's sardonic reply reflected his own pessimism:

Andrew Lang. John Sloan, Oxford University Press. © John Sloan (2023). DOI: 10.1093/oso/9780192866875.003.0006

Who will read the Victorian piper two or three hundred years hence? Who? Save one with plenty of leisure. Perhaps only a mangled copy of *New Poems* will survive, and will be attributed to John Payne, better known as a novelist. Such is history.[4]

Few long narrative poems gained complete critical approval in the Victorian period. The age valued the lyric more highly than the long poem. Lang himself, writing of the third flowering of nineteenth-century poetry which began with William Morris, admitted his preference for Morris' dramatic lyrics and monologues 'vastly above' his long narrative poems, which he found 'deficient in dramatic vigour'.[5] Reviewers said the same about his *Helen of Troy*.

Critics conceded that Lang's description of the dream-like meeting of Helen and Paris in the gardens of Menaleus was beautifully done:

> So hands met hands, lips lips, with no word said
> Were they enchanted 'neath that leafy aisle,
> And silently were woo'd, betroth'd, and wed.[6]

But there was almost unanimous agreement that his departure from Homer's 'white-armed Helen' as unfaithful wife, and decision to make her blameless, robbed her character of psychological interest, and the story of its most dramatic elements.[7] In Lang's version, Helen elopes with Paris under the spell of Aphrodite, forgetful of her old life, of her husband, Menaleus, and of her child, Hermione. In fact, Homer's *Iliad* leaves more open to question than reviewers supposed—whether Helen willingly eloped or was forcibly abducted by Paris. Homer's focus is on the pathos of Helen's suffering and self-blame. She is ostracized by the Trojan women, and humiliated that Paris treats her as a piece of property. Lang amplifies this sense of powerlessness in the character of Helen, giving it heightened dramatic treatment in the scenes involving Paris' deserted first wife, Œnone.

The Œnone-Helen rivalry, which forms the central narrative in Books 4–6 of *Helen of Troy*, has its source in post-Homeric poetry and story. In Lang's version, Helen receives a letter from the embittered Œnone and learns that the bearer, Corythus, is Paris' son. Œnone's letter reads:

> 'Ay, soon 'twixt me and death must be his choice,
>   And little in that hour will Paris care
> For thy sweet lips, and for thy singing voice,
>   Thine arms of ivory, thy golden hair.'[8]

Œnone's letter breaks Aphrodite's spell, waking Helen to painful memories of her old life and her abandoned child, Hermione. Paris, finding Helen and Corythus together, drives his sword through Corythus's neck, not realizing he is his son. The river of blood on the marble floor puts Helen forever beyond his reach:

> Nay, love had fallen when his child did fall,
> The stream love cannot cross ran 'twixt them red;
> No more was Helen his, whate'er befall,
> Not though the Goddess drove her to his bed.[9]

Reviewers admired the Paris and Œnone episode, but neither this, nor the fact that the book went to a 'more nicely got up' second edition,[10] could dispel his disappointment. Gosse believed an 'ambition to shine' as a poet had supported him from his Oxford days.[11]

Lang took little comfort in a letter from Symonds thanking him for the copy of *Helen of Troy*. Symonds was translating Sappho's fragments for a new 'Memoir' and asked what he thought of the controversy about Sappho's morals. Lang replied that he was a 'philistine in that lore' and preferred to stick to 'internal evidence'.[12] Symonds's letter only intensified his envy of those with sufficient private means to devote themselves exclusively to scholarship and poetry. He would have given anything to have a year to himself to write his life of Molière and finish his myth book. He had told Stevenson years before not to marry if he wanted to write 'what he cared for writing'.[13] Stevenson, now married but supported financially by his father, was able to write what he liked. Lang had to concentrate on 'bread and butter work'. When he did find time for his life of Molière, he sat forlornly 'among ruinous heaps of Molière books', like Pater's 'Marius in the ruins of Carthage'.[14] The myth book overwhelmed him even more. There were days he felt like the dusty Mr Casauban in George Eliot's *Middlemarch*, futilely labouring on 'The Key to All Mythologies'.[15] He told Stevenson, 'My myth book crawls on, but every now and then a coral insect adds a cell to the structure'.[16]

He inclined to be more sardonic than before about the writer's trade, describing himself as a 'penny and liner' and *Helen of Troy* as 'the imitation of poetry'. The coming of spring prompted verses mocking the new wave of innocent, fledgling poets:

> Down the Row the fleet bard rushes,
> Popular, pure, as Eliza Cooke;

> The harmless hope of the freshman flushes
>   In Blackwood or Longman to find a nook.[17]

His friends tried to raise his spirits. Gosse, who was London agent for the American *Century Illustrated Magazine*, asked him to write a piece on 'Edinburgh Old Town'. He agreed 'if they can wait till May',[18] but the article only added to what he disparaged as his 'seedy stark pot-boilers'.[19] He was grateful to Brander Matthews for persuading Scribner's to publish an edition of his poems, to consist of a selection from his *Ballads and Lyrics of Old France* and *Ballads in Blue China*, together with some new and uncollected verses. Dobson took on the task of selection, and they hit upon the title *Ballads and Verses Vain*, from Edmund Spenser's celebration in *The Faerie Queene* of 'Ballads, virelayes, and verses vaine'.

   Lang included his moving, recently written memorial poem 'Almae Matres (St Andrews, 1862. Oxford, 1865)', composed in a London hansom cab. 'Almae Matres', like 'Clevedon Church', was an elegy to Henry Brown, his friend in his first year at St Andrews, in whom he had confided his ambitions. The elegiac mood is intimated in the opening description of St Andrews as a 'haunted town'. Memories of its grey 'melancholy' streets, and 'ghostlike and shadowy' towers bring remembrance of an April day they 'loitered idly' in the 'ruined chapel' overlooking the bay, unaware that the future would soon separate them:

> We did not dream, we could not know,
>   How hardly fate would deal with us!

'Dream' in the sense of 'foresee' has a finely ironic edge in the context of youth's obliviousness to life's harsher realities. The 'ruined chapel' suggests, as in 'Clevedon Church', decay of traditional faith, although there is a preserved sacredness too in the memory of the 'broken minster'. It is, the poet writes, 'as if I touched your hand'. His picture of Oxford's 'flying terms' is more idyllic and joyful—'the summer's rides by marsh and wold', and crimson autumn clouds rolling 'about the towers of Magdalen' bring back thoughts of 'friends of old'. But his Oxford is one that calls on him to love the spirit of the place—its 'strong Traditions' and 'strange enchantments of the past', rather than to love those he knew there. His heart returns at the close to St Andrews:

> But dearer far the little town,
>   The drifting turf, the wintry year,

The college of the scarlet gown,
St. Andrews by the northern sea,
That is a haunted town to me![20]

Oxford still drew him back, however. When he dined 'with a lot of contemporaries at Balliol', they 'seemed as undergraduate as ever: only a little bald'.[21] Among undergraduates, he was already a legendary figure. An irreverent parody of him, 'The Ballade of Andrew Lang', addressed to an imagined freshman of Merton College, appeared in the newly launched *Oxford Magazine* in February 1883:

You ask me, Freshman, who it is
    Who rhymes, researches, and reviews,
Who sometimes writes like Genesis
    And sometimes for the Daily News;
    Who jests in words that angels use,
        And is most solemn with most slang
Who's who—whose which—and which is whose?
    Who can it be but Andrew Lang.[22]

He travelled to Scotland in April to write his piece on 'Edinboro Old Town' for Gosse and 'get a holiday'.[23] It was a relief to escape London, where the Fenian bombing campaign had made daily life in the capital perilous. Just before he left, a bomb was found in the offices of the *Times* newspaper. He tried to stay independent of politics but had come to dislike his work at the *Daily News* for its strong support of Gladstone's alliance with Parnell. He felt only contempt for Parnell's fund-raising in America which helped bankroll the dynamite campaign on the British mainland. He told Stevenson, 'I feel a whoresome longing not to go to the D. N. [*Daily News*] anymore, "whateffer"'.[24] He stayed in Edinburgh with his collaborator on the *Odyssey*, Henry Butcher, and Butcher's wife. He thought Butcher's wife 'quite perfect'; Butcher too, though he found Butcher 'very Protestant'.[25] He thought Butcher 'deserving but fortunate' to have landed a prestigious post as John Stuart Blackie's successor as Professor of Greek.[26]

Although his life seemed small beer in comparison with Butcher's elevation to a professorship, he took some comfort in events. His translation of the *Iliad* in collaboration with Walter Leaf and Ernest Myers had sold 2,500 copies in America between January and July, and they had cleared about £225. 'Floreat America', he wrote to Matthews.[27] He was also gaining a position of no small influence in the literary marketplace. His success as a journalist and reviewer lay in saying what he thought in a straightforward way, without malice or special favour, and writing for the enjoyment of doing it, rather than for effect. He said of the 'dreadful trade' as he called it, 'The work as in all the arts, is a pleasure. Have we to live by writing paragraphs? Then it is a delight to write good paragraphs, or paragraphs that seem good to us'.[28]

Poets and novelists sent him copies of their books, believing that a word of approval from him would advance their reputation and sales. He was delighted when *Treasure Island* came his way. He wrote enthusiastically to Stevenson, 'They have sent me *Treasure Island*, over which I have spent several hours of unmingled bliss. This is the kind of stuff a fellow wants ... I don't know (except *Tom Sawyer* and the *Odyssey*) that I ever liked any romance so well. No love making, nor rubbish, and no padding of any description'.[29] When Stevenson enquired who had written the doting review of the book in the *Pall Mall Gazette*, he replied, 'I did'. He helped Stevenson secure a contract with Longman for *A Child's Garden of Verses* which he thought 'quite as good as Blake in their line' and praised 'Windy Nights' as 'the most mythical thing a civilised man ever wrote'. He believed in being honest. When Stevenson sought his approval of 'The Pirate and the Apothecary', a narrative poem in octosyllabic couplets, Lang advised him not to publish it: 'To be abominably plain, the P. & A. is not within three stone of your public form, and if I were you I'd let it bide in MS. I don't believe Henley, whom I have always found excessively frank, could rival *this* for pure rudeness. But I am such a consistent and unblushing admirer of yours that I venture to speak my mind on this'.[30] Robert Bridges, a friend and fellow member of the Savile Club, asked for his verdict on poems by his friends Gerard Manley Hopkins and Richard Watson Dixon. Lang confessed he did not like the pieces by Hopkins, but he was initially quite taken by Dixon's *Mano*, a narrative poem of the Middle Ages in *terza rima*: 'I am delighted with *Mano*, as far as I have gone: capital reading too, which poetry is not always'.[31] But his final verdict, delivered in the *Saturday Review*, complained that he found the digressive intricacy of the story difficult to follow.[32] The review alarmed Bridges, whose *Prometheus, the Fire Giver: A Mask in the Greek Manner* had just come out. Bridges told Dixon, 'I have I think prevented Lang from reviewing it'.[33] Lang, had Bridges only known, was an unreserved admirer of his *Prometheus*, particularly the translation of Homer's description of Niobe and her children turned to stone, from the *Iliad*—for Lang, a striking example of the survival of savage myth in classical poetry.[34]

Henry James, back in London after a year in the United States and enjoying literary acclaim as the author of *The Portrait of a Lady*, came to dinner and was 'very good company'.[35] Nora and Louisa Wolseley were attending cookery lessons, made fashionable by Mrs Beaton's *Book of Household Management*, and they planned to hold a dinner party at the Wolseley's house in Portland Square, Mayfair, after Christmas. James wrote flatteringly to Louisa Wolseley after sampling one of their experiments, 'It is wonderfully good & I am still smacking my lips. I had already lunched when it arrived, but I immediately voted an extension & consumed the precious pudding at a single sitting ... It was very generous & self-sacrificing of you & your other *cordon*. If I had cooked such a pudding, I should have sent it to the Queen, & expected the Star of India, or some such recompense. It was the poetry of food—the ideal of nutrition! I don't speak, here, of Mrs. Lang. She shall have a chapter to herself'.[36] Lang viewed the dinner party, to take place in the new year, on 25 January 1884, with some nervousness. Among the guests with their wives were Lord Arthur Russell, the Liberal party politician, and Colonel John Frederick Maurice, who had been Garnet Wolseley's private secretary during the Ashanti Campaign and Zulu War. The Wolseleys' collection of Queen Anne bric-à-brac, rare books, old armoury, and Limoges enamel, filling the great house, inspired Lang's poem 'The Palace of Bric-à-Brac', which poked fun at the collector's dream of perfection in 'flawless cup and plate'.[37] Wolseley, though a man of action, had literary ambitions. He had already produced a novel under an assumed name, which, in Lang's judgement, was best left that way,[38] but he encouraged Wolseley's planned biography of the Duke of Malborough and offered his editorial help.

Lang hoped to increase his influence and income by agreeing to take on the grandly titled position of 'English editor', in truth agent, for *Harper's Magazine*. The task of reading submissions meant days when he did not leave the house and having to turn down invitations which he knew he ought to accept. He made an exception for a 'huge and magnificent dinner party' thrown by Edwin Austin Abbey, the American illustrator for *Harper's Magazine*, and Alfred Parson, a landscape artist and designer, at their home at 54 Bedford Gardens, Kensington. He liked Abbey, which was his main reason for going. He reported to Matthews, 'It was a beautiful dinner, and [W. S.] Gilbert made a nice speech. Henry James also spoke—he is not given to speaking'.[39]

With so much to do, Lang put his ambitious work on mythology on hold and settled instead on bringing out an interim collection of essays, five of which had already appeared in periodicals. He thought of calling it 'Totem and Taboos' but decided in the end on *Custom and Myth* as 'more "high-toned"'.[40] He felt his final choice of title conveyed more accurately the central idea that ran through the fourteen articles that made up the volume—that the meaning of myths is to be found in the customs, prohibitions, and habits of mind of savage mankind, and not, as the philological school would have it, in the names of gods and heroes as linguistic corruptions of nature concepts—sun, moon, stars, and the like. Analysis of names was a 'foundation of shifting sands',[41] with comparative mythologists unable to agree even on the original root of a name, let alone its meaning.

In his essay 'Cupid, Psyche and the Sun-Frog'—one of the gems of the collection—Lang showed that the story of separated lovers, in its many forms and incarnations, might well have arisen from an ancient custom which survived among some peoples into historical times forbidding a husband or a wife from seeing the other's face or body, or, in some cases, uttering the other's name in the presence of strangers. The story evolved in effect to illustrate and give sanction to the rule. In several essays, he combined classical and anthropological knowledge with contemporary folklorist details in an entertaining way. In 'The Bull-Roarer: A Study of Mysteries', he connected the hideously noisy toy slate on a long cord, known as a bull-roarer, and used by British boys in his day, with the ancient rhombus used in secret rituals by primitive tribal men to warn away women. In 'Moly and Mandragora', he found an amusing analogy between the belief of a lady he met at a Kensington dinner party, who was convinced a stolen potato carried on one's person can cure rheumatism, and the crediting of herbs and roots with magical properties in myths and legends. For all the enlivening wit, he never lost sight of his larger purpose. He discounted the philological interpretation of the 'moly'—the 'herb of grace'—in the *Odyssey*, as the 'dog-star' (Sirius) derived from Aryan meteorology, concluding with irony, 'People have their own simple reason for believing in these plants, and have not needed to bring down their humble, early botany from the clouds and stars'.[42]

The essay form, with its traditional openness to fresh reflections about man's experience of the world, proved highly suited to Lang's widened field of 'cultural archaeology' and mixing of the distant and near. It also accommodated his sense that scientific knowledge was always provisional and incomplete, especially in the reconstruction of pre-history. Unlike comparative mythologists, he did not 'pretend to explain everything'.[43] His attempt to account for the diffusion of the same stories round the world remained inconclusive. Ambiguity surfaced, too, in his effort to unravel the tangled thread of the origins of religion. He dedicated the book to Tylor and flew the flag for him when he dismissed Müller's view of fetishism as a corrupted, 'parasitical' form of an older, contemplative adoration of the Infinite.[44] The editors of the recent edition of Lang's *Selected Writings* insist, rightly, that in *Custom and Myth*, Lang took for granted Tylor's view that animism, fetishism, and magical practices formed an early primitive phase in the evolution of religion.[45] Yet Lang also freely admitted that 'what truly "primitive" religion was' he made 'no pretence to know' and quoted the passage in Charles de Brosses's *Culte des Dieux Fétiches*, in which the eighteenth-century French ethnologist claimed to have found that many African tribal peoples 'have a higher conception of the Deity than any which are implied in fetish-worship'.[46] This recognition of the 'confused and manifold character of early religion' as 'a tissue of many threads', was to become a fault-line which resulted eventually in the 1890s in Lang's defection from the consensus among evolutionary anthropologists about the development of religion.

That shifting perception found expression in his poetry. He was intrigued by the data on Bushman mythology collected in 1873 by a colonial administrator from Qing, King Nqsha's huntsman. Their chief god was a mantis or grasshopper god, Cagn, 'who made all things'. In his sonnet 'Natural Theology', Lang recreated the campfire spirit of the South African Bushmen and Qing's account of their prayer to Cagn, 'a father, kind and good':

> '... we cry to him,—*We are thy brood*—
> *O Cagn, be merciful!* and us he brings
> To herds of elands, and great store of food,
> And in the desert opens water-springs.'
> So Qing, King Nqsha's Bushman hunter, spoke,
> Beside the camp-fire, by the fountain fair,
> When all were weary, and soft clouds of smoke
> Were fading, fragrant in the twilit air;
> And suddenly in each man's heart there woke
> A pang, a sacred memory of prayer.[47]

Lang prefaced his poem with a Greek epigraph, quoting the words spoken by Peisistratus about his young guest Telemachus in Book 3 of the *Odyssey*, ἐπεί καί τοῦτον ὀίομαι ἀθανάτοισιν/ εὔχεσθαι· παντες δὲ θεῶν χατέουσ' ἄνθρωποι ('He too, methinks, prayeth to the deathless gods, for all men stand in need of the gods').[48]

Complementing his work on *Custom and Myth*, Lang agreed to write a scholarly introduction to Margaret Hunt's two-volume edition of *Grimm's Household Tales*, due for publication at the end of the year. His essay 'Household Tales: Their Origin, Diffusion, and relation to the Higher Myths' was one of his most seminal contributions to what he called the 'science of fairy tales'.

Contrary to the 'orthodox' account of fairy tales as degraded versions of the higher mythology, given in Max Müller's influential *Oxford Essays*, and Sir George Cox's *Mythology of the Aryan Nations*, he argued that the tales of the 'untutored' European peasantry occupied 'a middle place between the stories of savage peoples and the myths of early civilisations'. The monstrous, fantastical, and irrational features of both myth and *märchen* derived from savage man and the 'uncivilised imagination'. On the problem of explaining the similarity and diffusion of the same tales in widely scattered races, Lang confessed himself much less certain. He saw two possibilities. Neither excluded the other. Similar incidents might have originated independently from similar conditions of life and similar workings of the human mind. The diffusion of plots was much harder to explain, but without conceding to Müller's hypothesis of a single origin, Lang allowed for the possibility of some transmission from people to people and from place to place by traders, mariners, slaves passed from owner to owner, and brides, who, by the primitive law of exogamy, had to be chosen from an alien clan. He refused payment for his contribution, telling George Bell, the publisher:

> I only meant my preface as a contribution to the study of the *märchen*, and I hope you will not think it discourteous if I return your cheque. I had not any other purpose in writing except to set the subject as clearly as possible before the reader. If you like to send me a copy of your book on Fencing, I shall consider myself more than paid, especially as part of my essay may come into a large book on which I have been long at work.[49]

He received word from Henley in May that Stevenson was desperately ill at Hyères in southern France and likely to die. He wrote immediately to Stevenson, saying he hoped that Henley was 'disquieting himself and me, in vain. He often does'. He and Nora considered travelling to Hyères, but the cost proved prohibitive, and they settled instead for a week in Eastbourne, which he characterized as a 'cockney place, all esplanade dirty, crumbling chalk cliff, dirty sea, and howling wind!'[50] During their stay, he corrected the proofs of *Dissolving Views*, Nora's coming of age courtship novel, to be published by Longman in London and Harper in New York. Nora attempted to disclaim an autobiographical origin for her story by having her heroine, Eleanor Winton, humorously declare of novel-writing that 'however carefully you invented your characters and plot, your friends will be certain the book was autobiography'. The parallels between Nora and her heroine are too close to be coincidental. Her heroine has her gift for languages, and Kingston, where she lives, described as a 'forsaken spa' populated by 'old generals, old civil servants', is a thinly disguised Clifton.[51] Eleanor's mother is an invalid, and Eleanor finds a second mother in her aunt, just as Nora, in the same circumstances, had a friend and second mother in Hannah Kelly, a lady's maid in the Alleyne house. Eleanor also takes part in amateur dramatics, wearing a 'nebulous costume' for her role in Aristophanes' comedy *The Clouds*. A photograph survives of Nora posing against a classical balustrade in just such dress (see Figure 5.2). Lang, in correcting the proofs, had the comical but chastening experience of seeing ghosts of his old self depicted in Eleanor's suitors, the first, Ivan Russell, 'handsome, fair-haired, well-made', characterized as having 'the Oxford way of seeming to have been through everything, "phases", and "convictions", and "aspirations", and of looking back on them with a smile from an attitude of acquiescent indifference ... Fishing was an amusement which seemed made for him.'[52] Ivan's undergraduate poems, which Eleanor reads in an old copy of 'College Lays', are mocked as stilted and feebly aesthetic. The heroine's final choice is Lionel Beaufort, an older, more restrained figure, whose 'continental experiences' have turned him against 'aesthetic eccentricities'.[53] Their chance meetings at London society gatherings, at a Varsity match at Lord's, and at a shooting party in the Highlands, read like imaginative reworkings of real-life early encounters. The obstacle to their union, in the end overcome, is Beaufort's attachment to a dream of a young girl he once loved, a veiled allusion, perhaps, to Lang's early attachment to his cousin. The novel received disappointing reviews— rather unfairly, as the novel is livelier and more accomplished than many novels popular in the circulating libraries. Had she used a pseudonym, the novel, one suspects, may have perhaps passed unnoticed, or received more favourable reviews. The *Spectator*, claiming almost too insistently not to know the author personally, surmised from 'internal evidence' that she was 'clever, well-educated, intelligent' and 'endowed with a sense of humour', but judged the novel 'not strong food'.[54]

Lang and Nora returned from Eastbourne to news that Gosse had been simultaneously appointed to succeed Leslie Stephen as Clark Lecturer at Cambridge and invited to give a lecture tour of America. Lang wrote to congratulate him, quoting from Virgil's first eclogue, '*Haud equidem invideo, mirir magis*' (Well I don't begrudge you; I marvel at it'), adding, 'Every one either a professor, like Henry Butcher and you, or an Editor, and this wretched smatterer patauging in the bourbe (i.e. wading in the mire) of copy forever, till Death or Idiocy relieve him.'[55] Gosse's jubilation caused him some soul-searching. His 'Ballade of Neglected Merit' in *Century Magazine* that month reflected his wry view of the desire for public approval:

I have scribbled in verse and in prose,
I have painted 'arrangements in greens',
And my name is familiar to those
Who take in the high-class magazines.
I compose; I've invented machines;
I have written an 'Essay on rhyme';
For my country I played, in my teens,
But—I am not in 'Men of the Time'![56]

Stevenson, as he had hoped, was alive and well and on his way back to England. Lang promised to 'whip up' as many people as he could for the first-night performance of Stevenson and Henley's melodrama *Deacon Brodie: or the Double Life* at the Prince's Theatre on 2 July. He tried to interest Augustus Sala, one of the most popular journalists of the day, and Moy Thomas, the drama critic at the *Daily News*. Henley sent him a printed copy of the play for comment, and though he liked the character of George, a robber in the Deacon's gang, he joked that it would have been a more striking example of the double-life if the Deacon had been someone more distinguished, like an Archbishop or a Lord-Provost.[57] Lang had dutifully attended the disastrous opening night of Brander Matthews's comedy *Marjory's Lovers* at the Court Theatre in February earlier that year and had been almost in tears for his friend by the end. A brief notice in *The Theatre* magazine reported simply that the cast of *Marjory's Lovers* 'did what they could to prolong a miserable existence' but the 'unfortunate play ... was not sufficiently robust to outlive the sorrowful astonishment of the first night audience'.[58] The experience seems to have cured Lang forever of any ambition he might have had to write for the public stage. He bought tickets to *Deacon Brodie* for Nora, his sister Helen, and his cousin Eppie. Nora was glad she had gone. She remembered long afterwards the shudder of excitement she felt when she saw 'the thin evil figure' of Andrew Ainslie, a member of Brodie's gang played by Fred Desmond, 'with his lank black hair, stealing across the empty stage'.[59] Lang was fishing that week in Sutherland with his brother Bill, a young doctor and keen sportsman 'gone wrong in the chest'. Lang hoped they 'might take care of each other'.[60] He had turned 40 that year; Bill, 25, the same age as Keats when he died. His 'Ballade of Middle Age' that summer sought to supplant such gloomy thoughts:

Though youth 'turns spectre-thin and dies',
To mourn for youth we're not inclined;

We set our souls on salmon flies.
We whistle where we once repined.

The poem had for its cheerful refrain, 'Life's more amusing than we thought!'[61]

Sadly, life proved otherwise. Nora's sister Fanny, age 47, succumbed that summer to an aggressive, incurable, horribly painful illness. Charlotte Green, a friend since childhood, helped to nurse her in her final days. Fanny died on Saturday 16 August after prolonged and terrible suffering. She was buried the following Thursday at St Paul's, Clifton. Lang loved and admired her. His elegy 'Desiderium, In Memoriam S. F. A.' recreated the calm churchyard at her burial in the autumn twilight—the 'clustered rowan berries'; the drooping 'clematis', and the 'call of homing rooks'. There is a forlornness to his wish at the close of the poem that her soul might find pleasure in that peaceful place:

> But could I know
> That thou in this soft autumn eve,
> This hush of earth that pleased thee so,
> Hadst pleasure still, I might not grieve.[62]

They travelled north after the funeral to pay their final visit to Embleton. Mandell Creighton had been appointed to the newly created post of Professor of Ecclesiastical History at Cambridge and he, Louise, and the children were moving to Cambridge in November. The occasion was an emotional one for all of them. Their visits had been an annual event in their lives from the time the friends left Merton College a decade earlier. Robert Bridges was also visiting, though Lang found him 'very truculent'. In reply to a letter of condolence from Gosse, he told him that Nora was 'still rather tired and nervousy' and intimated the terrible suffering of Fanny's last days, 'Apparently, the sooner the horrid disease ended the better, that is all that can be said.'[63]

Louisa Wolseley helped to lift Nora's spirits on their return to London. They went to see Victorien Sardou's amusing comedy, *Les Pattes de Mouches* ('A Scrap of Paper'), which they found 'most amusing' and, contrary to reputation, 'not improper at all.'[64] Just five days later, Nora sank again into neuralgia and depression. Her brother Percy, just 29, had followed Fanny to the grave, leaving a wife and two-year-old baby daughter. The deaths of Fanny and Percy Alleyne; Nora's illness and depression; his brother's lung affliction: the 'series of misfortunes' seemed endless.[65]

The transience of life served as a spur to work. He saw *Custom and Myth* and a new collection of verse, *Rhymes à la Mode*, through the press and completed a verse version of 'Beauty and the Beast' for the Christmas number of *Longman's Magazine*. At Charles Longman's suggestion, he also produced a fairy tale of his own, his first, *The Princess Nobody*, to accompany a new edition of Dicky Doyle's picture-book, *In Fairyland: Pictures from the Elf World*. *The Princess Nobody* combined a medley of motifs and figures from fairy-tale and folk legend: a fairy godmother, the Water Fairy, who saves Princess Niente ('Nobody' in Italian) from a wicked dwarf; a Prince Charming, who discovers Princess Nobody's real name and speaks it, at which the princess vanishes away and he is turned into an old and ugly Prince Comical. In the end, the Water Fairy restores Princess Niente (now Gwendoline) to him, and he regains the form of the handsome Prince Charming. For all its incident and whimsy, *Princess Nobody* seems at times more contrived than inspired. The central folk motif of the forbidden name and separated lovers clearly owes something to his essay on 'Cupid, Psyche and the Sun-Frog'. There are echoes, too, of the *Odyssey* in the name 'Princess Nobody'—Odysseus takes the name Οὖτις ('Nobody') in the land of the Cyclops—and the enchanted sleep that falls upon Prince Comical's companions in Mushroom Land is Lang's fairy tale version of the Lotus-Eaters.

Doyle's amusing illustrations of harmless, wing-tearing battles between elf and fairy seemed to have their real-life counterpart in the undignified feud of two Anglo-Saxon scholars, John Henry Hessels and Henry Sweet, in the correspondence pages of the *Academy* in the months before Christmas, with Sweet dismissing Hessels contemptuously as a 'critical blue-bottle', and Hessels scornfully denouncing Sweet's transcription of Early English Texts as 'a calamity inflicted on the literary world'. Lang sent a copy of his knockabout verse on the Oxford (Sweet) versus Cambridge (Hessels) battle privately to Gosse and Symonds:

> Here's a combat; here's a treat,
> Hit him Hessels! Go it, Sweet!
> Fellows jump on chairs and tressles,
> Yelling, 'Go it, Sweet and Hessels.'
> 'Come on, Furnivall and Skeat,
> Here's old Hessels, mauling Sweet,'
> This one punches, t'other wrestles,
> Go it Sweet, and go it Hessels.[66]

By December, he felt he had done 'enough for one year', only to quickly change his mind after reading Arrowsmith's Christmas best-seller, *Dark Days* by Hugh Conway, whose shilling shocker *Called Back* had killed off his collaboration with Stevenson, 'Where is Rose?'. He thought Conway's novels 'desperately bad'—'perfect lunatic asylums without keepers'.[67] He responded with a parody, written and on sale within weeks, *Much Darker Days*, a tale of bigamy, murder, and 'original types of lunacy', by 'A. Huge Longway'. Walter Pollock, the editor of the *Saturday Review*, guessing the author, handed it to Lang for review at a staff meeting and watched with amusement the 'various expressions which chased each other about his face' and Lang's attempt to speak of the book 'as a stranger might do' before finally throwing it down on the table with a laugh, and saying, 'What's the good of beating about the bush? You know I wrote it!'[68] *Punch* unmasked the author days before Christmas, declaring, 'Who wrote *Much Darker Days*?—Mr. Merry Andrew Lang, of course. It's Lang syn' we've come across a better parody'. The book sold thousands of copies and, in his words, earned him 'a lot of tin'. He used it to buy Nora a 'swagger jewel'.[69]

The popularity of *Much Darker Days* brought in an invitation from F. C. Burnand, the editor of *Punch*, to contribute one of a planned series of parodies of some of the leading English and American novelists of the day. Lang pitched to Stevenson the idea of them writing a piece together in the manner of *New Arabian Nights* about a 'bewildered Yank' in London, who would, he declared mischievously, bear 'no resemblance to Henry James'.[70] Stevenson was busy on a ghost story for the *Pall Mall Gazette Christmas Extra*, so Lang pressed ahead on his own. The 'heroic novelist' of his 'Quite the Wrong Man', William Van Donop O'Dwyer, an American abroad, curious and amazed at all things English, is unmistakeably James. A courteous English stranger takes the innocent O'Dwyer to see the bewitching actress Miss O'Botherton in her role as Hermione in *A Winter's Tale* and, in a suggestive denouement, invites him backstage afterwards to join her for 'champagne and chicken ... when the lovely statue descends and is stone no more'. Sexually, the fastidious O'Dwyer, as the title suggests, is 'quite the wrong man' for romantic adventures.[71] James never commented on the piece, but the reference to Mary Ward's first adult novel, *Miss Bretherton*, written after she went with James to see the London stage performance by the American actress Mary Anderson, would have suggested to James that the author was someone who knew him personally.

Lang undertook more serious work when invited to become general editor of a planned series of biographies of 'English Worthies', to be published by Longman in partnership with Daniel Appleton & Co. of New York. He discovered immediately the delicate diplomacy needed for the job, when Dobson told him that Gosse, still lecturing in America, wanted to do Ben Jonson. He acted swiftly by writing to Symonds:

Longman contemplates biographies of *English Worthies*, and I am trying to start them. About the size of your *Shelley*, and lucre not *less* than £100. I wonder if you would (to oblige me) do Raleigh, or anyone you like, if it goes beyond a project. I'd like Raleigh for you, and Ben Jonson. I hear Gosse has a fancy for Ben, but then Ben was a scholar, and I don't think anyone but a scholar should do him.[72]

With Christmas nearly upon him, he finally wrote to Gosse, to say that 'provisionally, hopefully' he could put him down for one of the 'English Worthies' but adding with a disingenuousness that was unlikely to fool Gosse, 'Symonds would do no one but Ben'. He wished Gosse well on his lecture tour: 'I hope you are a tremendous Dog … and worshipped by the Dog Indians, and the Smithsonian Institute … Love to Brander, and Any Admirers of mine you may meet. Judicious puffs will be valued.'[73]

Lang may not have counted himself among 'Men of the Time', but he was fast becoming one. He received an honorary degree from St Andrews University. His portrait in oils by William Blake Richmond was exhibited at the Grosvenor Gallery Winter Exhibition at the beginning of the year. The *Magazine of Art* placed it in 'the first rank among the portraits of the year and praised its 'subtle apprehension of the idiosyncrasies of the subject … seen in many happy touches, notably in the languorous and graceful form, the drooping *abandon* of the right arm, the characteristic poise and turn of the head' (see Figure 6.1).[74] A verse tribute in *Punch* to his *Rhymes à la Mode* was another sign of his growing celebrity:

> A brighter, lighter seldom sang,
> Than laughing, lilting ANDREW LANG![75]

It was written by May Kendall, a young Yorkshire-born undergraduate of the recently founded Somerville College, Oxford, one of an emerging cohort of bright 'new women'. Lang had just accepted one of her poems, 'To Beatrice: The Squire's Daughter', for *Longman's* and sent others to the editor of *Punch*. Lang's name featured regularly in *Punch*. In the March issue of *Punch*, a verse parody of his 'Beauty and the Beast' accompanied a cartoon of France cosying up to Russia. His original celebrated the flowering of the timeless, universal moral of 'Beauty and the Beast', that 'from ugliness you need not shrink'.[76] *Punch* had a different, warning message for France:

> Madame Villeneuve and old Vedic priests
> (Ask learned ANDREW LANG) may slightly vary,

Figure 6.1 'Andrew Lang'. From a painting by Sir William Blake Richmond.
Photograph by Frederick Hollyer. © National Portrait Gallery, London.

> And here the tale of Beauty and the Beast
> Points a new moral. One need be wary.[77]

Any amusement or private satisfaction Lang may have felt was overshadowed by concern for Garnet Wolseley. After months of indecision, the government had finally bowed to public opinion and Wolseley was put in command of the 'Nile Expedition' to relieve General Gordon at Khartoum. Nora went with Louisa Wolseley to Sunday afternoon service at St Paul's Cathedral to pray for his safety and hear Canon Henry Liddon preach. Lang wrote to assure Louisa Wolseley of everyone's great faith in her husband: 'I heard someone observe, at the club, that if Lord Wolseley were to bring the D[evil] out of his own place he would do it. Everyone seems extremely pleased, even in the least military places'.[78] Tragically, Khartoum fell two days before the relief forces arrived. The entire garrison, including Gordon, was slaughtered. Lang wrote an elegiac verse on the vain hope of many in England that Gordon was still alive:

> Vain is the dream! However hope may rave,
> He perished with the folk he could not save;
> ...
> Nay, not for England's cause, nor to restore
> Her trampled flag—for he loved honour more.[79]

He shared the bitterness of the British public towards Gladstone's government for its failure to send troops sooner: 'I wish I were American, a German, even an Australian almost, to be out of this world of political quacks, and cowards, and liars'.[80] It bothered him as a writer that he did not speak out. Hearing of Louisa Wolseley's upset at false rumours that her husband advised withdrawal from the region, he reassured her:

> I am sure no one here dreams that Lord Wolseley advises withdrawal, and the desertion of our allies. These are the disgraces with which Mr. Gladstone makes us familiar every day ... I have a chance of saying, in journalism, what I think, as I never write on politics. I disagree, of course with the *Daily News*, and can only express myself in *Punch*, where it goes for little, being mainly in verse. If I were a bachelor, I would go to Australia or America, I am so ashamed of England, but the tree must lie where it falls.[81]

He expressed similar feelings to Stevenson: 'Certainly, I am one of the British Public, and beyond very mild remonstrances, never said a word. But what can one ever say? These things are in the hands of the howlers of this world ... I wish I lived in quieter times. I am sick of 'Great Slaughter'.[82] With a topical political significance that is generally missed, his melancholy poem 'Νήνεμος Αἰών' ('A Quiet Life') opens with an allusion to Ancient Egypt and the Nile region:

> I would my days had been in other times,
> A moment in the long unnumbered years
> That knew the sway of Horus and of hawk,
> In peaceful lands that border on the Nile.[83]

His peace of mind was further shaken by the explosion of a bomb at the Houses of Parliament on 24 January 1885, just a mile from where he sat having lunch at the Savile.[84] Stevenson's darkly comic *The Dynamiter*, out that spring, sought to make the Fenian and anarchist dynamite campaigns a subject of ridicule and contempt. Lang, seeing 'a dummy'—an advance review copy—in the offices of Longman, thought the title too 'catch penny', given the terror and injury terrorism had brought to the streets.[85] Yet a similar humoristic absurdity and exaggeration featured in *That Very Mab*, which he co-wrote anonymously with May Kendall. Their satire reflected a growing mood of irreverence and futility, following the debacle in the Soudan and the low regard for politicians and government policy at home and abroad. As in Shelley's poem *Queen Mab*, the present is seen as a time when human folly, vice, and vanity flourish. Through the eyes of their Queen Mab, returned to England after centuries of exile in Samoa, every aspect of modern civilization—Home and Foreign Policy; the New Democracy; the religious revivalism of Sankey and Moody and the Salvation Army; the triumph of machinery; art and literature—comes in for impartial ridicule. Grant Allen, reviewing *That Very Mab* in *Longman's*, identified May Kendall as the principal author, although noting that the verse parts were sometimes 'absurdly suggestive of a well-known hand in collaboration'.[86]

Stevenson, still grateful for Lang's help with *A Child's Garden of Verses*, suggested he publish some of his old *Spectator* articles on book hunting and book production. Lang was taken aback, having never considered his articles as book material, but he quickly warmed to the idea. Stevenson helped in the selection, and Brander Matthews found an American publisher for *Books and Bookmen*, as they titled the collection, in George J. Coombes of New York. Lang really wanted above all to publish a volume of short stories. He already had two magazine stories he could include in the collection: 'The Romance of the First Radical' from 1880, and a more recent tale in *Fraser's Magazine*, 'In the Wrong Paradise', in which the agnostic narrator is carried in the after-life to the Happy Hunting Grounds of the Ojibbaway Indians and discovers that in the 'traffic between the earth and the next world ... many a man finds himself in a paradise of a religion not his own'. In the Fortunate Isles, the paradise of the Ancient Greeks—he encounters a modern Hellenist, who complains that the Greek Elysium is 'a blooming fraud', a kind of punishment in the disguise of a reward. In Araby, the paradise promised by the Koran, he meets his old college professor of Arabic, 'the most shy of university men ... who had not survived the creation of the first batch of married fellows', looking miserable in the midst of an innumerable host of dancing houris. Though a transparently humorous yarn, 'In the Wrong Paradise' draws cleverly on Tylor's anthropological account of differing concepts of virtue and eternal reward to offer an ironic corrective to Christian absolutism.

His desire for some success as a writer of fiction received fresh stimulation in the early months of 1885 by his discovery of another new writer, who seemed to have something of Stevenson's flair. He had just read Rider Haggard's three-decker novel, *The Witch's Head*, with great enjoyment, when Haggard's story 'Bottles' came his way as London's editor of *Harper's*. He wrote to Haggard, 'I am much pleased with it, but I am unable to accept anything except by permission of the American editor ... I am glad to take this opportunity of thanking you for the great pleasure *The Witch's Head* has given me. I have not read anything so good for a long time.'[87] *Harper's* declined 'Bottles', which later appeared in *Cornhill Magazine*, titled 'The Blue Curtains'. Haggard tried Lang again with the manuscript of his new novel, *King Solomon's Mines*. Lang responded enthusiastically, 'I will find out what *Harper's Boys Magazine* is able to do ... I almost prefer it to *Treasure Island*.'[88] *Harper's* again declined, and *King Solomon's Mines* went to Cassell's, who had published *Treasure Island*. Haggard had been encouraged to write *King Solomon's Mines* by the success of Stevenson's novel. Lang and Haggard had a hugely entertaining lunch together, and the two became close friends. It turned out that Haggard's brother John Haggard, the British Consul in New Caledonia, knew Lang's cousin, James J. Atkinson. Haggard was one of the few men with whom Lang found himself in complete sympathy, though he joked, 'H.R.H. is so pessimistic that he always makes me wish I were dead, to which I am naturally prone.'[89] Lang's affection for Haggard was reciprocated. Haggard felt that Lang manifested a special light when he 'dropped his shield of persiflage with which he hid his heart'.[90]

Critics often claim that Lang was attracted to authors such as Stevenson and Haggard because they promoted the romance of heroic masculinity and imperial ideals. But what really captured Lang's interest in *The Witch's Head* was an echo of his own anthropological conclusions in Haggard's authorial insistence on the affinities between 'savage' and 'civilised' man. Haggard prefaced the chapter describing a David-and-Goliath fist fight in the Transvaal with an address to the reader:

Now, you, my reader, may think that there is a considerable distance between human nature 'in the rough', as exemplified by a Zulu warrior stalking out his

kraal in a kaross and brandishing an assegai, and yourself, say, strolling up
the steps of your club in a frock-coat, and twirling one of Brigg's umbrellas.
But, as a matter of a fact, the difference is of a most superficial character ...
Scratch the polish, and ... observe how powerless high civilization has been
to do anything more than veneer that raw material, which remains identical
in each case.[91]

Inspired by Haggard, Lang took as his subject, in three new short stories, the
encounter between civilized man and nature in the raw, but in his case to satirical, and at times, disquieting effect. In Haggard's fiction, natural man is seen
through the eyes of the sympathetic sportsman and adventurer; in Lang's stories, through the distorting lens of 'civilised spectacles'. 'The End of Phæacia'
is at once a hilarious send-up of eighteenth- and nineteenth-century missionary narratives and a darkly Swiftian satire on the destructive effects of western
imperialism's 'civilising mission'. In 'My Friend the Beachcomber', the beachcomber of the title is a shameless braggard, reeling off tales of his squalid
adventures in the Pacific and boasting of having tricked superstitious islanders
out of their property—themes that Stevenson would also take up in his tales of
the South Seas. The third of Lang's stories, 'A Cheap Nigger', a title undoubtedly uncomfortable for today's readers, gives a savagely ironic turn to a folksy
American tale of rival plantation owners in the pre-Civil War South. Lang
claimed to have been influenced by 'a combination of hints from Edgar Poe
and researches in Aztec antiquities',[92] but the irony of the tale is reminiscent
of Mark Twain's *Huckleberry Finn*. The narrator, an innocent northerner who
finds the spectacle of the slave-market 'painful and monstrous', imagines in
his naïvety that his host has outbid his rival for an old, broken-down slave
called Gumbo out of a hatred of cruelty and oppression, only to discover, in a
grotesque denouement, that Gumbo's real value is the treasure chart tattooed
on his head by his former master.[93]

Lang also began work on a crime novel which had a tattoo as its central
motif, in the figure of an improbably extravagant villain who has his whole
body tattooed with the same savage markings as the man he plans to murder in order to claim the murdered man's inheritance. Lang wrote excitedly to
Stevenson, 'I have been haunting the riverside in search of a proper house for
my murder: I have found the very thing, dormer windows, high pitched red
tiled roof, waste land behind hoardings, alley leading through into slums, and
everything you can desire'.[94] He enclosed a sketch. *The Mark of Cain* was published as number thirteen in Arrowsmith's Bristol Library. The third in series
had inspired Lang's parody, *Much Darker Days*, the previous year.

Lang's hero, Robert Maitland, a young, naïve fellow of St Gatien's College, Oxford, takes over as owner of a London riverside public house after his 'college "coach", philosopher, and friend'—a Benjamin Jowett figure—urges him 'out of his Alma Mater' to 'practice benevolence' and 'improve his acquaintance with humanity'. Comically, Maitland hopes 'to civilise ... a bit' the working men who frequent his riverside pub, while 'insensibly' gaining 'some of their exuberant vitality'.[95] *The Mark of Cain* thus begins as an amusing send-up of the reforming zeal of the Settlement Movements of the 1880s for contact between the classes, and of the vogue for 'social problem novels' at the time. From these beginnings, it develops into a tangled generic mix of sensational crime story and social comedy of manners. In earlier decades, Dickens and Thackeray succeeded imaginatively in fusing diverse generic elements and narrative tones—sensational melodrama, humour, social commentary—in what Henry James referred to as the 'large, loose, baggy monsters' of Victorian serial fiction. But with changing tastes, increased sub-division of the classic Victorian novel into distinct genres, and rivalry between realism and romance, Lang's rich confection of fictional types and motifs bemused and confused, and disappointed reader's expectations. The essayist and critic James Ashcroft Noble, writing in the *Academy*, imagined that Lang, without intending to, had produced a 'caricature of the shilling dreadful class' of fiction he had meant to write; though he was complimentary about the passages in the novel which 'glow with a fine quiet humour, and ... polished scholarly wit',[96] Lang himself seems to have hoped *The Mark of Cain* would establish his reputation as a novelist, describing it as his 'realistic study of character, and analysis of emotion, a little sketch of middle class life in the suburbs'.[97] The description of Maitland's visit to Oxford and Mr Bielby, for instance, has a nostalgic glow. Maitland's journey from Oxford station past Worcester, up Carfax, and down the High Street to St Gatien's, recreates a journey Lang himself had made many times as a fellow of Merton College.

Merton College was much on his mind when Lang wrote the book. The college had decided to endow the first professorship of English Language and Literature at the university, with a salary of £900 for forty-two lectures a year on 'the history and criticism of English language and literature'.[98] There were high hopes in literary circles that the university would appoint a literary critic with a wide range of interests, rather than an Anglo-Saxon specialist. Lang's name was on many people's lips. From among his friends, Saintsbury, Gosse, and Churton Collins entered the race. So too did A. C. Bradley, and Edward Dowden, the Irish-born poet and Shakespearean scholar, in the eyes of some the strongest candidate, though with little chance, as A. E. Freeman, the newly elected Professor of Modern History at Oxford who was on the appointments committee, hated the Irish. Lang did not apply. Lang guessed with an insider's instinct that the university would appoint a language specialist. It came as no surprise to him when the post went to Arthur Sampson Napier, the only philologist in the final field of nine. Although he thought Napier a good choice, he took exception to Henry Sweet's letter in the *Academy* congratulating the electors for rejecting the 'mythic claims of the light literaries' and choosing an Anglo-Saxonist.[99] He retaliated:

> May a humble 'light literary' (as Mr. Sweet puts it) say a few words about the Merton Professorship? ... A man may be deeply and seriously versed in the language and works of English authors from Surrey to Shelley, without being versed in almost prehistoric English. Such a man should not be regarded as a mere trifler, with claims as mythical as 'Grendel' ... A man of real capacity and knowledge, and worthy to be endowed, is sometimes driven into periodical literature just because he is not endowed. He must write what people at large can read, or he must starve.[100]

The year ended with rapid shifts of fortune. *Harper's Magazine* fired him without warning as their English agent. The reason given was that they had engaged William Dean Howells to write a regular column and had to sacrifice Lang's English department. Lang wrote bitterly to Gosse, 'Sacked! your old Howells has bowled me out at *Harper's*. I wish his taut clothesline was round his neck'.[101] He was upset, telling Matthews, 'I daresay in a week I shall have ceased to feel like a thing that is raw ... I was an atrophied organ and am now amputated'.[102] Then, in a sudden lift to his spirits, Charles Longman gave him the go-ahead to write a monthly 'causerie' in *Longman's Magazine*. He was given a budget of £10 a month. It offered him the peace of mind of a regular income and a means to attract a regular following of readers. New monthly and weekly miscellany magazines were coming on the market to rival *Longman's*, and *Longman's* needed to up its circulation. The causerie format, which consisted traditionally of an 'unforced flow of remarks, fancies, feeling, or thought' without stridency of argument, exactly suited his manner.[103] They decided to call it 'At the Sign of the Ship', from the firm's business premises at the Ship and Black Swan in Paternoster Row. His column appeared for the first time in the January issue of 1886. He hoped anxiously for its success. His future at *Longman's* depended on it.

7

Captaining 'The Ship'

Six months after the appearance of his first 'At the Sign of the Ship' feature in *Longman's Magazine*, Lang applied for the post of Secretary to the University of London. A letter from Margaret Oliphant to say his novel *The Mark of Cain* 'made her grin' decided him he would have to regard it as his 'Folly'.[1] He sent Stevenson a presentation copy with the inscription:

> Andrew Lang can scribble, A. L. can scrawl,
> A. L. can rhyme all day,
> But he can't hit it off with a shilling romance,
> For,—
> He never was built that way![2]

Stevenson thanked him for the book but did not disagree with his verdict: 'I do not believe in your crimes or your criminals; belief is not at command; I wish I could, but I don't.'[3]

The disappointment of *The Mark of Cain* was not the only reason Lang had to doubt his future in the writing business. The atmosphere in London social and literary circles had become more abrasive and factional with Gladstone's push in Parliament for Home Rule in Ireland. Divisions in political and social life had hardened. Lang was dismayed when Frank Hill, his editor at the *Daily News*, was sacked in January for disagreeing with Gladstone's Home Rule policy. He exclaimed drily to Matthews, 'My turn next I fancy: *vile damnum* ('small loss').'[4] He wondered too how he would cope with the constant deadlines and demands of the trade as he got older. He felt age catching up with him, and the effort required to make a decent living from literature was taking its toll. He confessed to Stevenson, 'I am not only *growing* but grown old, and life is no longer all sweet smiling satisfaction.'[5] To his astonishment he had made great progress on his 'big book' on myth over the dark winter, due in part to the fact that he 'felt bound' to keep his newly employed lady-typist in copy. He was still ambitious for the book's success. He told Gosse, 'I am sick of seeing my own name attached to trifles.'[6]

Andrew Lang. John Sloan, Oxford University Press. © John Sloan (2023). DOI: 10.1093/oso/9780192866875.003.0007

He did in fact enjoy some critical success with his *Letters to Dead Authors*, a collection of witty 'letters' to dead poets and novelists, written originally for the *St James's Gazette* in 1885 at the request of its editor, Frederick Greenwood. In his 'Shelley' letter, he condemned the prurient fascination in the 'art and morality' debates of the 1880s with the sexual life of Shelley and his circle: 'They swarm round you like carrion-flies round a sensitive plant, like night-birds bewildered by the sun'. He admired Shelley as a visionary poet of human liberation and love, 'whose genius burned always with a clearer and steadier flame to the last'.[7] He dedicated the book to Anne Thackeray, the novelist's eldest daughter, now Mrs Thackeray Ritchie, and quoted her declared delight in Jane Austen's novels in his letter 'To Jane Austen': 'Dear books! Bright, sparkling with wit and animation, in that the homely heroine's charm, the dull hours fly, and the very bores are enchanting'.[8] He reserved the highest compliment in the letters for Thackeray as 'without a rival' in his 'many-sided intelligence'.[9] Lang had to turn down an invitation to visit Mrs Ritchie that summer because of a prior engagement.[10] Apart from the reviewer in the *Spectator* who complained that Lang was 'a little too ready to believe that a sneer adds brightness to a sentence',[11] the many notices of the book paid generous compliments to his versatility, humour, and his shrewd, occasionally brilliant criticisms. Stevenson congratulated him on 'the best thing you have done … witty and graceful and tender', and attached a verse letter 'To Andrew Lang' in tribute:

> An equal craft of hand you show
> The pen to guide, the fly to throw.
> …
> Still like a brook your page has shone,
> And your ink sings of Helicon.[12]

Even so, Stevenson addressed him in his opening line as, 'Dear Andrew of the brindled hair'—a reminder that he was no longer young.

Benjamin Jowett was happy to provide a reference supporting his application to the University of London and wrote a brief, uneffusive testimonial of the kind written even today by Oxford dons, who imagine that the merest nod of approval from them will carry weight:

Hearing that Mr. Andrew Lang is a candidate for the Secretaryship to the University of London, I have great pleasure in stating that I know of him. He is a most amiable person who is greatly regarded by his friends and acquaintances. He is also distinguished as a literary man, and in my opinion is likely to become more so. I think that his appointment would reflect credit on the University.[13]

Whatever his hopes of the London University post, it came to nothing.

To his relief, his monthly causerie in *Longman's* proved popular with readers. His main topic was the current literary world, with commentary on new books and debates of the day. One of his roles was that of a scholar in the marketplace, a mediator between the world of learning and the wider society, drawing the attention of his readers to developments that interested him in education, language study, anthropology, and many other topics. Although he did not shirk controversy, he remained true to Saint-Beuve and the traditions of the French causerie in saying what he thought and felt, but without 'strenuous display or stridency of argument'.[14] He soon had a large following of devoted readers. Many assumed he was editor of the magazine and addressed their manuscript poems, stories, and articles to him as editor. He had eventually to print a disclaimer in the magazine informing subscribers, 'The Skipper of the Ship is NOT the editor of *Longman's Magazine*'.[15] The truth was that although he enjoyed his position as 'Skipper of the Ship' and the influence it gave him, he remained disappointed he was not made editor. An almost heaven-sent consolation was his reinstatement as English editor of *Harper's*.

He and Nora spent longer than usual that summer and autumn away from London. He put together his first collection of short stories, *In the Wrong Paradise*, while staying with Frederick Locker at the Norfolk coastal resort of Cromer. They made this a stopping-off place now that Embleton was closed to them. They had visited Redcar the previous summer when the Wards were also guests, and he had been driven to distraction by Mary Ward's constant chatter about the help she had received from Edmund Scherer, a French critic.[16] He felt Mary Ward 'would be nicer' if she didn't talk so obsessively about her work.[17] He took his revenge in his *Letters to Dead Authors* by poking fun at Scherer in a verse letter, 'To Lord Byron':

> There's a Swiss critic whom I cannot rhyme to,
> One Scherer, dry as sawdust, grim and prim.
> Of him there's much to say, if I had time to
> Concern myself in any wise with *him*.[18]

From Cromer, they continued north to Redcar to visit Hugh and Florence Belle, who shared his interest in fairy tales. After Redcar, Nora returned south to Clifton; Lang went for a fortnight to Glen Urquhart in the Scottish Highlands. While there, he witnessed what may have been one of the last house-burning evictions in Scotland, despite a law having been passed at Westminster before the summer recess, the Crofter's Holding (Scotland) Act, granting security of tenure to crofters. The first indication, as he returned with his gillie from a day's fishing, was the sight of 'great brown smoke hanging in the wet air' above a high, wooded hill. Drawing closer, they saw 'the black gables of the burning cottage' and 'on the grass near the roadside a woman ... trying to cover her property'. His gillie, 'full of pity and anger' at the eviction, told him that the farmer had been unable to pay his rent, and that his stock and cattle had already been sold up. Lang heard later that the burning of the house was the result of over-zealousness on the part of the factor, who had exceeded his instructions. It was an unsettling reminder of his grandfather, and the sins of the past. He thought the whole business 'miserable and ill-advised', but he still clung to the economic justification that 'land cultivated ... in small lots does not pay in some places'. He tried to shift some of the blame to the tenant, in choosing to regard the 'wretched business' as an example of Matthew Arnold's distinction between the pragmatic Anglo-Saxon and impractical Celt spirit exhibited in literature, displaying itself in the land question: 'An Englishman would have perhaps thought it well to leave a farm which he could not make profitable, when he had money and stock. But the Celtic tenant simply refused to leave, in spite of many requests and warnings'.[19] He gradually over the years came to disown the insidious, nonsensical racial prejudices and assumptions of this outlook.

He joined Nora in Bristol in September, and they travelled to Paris. Prior to their departure, he was alarmed by Gosse's threats of retaliation against reviewers of his *From Shakespeare to Pope*, who questioned his competence as a literary historian. He had tried to calm Gosse when the first reviews had appeared, jokingly comparing Gosse's outrage to recent press hysteria about the threat from rabid fighting-dogs:

> Your lectures have been excellently received, and only one or two unimportant people snarled at your verses. You have been rather too successful to please everyone ... Don't worry about the critical hydrophobia, it really is not worth a moment's thought. I wouldn't read reviews if I saw people were trying to rile me.[20]

He alerted Symonds:

> 'Weg' has had a facer, but no one can know what mischief he has in his heart. He is apparently quite reckless—his voice and his vanity have survived any

character he may ever have possessed. It is a misfortune for everyone that he has so much vitality,—he ought to be tonsured and sent to a monastery.[21]

Lang inclined to believe that those with a university education had an advantage in the literary trade. Haggard's imaginative ability amazed him, but the 'slipshoddity' of Haggard's style made him wince.[22] With Henley, the fault was reviewing books without sufficient learning or knowledge of the subject. Henley, who could be frank to the point of rudeness in his criticism of others, could not bear being criticized, and Lang made him 'rather mad' by saying an article of his was 'blethers', and that it could 'hardly be right' to review a history of French literature without knowing what a *pastourelle* was.[23] The value of university training was brought home to him with the arrival of the first completed manuscripts for the 'English Worthies' series. Gosse's *Walter Raleigh* needed extensive editorial intervention. 'I fear some of Raleigh must go', he wrote, marking the passages in the manuscript 'that might perhaps be sacrificed'.[24] Symonds' *Ben Jonson* in contrast required little editing before going to print. Lang's only mild suggestion was that Symonds might 'hedge a little' in his comments on literary representations of Puritan dissent from Jonson's *Bartholomew Fair* to Dickens's *Pickwick Papers* and *Bleak House*: 'The Dissenters are awfully touchy, and of course S.[tiggins] & C.[hadband] are not fair publicity of the common man, any more than the parsons who carry on critiques in cipher in the *Christian World* are examples of the clergy'.[25]

In Paris, Lang enjoyed browsing the French capital's riverside *bouquinistes*, but he felt, as before, 'a Babe in the Wood in Paris, an Idiot abroad'.[26] He was soon anxious to return to England, which he thought 'distinctly a good deal cleaner than la belle France'.[27] When he did get back, he had to intervene in a fresh row that erupted over Churton Collins' damaging review of Gosse's *From Shakespeare to Pope*. Collins, still smarting from his failure to obtain the Merton professorship, exposed Gosse's numerous inaccuracies and blindspots to prove Gosse's 'utter incapacity for the task he had undertaken', and to express grave concern that men like Gosse—journalists, reviewers, and professional critics with pretentions to learning—were being taken for genuine literary scholars.[28]

Collins' attack on Gosse was, to Lang's mind, simply the latest outbreak of the 'old quarrel' between Oxbridge scholars and non-university writers— a feud which early in the century had set Lockhart and Wilson against Leigh Hunt and Keats. He himself sided on occasions with university men, although he admitted to feeling 'like one of those bad, bold preachers ... who mightily moves his congregation to righteousness while hiding a bottle of whisky in the vestry'.[29] He was too aware of his own carelessness, and the blunders even the best scholars made, to be too harsh on others.[30] Gosse's flaw, in his view, was vanity, not ignorance; Collins', arrogance.[31]

Lang knew that one literary quarrel often led to another. When Gosse scornfully dismissed Collins' accusation of 'incompetence and even of imposture' as 'utterly contemptuous', particularly coming from someone who was once his 'intimate companion',[32] W. T. Stead, the crusading editor and lover of controversy at the *Pall Mall Gazette*, dubbed Gosse a 'log-roller' for assuming that 'friendship should be a bar to a reviewer's engaging in "outspoken criticism" of an author's work'.[33] Lang came to Gosse's defence in *Longman's Magazine*, declaring that 'log-roller' was a meaningless term of abuse, paraded by false moralists who held that a reviewer 'is never to praise his friends when they do well', but is bound 'to censure them when they do ill'. Instead, he advocated an 'ethics of reviewing' that chose silence, rather than exposure of 'ill-doing', especially of a friend, but of personal enemies too.[34] Stead hit back with relish, accusing him of 'moral cowardice which shrinks from plain speaking' and of turning literature into 'a lounge for the dilettanti'.[35] Lang shrugged off the stab from the 'accursed rag', as he called it,[36] but said to Matthews about Gosse, 'In truth he is no scholar, and should avoid airs of learning, and be content with a native love of literature and the power of interesting people. That's the short and the long of it'.[37] Matthews at the time was compiling the final selection of Lang's *Spectator* articles for *Books and Bookmen*, which included Lang's 'Literary Quarrels', in which Lang said, 'Men slander and hate each other on very slight provocation', but that 'what they are fighting about is, to them, no slight matter. It is success and reputation'.[38] He asked Matthews to leave it out, fearing it would only fuel further feuds.

He did not shrink from taking sides in the bigger battle between the so-called realists and romancers. The seeds of the conflict went back to William Dean Howells' attack on Dickens, Thackeray, and the romantic sentimentality of English fiction. Howells believed the future of the novel lay with his own and Henry James' brand of minute, psychological realism.[39] Lang held fire publicly but remarked in private that Howells 'might have waited for someone else to say that he and his friends are masters of fiction'.[40] When he did respond in print, he did so at first in light verses in his 'At the Sign of the Ship'—one, 'The Restoration of Romance', lauding Stevenson and Haggard as knights errant of 'King Romance';[41] the other, 'A Ballade of Railway Novels', taking a shot at Howells, James, and the 'cultured' set:

> Let others praise analysis
> And revel in a 'cultured' style,

And follow the subjective miss
From Boston to the banks of Nile,
Rejoice in anti-British bile,
And weep for fickle hero's woe;
These twain have shortened many a mile,
Miss Braddon and Saboriau![42]

ANDREW LANG

Figure 7.1 Drawing by Ernest Haskell.
Reproduced courtesy of the University of St Andrews Libraries and Museums.

He enjoyed being in the captain's tower when the enemy was cultural snob-
bery. To show he was not a snob, he went to 'Buffalo Bill's Wild West Show'
when it opened at Earl's Court, with Queen Victoria in attendance, telling
Matthews, 'Buffalo Bill is a great card here: he does not powerfully excite me.
But he *can* ride'.[43] When the *Contemporary Review* asked for an article on
American literature, he decided it was finally time to have his say on 'Realism and Romance'. His article made clear that his enemy was not realism, but
realism to the exclusion of everything else, and that realism and romance were
not divisible but complementary sides of fiction:

> Fiction is a shield with two sides, the silver and the golden: the study of man-
> ners and of character, on one hand; on the other, the description of adventure,
> the delight of romantic narrative. Now, these two aspects blend with each
> other so subtly—and so constantly, that it really seems the extreme of perver-
> sity to shout for nothing but romance on one side, or for nothing but analysis
> of character and motive on the other. Yet for such abstractions and divisions
> people are clamouring and quarrelling.

He saw no rational grounds for Howells' assumption that the new realism was
intrinsically of more value than popular romances. If people preferred Stevenson to Henry James, or, for that matter, Buffalo Bill's romantic Wild West
extravaganza to the latest historical or theological romance, it was simply a
matter of taste: 'We may not agree with their taste, but that *is* their taste'. It
was clear to him from his study of myths that the taste for the marvellous and
sensational regarded by Howells as 'childish' had its roots in primitive man's
attempt to understand and control nature, and what was more, still satisfied
deep-seated primitive needs and longings in civilized man:

> The advantage of our mixed condition, civilised at top with the old barbarian
> under our clothes, is just this, that we can enjoy all sorts of things ... Do not
> let us cry that because we are 'cultured', there shall be no Buffalo Bill ... If we
> will only be tolerant, we shall permit the great public also to delight in our
> few modern romances of adventure. They may be 'savage survivals', but so is
> the whole of the poetic way of regarding Nature.[44]

Lang's article became one of the defining contributions to the debate. His
advocacy of romance and the 'joy of adventurous living' as an antidote to over-
refinement was humorous, good-natured, and conciliatory. In the same year as
'Realism and Romance', he and Walter Pollock collaborated on *He*, a burlesque

of Haggard's *She*. They finished it at great speed sitting at opposite sides of the table, each taking up the story from where the other left off.[45] Lang gave his sense of fun full rein in 'The Avengers of Romance', a magazine skit of Stevenson's *The Black Arrow*, in which an arrow carrying a message shatters the window of the castle of Harpers in New York, the stronghold of Howells and his armed warriors:

> Under my belt I have four black arrows,
> That shall spit ye all as sparrows.
> One shaft shall De Howells slay
> That spake ill of Thackeray.
> The others are for all the lot
> That like not Poe and blaspheme Scott.

The ensuing battle between the warriors of American realism and the 'Avengers of Romance', led by Robert of Samoa, concluded in comic style with both sides at dinner at Delmonico's 'seated round the same mahogany ... swapping stories'.[46]

Lang has been characterized wrongly by some present-day critics as a strident advocate of heroic masculinity and imperial adventure. Much is made to rest on his statement, 'Not for nothing did Nature leave us all savages under our white skins; she has wrought thus that we might have many delights, among others "the joy of adventurous living" and of reading about adventurous living'.[47] He made no secret of his preference for 'swashbuckling' novels of action over the gloomy 'psychological vivisection' of character by the new realists[48]; but his views are not to be confused with those of other propagandists of romance who followed his lead, such as the author of 'Romanticism and Realism', who equated the preference for the romance novel in England with the spirit of the English as an adventurous, colonizing race.[49] We find the very opposite of belligerent masculinity in Lang's own writings. In his epical romance, *Helen of Troy*, his retelling of the Trojan War shifts attention from the battlefield and world of male violence and codes of honour to sympathetic treatment of the woman's perspective. His taste in literature was anything but one-sided. He insisted, 'What is good, what is permanent may be found in fiction of every *genre* and shall we "crab" and underrate any *genre* because it chances not to be that which we are best fitted to admire?'[50] As his *Letters to Dead Authors* make clear, Jane Austen was among his favourite authors—the 'deathless Jane', he called her. Among modern authors, he admired Rhoda Broughton, best-selling novelist of New Woman fiction, as Austen's 'female rival in English fiction.'[51] He singled out her ability to make 'you believe and know her persons are in love' to be her special gift as a novelist, telling the readers of *Longman's*, 'The passion of her Joan is as true in its way as that of Miss Austen's Anne Elliot.'[52]

He met Broughton for the first time in November 1886 when he and Nora were in Oxford as Jowett's guests. Broughton lived at 27 Holywell Street, just minutes from Balliol College, where she sometimes attended chapel. She was friends with Henry James and Louisa Wolseley. Her verbal sharpness was liked by some, disliked by others. Some in Oxford—Charles Dodgson was one— showed her the cold shoulder, but Jowett was among those who welcomed her to Oxford.[53] She and the Langs made instant friends. There was no need for Lang to engage in tiresome inconsequential conversation. They talked books. Lang wrote to Louisa Wolseley following their visit, 'We had a pleasant time in Oxford, and found Miss Broughton very affable.'[54]

Broughton undertook to read Lang's latest book, *In the Wrong Paradise*, and offered to send one of hers, to which he replied, 'If you are really so kind as to send me one of your books, I think I prefer Nancy, but I know Mrs Lang prefers Joan; so please let it be Joan!'[55] Broughton sent both. He reciprocated by sending her a large paper copy of *The Mark of Cain*: 'It is not necessary to *read* it, but some day the l. p. copy may be "very scarce". If read, I fear it is not to be taken seriously.'[56] He also wrote her a light-hearted poem, 'Doris's Books', celebrating the popularity of her writings compared to his: 'Here is a small madrigal, in which your works have a part. "Doris" is, of course, a creature of fancy bred, or rather a representative of the majority which leaves my volumes "quite uncut"':

> 'Quite uncut', 'unopened' rather
> Are my edifying pages;
> From this circumstance I gather
> That some other Muse engages,
> Doris, your untutored fancy.
> Yes, I thought so—deep in 'Nancy'![57]

He and Nora were in Oxford again to visit Rhoda Broughton over Christmas. They played golf on Christmas Day after church.[58] Jowett had acquired a fur coat that was too large for him, and Nora took it back to London to be adjusted. Jowett contacted her in January to say, 'The fur coat has arrived and fits perfectly now.'[59]

During the early part of 1887, Lang's championing of romance took a more scholarly direction. In his introductions to several works—to a new edition of William Adlington's translation of *Cupid and Psyche*; to the verse version of *Beauty and the Beast*, thought to be by Charles Lamb; and to Charles Perrault's *Popular Tales*—he hoped to further appreciation of the recurrence and ubiquity of the same tales in different ages around the world. There was high praise in the *Saturday Review* for his introduction to *Cupid and Psyche*: 'A more interesting and suggestive paper on the subject of Märchen has never been written'.[60] His introductions were intended as a foretaste of his two-volume *magnum opus*, *Myth, Ritual and Religion*, then with the printer. Neither he nor Longman expected much 'lucre', but he fretted about its critical reception, telling Matthews in January, 'Correcting proofs for my *Big* book, *o ciel!*'[61]

His translation of the Old French medieval romance, *Aucassin and Nicolete*, came out in June. He had undertaken the work at the prompting of William Russell Lowell, the American scholar-poet, after meeting him at the Academy dinner the previous May. Lang remembered writing it 'rapidly in summer gardens'. He paid tribute to Walter Pater, 'But for Mr. Pater who wrote excellently on Aucassin in his first book "Studies of the Renaissance", I doubt whether we should have heard of these two lovers'.[62] A final London social invitation before they left for Scotland that summer was a celebratory dinner with James Russell Lowell. Lang escorted Nora and Charlotte Green, now a widow. He sent Louisa Wolseley a humorous account of the rivalry between the two women in trying to gain the attention of the celebrated poet:

> Last night was the triumph of *la veuve* Green ... she cut out Mr. Lowell from under Nora's guns, and towed him, a prize, into the harbour of a sofa ... Nora did not stand her guns, I admit, indeed *la veuve* brandished a flag of the American war, and made the Yankees tell us all the atrocities of the South ... Nora's only comfort was that when *la veuve* told stories, she left out the points which were kindly supplied when she was quite done.[63]

He conveyed a less benign view of Charlotte Green's behaviour in reporting to Matthews: 'An ass of a woman trotted him [Lowell] out on your old war. I wish all tomahawks were buried, after that woman was well scalped'.[64]

In Scotland, on 26 September, his cousin and first love, Florence, became Mrs John MacCunn at Dalry in Galloway. The groom, like Lang himself a former Snell Exhibitioner at Balliol, was Professor of Philosophy at the newly founded University College Liverpool. The Sellar family had experienced a distressing two years. His Uncle Willie's health had broken down. Lang told

Stevenson it was a recurrence of 'some old hypochondriac ideas, that had been hanging about him for many years, always ready to jump up when he was ill'.[65] Travel in France, Italy, and Switzerland had brought partial recovery, but further family upset had been his youngest daughter May Violet's 'disengagement'. Jowett, a family intimate, consoled them on hearing of it, 'Bad lovemaking is better than an unhappy marriage. The young man seems to have behaved disgracefully'.[66] Lang brought some joy to the family by dedicating his *magnum opus* to his uncle. He also wrote a humorous but touching ballade to Florence, 'Ah Fortune, thy wheel', lamenting the changes marriage might bring:

> For the fields and the foxgloves aswing,
> For the Glen where the Rain and the Sun
> Will be scarcely the same sort of thing
> When Florence is Mrs MacCunn?[67]

He and Nora spent the week before the wedding at the village inn at Ballantrae on the Ayrshire coast. Lord Archibald Campbell was staying at the Manse with his wife, formerly Janey Sevilla, famous for her Orlando in the Pastoral Players' open-air production of *As You Like It* at Coombe Park in 1884. Lang sent word to Matthews, always eager for news of anything theatrical: 'We are at a pothouse on the Ayrshire coast; Lady Archie Campbell of Pastoral renown is at the Manse. Her lord—who has been a capital companion in the wilderness— has gone to town. I've caught a good many trout, and Mrs. Lang has stared at the sea: no land between you and us'.[68]

Lang's thoughts as he gazed out across the ocean were of Stevenson, who had sailed for America with his little clan in August. *Underwoods*, Stevenson's second collection of verse, published days before he sailed, included his irreverent verse letter 'Dear Andrew, with the brindled hair'. Lang responded at Ballantrae with his equally irreverent, 'Dear Louis of the awful cheek', which he sent for inclusion in his 'At the Sign of the Ship' for October. Copy went in a month before the magazine appeared. Much more quickly than this, on 16 September, the *St James's Gazette* published his 'Ballant o' Ballantrae', written while there, and dedicated to Stevenson. The poem, in the crotchety manner of Stevenson's poems in Scots, painted a grimly captious picture of 'the coast o' wasteland Ayr/ ... unco bleak and bare' in wet weather.[69]

On their return to London, he visited Henley at his house in Campden Gardens, Shepherd's Bush and was shown a letter in which Stevenson reported jubilantly that he had been offered a handsome £720 to write twelve articles for *Scribner's Magazine*. Lang was aware of tensions in Henley and Steven-son's friendship. A month before Stevenson sailed for America, he informed Matthews, 'RLS really has been very ill; Henley seems to think his illness a romance invented to keep him, Henley, remote! I should not care for W.E.H. about me much, if I were an invalid, more of an invalid, rather'.[70] Henley seemed annoyed by Stevenson's success. Lang, for his part, worried that Stevenson might waste his talent on lesser work. He wrote to congratu-late Stevenson on his good fortune: 'They don't pay *me* as much as *that* at *Longman's*'; but added, 'Are you really ready to write statedly in *Scribner's Magazine*? You should leave that kind of thing to drudges like

> 'The Heartbroken
> Translator
> Man of all work
> Hack
> Log Roller
> A. Lang'.[71]

He told Stevenson he had published an ode to him, 'The Ballant o' Ballantrae', in the *St James's Gazette*. Stevenson, at work on a historical novel of the Jaco-bite Rebellion, with the provisional title 'Brothers', retitled it *The Master of Ballantrae*. Lang, when he came to include 'The Ballant o' Ballantrae' in his collection *Ban and Arrière Ban*, apologized in a tongue-in-cheek note for the grim picture of Ballantrae which provided the setting for Stevenson's novel: 'Written in wet weather, this conveyed to the Master of Ballantrae a wrong idea of a very beautiful and charming place, with links ... good sea-fishing, and ... a ruined castle at every turn of the stream'.[72]

Lang was out of sorts on getting back to 'black, unseemly' London, the 'cen-tre of stinks'.[73] Jowett came to stay with them in late October to sit for his painting by George Frederick Watts. The portrait had been interrupted the previous year because of Jowett's failing health. Lang and Jowett disagreed about the controversial proposal for a new school of Modern Languages at Oxford which would include the study of English literature. Lang felt there was need for a School of Modern Languages but opposed the teaching of English literature at Oxford, which he thought would become 'chatter' about the pro-nunciation of prehistoric English.[74] Jowett supported the idea of including a study of English authors within the Classics curriculum.[75] Nora, a devoted admirer of Richardson, was undoubtedly the 'young lady, a friend' mentioned in Jowett's letters at this time, who introduced him to *Sir Charles Grandison*.[76]

She also gave him to read her novel in manuscript, 'Country Conversations', set in the 1850s and 1860s, a series of amusing dialogues between gossiping farmers' wives, daughters, and servant girls on the subject of abusive men, marriage, making ends meet, and country matters.[77] The first reviews of *Myth, Ritual and Religion* came out that month. Lang regarded *Myth, Ritual and Religion* as the 'great book' Jowett had urged him to write on leaving Balliol twenty years before, although he came to suspect that Jowett never read it.[78]

Myth, Ritual and Religion enhanced the reputation Lang had already gained in the field of comparative mythology three years earlier with his *Custom and Myth*. A French translation of his article on 'Mythology' in *Encyclopaedia Britannica*, with material added from *Custom and Myth*, was extending the influences of his ideas abroad.[79] *Myth, Ritual and Religion* surpassed his earlier work in its detail of man's myths and beliefs from the old savage state of nature to more civilized ages, but his purpose remained the same: to show, by the anthropological method, that the crude, anomalous, seemingly irrational elements of myth and ritual among advanced peoples were survivals or relics of savage imagination. What distinguished the book from his previous writings on the subject was his wonder and appreciation at the complexity and moral implications underlying the apparent confusion and credulity of the savage mind in which man 'regards himself as literally akin to animals and plants and heavenly bodies'. Drawing again on his uncle Gideon Scott Lang's evidence that the South Australian aborigine 'looks upon the universe as the Great Tribe', a body of which 'he himself is part', Lang concluded that 'This extraordinary belief is not a mere idle fancy—it influences conduct'.[80] He remained on the side of Tylor and the evolutionary assumption of man's progress from 'low' to 'high', 'savage' to 'civilised' in the provinces of myth, ritual, and religion. He found in savage beliefs only 'the small change of the idea of God', and 'nothing like the notion of an omniscient invisible being, the creator of our religion'.[81] Even so, he admitted to the difficulty of determining with certainty 'whether the religious or the mythical, the irrational or the sympathetic, element is earlier, or whether both are of equal antiquity'.[82]

Almost all the reviews were laudatory. An exception was the reviewer in the *St James's Gazette*, a died-in-the-wool advocate of Müller's solar theory.[83] The majority admired his vast accumulation of evidence, scholarly authority, and lucid, engaging literary style. The book especially pleased specialists in the field. Samuel Ball Platner, the American classicist and archaeologist, praised Lang's explanation of the evolution from savage state to civilized mythology as 'far more comprehensive and satisfactory than any yet discovered'.[84]

The *Unitarian Review* saluted him as a 'worthy disciple' of Tylor and quoted approvingly his declaration that 'man can never be certain that he has expelled the savage from his temples and from his heart, yet even the lowest known savage, in hours of awe and need, lift up their thoughts to their father and ours, who is not far from any of us'—the first part of Lang's statement, from a Unitarian perspective, an implicit reproach to what they regarded as irrational elements in mainstream Christianity.[85]

Lang took little comfort in the applause. He characterized the reviews as being 'in the spirit of young Pottingen ... "waving his hat but clearly not understanding what is going forward"', an allusion to the amiable young man in George Canning's eighteenth-century, anti-Jacobin drama, *The Rovers, or The Double Arrangement*. He would have liked, as he put it, 'to have the slating' of his own book.[86] He could see, better than reviewers, gaps in his argument. More than this, the evidence increased his doubts about the evolutionary theory of religion on which his writings until then were premised—the conviction that mankind's long and slow evolution was from savage to civilized—from totem worship and animism to a higher form of ethical monotheism. His findings opened his mind to the possibility that 'comparatively pure, if inarticulate religious beliefs' coexisted from the beginning alongside savage customs and rituals, and served, as in advanced civilization, to counter the selfish, unscrupulous, and violent tendencies in man. This is what he meant by 'going forward'. In his revised, second edition of *Myth, Ritual and Religion* in 1899, he replaced the sentences at the end of volume one, quoted approvingly by the *Unitarian Review*, with the corrective reflection, 'Religion does its best, in certain cases, to lend equilibrium, though the world over, religion often fails in practice.'[87]

Lang already had his eye on the post of Gifford Lecturer at St Andrews, one of four newly endowed lectureships on natural theology at the Scottish universities, founded at the bequest of Lord Gifford, a wealthy Scottish advocate. Appointment was initially for two years. Lang was not a university postholder, and therefore not a natural choice for the appointment, but he had friends at the university and was busy behind the scenes seeking support for his nomination. He was on good terms with the Bishop of St Andrews, Charles Wordsworth, the poet's nephew. Lord Archibald Campbell's parents the Duke and Duchess of Argyll, had influence at the university, and Lewis Campbell, the Professor of Greek and a former Snell Exhibitioner, remained in close touch with Jowett. Lang also corresponded with Sir John Lubbock, First Baron Avery, who was doing much to promote archaeology and anthropology as respectable disciplines. He discovered that his main rival was his old adversary, Max Müller. He kept his activities from Nora, who was having her portrait painted by Sir William Blake Richmond. He let Louisa Wolseley know only after telling Nora of his plans:

> The wicked old Max Müller is coming between me and my St Andrews. To him that shall be given. I think Scots might prefer a Scot to a German. I'd rather they chose anyone, now, than the pluralist. I have confessed my intrigues (with Alma Mater) to my wife.[88]

As he waited to learn his fate, he collaborated with Henley on a comic satire in which the figures in the pictures at the Royal Academy step out of their frames after the galleries close for the night, 'stroll about, and exchange their ideas about Art and Life'. Their *Pictures at Play*, published anonymously 'by two Art-Students', with illustrations by Harry Furniss, contained some entertaining scenes, notably Albert Toft's marble bust of Gladstone, a 'stainless moral' Dr Jekyll, regarding with horror his Mr Hyde in Frank Holl's portrait of his seventy-nine-year-old self. Lang and Henley trumpeted their differing artistic preferences in the Preface—Lang's decorative; Henley's pictorial—and made it part of the knockabout humour of the book.[89] Henley was not an easy man to get along with. He went on the warpath when he suspected Lang to be the anonymous reviewer of his *A Book of Verse*, who declared himself 'no partisan' of Henley's 'sometimes deliberate and crudely realistic' style and diction and complained that Henley's use of old French metrical forms lacked lightness.[90] Henley wrote in fury to his lieutenant, Charles Whibley, 'I didn't think A. L. would, or could have played it so low down on a pal like that. However, I've writ to him & burned the letter; & I've writ to him again, & it goes with this'.[91] A split was avoided on this occasion. Lang felt sympathy and admiration for Henley who had battled on after tragically losing a leg to tuberculosis, but professionally he thought Henley too easily offended for a man of letters. Lang always took his cue from Thackeray, who believed that 'authors should make up their minds to a great deal of honest enmity'. That, Lang felt, was 'the right way to look at these things, to take appreciation as kindness, and opposition, not as a "stab" of the "enemy", but as the inevitable, natural, even desirable, result of the blessed differences in human temperament, tastes, opinions'.[92]

He sat next to William Courtney at a Merton College 'Gaudy' that spring. Courtney taught Logic at New College, but he had had enough of the disapproval by 'serious Oxford', because he wrote for the popular press. Lang heard from him shortly after asking about possibilities in journalism or editing in London. Lang replied that he did not know of any opening worth his while and advised him to stay where he was as London journalism was 'a case of scribble for ever and ever … unless you have some certainty, on a paper or an editorship'.[93] At Balliol, he enjoyed seeing the 'Humphry Elsmeres', as he humorously christened the Wards that year on the publication of Mary Ward's crisis of faith novel, *Robert Elsmere*. He poked fun in his review of the novel by describing her as a writer of 'good promise … when some fairy adds the gift of narrative style' to 'the style of an essayist'.[94] He reported with amusement to Haggard of his Oxford visit, 'Mrs Ward thinks it a very wicked thing to have fights in novels and has never read a saga'.[95]

The result of the elections for the Gifford Lectureships was announced. His intrigues had been effective. Max Müller was elected to the lectureship at Glasgow, Lang, to the lectureship at St Andrews. He shared his good news with Matthews: 'Did you ever hear of my luck in getting a lectureship on my myths at St. Andrews, a place I'm very fond of?'[96] The appointments caused some consternation in Scotland, particularly among Presbyterians, who questioned whether the intention of the Gifford Lectureships was to sap religious faith rather than to buttress it.[97]

With the country in the 'horns and hoofs' of a blizzard, he and Nora travelled to Italy in March, hoping to escape the foul weather, only to find themselves in the tail of the blizzard in the shape of rain.[98] He wrote to Rhoda Broughton from La Spezia in northern Italy, 'When it rains in Italy, it does rain!' He was reading her novel *Belinda* and planned to write a letter from her characters to George Eliot's Dorothea and Mr Casauban, to conclude his series of imaginary letters from 'Old Friends in fiction' in the *St James's Gazette*, with the promise that 'the Middlemarch people shall not have the best of it'. He explained:

We are here (and there, and elsewhere) chiefly because Messrs Harper of New York pay part of our expenses. With the baseness of Capitalists they do *not* provide funds for Roulette! … "My wife, poor wretch," gets on wonderfully well, considering that our tastes are contrary as the Poles … I like to loaf in the sun, and she likes to see the works of Basano (I thought he was a photographer—no such luck) in chill palaces.[99]

Their holidays abroad seemed always to end in disaster. In Florence, the Arno was in flood and nearly rose over the bridges, and at Bologna he thought he would die from dysentery. There was little left of him when they arrived in Venice. Symonds was there, but practically an invalid, and stayed 'pretty clear' of them. Nora, worn out with anxiety and fatigue, had a cold. News from England was that Mary Ward's *Robert Elsmere* was a runaway bestseller with the reading public. Lang was amused rather than pleased, telling Broughton, 'I don't care for Sunday books in disguise, and never could stand *John Ingelsant*. The fact is the clever-dull section of the public is never really happy except with politics and religion!'[100] He read of Matthew Arnold's death in the evening papers while waiting at Venice station.[101] He sent condolences to Mary Ward, expressing his dismay at the obituary notices he had read: 'Nobody seems to know that *he was a poet*'.[102] He regretted that Balliol College had not raised funds to have Arnold's portrait painted during his lifetime. Now it was too late.

They made the long journey to St Andrews in August to look for a house. They would have to swap their London home for lodgings in St Andrews from January to March when he was to give the Gifford lectures. They settled on 'Castlecliffe', a two-storey house in Scots baronial style on a 'beetling cliff above the sea'. The weather was lovely, although he continued to feel unwell. He told Stevenson, who was sailing in the South Seas, 'My peepers and my peptics are going downward way pretty fast'.[103] Bad eyesight and poor digestion did not slow down his literary output. The *Athenaeum* expressed astonishment at the rate his books were appearing 'so closely on each other's heels' and likened it to 'the brave days of Alexander Dumas'. He had a new collection of verse, *Grass of Parnassus*, and a fantasy novel for children, *The Gold of Fairnilee*, out in time for the Christmas market.

His tale, set in the Border country of his boyhood in the period after the Battle of Flodden of 1513, combined history and the old fairy-legend of Tamlin, spirited away to fairyland. He wrote the story partly out of impatience with the fashion in modern fairy-tales for ethereal, 'fangless' fairies with wings— the fairies, in effect, of Dicky Doyle's *In Fairyland*. He wanted to return to the wide-awake' world of the old *märchen* where heroes and heroines had 'sorrows to suffer ... and difficulties to overcome', where the fairy world was darker and more ambiguous. He was not the first to recreate the fairy-seduction theme of the Border ballad in normal, everyday characters and setting. In Maria Mulock Craik's *Alice Learmont, or A Mother's Love*, Alice, the heroine, a descendant of Thomas the Rhymer, is stolen in infancy by the fairies. There is no evidence that Lang knew the novel, one not intended specifically for children. He had that year edited a new edition of *Border Ballads*, with 'Thomas the Rhymer' and 'Tamlane' first and second in the list of contents. There are, nevertheless, close parallels between *Alice Learmont* and *The Gold of Fairnilee*. In Craik's story, Alice, recaptured and dragged away by the fairies while fetching water for her sick mother, sees her captors for the first time as they really are, not beautiful, carefree spirits, but ugly, wrinkled creatures. In Lang's tale, the spell is broken when his boy-hero Randal Ker sprinkles water from a fairy bottle on his eyes and sees the ghastly reality of fairyland:

> The Fairy Queen, that had seemed so happy and beautiful in her bright dress, was a weary, pale woman in black, with a melancholy face and melancholy eyes ... And the knights and ladies were changed. They looked but half alive; and some, in place of their gay green robes, were dressed in rusty mail, pierced with spears and stained with blood. And some were in burial robes of white.[104]

'Visitors to Fairyland', Lang remarked in his criticism of modern fairy tales, 'are really among the dead'. *The Gold of Fairnilee* has a happy ending. After seven years, Randal's child-companion Jean, now grown up, seeing him mirrored in the waters of the Wishing Well and braving the menace of an ugly dwarf, wins Randal back through the sign of the cross. Fairy tales depicted 'our wayfaring in a world of perplexities and obstructions', Lang wrote, but 'all ends well'. Although he worried that *The Gold of Fairnilee* would 'frighten the kids into fits',[105] the book proved a success. Lang's importance as a writer for children, as Lancelyn Green recognized, lay in the influence he had in displacing the 'novel of child life' and substituting for it the new kind of children's fairy tale and fantasy.[106] After came many classics of children's literature which mixed flesh-and-blood characters and situations with fairy-tale elements—Edith Nesbit's *Five Children and It*, for example, J. M. Barrie's *Peter Pan*, and later, C. S. Lewis' *Chronicles of Narnia*.

Lang accepted an invitation to give the Sunday afternoon lecture on 2 December at South Place Chapel in Finsbury, home to the free-thinking Ethical Society. Before the lecture, there was an organ recital, and when the applause died down, Lang was escorted in. He drew some smiles with his opening remark that as it was Sunday afternoon, he thought it best to consider not the mythology but the religion of ancient Greece. The audience, he noticed, was made up not of West End intellectuals but of lower middle class 'with a sprinkling of well-to-do working men'. Elizabeth Robins Pennell, an American correspondent for the New York press, who knew him, reported that his 'usual languor of manner' disappeared when he spoke, and that the ease and sympathy of his delivery drew in his audience. The meeting struck her as 'more genuine than anything of the kind' she found in London.[107] The lecture was a rehearsal for his Gifford lectures. Lang reported humorously to Gosse the next day, 'I preached on Greek religion on Sunday in Finsbury: my cook was much edified'.[108]

He worked over Christmas on two new books which could not have differed more in genre and approach. On the death of Sir Stafford Northcote, Lord Iddesleigh, the Conservative politician, in 1887, he had agreed at the family's request to write the official biography, only to realize afterwards the huge amount of work life-writing entailed. The task threatened to overwhelm him. He felt particularly ill-suited to the task. He had never met Stafford Northcote, detested politics, and was disinclined to interview people who knew him after seeing Gladstone, who 'did not seem interested'. He confessed to one interviewee, 'The row is not only long but difficult to hoe. I wish someone else were hoeing'.[109] He found collaboration with Haggard on an adult fantasy novel, *The World's Desire*, with Odysseus as hero, much easier going. His idea was for a tale of Odysseus' final voyage of adventure to seek his ideal beauty, Helen of Troy, 'the world's desire' of the title. Haggard began working on the idea in March 1888 and wrote the central portion of the book describing Odysseus' arrival at the decadent Egyptian court, where the Pharaoh's sinister wife Queen Meriamun seduces him in the semblance of Helen. Lang enjoyed telling Stevenson that the hero of their 'improbable' tale 'having gone to bed with Mrs. Jekyll, wakes up with Mrs. Hyde'.[110] Feeling that the veteran Odysseus was introduced 'rather perfunctorily and abruptly on the scene', he began the narrative with four chapters, in which Odysseus, prior to his final journey in search of Helen, returns from an earlier voyage to find his kingdom of Ithaca sacked and his wife dead.[111] There were some who questioned why he chose to waste his time on 'such unreal stuff'. The truth was he was envious when he saw the eye-watering sum Haggard received for his novel *Colonel Quaritch, V.C.*, and reflected that 'two or three' of the same would allow him 'to retire from business'.[112]

He and Nora left for St Andrews in mid-January for his inaugural lecture. Müller had already given the first of his Gifford lectures in Glasgow. The *Scots Observer*, an Edinburgh-based weekly with Henley its newly appointed editor, predicted that before long the public would 'enjoy the pleasing spectacle of one Gifford lecturer knocking his brother lecturer's conclusions into the limbo of exploded fallacies'.[113] Life for Lang was about to take a new turn.

8

A Double Existence

The sea winds and wide sky of St Andrews Bay were a joy after the London fogs in winter. Lang delivered the first of his Gifford lectures in St Leonard's Hall in the evening of Thursday 17 January 1889. A procession of professors led him in. There was a great crowd in attendance. He spoke in a clear, high-pitched voice. There was a disturbance by a group of rowdy students who were there for that purpose, but order was soon restored.[1] One who was in the audience described the lecture as combining an extraordinary amount of knowledge with a 'wonderful brightness and liveliness of treatment'.[2] Lang was good at communicating complex ideas and arguments in a manner that interested non-specialists. He was more successful in this than John Hutchison Stirling, the Gifford lecturer at Edinburgh, who was reported in the *Scots Observer* to have 'nothing better to offer than scraps of musty metaphysics'.[3] He also avoided causing the kind of outrage Max Müller had provoked in Glasgow, where his lectures on 'natural religion' were condemned both by Presbyterian and Catholic leaders for spreading pantheistic, anti-Christian views among the students. Müller's view was that religion originated not in divine revelation, but in man's sense of the infinite, of something beyond the physical world.

Lang broke rank for the first time from the theory of Tylor, Herbert Spencer, and Darwin, that the idea of God, the 'soul', and future life evolved out of early man's worship of ghosts and ancestors, and arose from his primitive mis-understanding about the materials of dreams and hallucinations. His logic was simple: 'If religion, as now understood among men, be the latest evo-lutionary form of a series of mistakes, fallacies, and illusions, if its germ be a blunder, and its present form only the result of progressive but inessential refinements on that blunder, the inference that religion is untrue—that noth-ing actual corresponds to its hypothesis—is very easily drawn.'[4] He aimed to challenge and provoke. One thread of Tylor's *Primitive Culture* on which he strung his alternative theory was Tylor's passing notice of a similarity between primitive beliefs and practices and those indulged in by contemporary spiri-tualists and clairvoyants—a parallel which Tylor had left 'hanging in the air'. As an opening gambit, Lang picked holes in David Hume's famous essay on 'Miracles', which discounted superstitious belief in miracles as a violation of

Andrew Lang. John Sloan, Oxford University Press. © John Sloan (2023). DOI: 10.1093/oso/9780192866875.003.0008

common-sense experience and the uniform and exceptionless laws of nature. Lang pointed out, as others had done, Hume's circular logic, since the laws of nature can only be deemed exceptionless by excluding accounts of miracles without bothering to examine the evidence. From there, Lang followed two lines of argument: first, that anthropologists needed to examine the facts of early mankind's supranormal experiences and beliefs with the same open-mindedness and scientific rigour as the newly founded Society for Psychical Research (SPR) in its investigation of modern-day psychical occurrences, and not prejudge them as fantasy, resulting from credulity, ignorance, or deception. When writing up his lectures for publication, he found an echo of his thoughts in William James' pioneering writings in the new science of psychology. James shared his attraction to psychical research, declaring in the Preface to his essay *The Will to Believe*, 'I was attracted to the subject ... by my love of fair play in science'.[5] Lang, for his part, hoped to make converts in the anthropological community, naïvely so perhaps, given that investigation of the paranormal in an age of science was not academically respectable, and anthropology by his own admission was only just emerging as a subject from the 'limbo of the unrecognised'.[6]

Lang's second line of argument was equally controversial. Although disclaiming belief in 'primitive monotheism', he provided tentative evidence for what he called 'high gods of low races', a belief in an 'All Father' even among the lowest savages, evidence currently denied by anthropologists or explained away as borrowings from missionaries, or remnants of European or Islamic influences. He attributed primitive man's dim surmise of a Supreme Being not, as in Judaic-Christian tradition, to direct Revelation, nor, as Müller did, to man's innate sense of the infinite, but more matter-of-factly to man's natural conjecture on a 'Maker of things' he himself could not make.[7] He felt that if his ideas succeeded in convincing, it would be because they showed that both belief in psychical phenomena and the 'Argument for Design'—in effect, the raw material of religion—were not mystical in origin, but man's response to actual experiences in the world. Inevitably, he was uncertain how far his mixed audience, some with no knowledge of ancient or modern languages, followed the direction of his arguments.[8] Controversy would erupt nine years later when he published his long-considered version of his Gifford Lectures, *The Making of Religion*, which retained the substance, though not the actual words of his talks.

He was in Selkirk at the end of May to open the town's first free public library and be presented with the Freedom of the Borough. He was overcome with memories as he drove past Viewfield on the morning of the ceremony.[9] He wrote afterwards to Thomas Craig-Brown, a local historian and his host during his stay, 'A little less brass band might have been suggested by diffident souls, but I was steeled to walk even on a purple carpet, which Agamemnon thought too swagger, when he came marching home'. Of the official photograph, he added, 'I was trying not to laugh which begets a stern expression, but all photographs are horrors'.[10] He sent hampers of books from London for the new library.

That summer the Chair of English Literature at Glasgow University became vacant on John Nichol's retirement. The *Scots Observer* voiced strong support for Lang's election to the chair, declaring that the choice of 'so eloquent and various a man would delight the nation'.[11] Lang flirted with the idea of applying, but decided it was too much hard work. He was offered the post nevertheless by the 'Crown', as he put it, in the person of Lord Lothian who 'stalked me at Lord's, at the University Match'.[12] He heard afterwards it had gone to Andrew Bradley, whom he knew from his Oxford days.

In London, that July, he helped 'Graham R. Thomson' prepare for publication a selection from *The Greek Anthology*, containing some of his translations. He had, so to speak, 'discovered' Graham R. Thomson when reading submissions from would-be contributors to *Harper's Monthly*. He thought Thomson's poems successful in capturing the Greek spirit, exclaiming, 'My wig; there's poetry there'. He liked to advance the careers of fledgling poets. He used his causerie in *Longman's* magazine to showcase May Kendall's talents, and to introduce to a wider public the early verses of Violet Hunt, whom he got to know when writing the introduction to her mother's edition of Grimm's fairy tales. He also helped Alice Shield with an historical article on the Stuarts for *Blackwood's Magazine*, and even attempted to erase his role in its production, suggesting to Blackwood that he print it in her name, as 'it would be useful to her, if she does not object. The finds are almost all hers, I only top-dressed it'. Blackwood turned down the suggestion, telling his editorial team, 'This is rather cool! We know the young woman ... had heaps of trash from her.—I have told him his name must be given as well as hers, or it would be misleading'.[13] In the case of Graham R. Thomson (in fact, Rosamund Thomson), he printed and praised her verses, thinking that she was a man. He only discovered the truth when anthologizing some of her Greek translations for a collection of *Ballads of Books*. He and she were soon on easy, intimate terms. He teased her about her new-found socialism: 'A pretty socialist *you* are, why don't you go to Box Hill on Bank Holiday. I believe your socialism is about as sincere as our Grandmother's Tauschnitzes'.[14] Her socialism and male pseudonym were not her only deceptions. Her knowledge of Greek was also a pretence. After correcting the proofs of her translations for *Selections for the Greek Anthology*, Lang wrote to a young Oxford friend, Gilbert Murray, recently elected Professor of Greek at Glasgow, 'I may possibly have to ask *you* to look over a few pages of print of a lady who, not knowing Greek, has adventurously edited a book of English versions of the Anthology. I have weeded out her howlingest errors, but many may have escaped me'.[15] Earlier that summer, he had recommended Murray's first novel, *Gobi and Shamo*, to Longmans, after it had been rejected by several publishers.[16]

He and Nora holidayed that August at Loch Awe, where Nora made him return the fish he caught when she went in the boat with him. The weather turned bad, and with nothing to do except write, he made 'prodigious' progress on his life of Northcote.[17] He thought the trend for lengthy biographies had got out of hand with Francis Darwin's vast, three-volume life and letters of Charles Darwin: 'Why should biographies, in this age, give such prodigious deal of paste to such a scantly allowance of plums?'[18] There was heated dispute in the literary world about the other trend in biography towards intimate revelations of the subject's private life. There had been a storm of protest at James Froude for divulging details about Carlyle's unhappy marriage, even though this had been sanctioned by Carlyle himself who wanted to strike a blow against mealy-mouthed biography. Lang thought it right for biography to be candid about the faults of the subject, but he felt too that a single moral lapse in an honourable life should be let slip by, otherwise the fault would 'swell blackly all over the canvas, like a genie streaming out of his vase', a prediction that came true with the biographical fixation with people's sexual secrets. He thought the argument that 'the public has a right to know', the 'most odious cant of all', an excuse to satisfy the public taste for 'spicy revelations' and give writers and publishers a '*succès de scandale*'. He was aware of the danger of bias and self-projection in biography: 'A man forms, perhaps unconsciously, an idea of his subject, and that idea dominates the portrait which he draws. Quite unintentionally he selects all that bears out this theory and has a tendency to omit a good deal of what makes against it'.[19] In his case, the art of biography was less projection and more an act of discovery, a recognition of himself in a life he thought to be different from his own. He might have been speaking about himself when he wrote of Northcote's childhood, 'Some children are born bookworms, and make themselves happy with the pictures of fairy tales even before they can read'. His record of Northcote's undergraduate days at Balliol were shot through with bitter-sweet personal recollections—the Sunday evening wine-parties; the essay societies in which essays were never read; and the 'beautiful agony' of schools, after which 'the sparkle is out of the champagne, and the road for the rest of us—not for Northcote—runs "long and dusty and straight for the grave".[20]

That October he made a new friend in the young Rudyard Kipling who had just arrived in London from India. Lang had spotted Kipling's talent as far back as 1886, when the original *Departmental Ditties*, published anonymously in India, came into his hands.[21] He likened some of the verse as 'worthy of Bret Harte' and reprinted 'In Spring-Time', which he thought the best poem in the collection.[22] Shortly before Kipling's arrival in London, he wrote a review of Kipling's Anglo-Indian stories, describing their author as 'so clever, so fresh, and so cynical'.[23] On 26 October, after their first meeting, Kipling sent him a humorous verse parody in the style of Bret Harte, describing an imagined lecture tour of the United States by Lang and Haggard to promote *The World's Desire*, during which the American public confused Lang for Haggard and Haggard for Lang. In Lang's case:

> The prohibition party made him lecture on the fate
> Of the female Cleopatra who imbibed her poison straight,
>
> ...
>
> But the straw that broke the camel was Chicago's mild request
> For a Zulu dance in character—appropriately dressed.[24]

Lang finally got to meet Anne Thackeray Ritchie that autumn at Beaver Lodge, William Blake Richmond's house in Hammersmith. Among the other guests were William Morris' widow, Jane Morris; Marie Stillman, a pre-Raphaelite artist; and Henry James. He enjoyed astonishing Anne Ritchie by revealing that Becky Sharp, at least the person who inspired the character of Becky Sharp, Miss Theresa ('Tizzy') Revis, was no less a person than the notorious Countess de la Torre, who had been up before the magistrates for turning her Kensington lodgings into a refuge for stray cats and dogs—the subject of frequent press reports.[25]

Lang had two books out in time to catch the Christmas market—*The Blue Fairy Book*, his first anthology of fairy stories from around the world, and a new fairy story of his own, *Prince Prigio*, one of the first of a new wave of children's fairy tales, combining, as Oscar Wilde's *The Happy Prince and Other Tales* had done the previous year, the approved moral lessons of conventional stories for children with humorous, ironic, deflationary techniques poking fun at authority. His *Blue Fairy Book* was a compilation of many of the best-known and best-loved modern literary fairy tales. He stated in his Introduction that the collection had been made for the pleasure of children, and 'without scientific purpose', but his editorial policy was guided by two principles of his theory of folklore, or the 'science of the lower mythology' as he liked to call it. Firstly, he believed that all nursery tales, like all myths and legends, had a common source in primitive *märchen* from the earliest age of man, and that it was doubtful whether any surviving tales were 'absolutely pure from literary handling, absolutely set down as they drop from the lips of tradition'. Secondly, he followed Tylor and the comparative evolutionists in regarding children as closer in imagination to the 'young age of man', and therefore responsive to the oldest, most elemental forms of story. In *The Blue Fairy Book*, Winnie Wright's translations of the French *contes de fées* are 'abridged and stripped of their frippery'; Violet Hunt dwindled down her version of 'Aladdin' and 'The Forty Thieves' to something imagined to be closer to their original source and so more in touch with children's tastes; and Lang's rendering of the Perseus legend, 'The Terrible Head', drops the personal and local names in order to 'reconstruct an old impersonal and unlocated story' of a 'Jack the Giant Killer' type. The inclusion of May Kendall's condensed version of Swift's 'Gulliver in Lilliput' struck many as oddly out of place in a book of fairy tales, yet even in this, Lang's eye, as editor, was on the connection between the alternative world of fairy and tales of voyages to strange, magical places, so 'Gulliver in Lilliput' was given a place with the marvels left in and the satire 'subdued'.

The *Blue Fairy Book* was a success and did much to shift the taste in children's fiction from the tales of real life to fairy tale and fantasy.[26] The book owed much of its popularity to Henry Justice Ford's colourful, richly detailed pre-Raphaelite illustrations. The *Red Fairy Book* followed a year later, with the print run doubled from five to 10,000 copies. Lang thought the *Green Fairy Book* of 1892 would 'probably be the last', but the series proved a moneyspinner for Longmans, and a new coloured story anthology appeared in Lang's name on average every two years for the rest of his life. As with most popular publishing series, the editor and contributors received a once-off fixed fee and did not share in profits from royalties. Lang was paid £100 for editing each volume; his team of friends and relatives who served as editors and adaptors, £3 for each tale—a fee that remained unchanged throughout the series. Ford was better paid. He received four guineas for a cover design and about £300 for a hundred drawings. The illustrations served not only to attract children; they made the books less easy to pirate. Nora took over as editor after the first four in the series, although his name for commercial reasons remained on the cover, a situation she came to treat with sardonic humour. They were a real husband and wife partnership, complaining behind closed doors, as families do, about who borrowed whose pen—she, exasperated by his disorganization; he, saying she was fussy.

His own fairy tale, *Prince Prigio*, was a medley of fairy-tale motifs which simultaneously paid homage to the genre while comically sending it up. Lang was undoubtedly influenced by earlier burlesque fairy tales—F. E. Paget's *The Hope of the Katzekopfs* and Thackeray's *The Rose and the Ring*—which he loved when he was 10. Lang begins his tale with the christening of baby Prigio and the appearance of a malicious fairy, cross at not being invited, whose curse is that he will be 'too clever' and grow up disliked by everyone for being always right. As in Thackeray, Lang's allusions to 'a host of previous *märchen*' and flaunting of literariness, as Sanjay Sircar observes, have a comically lowering effect.[27] When the dreaded Fire-drake monster brings drought to the land, Prigio ensures that his two younger brothers are sent to face it, on the logical principal that the monster in fairy tales kills the first two before being beaten by the third. Ennio, the youngest, writes a poem about the advantages of dying young before going to meet his doom. Prigio finally destroys the Fire-drake by getting it to fight the Remora, or Ice-Beast, which he discovers from reading Cyrano de Bergerac. The ending of *Prince Prigio* is charged with comic irony. Urged by Rosalind, his bride, to reverse the fairy curse with the aid of a magical Wishing Cap, Prigio, reflecting that 'every man has one secret from his wife', wishes only that he 'SEEM no cleverer than other people'. In the end, we are told, he became 'the most popular Prince and finally the best beloved King who ever sat on the throne of Pantouflia'.

Burlesque and parody are generally ranked on a lower level than fairy tales which take themselves seriously. J. R. R. Tolkien, in his highly regarded essay 'On Fairy Stories'—originally the 1939 Andrew Lang Lecture at St Andrews—argues that 'since the fairy-story deals with "marvels", it cannot tolerate any frame or machinery suggesting that the whole framework in which they occur is a figment or an allusion'. The one touchstone of the fairy story as a legitimate literary genre, as opposed to its use for 'lesser or degraded purposes', is that it should be presented as 'wholly credible ... as true'.[28] Lancelyn Green shared that view and judged Lang's Pantouflia stories to 'belong to a lower and commoner form of art than *The Gold of Fairnilee*', although conceding, uneasily, that *Prince Prigio* was more popular with children.[29] Lang himself at times was in two minds. He loved *The Rose and the Ring*, and at Oxford, in his student days, he delighted in the 'happy surprise' and 'entire novelty' of Lewis Carroll's first *Alice* book,[30] but on taking up the study of folklore he adopted a high-brow disdain for modern, artificial fairy tales and praised Julia Horatio Ewing, author of *Jan of the Windmill*, because she never

'burlesques things old' the way other children's writers did.[31] He soon dis-
owned this attitude as the 'fanaticism of pedantry' and expressed approval
of popular literary adaptations of the genre from Madame d'Aulnoy's witty,
seventeenth-century *contes de fées* to the familiar *fées* of modern fairy-tale: 'It
is from Madame d'Aulnoy that *The Rose and the Ring* of Thackeray derives its
illustrious lineage. The banter is only an exaggerated form of her charming
manner.'[32]

The *Blue Fairy Book* had its critics. The sternest were the purists in the Folklore Society who worried that his adapted tales from different sources and
different times might confuse later students of mythology. Laurence Gomme,
a founder member of the Folklore Society, dismissed his fairy books and their
accompanying illustrations as inaccurate and misleading. Lang gave a lecture
to the society in November 1889, after the *Blue Fairy Book* came out, and
shrugged off the objections, happy that the books were enjoyed by children
and helping to promote the popularity of folk tales, myths, and legends—but
dissatisfaction remained. He said of those who took the purist line, 'To listen
to some persons, one might think that gaiety was a crime.'[33]

In fact, the fairy books remained closer to their sources than most adaptations of folk and fairy tales for children, doing little to soften or sanitize the
sometimes uncomfortable and violent features of the original tales, particularly as the series progressed. H.J. Ford's illustrations did not spare children
the darker elements. His frontispiece for the *Grey Fairy Book* represented the
disturbing image of 'The Dervish drowning the pigs' from 'The Story of the
Fair Circassians', while his full-page illustration of 'The Turtle and his Bride'
in the *Brown Fairy Book* pictured the grisly scene of the girl about to drop the
turtle into a cauldron of boiling water (see Figure 8.1).

The day after his lecture to the Folklore Society, Lang gave a talk at the South
Kensington Museum on 'How to Fail in Literature'. The proceeds were to go to
Mrs Sitwell's College for Working Men and Women. With the rise of literacy,
advice on how to write for a living was a popular theme in the magazines.
Stevenson's 'Letter to a Young Gentleman Who Proposes to Embrace a Career
in Art' featured in *Scribner's Monthly* the previous September. Lang turned
the subject humorously on its head by offering advice on 'how to fail', with
comical examples of amateur, aesthetic verse, and warning would-be writers:
'Faint and fleeting praise, a crown with as many prickles as roses, a modest
hardly-gained competence, a good deal of envy, a great deal of gossip—these
are the rewards of genius which constitutes a modern literary success.'[34] He was
pleased to see good 'half-crowns' at his lecture, 'if not "paper".'[35] An account
of the lecture in Henley's *Scots Observer* applauded his criticism of 'toppery

Figure 8.1 'The Turtle Outwitted'. Illustration by H.J. Ford for
The Brown Fairy Book.

and dilettantism' in modern literature, but added reproachfully that 'his own
Muse has not always been so clean as one would wish'.[36] His reconciliation
with Henley after the misunderstanding over Henley's *A Book of Verse*, and
the effusive tributes to him in the *Scots Observer* as 'the Admirable Crichton of

modern letters' after his appointment as Gifford lecturer,[37] had proved short-lived. When the *Athenaeum* announced that Lang was to be general editor of the Tudor Library reprints and translations, a role Henley had already signed up for with the publisher David Nutt, Lang had to go in person to the office of the *Scots Observer* in Edinburgh and assure a furious Henley that he 'knew nothing of any "Tudor" series or of any general editorship'.[38] A break between them was again prevented, but news and reviews of Lang's work in the *Scots Observer* were less complimentary from then on.

The precariousness of the writer's trade was never far from view. When Gosse's salary as English editor of *Century Magazine* was cut in half, he came to Lang for help. Lang himself was dropped in November as English editor for *Harper's*, there being too few manuscripts accepted to justify the post. The news was disappointing but came as no surprise. He had never received more than a handful of submissions of 'ordinary magazine cali-bre'.[39] He had been asked by the Wolseleys if he knew of anyone suitable to tutor their sixteen-year-old daughter Frances. He put the prospect to Gosse: 'I have not heard a word on the matter of finance. Mrs Lang is writing to Lady Wolseley and will ask her downright, and so you needn't come into it at all, unless it seems adequate'.[40] Gosse came to an agreement with the Wolseleys and passed two pleasant years as Frances Wolseley's tutor. *Harper's* meanwhile tried to make up for Lang's loss of the editorship by commissioning him to write a series of articles on 'The Comedies of Shakespeare', to begin with the festive *The Merry Wives of Windsor* for the Christmas number.

In January 1890, he and Nora were again at Castlecliffe for his second session of Gifford Lectures. William Robertson Smith's *History of the Semites*, just out, a brilliant cross-cultural study of the affinities between ancient Semitic peoples and other ancient races, reinforced the line of argument he was taking in his lectures: the primacy of social customs and institutions over myths and beliefs. But Smith believed that the tribal god developed later than ancestral totems; Lang, in line with evidence for 'high gods among low races', regarded the two as coexisting, as complementary.[41] He felt at home in the quiet, grey streets of St Andrews, with their medieval towers and monuments, and blue hills in the distance. From his experience of lecturing the previous year, he suggested that he lecture once a week or hold a more informal discussion group at home, but disappointingly he reported back to the principal, James Donaldson, of the experiment, 'Not one person came to my theological at home'.[42] He and Nora did however entertain students at their lodgings on the Scores, and he helped boost the circulation of the newly launched *College Echoes, St Andrews*

University Magazine with his anonymous verse and prose. He was rewarded with an irreverent limerick:

> There is also a poet named L—,
> Of the dear little city who sang;
> If he wouldn't be funny
> Nor make so much money,
> He might be immortal, might L—.[43]

Being credited with opulence always amused him. He liked to remind people that writers earned less than barristers, doctors, and painters. Taking a house at St Andrews for the winter was an added strain on his purse. He wrote to Matthews at the end of his second course of lectures with a mixture of joy and irony, 'After a perfectly lovely winter, the weather has turned fiendish. We had plenty of sun, and beautiful lights on the sea and the hills. I doubt if my bankers account takes much by it all though. The expenses are considerable.'[44] The Gifford lectureship was normally for two years, but he was a popular figure, and when it became clear he was to be invited to stay on, he wrote to James Donaldson that he hoped he would not be asked to do more lectures next year and that everyone could do with a change.[45] The position was filled by Edward Caird from Glasgow University, like himself a former Snell Exhibitioner and fellow of Merton College.

News of his success at St Andrews preceded him to London. The popular monthly *Temple Bar* celebrated in French verse his knowledge of 'the Laws of superstition', addressing him as '*charmant persifleur*' ('delightful wit'),[46] translated as 'jokist' in an English rendering which appeared in the *Evening Telegraph* later that month:

> Oh jokist! 'tis thy part
> To flit, and skim, and dart
> With gaiety of heart
> O'er these abysms.[47]

While in London, he dined with Dowager Lady Iddesleigh and was able to report that his biography of her husband was almost ready for the printer. He also served as a steward at the wedding at Westminster Abbey of Sir Henry Morton Stanley, the explorer, to Dorothy Tennant, the artist-sister of Frederic Myers' wife, Eveleen. He was glad not to be 'party to it'.[48] He watched the guests as they trod over the flagstones that marked the burial place of two famous women—Mrs Aphra Behn, the playwright and wit, and Mrs Anne Bracegirdle, the actress and beauty. He heard one lady ask, 'Who is Mrs Bracegirdle?'—a sobering reminder, he reflected, that 'fame is vanity, and wit and beauty ... perishable goods'.[49]

Lang was heartbroken when his Uncle Willie died that October. He and Nora had been to Kenbank, and his uncle had seemed in better health and to be getting on with the final volume of *The Roman Poets of the Augustan Age*. Lewis Campbell, in an unusually frank obituary for the times, laid the blame for his friend's unhappy boyhood on Patrick Sellar for having his son 'under strict and somewhat severe surveillance with the single motive of excelling to please his father'.[50] Lang was more reticent in his 'Memoir' of his uncle for the posthumous volume of *The Roman Poets of the Augustan Age*, merely saying, 'The elder Mr. Sellar was a man of great energy, and expected great energy and industry from others', and 'considered it a positive duty' that his son 'should be head boy'.[51]

His hope that he and Haggard would have a critical and popular success with *The World's Desire*—their 'flaming Homeric romance', as he called it[52]—hit the dust when the reviews came out. The book sold well because of Haggard's name, but the critics panned it. Their praise for the finish and grace of the lyrics woven into the narrative was no consolation, accompanied as it was with ridicule of the torrid story and its toplofty style. Lang blamed himself for the failure. He sent news of its doleful reception to Stevenson: 'Such a universal slating never book received before'. He added, 'The other critics slew it, and Henley jumped on it, in rather muddy boots, to my mind. I am *porte malheur* ('bad luck') as a collaborator'.[53]

Henley's *Scots Observer* was haemorrhaging money, and Henley, under pressure from the owners to attract a wider readership, adopted a populist tone of imperial Britishness and masculinity, which targeted decadence and 'foreign' influences on the arts. Its offices were moved to London, and the magazine retitled *The National Observer*. Lang was goaded into a quarrel in the correspondence pages when he questioned a review which disputed the prevailing theory of Asia as the cradle of Aryan civilization. The review claimed that a blond race from Britain, speaking a primitive Aryan tongue, had conquered the Indo-Europeans.[54] Henley, unknown to Lang, was egging the reviewer, Charles Whibley, to 'pickle the Andrew as you please' and get him in a 'tight place'.[55] For Henley, personal animus and practicality combined: controversy sold magazines, when a well-known name could be goaded into protest. He used the same trick that year against Wilde, who was baited into retaliating against the magazine's attack on *The Picture of Dorian Gray*.

Henley described *The World's Desire* in a mocking parodic review as 'the most complete artistic suicide it has ever been his lot to chronicle'.[56] Lang tried to be fore-bearing: 'I may be, and probably am, prejudiced against Master Henley, his works and ways, but we must take him as we find him. "There will be no other" Henley'.[57] He was shocked, however, by Henley's uncomplimentary comparison of Stevenson's *Ballads* with Kipling's 'The Ballad of East and West': 'How furiously Henley has been sacrificing all his old friends on the altar of Kipling. Even Stevenson. All must go. Not that I don't admire Kipling, but one can do that without making odious comparisons'.[58] He made up his mind not to write again for Henley's 'rag',[59] and told Gosse, 'I think Henley has been rather brutal and personal in unexpected directions; however, that is much more his look out than mine'.[60]

More gratifying were the generally complimentary notices of his life of Northcote, although some reviewers were suspicious of the family's motives in choosing him as biographer, with his handling of political events compared by the *Saturday Review* to the bashful insinuations of Dickens's Rosa Dartle in *David Copperfield*: 'Mr. Lang contrives ... to represent himself as a kind of male Rosa Dartle in politics, really anxious to know, and sorry to make a little confusion ... Thus he disarms the most ferocious criticism'.[61] All agreed about his sensitive character study of Northcote the man, who came out better than he seemed to many in life. Garnet Wolseley, who knew Northcote personally, certainly thought so, telling his wife:

I have been deep in Andrew Lang's Introduction—a charming piece of literature—and his story of Sir Stafford Northcote's boyhood and early life. He contrives to throw a charm over his narrative that makes me forget the subject of his book was so essentially my opposite (so much about him of the Tomcat that cared neither to fight nor make love) that I never met him without thanking God, like the Pharisee, that I was not as he ... Andrew L. does his job so well that he throws a halo of heroic interest about a man who was certainly filled with placid virtues and wearisome good qualities. I am so struck with the power to make the commonplace interesting that I felt, and feel, low at the thought of how utterly unable I am to write about one whose very name recalls national triumph ... If Lang knew as much of Malborough as I do, what an epic he would make of it.[62]

Lang replied to a letter from Wolseley, which evidently conveyed the same praise: 'Apparently it is well that I never knew my hero in the flesh ... John Churchill is a very much more entertaining figure, but much harder work: I hope you are in sight of heaven.'[63]

Lang's health broke down that winter. There had been earlier warning signs. He woke one morning in September spitting blood.[64] A specialist judged that his lungs were clear, but he was advised to give up all lecturing. In November 1890, when illness forced him out of London, he took a house in St Andrews for the winter, even though his time as Gifford Lecturer was over. He had always lived a kind of double life since his Oxford days, dividing his time between works that required scholarly patience and writing for the newspapers and magazines. The move to St Andrews heightened his double existence. For the rest of his life, he lived in two worlds, passing half the year in the small Scottish university town where he belonged within a close-knit academic community, the other half, in the bustling metropolis, contending with those at the centre of press, magazine, and book world. The undergraduate magazine reported that his successor Professor Caird's poorly attended lectures were 'not only uninteresting but unintelligible' and that students 'preferred those of Mr. Lang'.[65] At St Andrews he enjoyed a quasi-academic status. Even the caddies at the Royal and Ancient Golf Club, where he was a member, addressed him as 'Professor', no matter how often he told them, 'Emeritus Lecturer only, if you please'.[66] 'A Lang Shadow', a comic verse in *College Echoes*, described his

> languid air,
> The eye-glass always falling
> The super-borèd stare
> And pockets hand enthralling,

and revealed that his secret double, the 'Lang Shadow' of the title, contributed regularly to its pages:

> You ask the double's name?
> I hope you will condone a
> A modicum of fame—
> He is sometimes called C-r-a.[67]

He used the anonymity of the student magazine to give comic vent in a Popean verse-satire, 'The Log-Rolliad', against the foibles and excesses of literary London. He began, under cover, by making himself a target of ridicule:

Still am I mute, while Logs go Rolling round
And fill the Weekly papers with the sound,
...
While yet Lang tells, and illustrates the tale
By precept and example—How to fail.

His poem upbraids the leading writers of the day: Mary Ward, whose *Robert Elsmere* sends parsons to sleep; Kipling with his 'Hindustani jargon'; Meredith's unintelligible grammar; Hardy's 'tedious rustics'; and Oscar Wilde's self-trumpery:

The infinitely Little let me sing,
My tiny tribute to the Trumpery bring,
To Oscar's locks apply the tardy shears,
Hum a mosquito, in the longest ears.
He saves his parting reprimand for Stevenson's child's play:
But ere the evening's discipline be done,
Lock up the tops and toys of Stevenson.[68]

Gosse was shocked when he learned of the existence of the poem, and Lang had to explain to him that it was a 'satire on satire', a '*genus irritabile*' against the whole jealous, back-biting literary trade.[69] When William Helm, editor of the *Morning Post*, wanted to reprint it, Lang asked him not to, claiming again that it was a 'satire against satire', not against the writers named. He added, 'Some persons with no sense of irony, or with very little sensitive minds, felt injured'.[70]

St Andrews had its drawbacks. He was disappointed to receive only one entry when he introduced an essay competition for undergraduates on the lines of the Stanhope Prize at Oxford, forgetful perhaps that undergraduates at Oxford showed the same lack of interest in topics unrelated to their examinations, and that the Stanhope Prize itself 'rarely attracted more than a handful of participants'.[71] On announcing the result, he impressed on students that the most fruitful work at college was often on subjects outside the curriculum.[72] For all his dissatisfaction with London, he still enjoyed filling column space and writing reviews and articles to deadlines, as much as he had done in the youthful days. When George Gissing's *New Grub Street* came his way for review that spring, he objected to its grim, despairing picture of London literary life, complaining, 'In Grub Street there are many mansions; they are not all full of failure, and envy, and low cunning, and love of money, and hatred of success'.[73] Gissing's 'cultured' heroes believed their classical education earns them a place in society free from the mere struggle of necessity: theirs was a fantasy of scholarly refinement and gentlemanly ease. Lang, in contrast, saw classical schooling as ideal training for the literary trade, and London the place where you made 'useful acquaintances' and could reach the front as a writer.

Even so, he was always sad when spring came, and it was time to leave St Andrews and return to London. He expressed his mood in 'The End of Term':

> Farewell! for turning a reluctant face
>   Once more we seek the din,
> The lurid light of that abhorrent place
>   Of luxury and sin.[74]

Nora felt the opposite. To her, the St Andrews winters were 'months of banishment' from London which she loved, and she was always happy to return to the capital. But she made the most of her new life and became part of community life at St Andrews, taking over as manager of the amateur dramatic society, and playing in successive winters Mrs Malaprop in Sheridan's *The Rivals*, and Mrs Hardcastle in Goldsmith's *She Stoops to Conquer* at the Town Hall. The university magazine praised her natural style and comic timing as Mrs Malaprop, but the following year complained that her hurried delivery as Mrs Hardcastle 'left something to seek in the way of distinctness' (see Figure 8.2).[75]

Corby Castle, Carlisle, the home of Anna Hills and her husband Herbert, an appeals court judge in Cairo, became their new port of call on their journeys to and from Scotland. Lang knew their son Jack, a young London solicitor and former Balliol man, with whom he sometimes went fishing. He dedicated his *Angling Sketches* to Anna Hills 'in memory of pleasant days at Corby'. His 'sketches', though mainly humorous accounts of the experiences of 'the incomplete angler', also voiced his environmental concerns about over-fishing and river pollution and condemned the use of poisons and dynamite, and the 'dies and dirt' of the mills and factories for the death of trout.[76]

Lang's residence at St Andrews involved him increasingly in Scottish social circles. It also drew him imaginatively to Scottish themes and subjects. He began work on a new twenty-four-volume Border edition of Walter Scott's Waverley novels in October 1891. He was on friendly terms with Mrs Maxwell-Scott, the novelist's great granddaughter, who had inherited the Abbotsford estate, and helped with her catalogues and guides to personal relics and antiquarian treasures at Abbotsford. He stayed at Chiefswood Cottage, the former summer retreat of her grandfather, Scott's son-in-law, John Gibson Lockhart.

Figure 8.2 Nora as Mrs Malaprop in Sheridan's *The Rivals*, 1893. Nora's hand embroidered dress was made in the 1770s, the decade in which *The Rivals* was first performed.
Reproduced courtesy of the National Library of Scotland.

Lang wrote on 9 October to tell her that he had made his first visit to the manuscripts that day and read various correspondence from 1805, when Scott began *Waverley*, to 1814 when he finished it.[77] The intention of the Border edition was to throw fresh light on the historical setting of each novel and the circumstances in which the stories were written and published.[78] He made surprising discoveries. Documents at Abbotsford, and state papers at Windsor Castle and the British Museum, contained accounts of Charles Edward Stuart's 'secret adventures', travelling incognito, an exile and fugitive in Europe, reported on by spies and the target of assassination, following the failed '45 uprising—material so 'Stevensonian' that Lang sent the information to Samoa, where Stevenson had settled, with suggestions for a story. Stevenson found it a 'gallant suggestion' and began work on a novel, based on Lang's idea, provisionally titled 'The Young Chevalier'.[79] Stevenson's progress, and Lang's hopes of a historical novel to match those of Scott and Thackeray, were suddenly put on hold, in a wholly unexpected way, with Hardy's publication of *Tess of the D'Urbervilles.*

In his review of *Tess*, Lang criticized Hardy's 'persistent melancholy' and clumsy displays of quasi-scientific language and classical learning. He found the narrator's high-sounding declaration, 'The President of the Immortals has finished his sport with Tess', at the end of the novel, particularly jarring and insincere.[80] Hardy, who had long courted Lang's seal of approval, wrote to Edward Clodd, who had Lang's ear, 'If Andrew, with his knowledge & opportunities, had a heart instead of a hollow place ... he would by this time have been among the immortals of letters instead of gnawing his quill over my poor production'.[81] Hardy hit back in his preface to the single volume edition of *Tess*. Hardy dismissed his 'great critic' as too 'genteel' to endure the truth of the novel and claimed literary precedence for declaiming against the gods in Shakespeare's 'as flies to wanton boys are we to the gods'.[82] Lang, coming upon an extract from Hardy's 'Preface' in the *Illustrated London News*, returned to battle in *Longman's*, with a rejoinder that Gloucester's words were the distraught outcry of a character in the depths of despair, whereas in *Tess*, Hardy's illogical outcry against divine malice was made the 'moral and marrow of his romance'.[83] He brushed aside the charge of 'gentility', which he took to be Hardy's way of calling him a snob and a prig, and insisted that the reasons he disliked *Tess* were the improbability of the action and Hardy's treatment of the seduction plot. He wrote, 'Other girls in fiction have been seduced with more blame and have not lost our sympathy'.

Lang, in writing to Stevenson, made explicit his distaste for Hardy's voyeuristic male sexual fantasy of rape and violated innocence, which Hardy's novel blamed, hypocritically, on the malice of the gods. He praised Stevenson's treatment of the young David Balfour's love for Catriona as a 'blessed relief a wilderness of Tess's', 'Hardy can't even look at a flint quarry, but he falls to talking about phalluses'.[84] Stevenson, he learned, detested *Tess* even more strongly than he did and thought the rape scene 'unworthy of Hardy' and 'false to every fact and principle of human nature'.[85] Their agreement gave Lang no satisfaction, as it resulted in Stevenson shelving 'The Young Chevalier' to begin work on a novel, 'The Justice-Clerk' (later, *Weir of Hermiston*) which would offer an alternative to Hardy's treatment of the 'fallen woman' story. Stevenson planned that his 'maiden-no-more', unlike Tess, would be the willing victim of her seducer, but in the end be loved by a resolute young lover, who, unlike Angel Clare, would stand by her despite her past.

Lang was grateful to Stevenson for encouragement with his own writing. Stevenson sent photographs of upright stones, and accounts of burial customs, totem-worship, and sorcery, gathered during his Pacific voyage in 1889 from the Gilbert Islands to Samoa. Lang used the information to refute Grant Allen's claim that 'all worshipped or sacred stones were once ancestral grave-stones', and that Jehovah was originally nothing more than 'the ancestral fetish stone of some early Semitic' chief.[86] He thanked Stevenson, 'Delighted to get the Gibby island materials, for arguing with people like Allen you have to supply them with the facts'.[87] Many years later, he told Oliver Lodge that in demolishing Allen's hypothesis, 'I was mean enough to get Robertson Smith to coach me in the Hebrew department'.[88] He admired Allen's 'private qualities', but regarded him as a 'sciolist', who pretended to knowledge without taking the trouble 'to get up the facts'.[89] Although Lang did no field work, he always drew where possible upon evidence gathered by those who did—Tylor in Mexico; his cousin J. J. Atkinson in New Caledonia; Stevenson in the Pacific. He was delighted by Stevenson's gift of the 'devil box of Apemama', a South Seas totem-shell in a home-made wooden box. He protested, 'The Devil Box is too good for me, and should be in a museum. But I don't mean to part with it'.[90]

Lang, elected President of the Folklore Society in 1891–2, sought to ensure that the two camps of the society—the anthropological and the literary—worked in harmony, and that attention to tales, legends, and sagas were not privileged over a study of social conditions, customs, and beliefs (see Figure 8.3). He arranged for the delegates at the International Folklore Congress in London in October 1891 to visit the Pitt Rivers Museum in Oxford, with its unmatched collection of cultural artefacts from all over the world. August Pitt Rivers, though an amateur, had given archaeology academic respectability by rejecting the treasure-hunt aspect and showing that 'the common objects rather than the rare and beautiful were the raw material of the subject'.[91] Despite that gain in respectability, a separation of the literary and scientific continued to divide classical studies at Oxford, where

Figure 8.3 Lang delivering his Presidential Address at the opening of the International Folklore Congress at Burlington House on 1 October 1891. *The Daily* Graphic, Friday 2 October 1891.

the archaeological discoveries of Heinrich Schliemann at Hissarlik and Mycenae had made little impact, and the course in Literae Humaniores remained rooted in a textual approach to antiquity. Lang wanted to change that. Paradoxically, he employed astute textual analysis and close reading in his *Homer and the Epic*, in which he set out to demonstrate the unity of Homer's epics as single-author compositions, a question he had first tackled for Jowett in his undergraduate days. He applied his considerable knowledge of folklore and literary form to refute the theory of Friedrich Wolf and the German analytical school—the 'microscopic men', he called them—that Homer's epics evolved from a vast mass of pre-existent lays and sagas, polished and unified by many hands over several centuries. There was an academic competitiveness to the book. Walter Leaf, his co-translator of the *Iliad*, wanted to have it both ways, adopting Lang's understanding of the difference between folk poetry and epic poetry, while simply modifying Wolf's theory of composite authorship by supposing a 'school' of poets who added to the Homeric epics over time.[92] Lang dismissed the idea of a 'school'. He declared that the idea of successive generations of inspired poets able to keep up the same sublime Homeric level was completely counter to what we knew of how great works of literature came to exist.

He used the critical weapon of good-natured ridicule to discredit the examples given by the German school as evidence of different authors at work in different ages. He dismissed as silly and illogical the idea that the magical transformation of Odysseus by Athene into a withered, old beggar in Book 13 of the *Odyssey* was added by a later writer who failed to notice the contradiction between his invention and the nurse Euracleia's recognition of Odysseus' scar in Book 19, and the report of this in Book 23. He protested, 'A scar on a fair limb remains a scar on the same limb when withered either by age or magic'. He added caustically:

> It seems that magic and transformation come *late* into fable, that natural causes are allowed to work in *earlier* poetry. Thus Odysseus, in the old story, was rendered unrecognisable by age and trouble, in the later poem by art magic. To say this is to reverse the order of the development of fancy, to prove *Tom Jones* earlier in order of evolution than the oldest *Märchen*.[93]

He entertained readers with a parody of the German method, which he had already used in *Longman's*,[94] one imagining the origins and authorship of Walter Scott's *Ivanhoe* to be unknown and the work of many hands across centuries. Jowett, on hearing what he was doing, confessed frankly that he thought it 'time to drop the Homeric question'.[95] Lang was less worried by Jowett than by the German analysts, telling Matthews, 'I'm afraid some German pedant may make sausage of me'.[96] Among English scholars, the Cambridge classicist, Arthur Platt, despite some reservations about Lang's occasional neglect of scientific evidence when it conflicted with his literary judgement, was satisfied that Lang had 'proved the German school wrong with as much cogency as can possibly be expected in a literary problem'.[97] The majority, however, remained to be convinced.

Lang had even less success in trying to persuade members of the Folklore Society that traditional folklore and contemporary psychical research were areas of study which ran together, and that contemporary reports of abnormal experiences ought also to be within their field of enquiry. He was equally critical of the SPR for neglecting historical evidence of spiritual and paranormal experiences. Folklore ignored the present, psychic research, the past. In an effort to jog the two sides, he brought out an edition of *The Secret Commonwealth of Elves, Fauns, and Fairies*, a tract by Robert Kirk, a seventeenth-century Highland clergyman and graduate of Edinburgh University, who had documented the fairy kingdom, neither as illusions nor as spirits from hell, but as 'a mere fact of nature' and 'a world with its own laws'. Lang dedicated the book in Scots dialect to Stevenson, whose ghost stories he enjoyed:

> O Louis! you that like them maist,
> Ye're far frae kelpie, wraith, and ghaist,
> And fairy dames, no unco chaste,
>   And haunted cell.
> Among the heathen clans ye're placed,
>   That kens na hell![98]

Paranormal activities—spiritualism, séances, telepathy, clairvoyance, and the like—continued to gain in vogue and public attention. Lang had followed closely the activities of the SPR from its foundation in 1882 and counted friends among its members. Through science, it was hoped, the mysteries of the paranormal would finally be discovered and explained. Lang's view shifted between scepticism and belief. The populist editor W. T. Stead sent him a complimentary copy of *Borderland*, a new quarterly magazine on spiritualism and psychical phenomena founded for the general public rather than the 'select few'. Lang, in writing to thank him, made plain his agenda: 'My interest in the "Research" is mainly historical and mythological: can you not get a qualified person to make an accurate study of the Cock Lane Ghost? The SPR people don't even know its own silly business, as far as its history is concerned. I have written an article on the 17th century SPR for the *Contemporary Review*'.[99] The article, 'Comparative Psychical Research',[100] was the starting-point of Lang's venture into the new field of 'psycho-folklore'. His *Cock Lane and Common Sense*, an extensive, comparative investigation into ancient and modern forms of spiritualism, witchcraft, hauntings, second sight, and other abnormal occurrences, attempted, as he put it, 'to reconcile these rather hostile sisters in science'. His mission made few converts. To the SPR, past events were not 'evidential', and so beyond scientific investigation and incapable of proof; to folklorists, and to the majority of reviewers, his conclusion that material science, physiology, and the new psychology did not satisfactorily explain all cases of abnormal occurrences was a regrettable retreat from his avowed sceptical and scientific attitude.[101] 'Such', Lang complained, 'are the natural results of two restricted specialisms'.[102] Clodd, a fellow member of the Folklore Society and an outspoken agnostic, who regarded spiritualism and occultism in the same way that he regarded Christian belief in miraculous birth and transubstantiation, as the persistence of barbarous survivals and superstitions, was especially dismissive. In his 'Presidential Address' to the Folklore Society the year after Lang's *Cock Lane and Common Sense* was published, Clodd ruled out any association with the pseudo-scientific spirit, which 'skulks in dark chambers that perhaps it may hear the twaddle of witless ghosts'.[103] Lang, in his private correspondence, urged Clodd not to show contempt for psychical researchers: 'They are not the idiots you suppose. It is all Anthropology, *quod semper, quod ubique*, and I, for one, can't play the ostrich about it'.[104] He saw things from both sides: 'To me it is plain that a furious desire for a future life, on the one hand, and a furious aversion to the notion, on the other, are the invisible obstacles to cool study of the subject'.[105] He and Clodd remained on friendly terms. When the two talked on the subject at the Savile Club, and Clodd threw in the quotation from the New Testament (James 2:19), 'The devils also believe, and tremble', Lang, echoing the final sentence of Fontenelle's 'On the Origin of Fables', with a twinkle replied, 'I don't believe, and I tremble'.[106]

Lang's approach to the supernormal divides modern-day critics. Marjorie Wheeler-Barclay points out that despite Lang's insistence on 'serious scientific examination' of the psychic region of human nature, 'in some way he preferred it to remain what it always had been, a category of which we know nothing'.[107] Leigh Wilson, on the other hand, argues that Lang's recognition that science relies on 'a notion of fact within which fantasy resides, not as a contradiction, but as an essential part of its construction', is the very reason for Lang's significance.[108] Lang explained his own attitude to abnormal occurrences in the clearest terms in his revised, second edition of *Cock Lane and Common Sense*, saying that the answer he gave when asked, 'But what do you believe yourself?' was:

> The author has little doubt that there is a genuine substratum of fact, probably fact of conjuring, and of more or less hallucinatory experience. If so, the great antiquity and uniformity of the tricks, make them proper subject of anthropological enquiry, like other matters of human tradition.[109]

In October 1893, while Lang was at work on *Cock Lane and Common Sense*, Benjamin Jowett died. Lang, deeply saddened, paid tribute in his column to 'the gentlest and kindest of mentors'.[110] By November, strangely, there was still no news of his successor. Lang did not know why.[111] Unusually for those days, it was a contested mastership, with some conservatives among the thirteen fellows supporting James Leigh Strachan-Davidson, the long-serving and popular dean of the college, but the majority in favour of a more liberal head of house to bring intellectual distinction and teaching strength to the college. The matter was settled finally and quietly six weeks after Jowett's death when Edward Caird, Lang's successor as Gifford Lecturer at St Andrews, was appointed the new Master of Balliol.[112] Lang followed events from outside. It seemed the destiny of others to advance to higher things.

His heart, in any case, was in St Andrews rather than in Oxford. That summer he undertook a history of the town for the general reader, based largely on secondary sources, a decision he came to regret. Surprisingly, given its modest aims, the book came under attack for failing to preserve historical impartiality and for questioning Knox's greatness and the benefits of the Reformation, which made Scotland Presbyterian.[113] 'Not a few of the author's countrymen will rise from its perusal with the feeling that he is not a true Scot'. So wrote David Hay Fleming, his most acerbic critic, a respected historian and St Andrews' resident, who dismissed the book as 'slipshod and superficial', full of 'errors and blunders of all kinds', and a 'gross caricature' of Knox and the Reformation.[114] They exchanged fire in the pages of the *British Weekly*, a skirmish that made them friendly, dedicated adversaries until the end of Lang's life. In Lang's words, Hay Fleming became his 'friend and constant trouncer'.[115] Publicly, in that first exchange, Lang stuck to his guns, insisting that the Kirk had crushed the 'joy of life' and that 'the belief in their abnormal powers' helped give Knox and the Reformers an undemocratic influence over moral and religious liberty.[116] Privately, he resolved from that time always to base his arguments on manuscript documents.

He and Nora planned that year to visit Ireland, where Garnet Wolseley was serving as Commander-in-Chief of the British forces. Lang was keen to meet the 'wild Irish Professors', who sought to verify through archaeology the social reality of the Celtic culture reflected in Irish folk poetry. Archaeological excavations, and an association of the bardic chronicles of pagan Ireland with the Homeric epics, were, to some, fashionable proof of the common racial inheritance of Celt and Greek. Lang found much to admire in the flowering of Irish literary revival, but he was critical of racial stereotypes of the Celtic spirit. Although he warmly reviewed Yeats' *The Celtic Twilight*, which combined tales of magical occurrences and fairy encounters that Yeats had heard from Irish folk with Yeats' own visionary experiences, he reminded the author that 'all the world has its visionaries', and that 'the great Celtic phantasmagoria is the world's phantasmagoria'.[117] He and Nora had already packed for Ireland when Nora fell ill. Lang wrote apologetically to Louisa Wolseley, painting a comic picture of his trials as a husband:

> She ... really is in such a state of aches and pains that she would be wrong to travel, and what I would undergo with her *I* can partly guess, from her feats when she is well, and in a train. I have steadied myself against these, endurance is the badge of all our tribe (besides I could have gone into a smoking carriage and left her to her fate), but I am afraid that she might incur serious danger from the cold. On the other hand, the crossing might have done her a world of good, though not in the way she likes.[118]

Nora herself confessed to Mrs Alice Stewart, a friend, 'You have a diploma from your husband for never being out of temper—a tribute my husband could not give me even for a single day'.[119] They eventually succeeded in making the crossing to Ireland the following May. That month, Garnet Wolseley was in London, receiving promotion to the rank of Field Marshall, but they had a delightful time with Louisa Wolseley at the Wolseley's lodgings at the Royal Hospital, Kilmainham, Dublin, and returned home via Holyhead on 'the most glassy of seas'.[120]

During the winter of 1893–4, Lang met J.M. Barrie for the first time. Barrie had come to St Andrews to recover after a serious illness. Lang liked Barrie but thought him 'a weird looking little cove' and 'not what you call a lady's man'.[121] It thus came as a surprise to him when he heard later of Barrie's marriage to the actress Mary Ansell. On finally meeting her, he could not make out whether Barrie was cross, or shy at having to introduce her. He told Emmeline Puller that 'Mrs. Barrie ... only left on me an impression of making play with her arms, though I don't know whether these limbs justified her obvious admiration of them'.[122] That first winter, he and Barrie were walking in the old parts of St Andrews when they ran into Anne Thackeray Ritchie with her husband, Richmond, who was recovering from illness. She had included a flattering tribute to him in the introduction to her *Madame d'Aulnoy's Fairy Stories*, published shortly before his *Green Fairy Book*.[123] He, in turn, had written to congratulate her on her 'delightful' childhood reminiscences in *Harper's* magazine of Robert Browning and her father together. The affinity he had always felt with Thackeray increased on reading her memory that her father was very interested in hearing stories about ghosts and clairvoyant experiences, although he did not believe in them.[124] At St Andrews, she was anxious about money and asked his advice about using a literary agent. Lang took time before giving an answer:

> I am a kind of dove, as far as my own ventures go, but more or less serpentine in wisdom about other people's. I am inclined to believe that you would find Mr A. P. Watt a useful agent. He is Scotch, and, I believe, indifferent honest. He acts for an author as a solicitor with a client. He introduces no modesty, no personal feelings of any kind, into business, as we authors can't help doing ... The disadvantage in Watts, to my mind, is that he must higgle, and probably puffs the article he has to dispose of, in fact he trades for us. But most authors can't trade for themselves. If you can allow your business to be done for you, in the same manner as the publishers are doing theirs for themselves, then he is the man. People like us have no chance with the Macmillans of this world.[125]

Nora dated the years in a novel way according to his latest obsession, his 'small talk'. 1894 was the year of Jacobite conspiracies, and, in particular, the mysterious identity of a treacherous double agent, a close friend of Charles Edward Stuart, who signed himself 'Pickle the Spy' in his secret reports on the prince to the Hanovarian government in London. Lang initially believed him to be James Mohr MacGregor, Rob Roy's son, whom Stevenson had made the father of the Highland heroine of *Catriona* (in America, *David Balfour*). After a careful study of the Pelham Papers at the British Museum, his suspicion shifted to Alistair Ruadh Macdonnell, known as Young Glengarry, who had been active in the '45 and was revered as a valiant and devoted Jacobite and the noblest of the clan chiefs. If he was right, it was a striking historical discovery, one that he knew would raise violent objections, showing as it did how shabby a thing Jacobitism was. Although Stevenson was busy on other novels, Lang was hopeful he would recommence work on 'The Young Cavalier' and had transcripts made of the Pickle letters to send him. First, he sent the transcripts to Aeneas Ranald Wesdrop, the current Glengarry, titular head of the Clan Macdonnell, to give him the opportunity to disprove his findings.[126]

Cock Lane and Common Sense brought him into close contact with the SPR, which now considered him more an ally than an antagonist. Oliver Lodge, a scientist working on radio waves and one of the society's leading members, was convinced that the Italian medium Eusapia Palladino had supernormal powers after attending a series of her séances that summer in the Mediterranean. Richard Hodgson, an American psychical investigator, criticized Lodge and his team for failure to put in place sufficient controls. Palladino agreed to come to England the following summer to repeat the experiment. Lodge asked Lang's advice. Lang's mind was 'in a balance'. He confessed to disliking 'paid sorceresses in the dark', but he did not fancy his own 'powers of detection and seeing (or hearing rather) would not have been believing'.[127] He agreed to sound out Peter Guthrie Tait, the Professor of Natural Science at Edinburgh, on the question of adequate scientific controls. He also encouraged Lodge to take up the offer of help from the popular stage magician, John Nevil Maskelyne, who performed illusions and magic tricks nightly at the Egyptian Hall in Piccadilly, with his partner George Alfred Cooke. Part of their show was exposing the claims of fraudulent mediums to supernatural powers. Matters were left there for the time being.

At the end of October, he sent Stevenson a print of John Raeburn's portrait of Lord Braxfield, the famous eighteenth-century Edinburgh 'hanging judge', knowing Stevenson planned to introduce him as a character in the novel he was writing—*Weir of Hermiston*. He posted the transcripts of the Pickle letters separately a day or two after. Mail between Britain and Samoa took roughly a month each way. He received in mid-December a disturbing letter from Samoa which had crossed with his own. For the first time since he had known him, Stevenson wrote of personal anxieties and of haunting phobias—that he would be paralysed, become insane, but live on a burden to his family, 'no longer himself'.[128] There were reports in the press that very week that Stevenson was dead. There had been many false reports of Stevenson's death over the years. As soon as one newspaper said he was dying, another newspaper would report that he had begun work on a new novel. This time, news of his death seemed to ring true. Chillingly, Lang received a second letter written on 1 December, just two days before the date of Stevenson's reported death, thanking him for the Braxfield print, but saying that the transcripts of the Pickle letters had still to arrive. Lang wrote to Anna Hills:

> I am distressed about Stevenson. We were very friendly, though we were never friends. I mean he was never one of the four or five people one regarded as friends. There is nobody fit to tie his shoelace, and he was a good fellow. I fear I threw away his last letter last week, all about death; I could not guess he was to escape what he feared so soon, paralysis and loss of reason. It is not an unhappy end for him, but it is a great loss to us. Now there will be fountains of gossip let loose.[129]

Obituaries and critical assessments of Stevenson's life and work had already begun to appear in the press. The *Spectator*, while paying tribute to his skill and finesse as a writer, argued that his writings came up short of the emotional atmosphere and naturalness of Scott.[130] Lang wrote to Anna Hills:

> What the *Spectator* said was true, though it was not quite the time for saying it, or partly true. The beautiful edifices are not very solid; but I always attributed that to health and circumstances ... Apart from private liking, I could better have spared the whole writing generation from George Meredith to Mr. Richard Le Gallienne, but it would hardly do to say so in public.[131]

His own tribute in *Longman's Magazine* took issue with the *Spectator's* view that Stevenson valued language and style 'for its own sake', although he acknowledged as 'true enough' that Stevenson did not have the 'opulent genius of Scott', which he put down to Stevenson's lifelong struggle with ill-health. He observed too that the 'miscellaneous and varied character' of Stevenson's writings was perhaps why he did not enjoy a greater popularity with the wider public, compared with less talented authors. Stevenson 'has fallen under the reproach of versatility, so fatal in a country like ours'—a comment that applied to his own reputation. Measuring Stevenson with the greatest writers he judged him a 'Little Master', but of the Little Masters the 'most perfect and delightful'.[132]

His reflections on Stevenson, almost without meaning to, were a recognition that their whole generation, himself included, fell short of literary greatness. Stevenson, of all the writers he had known, had seemed the one with most genius. Even Kipling disappointed. Lang's early enthusiasm that Kipling had 'stuff in him' had been extinguished by *The Light that Failed*, which he hated.[133] No living writer seemed to have the commanding voice or personality of the first Victorian generation of poets and novelists. It saddened him that his own muse seemed to have deserted him. He ended his fifth collection of verse, *Ban and Arrière Ban*, with 'A Poet's Apology', lamenting 'the Muse has gone away/ ... Now he's grey'.[134] Still left in his hands, however, were the Pickle letters and enough historical material for a series of books that could rewrite the history of the Jacobite uprisings and relations between Scotland and England. What had begun as historical annotations for his Border edition of Scott's novels had deepened into a recognition of the *suppressio veri* of history itself, of what historians leave out. He felt under an obligation to do something with it. He knew that if he did, he would make enemies in his own country. He had come to another fork in the road.

9

Turning Historian

The winter of 1894–5 was unnaturally severe. In London the Thames froze, and thousands skated on the Serpentine in Hyde Park. Lang and Nora wintered in Scotland, where temperatures in the Highlands were the lowest ever recorded in Britain. At St Andrews they were pounded with fierce westerly gales, with slates flying off the roofs, and seagulls dashed to death against trees.[1] Lang and Nora decided to leave for the Continent. His historical and psycho-folklorist research had converged in an interest in Joan of Arc, burned as a witch by the English during the Hundred Years' War. There were widely polarized views and representations of Joan of Arc. Shakespeare in *Henry VI Part I* portrayed her as a cunning witch, but to many she was a saint and martyr. Lang's interest was not simply idiosyncratic. The availability of the original trial records in the early 1890s, and the publication in 1890 of J. B. Ayrole's *La Vraie Jeanne d'Arc: la Pucelle devant L'Eglise de son Temps* ('The Real Joan of Arc: the maiden-saint before the Church of her day'), made her life and visions again the subject of debate. That summer, Sarah Bernhardt thrilled audiences at Her Majesty's Theatre with her performances as 'the inspired Pucelle'.[2] In January 1894, Pope Leo XIII authorized the commission in Rome to examine the case for her canonization. Lang, determined to get to the truth, drove himself to distraction reading contemporary documents in dog Latin and Old French and concluded that even if Joan of Arc's voices and visions were hallucinatory, they were not to be sneered at. He had recommended her to Stevenson as the suitable subject of a novel: 'There was never such a brick of a girl, nor will be.'[3] Now that Stevenson was dead, Lang's thoughts turned to writing the novel himself, and he decided to visit the country along the Loire associated with her. The night after their arrival at Marloes Road, he rescued their cat Dickson from the top of a high trellis behind the house, with the help of a ladder. He woke the next morning feeling ill, and they had to cancel their trip.[4]

He attended Maskelyne's magic show in Piccadilly on 5 February and afterwards discussed with the magician the forthcoming Palladino séances, scheduled for August and September at Frederic Myers' house in Cambridge.[5] At St Andrews, Peter Guthrie Tait had expressed 'no interest' in Palladino or what he called 'charlatans and rapping tables', although as an experimental

Andrew Lang. John Sloan, Oxford University Press. © John Sloan (2023). DOI: 10.1093/oso/9780192866875.003.0009

scientist he warned that 'the more precautions one takes, the more one confides in them, and is, ergo, the more easily the victim'. Lang liked Maskelyne and advised Oliver Lodge, who was organizing the Palladino visit, that a professional conjurer might be a better critic than those with a 'training in physical science'.[6]

As winter receded, he and Nora made their escape, not to Loire country, but to the Mediterranean. They were staying at the Hotel Continental in Cannes when news broke of Oscar Wilde's arrest on a charge of committing indecent acts. Wilde's plays closed, and many in London's literary and artistic circles suffered by association. Lang was the unhappy observer of the extremes reshaping the London literary scene. He disliked the exhibitionism of the New Hedonists and Aesthetes and thought Wilde a 'churl', but he found equally objectionable the raids on private life, the hypocritical mix of salacious gossip and moralizing sentiment that marked the New Journalism, and the belligerently masculine, anti-decadent mission of men like Henley. He was unimpressed by the self-conscious eccentricity of the *Yellow Book*, which he thought 'commonplace'.[7] In private, he was scornful about the 'Yellow Book Donkey'—in fact, the young Max Beerbohm—dismissing Beerbohm's provocative 'A Defence of Cosmetics', which championed artificiality over reality, as derivative of Baudelaire's 'In Praise of Cosmetics' and John Donne's 'That women ought to paint themselves'.[8] He was equally dismissive of Grant Allen's sensational novel on the 'Sex Question', *The Woman Who Did*, which he described as 'skittles about holy matrimony', saying sardonically, 'I'm too old to go to Ostend with a very dear friend, so I take no interest in the apologia for that practice'.

There were, to Lang's mind, worse things than human 'passions and entanglements'. He condemned press reportage of the O'Shea versus Parnell divorce as hysterical and idiotic: 'Would they make such a fuss, on a man's own side, about an amiable weakness in the U. S.? He is stained with every crime, and *this* is the only one the idiots are about. Are they afraid of their own dissenting *mères de famille* going wrong?'[9] He also dismissed as bunk Max Nordau's medico-psychological study of fin-de-siècle *Degeneration*, which characterized Wilde as a pathological type of the degenerate artist. Popular pseudo-scientific theories such as Nordau's were, as he put it, 'talking in the air'.[10] His attitude to Wilde as a literary man had shifted since the days of Wilde's lecture tour of America. He had not retaliated when Wilde dubbed him 'The Divine Amateur' or mocked him as 'a poet who has the sweetest of voices and absolutely nothing to say'.[11] Nor did he resent it when occasionally Wilde passed off borrowings from his writings as his own, most blatantly the witty repartee on the discomforts of nature which opens Wilde's 'The Decay of Lying'. Lang even came to admire Wilde's ingenuity as a writer, particularly Wilde's decryption of Shakespeare's sonnets in the essay-story 'The Portrait of Mr W. H.', which identified the mysterious 'Mr. W. H.' of Shakespeare's Sonnets as 'Willie Hughes', a boy actor of the female parts.[12] Lang refrained from any direct comment on Wilde's trial and imprisonment, although he wrote afterwards that he thought it wrong to jump to unfavourable moral conclusions about a writer on the evidence of their work[13]—the method of attack adopted by Wilde's prosecutors during his trial who introduced the homoerotic inferences of Wilde's 'The Portrait of Mr. W. H.' as evidence against him. Stevenson, from the time when they were both single, was usually the only friend to whom he spoke frankly about sexual matters, and Stevenson was dead.

Lang made progress with his investigation into Joan of Arc. At the 73rd General Meeting of the SPR, at Westminster Town Hall, on the evening of Friday 17 May, Nora read his paper 'The Voices of Jeanne d'Arc'—a defence of the Maid of France from the charge of imposture, insanity, or hysterical illusion. Lang's essay highlighted the striking absence of 'dissociation' or 'physical disturbance' in Joan of Arc's 'voices', in contrast to the agitations of the modern-day seeress.[14] Though not himself a member, Lang attended the meeting of the SPR on 12 October when, as he colourfully reported, Eusapia Palladino was 'handed over, as it were, to the secular arm'.[15] Hodgson, at the Cambridge séances, had caught her in the act of using repeatedly a freed hand and foot. Maskelyne, annoyed that he was not mentioned in the report, released a press statement claiming to have sensationally unmasked the bogus marvels which had taken in Andrew Lang and the professors.[16] Lang calmed Oliver Lodge, saying, 'Maskelyne is only advertising'.[17] But he issued his own public disavowal, pointing out that his recommendation of Maskelyne as an observer was hardly the attitude of a credulous person.[18]

Before the year was out, he had completed his novel about Joan of Arc, *A Monk of Fife*, written in the form of the imagined memoirs of Norman Leslie, a fifteenth-century Scottish monk of Pluscarden Abbey, recalling his life as a young man, falsely accused of murder, his escape to France, and his adventures fighting under the banner of Joan of Arc against the English. To heighten the illusion of authenticity, Lang's name appeared on the title page as the translator from the French of Leslie's original medieval manuscript. He also forged extracts in Old French giving confirmation of his sources. The book was illustrated by Selwyn Image in the style of early English printed books (see Figure 9.1). The novel, a skilful blend of history and imaginative storytelling, is without question Lang's best work of fiction, his fairy tales for children aside. He adapted Scott's narrative device in *Waverley* of having a young in-between

Figure 9.1 'La Pucelle Blessée'.
Drawn by Selwyn Image for *A Monk of Fife*.

hero, ambiguous and uncertain in his allegiances to the conflicting forces shaping and making history. His Norman Leslie declares himself 'as true a Scot as any', but he has also earned the nickname 'English Norman' on account of his 'southern trick of the tongue', caught from having an English mother. Having a young, impressionable hero lent credibility to the elements of the marvellous in the novel, while allowing the reader a measure of doubt. Although overawed by the Maid's preternatural presence, Leslie takes up arms in her Scottish guard mainly to impress Elliot Hume, the daughter of the Maid's banner painter. Elliot's 'passion of faith in the Maid', he declares, 'made war on her love for me'. He comes to question 'how the saints, who, as then, guarded her, gave her no warning' of her betrayer Brother Thomas Noiroufle, a wolf in sheep's clothing. The same ambiguity haunts the novel's ending. At Elliot's insistence, Leslie visits Joan in her cell on the eve of her execution with a plan of escape, but she refuses to flee, and he is the grim witness to her burning. Though convinced he has witnessed the martyrdom, as he rides away he recalls uneasily her final prophecy, 'I shall be delivered, and with great victory'.

Lang's portrait of Joan of Arc differed from the image of suffering female innocence favoured by Victorian predecessors—a sentiment which gave birth to Browning's blameless Pompilia in *The Ring and the Book*, and Dickens' Little Nell. Lang remarked wryly of Dickens's heroine, 'I confess that Little Nell might die a dozen times, and be welcomed by a whole legion of Angels, and I would remain unmoved'[19]—undoubtedly the source of Wilde's often quoted witticism, 'One must have a heart of stone to read the death of Little Nell without laughing'.[20] Lang's Joan of Arc is a figure of female courage rather than victimhood. It was, in a sense, his answer to Hardy's *Tess*.

The critics loved it. William Robertson Nicholl, the editor of the *Bookman*, thought its Joan like 'a fair saint of some mystical glass-painter, or some pious tapestry artist'.[21] The *Athenaeum* judged it 'simple and quaint and beautiful, like a stained-glass window in some old English church'.[22] A dissenting notice, written more in the style of a *Punch* spoof than a standard notice, appeared in the *Saturday Review*. Lang himself may well have had a hand in it: his mischievous slating of his own work went back to his Oxford days in his review of 'Pulvis and Umbra'. The review described *A Monk of Fife* as 'mainly an offering to the memory of Stevenson' and compared its anonymous author satirically to 'the clever little boy at preparatory school' who displays 'the type of boyishness of Mr. Andrew Lang': 'He is naturally at his best in those chuckling leaders in the *Daily News*, bristling with allusions, apt misquotations, and clear mimicry. As a critic he is amusing when he is not imitating, and if he could only keep his hands from romance he would cut a very respectable figure among contemporary writers'.[23] Lang came to regard his forgeries in Old French as 'a blunder ... for a learned medievalist could not make out whether he had a modern novel or a fifteenth-century document in his hands; while the novel-reading public exclaimed: "Oh, this is horrid real history!"'[24]

In February 1896 there was distressing news from New Zealand. His brother Craig had not long to live. Lang hoped his letter to Eva, Craig's wife, would reach her before his brother died. It got there too late. Her account of Craig's last days was harrowing. He told John, who had emigrated to Australia, 'I could not feel it more had it occurred when I was young'.[25] T. W.'s health also gave cause for concern, and he sent word to Chattan House, Northumberland, where T. W. was staying, urging him to 'put himself in proper hands'. Death and illness were followed by more distressing news. His cousin Eppie's husband, Cecil Arkoll, a London solicitor, had 'bolted' with Eppie's ex-governess, 'having spent most of his money, and having taken to drink'. Lang travelled at once to Edinburgh to comfort his cousin and his aunt. How Arkoll could have 'escaped observation' for so long was beyond them.[26]

While in Edinburgh, he looked up George Saintsbury, who had succeeded David Masson as Professor of English Literature. Saintsbury had made sure Lang was not a candidate before deciding to stand. Lang had, in fact, turned down the post. Having to deliver 150 lectures a year was not to his liking, and he doubted that literature was a subject that could be taught. He warmly supported Saintsbury's application for the post, giving assurances of Saintsbury's interest in Scottish literature.[27] Saintsbury was elected over Henley and Walter Raleigh, his main rivals. Lang had celebrated his friend's success by making irreverent fun of his enthusiastic claims for the younger poets of the day, calling for them in his 'Ode to Mr Saintsbury' to strike up the lyre for Saintsbury:

> Touch, Thompson, touch the sounding string,
> With Johnson, Dobson, Davidson
> ...
> Build Rhymers' Club, the lofty rhyme,
> Great fancies mate with glowing words,
> Like Pembroke—in the Doctor's time—
> The land's 'a nest of singing birds'![28]

He heard gossip, during his visit to Edinburgh, of dissatisfaction and disturbances at Saintsbury's lectures and remarked to Gosse, 'Rather an old dog for a new trick, perhaps'.[29]

Lang preferred life in two worlds. He was on good terms with Clement Shorter. The two had first met when Shorter, then a reporter for the *Star*, attended Lang's lecture at South Place Chapel in 1888. Their growing friendship resulted in Shorter, now editor of the *Illustrated London News*, Britain's largest selling pictorial weekly, inviting him to write an informal weekly causerie. The two came up with several possible titles before finally settling on Shorter's suggestion—'From a Scottish Workshop'—echoing Lang's old adversary Max Müller's *Chips from a German Workshop*. He was also invited to write a survey of contemporary British literature for the first issue of *Cosmopolis*, a new international monthly to be distributed in London, Berlin, and Paris and to include articles in French and German as well as English. He had disregarded a request from Stead for his signature to a petition calling on the European powers to end the arms' race, saying to Mrs Hills, 'As if the European powers cared for me and such as me'.[30] But he was happy to foster cultural unity in the pages of *Cosmopolis*, giving free rein to his personal, multidisciplinary interests, with commentary on historical studies, on the use of popular science in 'novels with a message', and on French and English treatments of Joan of Arc. After a successful launch, Fernand Ortmans, the journal's German editor, commissioned him to contribute a bi-monthly 'Notes on New Books'.

He attended the *Cosmopolis* dinner at the Savoy Hotel on 25 June. George Gissing, also among the guests, was keen to be introduced, but they did not speak.[31] They met again at a lunch held by Gosse at the National Club, in Whitehall Gardens, just over a week later. Lang, fatigued with work and troubled by recent family events, was disinclined to conversation. He associated Gissing with the 'young scribes' who preferred French and Russian realism to the traditions of the English novel. Lang's dislike of their deliberate drabness and pessimism was well known. His objection to Zola's '*naturalisme*' was not just a complaint against Zola's concentration on the morbid and sexually explicit, but against the imposition of the positivist spirit and 'crude materialism' on literature in the name of 'science'.[32] He wrote, 'Even if we grant to M. Zola that the object of the art of fiction is "the scientific knowledge of man", we fail to see why that knowledge should dwell so much on man's corruption, and so little on the nobler aspects of humanity'.[33] Surprisingly, he recommended that people read *The Nether World*, arguably Gissing's grimmest novel of working-class life. From unfavourable remarks on bank holidays in Lang's letters, it is clear Gissing's lurid representation of bank holiday excess had for him a ring of truth.[34] Gissing, seemingly unaware of Lang's review of *The Nether World*, noted in his *Diary*, 'Lang justified his reputation of being crusty to new acquaintances. Not an agreeable type; lolling and languid'.[35]

By coincidence, though neither seems to have been aware of this at the time, Lang had agreed to edit the thirty-two-volume Gadshill Dickens for Chapman and Hall; Gissing, to write a critical introduction to Dickens' novels for Blackie's 'Victorian Era Series'. When Gissing's *Charles Dickens; A Critical Study* came his way for review two years later, Lang was pleasantly surprised to find in it a complete absence of any censure or derision of Dickens' melodramatic effects and appeal to public sentiment. 'One might have expected Mr. Gissing to be severe, in the modern way', he wrote, 'But Mr. Gissing is *not* severe. He sees but declines to chastise with scorn.'[36] Their views did not always align. Lang was unconvinced by Gissing's defence of *Little Dorrit*, a novel he found fatiguing. He preferred the irrepressible humour of Dickens' early novels. But Gissing shared his understanding of the social evolution of literary taste. Today's critics have argued that Gissing 'eclipsed' Lang as Dickens' critic.[37] The truth is that Gissing read and clearly benefitted from the early volumes of Lang's Gadshill edition. Gissing's acclaimed historical perspective on the distance between Dickens' day and his own may even have been indebted to Lang, who in his introduction to *Pickwick*, the first of the Gadshill volumes, said of Dickens, '"Naturalism" and the shadow of Darwinism, have not yet fallen upon him ... with Mr. Pickwick we inhabit "another world than ours"'.[38]

Lang's aloof manner often caused discomfort to new acquaintances. Sidney Colvin believed his 'habitual preoccupation with his own ideas made his manner ... often seem careless and abstracted, or even rude, when rudeness was farthest from his mind.'[39] He caused himself great embarrassment when Frederic Myers introduced him to an American couple at his club and invited him to join them for dinner. Oliver Lodge, also a guest, recalled:

> It gradually became evident during dinner that Andrew Lang either didn't know who they were or was treating them in a supercilious manner, not addressing a remark to them, though he talked to Myers a good deal. He was the first to leave the table, and I, feeling rather uncomfortable, went down to the cloakroom and said to him, 'Do you know who these people were? 'Oh,' he said, 'a Mr. and Mrs. Cummings, or something of that sort.' I told him that it was Mark Twain.[40]

Mortified, Lang rushed upstairs and invited Twain to Marloes Road to lunch with Lord Lorne, knowing the two were old friends. Twain and his wife Olivia were living in relative seclusion in London, following the death of their daughter Susy, and, with the support of Myers and Lodge at the SPR, were attending séances hoping to 'contact' her. Lang thought *Huckleberry Finn* 'the Great American novel, usually spoken of as a glory of the future,'[41] but found the great American humourist in person to be 'as funnily out of it as a man can be', leading him to conclude, 'It is not method or mechanism, or brag of Howells's, that makes a book live. The unconscious does that trick.'[42]

After finishing his novel on Joan of Arc, Lang turned from fiction to biography, taking as his subject another figure he felt had been unfairly treated by history—John Gibson Lockhart, Walter Scott's son-in-law and biographer, much maligned as a friendless, unfeeling man for his vicious book reviews in

Figure 9.2 Lang in 1895.
From Herbert Maxwell's *Evening Memories*. Alexander Maclehose & Co., 1932.

Blackwood's magazine and his infamous attack on Leigh Hunt, Keats, and the 'Cockney School of Poets'. From his work on his Border edition of the Waverley novels, he was confident he had enough evidence to show that the youthful Lockhart (known as the 'Scorpion'), had been made the 'solitary scapegoat' for the worst excesses of his older friend John Wilson (pseudonym 'Christopher North'), and others on the magazine. Anxious to avoid a public quarrel, he wrote informing Sidney Colvin, Keats' biographer, that he had letters which disproved Colvin's near certainty that Lockhart had written the offensive article on Keats: 'I am rather pleased, because I could not see Lockhart's hand in the Cockney rubbish, it was too *stupid* for him. Of course, it was morally bad to be in with the writer as to write the drivel, but dull rant the Scorpion, I think, is free from'. Lang posted a second hasty letter to Colvin that day, retracting the charge he had made against Christopher North, but insisting on Lockhart's innocence: 'I now see reason to suppose that the Leigh Hunt articles were by several hands, and, to my surprise, find J. G. L. writing in a most benevolent manner (in a private letter) about Keats'. He asked Colvin to burn both letters and not to mention what he had said. He said in signing off, 'Lord what a crew, literary fellows were to squabble among friends: I wonder they are still as bad. I could a tale unfold, not of Lockhart, but I won't'.[43]

Lang's planned defence of Lockhart's character soon threatened to fall apart. He admitted privately to Emmeline Puller, 'Generally amiable Lockhart was *not*. If I were much cleverer, and rather a literary ruffian, and able to eat and drink a great deal, and violently reserved, you would have somebody not unlike Lockhart'.[44] He found reason for sympathy in the circumstances of Lockhart's early life—his partial deafness from childhood; shyness that was often mistaken for coldness; and lack of a wise counsellor when he graduated from Balliol, age 19, and took to literature in Edinburgh—but he struggled to reconcile the earnest, considerate Lockhart, evident from his letters to friends and family, with Lockhart's loyalty to the end to *Blackwood's Magazine*—'that mother of mischief'. He exclaimed to Matthews in frustration, 'Such a Jekyll and Hyde of a man'.[45] Margaret Oliphant read the proofs and suggested he modify his criticisms of *Blackwood's Magazine* as a 'cankered witch' who had set her mark on his subject as a young man: 'This of course is an irrational sentiment, and unjust to the venerated Maga. She did not make Lockhart and Wilson write as they did. It was they who set their mark on her'.[46] More welcome was Anne Richie's childhood recollection of Lockhart in his last illness, sitting in a carriage on an autumn afternoon in Rome—the 'pale stern beauty of his face' and beautiful jet-black eyes—looking 'as if he were some medieval almost mystical figure out of one of the galleries'.[47] It confirmed other eye-witness accounts of Lockhart as 'a Beauty, an 'Adonis'. He obtained her permission to quote her in his book.[48] He was alone at St Andrews on 24 March 1896, the day he finished his life of Lockhart—'buried him with a tear in my eye', as he put it to Emmeline Puller, 'It was a very sad life, and very pluckily lived'.[49]

Few were convinced by Lang's defence of Lockhart's intrinsic good nature. *Blackwood's* hit back at his apology for Lockhart at the expense of the magazine, with a review by Margaret Oliphant, published anonymously, stating in print the view she had expressed privately: 'The Magazine, if unamiable in its youth, was not so by any set purpose of its own, but because Lockhart and Wilson made it so'.[50] The *Calcutta Review*, more circumspectly, noted Lang's closeness to his subject, describing both men as 'Balliol-Scotch' who united 'North-British particularism with the classical culture which marks the foundation of Devorgilla'.[51] William Robertson Nicholl declared frankly that Lang had allowed sympathy to affect 'his relations to the fact'.[52] There was some astonishment at the evident cost lavished on a book which was unlikely to sell many copies—two quarto volumes, handsomely bound in red morocco, ornamented in gold with the Lockhart crest, and with a red ribbon bookmark, usually reserved for the Bible or poetry. But there was recognition, too, that the work was a permanent contribution to English literature. For Lang it was a labour of love. He had not wanted to be 'too favourable' to Lockhart, but he believed that a 'leaning' to his subject in a biographer was 'better than a prejudice against him'.[53]

After the labours of Lockhart, Lang went fishing in the far north-east of Scotland, at Helmsdale, a coastal village established in 1814 to resettle the crofters his grandfather had evicted from the Straths on the Sutherland estate. He was astonished by the daily tally of salmon landed by his hostess, Miss Radcliffe, a 'white-haired, muscular being', who was fast becoming a legend in angling circles.[54] There were days he caught nothing and suspected he would not be asked back.[55] His thoughts were moving again in the paths of history. Now convinced of the identity of 'Pickle the Spy', he began to turn the material he had intended for Stevenson's use into a historical account of Charles Edward Stuart's European exile after the defeat in the '45. He retained a romantic nostalgia for the Jacobite cause. He had locks of Charles Edward's 'soft bright brown hair', and a portrait of him as a boy.[56] His poem, 'Three Portraits of Prince Charles', reflected sadly on the physical and moral decline mirrored in the change from the 'beautiful face of a youth' on the eve of the '45, to his face in old age, 'Hateful and heavy with wine'.[57] He believed the 'stress of exile'—a life that was no life—to be the cause of habits that alienated the Prince's friends: 'Who can wonder if he lost temper, and sought easy oblivion in wine!'[58] He sought to excuse the prince's 'love them and leave them' attitude to women, telling Anna Hills, 'The P[rince] I fear was *not* the Patriarch Joseph ... Ladies used to go from London to Paris, merely to see the P. in his box at the play and return the next day. No head of 25 could stand this adulation'.[59] In writing his history of *Pickle the Spy, or the Incognito of Prince Charles*, however, he resolved not to allow sentiment or sympathy to interfere with the facts. To do so would be a sin against truth.

He employed Violet Simpson, a young graduate with a history degree from St Hugh's Hall, Oxford, to help him decipher manuscripts in the British Museum and in the Queen's Library at Windsor.[60] That summer and autumn, as he put the finishing touches to the book, he was able to mix business with pleasure when he ventured into Glengarry's country, the country of Clan Mac-Donnell, north of Fort William, to fish and to get a sense of 'historical tradition' and 'local colour'.[61] Highland air and editing Dickens exhilarated him. At Glencoe House he wrote lyrics, which Lord Archibald Campbell's daughter, Elspeth, sang to the company, and at a volunteer ball, he allowed himself to be 'pushed through a dance, like Mr. Pickwick'.[62] After Glencoe, they went to Cumloden House, in Galloway. The house was 'full of young Lady Mary's and Agnes's', whose exact relations and surnames he could not make out. Jack Hills, recently engaged to be married, joined them with his bride-to-be, Stella Duckworth, the only eyewitness to an 'almost incredible event' when he landed a salmon.[63] She was Leslie Stephen's daughter, and her mother Julia had been Burne-Jones' 'Madonna of the Annunciation'. Julia Stephen had died the previous year, and Stella had stepped in to take on the role of mother to her half-sisters, Vanessa and Virginia, who were still young girls. She and Jack were to marry in the spring.

Lang's *Pickle the Spy* caused a stir when it came out in January 1897. The *Athenaeum* believed the book would bring 'sorrow and heart burning to many in Scotland and ... beyond the seas'.[64] The conservative *Spectator* judged it his 'most serious contribution to historical, if not to British literature', and congratulated him for tearing 'the mask from latter-day 'Prince Charlie Jacobitism' and, above all, for proving 'the chivalry of the Highland chieftains to have been an absolute imposture', and the Hanovarian Succession, 'an almost unmixed blessing to the country'. He was warned to 'be on the lookout for dirks'.[65] Lang wrote to the editor of the *Spectator*, objecting to the derogatory views attributed to him by the reviewer regarding the Highland chiefs and common clansmen, and the women who attended the prince in exile, 'I should indeed deserve to be dirked if I maligned ladies, or the Highlanders as a people'.[66]

The notice he received as a new voice on Highland matters took an awkward, personal turn when he was invited by Sidney Lee and the editors of the *Dictionary of National Biography* (*DNB*) to write Patrick Sellar's entry for inclusion in 'Volume 51: Scoffin to Sheares'. Lang felt pressure from two sides. Lee wanted an account of Patrick Sellar's arrest and trial for his role in the

Sutherland Clearances; the family objected to any further raking up of the past. Lang explained the difficulty:

> *In re* Patrick Sellar of Westfield, I can't re-try the case of my grandfather, who was honourably acquitted, though Prof. Blackie & Co libelled him, after he was dead. If anyone writes on my grandfather, he will find, I think, a full report on his case, with comments, in *The Sutherland Clearances*, by my late uncle Thomas Sellar (Longmans, about 1880–1885). But it is impossible to go into a minute comparison of contemporary documents, on one side, and Celtic mythology, on the other. Therefore, I think my grandfather might rest in peace, and not be re-tried after death. Perhaps you will kindly let me know your opinion.[67]

He agreed to do the article, but only on certain conditions. He refused to go into details of the trial: 'I can name books and other authorities on both sides, but naturally I cannot go with a perplexed controversy, and take sides: there is no room for it'.[68] He also told Lee he would submit the finished article to the family for approval: 'If they *still* fuss, I must drop it, *anybody* can do it: it gives me endless worry'.[69]

Lang was noticeably drawn to write about figures, not unlike his grandfather, who cast an ambiguous shadow over history, their character and actions, matters of controversy and dispute. His dismissal of the charges against his grandfather as 'libels' in his letter to Lee, and his protest against the 'impossibility of going into minute comparison of contemporary documents', are strikingly at odds with his assiduous sifting of evidence to get at the truth in other matters. His published entry in the *DNB* sidestepped mention of the financial interests that motivated the Clearances, and the costs in human suffering, stating simply that 'in consequence of the periodical failure of the crops in the straths or river valleys, the crofters were removed to the coast'. It included only a brief statement about Patrick Sellar's arrest and trial 'in connection with the removals', and his acquittal 'by the unanimous verdict of the jury'. He might be accused of bad faith or even dishonesty for refusing to examine the facts, yet we might be inclined to sympathize with him, too, for putting family honour above personal viewpoint, and for his unwillingness to go down in history, as he inevitably would have done, as a turncoat.

In March 1897, Gosse asked him to read Gilbert Murray's *History of Ancient Greek Literature*, for a 'Short Histories of Literature' series for the general reader Gosse was editing for Heinemann. Lang told him bluntly that

Murray's history was too technical in places for the general reader—Homer as literature 'rather elbowed out by the Homeric Controversy'—and too short to satisfy the more informed. He complained, too, that Murray put too much faith in Wilamowitz-Muellendorff, a German scholar careless with his evidence.[70] Lang responded in irritation when Gosse accused him of bias:

> I don't see why I should be prejudiced against Murray, whom I like. I shall, of course, keep my opinion of his book to myself ... Nobody has asked for it, and nobody will get it if they do ask. But a body may surely have his opinion on a subject with which he has a practical acquaintance![71]

Gosse lost no time in sending on his letter to Murray, with a note, 'The above is delightful. It is like a schoolboy, who sulks all afternoon, and comes home hungry for tea. E. G.' Lang had already written to Murray directly, stating candidly the same points he had made to Gosse. He found himself having to talk Murray out of annoyance and impatience with Gosse: 'Gosse appears to have conceived that I wanted to abuse your book. Nobody asked me, but it was never my intention. Gosse is not invariably sagacious.'[72] He reinforced this in a later letter: 'I daresay Humanity, in a lump, may have many fine qualities, but you can't expect them all in poor Gosse, you know. It takes all sorts to make humanity.'[73]

Murray's history reawakened old ambitions to bring down the whole house of cards of German 'separatist' theory of Homer, and to translate the *Homeric Hymns*. First, he had a more pressing task. He continued to track down fresh evidence to silence the doubters who refused to believe that Glengarry, a gallant young Highland chief and Jacobite, could be the infamous Pickle the Spy. 'New Pickle materials flew in', he reported to Matthews in April, '... incredible facts which happen to be true.'[74] His entry on his grandfather for the *DNB* had shifted his interest from uncovering the identity of Pickle the Spy to a wider historical consideration of conditions in the Highlands after the defeat of Jacobitism. Although he thought the British Museum 'a heart-breaking place',[75] it was there, in the King's Library, that he found Manuscript no. 104, a report by a government secret agent, a 'court trusty', on the dreadful servitude and backwardness of the people on the forfeited Jacobite estates, and the abuses of the old clan system. William Blackwood agreed to publish the manuscript with the title *The Highlands of Scotland in 1750*, with an introduction by Lang. Although Lang cautioned that the report was the work of a 'violently

Whiggish and Protestant' observer, and therefore had to be read with allowance for prejudice, he was persuaded by its account of the arbitrary power of the chiefs and the desperate poverty and ignorance of the people, which accorded with other reports of the social state of the Highlands in the period from the Jacobite uprisings to the great emigration to America. Lang drew upon the Duke of Argyll's history of the Highlands, *Scotland as It Was and as It Is*. Like Argyll, he laid much of the blame for the Highland Question on English negligence, claiming that 'Had Cromwell's policy been steadily carried through, had roads been made into remote districts, the clan system would not have lingered on', in the Highlands, 'the Clans would have accommodated themselves to new conditions, like the Clans of the Border'.[76] But Lang stopped short of Argyll's view that the 'power of ownership' had been the 'only engine' for reclaiming the Highlands from 'the anarchy of the Clans' and for rescuing the poorer classes from the oppression of Celtic feudalism.[77] Lang merely noted that as the power of the landlord increased, the 'romance of the Highland Celt ended' and 'a population ... made room for cattle, sheep, and deer'. He felt a sequel to *Pickle* was called for, one that would give a full and frank picture of the self-interest of the clan leaders, and the betrayal and double dealing by many in Scotland after the '45. 'I am shocked by the misdeeds of everybody concerned', he told Lady Wolseley, 'I blush all the time'.[78]

The Companions of Pickle, Lang's sequel to *Pickle the Spy,* is a curiously equivocal work. In his concluding chapter, 'Old Times and New', Lang declares Charles Fraser-Mackintosh, the Scottish land reformer and Crofters' Party politician, 'wide of the mark' in claiming that Government Commissioners on forfeited estates were the first evictors. Lang points out that the imagined good old times before Culloden were not quite the 'Celtic golden age' of clan myth, that evictions were not uncommon, and that 'on the whole, the distressed Highlanders need not, it seems, conceive that the old times were free of distress, or that the Chiefs were really always humane'.[79] Although not a justification of the Clearances ('Who does not sympathise with their emotions', Lang asked, 'holders of land, proud free men', forced to 'emigrate, or become labourers or artisans in towns?'), his *Companions of Pickle* shows the old Highlands to be a place of poverty and frequent famine, and that the hurry to improve, which people detested, was more benign in intention than the tyranny of the old clan system.[80] On the other hand, Lang also acknowledged that 'whatever the material conditions', the Highland people possessed a rich and dignified 'native culture', and that the forced removal of clansmen from ancestral lands had been justified on legal rather than moral grounds.[81] His picture of deprivation in parts of the present-day Highlands expresses a poignant, powerfully personal regret, one that recognized the division of Catholic and Protestant that still marred democratic life in Scotland:

> I have seen in the Highlands heart-beating destitution. I have seen an old shivering woman gathering nettles for food near Tobermory. On one side of a river I have seen scantily clad girls hanging about listless, in the rain, beside hovels more like the nests of birds than human habitations. On the other side of the water were comfortable cottages and thriving crops. The former were the Protestant, the latter the Catholic side of the stream, which the Reformation did not cross. In the bleak, cold June, on Haladale, I have said, 'Who would stay here that could go away?'[82]

More widespread in other parts were the poor on the Catholic side. A sense of injustice and loss—that perhaps all had not been for the best—weakened the optimism of his wishful, almost idyllic closing image of the present-day Highlands as 'a realm of forests, hills, and streams, deer and salmon', where the descendants of the clansmen, 'or most of them', seemed 'more fortunate than their cousins in the new times, or their fathers in the old days that were not really golden'.[83]

That Lang's personal view of his grandfather, Patrick Sellar, may have diverged from his public defence in the *DNB* is hinted at in his private correspondence during the writing of the book. Edward Nicholson, Bodley's librarian and an amateur folklorist, was compiling an anthology of the folk-lore of the Golspie district of north-east Scotland, and knowing Lang's family association with the region, asked if there had ever been reports of ghosts at Morvich House. Lang assured him that none of the family had 'ever heard of a spook there'. It was on this occasion that Lang remarked with candour, 'Spooks in a body would have given my grandfather a wide berth'.[84]

On one subject, Lang had decisively changed his position. Writing his Pickle books put paid to the popular myth of the spontaneous, imaginative, impractical Celt as opposed to the more pragmatic and prosaic Anglo-Saxon, fostered by the writings of Ernest Renan and Matthew Arnold. In 1893, he had warmly reviewed Yeats' *The Celtic Twilight*, which combined strange tales of magical occurrences and fairy encounters, told by Irish folk, with Yeats' own visionary experiences; but he also reminded the author that 'all the world has its visionaries', and that 'the great Celtic phantasmagoria is the world's phantasmagoria'. The review also had a mischievous sting in the tail for Yeats himself, noting 'an astonishing thing that, with all the poetry of the popular Irish imagination, the country had no great literary poet'.[85] Lang's writings on mythology and folklore had greatly influenced Yeats' account of Irish traditions, but Yeats' mystical vision of the supernatural spirit and primitive wisdom of the Irish peasantry went beyond anything Lang could countenance. Yeats sought proof of the supernatural; Lang merely argued that there might be something in it. By 1897, Lang was more openly at war with Yeats and writers of the Irish Literary Revival, dismissing the claim for the inherited blood of the Celt as 'self-conscious, *voulu* ('imposed')': 'Races have long been mixed, and the history of race is profoundly obscure. When we bring race into literary criticism, we dally with the lovely fluent enchantress, Popular Science'.[86] The article brought Yeats round to the view that what Ernest Renan and Matthew Arnold had characterized, and he had previously accepted, as distinctly Celtic, was after all the 'primitive' element found in many European folk literatures.[87] Their accord had a further unexpected result. Julian Sturgis, another Longman's author, sent him a manuscript of 'Poems' by Eva Gore-Booth, a friend of Yeats. Lang recommended them to Longman for publication.[88] This led to an invitation to Lissadell, the home of Eva's father, Sir Henry Gore-Booth, in Sligo, on the west coast of Ireland. Lang was keen to see first-hand something of rural Irish life, its landscape and its people, and to enlarge his knowledge of Irish folklore. He arranged to go in August.

Through spring and early summer, Lang prepared *The Making of Religion*, his much-revised Gifford Lectures, for the printer, and put the finishing touches to his *Companions of Pickle*. Working on two books at once reduced him to a shell, but the excitement of having something new and controversial to put before the public kept him going. He and Nora were deeply saddened by news that Jack's wife Stella, just three months married, had died after catching an illness on their honeymoon.[89] Before they left for Ireland, Lang was the target of an abusive attack by a Presbyterian minister at the annual meeting of the Gaelic Society of Inverness. Lang was denounced as an enemy of the Celtic race, who had not left 'unraked a dunghill in search of a cudgel ... to maltreat the Highlanders, particularly those who rose in the Forty-five'.[90] Lang kept his powder dry. His rebuttal would be his forthcoming *Companions of Pickle*.

On 15 August, they made the night crossing from Stranraer, Scotland, to Dublin. The noise from a gang of platelayers hammering all night to the flare of a gas lamp outside their cabin window made sleep impossible. Wolfe Tone celebrations in Dublin the day before their arrival had been the climax of centennial commemorations of the United Irish Rebellion of 1798, and a morning-after atmosphere hung over the city. They rested at the Shelbourne Hotel that morning before making the journey south in uncomfortably hot weather, in a railway carriage full of priests, to Henry Butcher's house at Danesfort, Killarney. News that Lang was in Ireland prompted comic verses in the *Sun* from the London-based Irish journalist, William Patrick Ryan:

> What inspired this Celtic trip,
> For from 'Longman's' and 'The Ship'?[91]

Lang had business matters to discuss with Butcher. Before attempting a translation of the *Homeric Hymns*, he received Butcher's reassurance that he was happy for him to undertake the translation on his own. He admired Butcher's house and the surrounding countryside of lakes and hills, although Scottish heather was more to his taste than the lush green Irish landscape. During his stay, his impatience with the myth of the Celtic character was roused by a piece on 'The Charm of the Stuarts' in the *Spectator* which referred to 'the Celtic strain in the Stuart blood'. He wrote to the *Spectator* to point out the error—the Stuarts were in fact a branch of the Anglo-Norman Fitzalans—and dismissed as unscientific the racial stereotyping of character, saying, 'As to the "Celtic type", I doubt if there is a Celtic type of character.'[92]

They left Killarney at the end of August for Lissadell in the far west. They spent a week there, visiting prehistoric sites and collecting tales of fairies and folklore from the locals. They learned that Yeats had been at Lissadell just before their arrival.[93] Lang was excited by what he saw and heard in Ireland. On his return to London, he urged Clodd of the need to keep looking for 'fresh facts'. He thought Clodd's latest study of folk tales simply repeated what had been said 'over and over': 'There is plenty of new stuff to find out ... Even if one gets lost, or hits blind paths, one must try to keep advancing.'[94] Through Clodd, he wrote a long letter to Yeats, reporting his folklore findings in Ireland and voicing his surprise that he had found no knowledge of second sight or of crystal-gazing in Ireland.[95] Lang published the material he had collected in 'A Creeful of Stories' in *Blackwood's*, noting that second sight, still common in the Highlands, seemed almost unknown in Ireland, while the Irish belief in fairies was a fading tradition in the Highlands.[96] Clodd tried to arrange a meeting between the two, but by the time Yeats got back to London, Lang had left for Scotland. He evidently met Yeats a year or two later. His novel *The Disentanglers* includes a burlesque portrayal of Yeats as the coming dramatist and poet of the Celtic Renaissance, Mr Blake, who believes 'the poetic gifts of the natural man ... still extant in Ireland'.[97]

Lang returned from his Irish trip to hostile reviews of *The Making of Religion*. His *Myth, Ritual and Religion* had already been placed on the *Index*

Expurgatorius of books Catholics were forbidden to read. *The Making of Religion* succeeded in offending both atheists *and* Catholic theologians. John Mackinnon Robertson, a rational secularist, accused him of professing primitive universal revelation, a charge which Lang categorically denied, insisting that his position was that 'the origin of belief in God is unknown'.[98] The Irish Jesuit George Tyrell, for whom Lang's heresy was the opposite, opened his attack on *The Making of Religion* by ridiculing all 'the Clodds, the Allens, the Langs and other popularisers of the uncertain results of evolution-philosophers' as 'a crowd of socialists who follow like jackals in the lion's (i.e. Tylor's) wake'.[99] At the Savile Club, Lang hailed Clodd as 'Brer Jackal', and had to disclaim afterwards in reply to Clodd's puzzled enquiry, 'I did not call you a *jackal*, see Father Tyrell in the *Month* for September'.[100] Lang sent Tylor an extract from the 'Papist rag', as he called it, and made known his frustration that no one whose views he valued had reviewed the book: 'I wish an expert would notice the book, but Frazer won't, Lyall seems to shirk it, and you must not bother with it, and—there is nobody else!'[101]

His wish for more informed reviews was answered, though not as he would have liked. Edwin Hartland, newly elected President of the Folklore Society, discounted his evidence for an indigenous belief in a 'high god' among the Australian Aboriginal people. Lang had relied on the Australian explorer and anthropologist Alfred Howitt's report of a belief in a 'Supreme Spirit' among the tribes of south-east Australia.[102] Hartland pointed out that Howitt strongly objected to the interpretation which Lang had placed on his account and had come to regret using the term 'spirit' to refer to the larger-than-life being of the Aboriginal story. There was, Hartland insisted, no such thing in the minds of Australian Aborigines as a moral, all-knowing Father-god.[103] Lang and Hartland skirmished for several months in the pages of *Folklore*. Lang found allies in Mrs Langloh Parker, a scrupulous and knowledgeable recorder of south Australian legends and beliefs, and Frederick Starr, Professor of Anthropology at the University of Chicago, but he conceded too there was need for further field work and enquiry. Hartland said of their difference, 'I do not desire, and I am sure he does not desire, victory, but truth. "More facts and more criticism", are, as he says, what we want'.[104] Lang was soon to discover that not all those engaged in the new discipline were so willing to admit disagreement.

Over Christmas, as people prepared to welcome in the last year of the century, Lang received a surprising gift. Charles MacGregor Falconer, a devoted admirer and collector of everything he wrote, presented him with *A New Friendship's Garland*, an anthology of complimentary poems to and about him by many hands. Some, like those by Stevenson and Henley, were of a personal nature; others paid tribute to his many-sided achievements and influence as a writer. The whole thing had been done without his knowledge. His first contact with Falconer had been in the 1880s, when Falconer, who managed a rope and sail company in Dundee, wrote to him enquiring about his rarer items. When the two met for the first time in 1889, Lang found him a 'brisk-mannered, alert-eyed, crisply-spoken' man of business.[105] Falconer by then possessed 495 of his titles.

Falconer's literary *liber amicorum* ('book of friends') felt in some ways like an encouragement to retire rather than to write more. Among the inclusions was a verse letter from the New York humourist John Kendrick Bangs, urging that he 'take a rest a week or two',

> Your books flow in so fast that I
> Cannot keep up, howe'er I try.[106]

Tributes in the press frequently made fun of his abundant writings, with jokes that his name was a 'mere badge or trademark of a syndicate'. To the question, 'Who is Andrew Lang?' in Hatchards' 'Books of To-day and To-morrow', the answer was, 'There is no Andrew Lang. It is only a name for trade purposes. Andrew Lang is really a Kensington secret society that exists to make good reading'.[107] *Lives of the 'Lustrous*, a spoof version of Sidney Lee and Leslie Stephen's *DNB*, by 'Sidney Stephen' and 'Leslie Lee', described him as 'the Prismatic Fairy King' who had 'established a company at St Andrews for the promotion of ballads, rondeaus, teetotems, pickles, Rider Haggard, shilling shockers, translations, leaders, criticism, epics, and other tropical and Jacobite *bric-à-brac*'.[108] Lang was amused to see himself described in the *Figaro* (Paris) as '*un ancient redacteur sportif*' ('former sports editor'), now a very popular Oxford professor, who had published a book of Positivist Philosophy, called *Les Myths et Les Religions*.[109]

Lang had no plans to retire. He busied himself on a second historical novel, *Parson Kelly*, centred on an abortive Jacobite *coup d'état* of 1772, the Adderbury Plot, to restore the Stuart monarchy to the throne. He enlisted the help of a young novelist and playwright, E. A. W. Mason. They had been introduced by Frederick Macmillan, Mason's publisher, over lunch in the spring of 1896.[110] Lang described his role good-humouredly: 'My part is to invent things which he takes out—thereby ruining the work of lop-sided genius. I do it with better grace, but he does it more natural, and in truth does most of it'.[111] The novel began serialization in *Longman's Magazine* in January 1899. He was satisfied with the result, the critics less so. Though rich enough in sexual and political intrigue, double identity, and changes of location between Paris and London to satisfy readers of serial fiction, in book form, the *Athenaeum* felt that Mason's 'good turn of narrative', and 'Lang's earnest zeal for historical accuracy' did not quite add up to a satisfactory novel.[112] Mason went on to have much greater success on his own with his best-selling novel of adventure, *The Four Feathers*.

Lang devoted the first half of 1899 to completing the first volume of *A History of Scotland from the Roman Occupation*, an ambitious undertaking conceived during the writing of his Pickle books. Scottish history at that time had shrunk to a small, insignificant chapter in the dominant narrative of Anglo-British history. There had been signs of a revival of Scottish national identity during Lang's student days. The Scottish History Society was founded in 1866 to promote the publication of ancient Scottish records and manuscripts. The 1860s and 1870s had also seen the appearance of Cosmo Innes' *Scotland in the Middle Ages* and William Forbes Skene's *Celtic Scotland: A History of Ancient Alba*. But history generally had ceased to be much read by the wider public, and the interest of the Scottish people in their own history was possibly as low as it ever had been.

In August 1899, with the first volume ready for publication, Lang announced his purpose in *Blackwood's Magazine*. His manifesto, 'History as She Ought to Be Wrote', was a witty and spirited call on historians to be guided by the example of earlier historians such as Macaulay and Froude, who combined accuracy with imagination and literary style. He criticized the 'new school' who renounced historical imagination for what they called 'science' and asked, 'Can science be pursued at all without imagination?' He lamented the trend towards history books written by specialists for specialists. He thought the subject in a 'parlous state' that historians should 'love to have it so'. He picked holes too in their claim for the superiority of 'scientific' knowledge because it was 'up to date'. In many branches, he argued 'science' was 'a set of mirages': new facts and new theories were constantly coming to light and evolving; the 'up to date of to-day', the 'exploded fancy of to-morrow'. Works of history endured because they were written with insight, style, and constructive imagination. Lang's article is his most direct and passionate statement of his generalist intellectual commitment and resistance to the ever-narrowing specialist tendencies of modernity. He adopted a colourful metaphor to describe the attitude of specialists to their own small, jealously guarded areas of specialism: 'Thus tiny bits of knowledge are to be the special property of a small class, someone owning "poffle or pendule", some another. No one has a right in the general folk land of the past'.[113]

Unfortunate timing resulted in the publication of the first volume of Peter Hume Brown's rival *History of Scotland* ahead of his own. Lang admired Hume Brown, who combined patient documentary investigation with readability and shared his belief that the 'passions, caprices, humours, and adventures of our ancestors, no less that the almost impersonal movements and tendencies of forces and ideas deserve their place in history'.[114] Like Lang, Hume Brown looked beyond politics and the actions of kings to the larger life and spirit of the people. Both made use of literature. Lang, however, also drew upon his extensive knowledge of archaeology, folklore, and anthropology. He believed he was the first historian to derive facts from so many diverse sources.[115] Of the precise and immediate cause of the amalgamation of Picts and Scots in the ninth century, Hume Brown could only plead that 'no satisfactory account has come down to us'.[116] Lang's lucid explanation, in contrast, was that the Picts were a totemic people, whose exogamous marriage laws led to this eventual fusion through Kenneth MacAlpine, a Scot of Dalriada, who became King of the Picts by maternal ancestry.[117] In his chapter on 'Early Culture in Scotland', Lang drew upon 'the neglected field of the comparative study of miracles', and on the evidence of burial rites, relics of iron bronze, language, place names, and the 'neglected field of the comparative study of miracles' to throw fresh light on the differences between 'Celtic' and 'Teutonic' customs, laws, and modes of life in the centuries after the departure of the Romans. He concluded the chapter with an eloquent, elegiac reminder of the 'unwritten, or little written records' of Scotland's past which 'sleep on museum shelves, or under the black water of lochans, or in howes and barrows. Grey stones on windy moors, green knolls in the *pastorum loca vasta*—the wide tablelands and hills of North and South—speak dumbly of forgotten kings and unremembered wars'.[118]

Where he differed most from Hume Brown was in his treatment of the history of Anglo-Scottish relations. Although he shared Hume Brown's view that Edward I's ambition and wilful disregard for Scottish sentiment destroyed the scheme of peaceful union between the two kingdoms, he recognized, too, that the vague and often disputed history of Scotland's feudal submission to England contributed to the difficulty. He regarded Edward I, as he had in his student days at St Andrews, not as the 'evil monster of early Scottish legend', but as 'the greatest of the Plantagenets, the brave warrior, the open-hearted friend, the true lover, the generally far-sighted politician'[119]—a favourable characterization that he knew was certain to displease Scottish patriotic sentiment. He also criticized Protestant historians for failing to give credit to the ancient Church as a source of culture and defender of Scottish independence before the Reformation, and for suppressing or glossing the tyranny and violence of the early Kirk. He anticipated his history would 'displease many, and content few'.

Frustratingly, the first volume of his *History of Scotland* was further delayed by the outbreak in October 1899 of war in South Africa. Lang shared the horror of the British people at the early setbacks of the Boer Campaign—the devastating defeats of 'Black Week' in December when almost 3,000 British soldiers were killed, wounded, or captured, and Ladysmith, Kimberley, and Mafeking were under siege. At the *Daily News*, there were in-fighting and resignations over the newspaper's change of policy from neutrality to support for the war. John Robertson resigned as editor out of sympathy for the Boers. Lang, though socially conservative and patriotic, remained resolutely non-political. He declined to take over as editor, confessing that he refused the 'opulent editorship ... for motives of "delixy" as Jeanne says: perhaps I should have been indelicate'.[120] He had planned to visit the Wolseleys to advise Garnet Wolseley about writing his memoirs, but with Nora unwell and Garnet Wolseley busy with military preparations, he bowed out gallantly, despite Louisa Wolseley urging him to come anyway:

> I fear you will find me an odious thing, a vagrom man about the house—a kind of superfluous Robinson Crusoe. So I fear I had better comfort my wife at home, and trust to a more congruous occasion. I have acted on the Golden Rule of the Gospel, and Adam Smith, of putting myself in your place by the exercise of the imaginative faculties, and I know you would wish to be unvexed by me, in the circumstances.[121]

Wolseley had urged a delay in sending troops to allow greater military preparation. Though his advice was ignored, as Commander-in-Chief, responsible for overseeing the mobilization, he was blamed for the early disasters and made to swallow the bitter pill of seeing his subordinate and rival Frederick Roberts ('little Bobs') sent in his place to take command of the forces. The British army began to achieve its objectives under Roberts, but military action included burning Boer farms and the internment of civilians in concentration camps where thousands—including women and children—died from hunger and disease. Lang, sickened by events, wrote to Louisa Wolseley on Christmas Eve after Garnet Wolseley retired from the army, 'This is the eve when Asses and other *betês* speak, so I may say my say. I wish Lord Wolseley had been at the front'.[122]

When the first volume of his *A History of Scotland* was finally issued, *Blackwood's* was quick to see an analogy between the failure of treaties to clarify the extent of British sovereignty in the Transvaal, which had led to the war in South Africa, and Lang's account of the disputed twelfth-century treaties between Scotland and England on the question of Scottish independence, which had led to centuries of war between the two kingdoms.[123] There was general appreciation of his care for scholarly detail and for his engaging literary style. There was much dissatisfaction, too, especially among Presbyterian critics, with his scant coverage of the errors of the Church before the Reformation. He answered his critics in the second edition, pointing out that the abuses of the ancient Church were already well-documented, whereas the intolerance, hypocrisy, and 'democratic tyranny' of the Reformation had too often been 'slurred over' by Protestant historians. He had a special message for his Scottish Presbyterian critics, declaring that if there was one thing especially remarkable in the Presbyterian form of faith he had learned in childhood, it was tolerance.[124] He had no intention of letting up on his protest against the unwillingness of Protestant historians to face the facts, or in his determination, in the forthcoming volumes of his history, to speak the truth.

10

Unexpected Honours

The new century brought sadness. In October 1900, Max Müller died at his home in Oxford. Lang paid tribute to him as an 'example very rare among scholars, who commonly are a race almost as irritable as poets'.[1] Asked by Müller's widow, Georgina, for his reminiscences for inclusion in her late husband's *Life and Letters*, Lang wrote warmly of how her husband 'always met my criticisms, often petulant in manner, and perhaps often unjust, with good humour and kindness perhaps unexampled in the controversies of the learned and half-learned'. He reflected elegiacally too on the transience of all learning and the lesson for human conduct:

> Our little systems have their day, or their hour: as knowledge advances, they pass into the history of the efforts of pioneers. But that history would offer reading much more agreeable, if discussions were always conducted (they almost never are) in the genial and humane temper which Mr. Max Müller displayed.[2]

His sense of a world passing away increased in January when he received word of Mandell Creighton's death at the age of 57, following two stomach operations. People believed that had he lived, he would have been made Archbishop of Canterbury. He left four unmarried daughters, all lovely girls, Lang thought.[3] Louise, his widow, was determined to continue her charity work. On 22 January, just days after Creighton's funeral, the London papers announced Queen Victoria's death on the Isle of Wight. Lang was surprised by how affected he was by the news. He said to Matthews, 'Dear old lady, I don't know how it is, but people miss her like a good old grandmother, without any humbug'.[4]

Even as Müller was being laid to rest, he faced a new, younger opponent in J. G. Frazer, a fellow Scot and Cambridge classicist. Frazer's interest in anthropology had been awakened, as his own had, by Tylor's *Primitive Culture*. Frazer's *The Golden Bough*, a wide-ranging account of primitive fertility cults, had impressed many in folklorist circles in 1890. Lang had been grateful to Frazer for valuable comments on the draft of *Modern Mythology*, Lang's

Andrew Lang. John Sloan, Oxford University Press. © John Sloan (2023). DOI: 10.1093/oso/9780192866875.003.0010

final salvo against Müller and the philological school.[5] One reviewer described Lang's book as 'a slaughter of the slain'.[6] Frazer's early support made his lack of response to *The Making of Religion* the more disappointing. That Lang's speculations about 'high gods among low races' differed from Frazer's strict evolutionary view of man's progress from primitive magic to religion and finally to science was to Lang's mind not a bar, but an encouragement to friendly rivalry and debate. He criticized Frazer in the 'Preface' to his translation of the *Homeric Hymns*, pointing out, in veiled terms, the 'danger of the abuse of system-making' by anthropologists.[7] He threw down the gauntlet in earnest when he disputed Frazer's conjecture that the isolated, godless Arunta people of Central Australia must be 'near the beginning', and their elaborate totemistic rituals, evidence of man's earliest, pre-religious beliefs.[8] Frazer's view of early man was largely equivalent to western civilization's colonial view of inferior races. To Lang's mind, savage man was more like us, people in whom barbarism coexisted with moral values, though values different from our own. The fact that among the Arunta, young male initiates learned that the 'supreme being' was a mere 'bugbear' to frighten women and children was, for Lang, evidence that the Arunta were far from the beginning, given the extreme unlikelihood of savage peoples becoming 'dupes of their own primitive jokes'. He directed his wit against the anti-Christian, anti-religious implications of Frazer's theory, by suggesting that the Arunta 'may well have lost an earlier theistic belief ... just as a man of science may lose faith in one way ... by dint of a scientific theory ... and, as a fanatical spiritualist may lose it another way by devotion to rapping spooks'.[9] The essay was Lang's first broadside in what turned out to be a long war.

Frazer's refusal to answer his critics in open debate exasperated Lang. His impatience increased when he read the second edition of Frazer's *The Golden Bough*. He was incredulous that a book so packed with learning could contain so many baseless conjectures and naïve, self-contradictory arguments. He exclaimed, 'Lord, what stuff and nonsense are in that book'.[10] He considered it 'the most learned and the most inconceivably silly book of recent times. To criticise it is really too [much] like hitting a child. And the gifted author thinks he has exploded all of Christianity that Mrs Ward had left ... One laughs out loud in bed at the absurdity of it'.[11] He sent Tylor a comic parody of Frazer's method: 'History is a more exact science than anthropology as illustrated in the G. B.: Vashti, I take for a variant of the wife of Candales who barred being exhibited in the buff. Riccio and Darnley were the spirits of vegetation, killed in spring to keep cabbage lively. Ditto the Regent Murray.

Observe the connection of Jeanne d'Arc with May and the spirit of vegetation'. He was especially scornful about Frazer's interpretation of the 'anecdote about Babylonian criminals being given the run of the Royal Harem before execution':

> Frazer, later, adds that the man had to 'enjoy the favours of the "sacred harlot",
> plus those of the ladies of the Harem as he had only one day',—Puzzle—to find
> out how many ladies of all sorts he "enjoyed". Frazer seems to have Herculean
> ideas, and there is no evidence for the sacred lady of pleasure.[12]

He tried to keep derision out of his reviews of *The Golden Bough*, but he sailed close in highlighting a glaring contradiction in Frazer's association of the Passion narrative and the Jewish Feast of Purim with the barbarous practice of human sacrifice, since Frazer's theory required that people knew that the yearly victim at Purim was a divine or sacrificial victim, while Frazer himself maintained that 'nothing of the sort was known to anybody'.[13] Clodd, who acted as a friendly go-between, learned from Frazer's Cambridge colleague, Alfred Haddon, that Lang's attacks had given 'the poor little man bad nights'.[14] But Frazer refused to enter the ring, merely confessing privately to Edwin Hartland that Lang was probably right in saying that his Purim theory of the Crucifixion 'would not have contributed to the deification of Christ' and that he would 'strike that out of a new edition'.[15] To Lang's mind, Frazer was 'no sportsman'.[16]

Magic and Religion, Lang's point-by-point criticism of *The Golden Bough*, left no one in doubt about his derisive view of Frazer's theory. Lang began his book by pointing out the 'danger of allowing too ingenious and imaginative hypothesis to lead captive our science' and criticizing the lack of historical evidence for Frazer's 'strange array of facts'.[17] He corrected Frazer's many inconsistences, errors of fact, and misinterpretations, not least Frazer's reliance on Virgil's comparison of his Golden Bough in the *Aeneid* to mistletoe, which, as Lang dryly remarked, was quite different from identifying it with a mistletoe: 'A poet does not compare a thing to itself'.[18] The *Saturday Review* headlined its review of Lang's *Magic and Religion*, 'Lopping the Golden Bough'.[19] Although Lang's objections were widely accepted as valid by reviewers and critics, Frazer's book went on to enjoy popular success as a stirring and frightening compendium of barbarous and superstitious practices among primitive and backward peoples. Frazer maintained a show of indifference. He told Hartland he doubted whether he would read Lang's book, as he had 'ceased to attach much importance' to Lang's utterances.[20] Behind the scenes, however, he sought allies. He wrote to Lorimer Fison, an Australian anthropologist:

> Lang ... has been charging at me here, there, and everywhere like a mad bull, and has now published his bellowings in a book, which I have not yet seen. But like Brer Rabbit I lie low and say nothing, which I imagine heats the furnace of his wrath sevenfold. I believe that what has enraged chiefly is that I have absolutely ignored his *Making of Religion*, on which he seems to pride himself, and which I have always thought a bad book ... I should particularly like to know what Howitt thinks of the capital Lang has made of his evidence as to the Australian belief in a moral creator of the world.[21]

Lang found the same lack of openness to argument and self-correction among historians. In the second volume of his *History of Scotland*, which covered the eighty years from the birth of Mary Queen of Scots to the death of her son James VI of Scotland and I of England, he stepped up his attack on Scottish historians for their failure to say anything about the untrustworthiness of Knox's *History*, or to acknowledge the 'persecuting violence' and destruction brought by the Reformation. He dismissed as absurd Hume Brown's claim that 'Calvinism had a kind of elective affinity for the Scottish national genius' and its relish for dialectic. Lang took his first step in challenging a general assumption in Scotland that the national character in Scotland—its thrifty, enquiring, extremely independent people, egalitarian educational tradition, and taste for argument—was the legacy of the Reformation. In Lang's view, the character of the Scottish people had been formed *before*, not *by* the Reformation.[22] Scotland chose Calvinism, he suggested provocatively, because it was 'the cheapest system, entailing no expense on archbishops, bishops, deans, canons, cathedrals, and other luxuries'. He remarked dryly, '*Au fond* the Scottish mind is practical'.[23] The American constitutional historian Gailland Thomas Lapsley recognized Lang's corrective purpose in emphasizing the darker, violent side of the Reformation. He praised Lang's 'delectable humour, his lightness of touch, and his never-failing wit'; but he was critical of Lang's neglect of constitutional issues. He thought the main weakness of Lang's history was his failure to take account of the 'virtually complete lack of constitutional machinery' in Scotland at that time, through which 'opposing forces could peacefully check or modify one another'.[24] His old adversary on the subject, Hay Fleming, stout Sabbatarian and defender of the Reformation, was less forgiving. In private, he thought Lang a 'wonderful chap', but on the strength of the St Andrews book, judged him an 'unreliable historian'.[25] He responded to Lang's criticisms of Knox and the Reformation by numbering Lang among the philistines, who paid lip service to truth, while lacking in 'impartiality and fairness'.[26] The truth, according to Hay Fleming, was that Presbyterian dissent had promoted freedom in Britain as a whole, and the actions of the Reformers in suppressing certain religious observances had been prompted not by 'morose temper', as Lang suggested, but by 'their hatred of superstition'.[27] The majority of Scottish historians attributed Lang's criticisms of the Reformation to his deep dislike of Presbyterians. William Croft Dickinson, in his Andrew Lang lecture in 1951, stuck to this view, adding his belief that 'still more', Lang sympathized with aristocracy and feared the 'democratic' energies Knox had raised in the Scottish people.[28] There has been a noticeable shift since then. There is now recognition of Lang's critical significance as a historian, not only as the first to subject the consensus Presbyterian history of the Reformation to 'sustained criticism',[29] but, more generally, as an independent, critical mind who 'cast doubt on many of the grand narratives and paradigms conventionally used to make sense of Scottish historiography'.[30] Lang freely acknowledged being on the side of Episcopalians and Catholics who suffered persecution and deprivation of civic and religious liberty at the hands of the Reformers. Of bias generally, he exclaimed, 'Bias! No mortal is without it, scientific or layman. Not to understand that one has lashings of bias is very dangerous, I think. I observe that people always accuse their opponents of bias, but I accuse myself and all humanity'.[31]

The mass of evidence and material Lang had gathered while working on the second volume of his history resulted in two spin-offs books. In these, he pioneered the modern 'cold case' or 'true crime' genre. The first, *The Mystery of Mary Stuart*, investigated Mary's guilt or innocence in the murder of her husband, Lord Darnley. Lang likened his method to that of a detective going over 'every inch of ground ... on the scene of a recent murder'. It involved a careful reconstruction of events, examination of witness statements and motives, and a search for missed clues and for evidence of events 'behind the scenes'.[32] *The Mystery of Mary Stuart* opens like the *mise-en-scène* of a detective novel or stage play by introducing the main characters—Mary, 'the centre and pivot' of the mystery, a 'lady to live and die for'; Darnley, 'The Young Fool'; Bothwell, 'The Furious Man'; Murray, 'The Puritan Brother'; and Maitland of Lethington, 'Machiavelli'. Lang documents the events leading up to the murder of Rizzio, Mary's secretary and favourite, on the orders, it seemed, of the jealous Darnley; then the murder of Darnley, smothered, it appeared, his night-shirted body discovered in the orchard of a house on the remote outskirts of Edinburgh where Mary had suggested he stay. Lang included a map of the house and the murder scene to help readers visualize the crime, with 'x' marking the spot where Darnley's body was found. The book then becomes an exhaustive analysis of conflicting witness testimonies, dubious motives, and the doubtful authenticity of the infamous Casket Letters, allegedly from Mary to Boswell, implicating her in her husband's murder. He described the second of his historical crime books, *James VI and the Gowrie Mystery*, to Matthews as 'a regular Sherlock Holmes affair',[33] although he worried that it would be 'much less exciting' for readers, there being 'no woman in the case'.[34] In fact, his recreation of the alleged kidnap and failed attempt on James' life at Gowrie House, which left John Ruthven, the young Earl of Gowrie, and his brother, Alexander, dead, proved an even more gripping and suspenseful mystery. He again included a map of the crime scene. The problem for the reader was whether to believe James' story that he had gone there on the promise of a pot of gold and had been set upon in the turret-room, or the claim by conspiracy theorists that the so-called plot was the king's elaborate device to rid himself of the Gowrie family. Lang's verdict was that despite its glaring improbabilities, James' story was true, and that the Gowrie brothers, with a grudge against James, devised their plot, but blundered over its execution.

Lang's investigations of historical crimes and mysteries became a regular feature of the magazines. They were later collected and published as *The Valet's Tragedy, and Other Stories* and *Historical Mysteries*. Émile Fuguet, a French critic, observed of Lang's historical mysteries that he tended 'towards a solution which is farthest removed from the legend'.[35] While it is true that Lang's case studies often offered a corrective to far-fetched fancies and fabrications, he was not immune to the strange and extraordinary. In his historical practice, as in his study of psycho-folklore, Lang remained alert to the limitations of nineteenth-century common sense that held that what is strange cannot be true. He said to Oliver Lodge, 'The practice of history shows me that the cleverest guesses are upset by the discovery of a manuscript containing the real facts, which no mortal genius would have conjectured to be what they actually were'.[36]

Coming up with new ideas was a trick of survival in the writing business. Lang remained confident but not complacent of his position in a trade where no one had 'security of tenure', where newspaper and magazine editors were ousted regularly, and staff replaced.[37] The demand was always for young men with fresh ideas to attract readers and drive up circulation. He had no quarrel with this. What bothered him was the growth of press intrusion into private life. A feature of this was the trivial glamorization of people in the arts and entertainment, with gossip about their travel plans, their acquaintances, their fabled earnings, and photographs of their homes, gardens, even bedrooms. It did not surprise him when Gosse joined the trend, with articles on Pater and Stevenson which mixed criticism and titillating personal anecdote with an element of vanity and self-congratulation. Lang sent him a warning in verse:

> Come not to me when I am dead
> To write a pleasing essay on my grave,
> Or a melodious stave.
> These let the paragraphist lie,
> But thou, go by![38]

He was dismayed by the inclusion in Margaret Oliphant's posthumously published *Autobiography and Letters* of a paraphrase of some unflattering remarks he had made about Robert Burns in a letter to her. This prompted his outburst in *Longman's*, 'Think what letters are; hasty, indiscreet, inaccurate. Authors ought to write nothing and burn everything, in the way of letters.'[39]

His distaste for Gosse's tittle-tattle and annoyance at having his views taken out of context in Margaret Oliphant's *Autobiography* were nothing in comparison to his shock on reading Henley's bitter attack on Stevenson's character and reputation in the *Pall Mall Gazette*.[40] Henley denounced Graham Balfour's official biography of Stevenson as a whitewash. He painted an unflattering picture of his dead friend as a vain, self-righteous egotist and hypocrite who hid his unsavoury personal life from the public. Henley hinted darkly at future revelations: 'I know too much. In the days to come I may write as much as can be told'. Lang suspected that Henley had recognized himself in a letter unwisely quoted by Balfour. In it, Stevenson made scornful comments about someone named 'x' who was benefitting from his generosity. Lang begged Gosse not to retaliate, dreading this would provoke Henley to carry out his threat of further revelations. He referred Gosse to 'benefits forgot', a phrase from the melancholy song in Shakespeare's *As You Like It*, 'Freeze, freeze, thou bitter sky,/Thou doth not bite so nigh/As benefits forgot/ ... As friends remembered not'.[41]

> I had vaguely conjectured that x. was Henley, and *hic illae lacrimae* (i.e 'hence these tears'). About one thing I am sure, there should be no raking up letters and no mention of 'benefits forgot'. If one does a love a good turn and acquires merit, the merit evaporates the moment it is mentioned. Again, if there is any digging up of bygones, then H. comes in with all he says he has up his sleeve, and who knows how *that* might strike the public?[42]

It saddened him to remember how different things had been when, as young men, they had all looked out for each other. When Matthews wrote that Henley's outburst was typical of the man, Lang sadly agreed, 'Henley, as you say, wrote in character on Stevenson. A more loathsome exhibition I never saw'.[43]

Eighteen months later, Lang left a tennis party in Kensington on hearing that Henley was dying, and went to Henley's house in Addison Road to 'ask after him'.[44] He would not allow bad feeling to reach beyond the grave, although after Henley's death he turned down a request to write the entry on him for *Encyclopaedia Britannica*. He told Gosse, 'It is *awful* writing about the recently dead, whom one rather barred while they were in the flesh. 'Henley!' I think I won't'.[45] Lang had always dreaded false representation of himself, his family, and his friends after his death. Entering the new century, with its taste for sensational biography, served only to heighten his dread.

Lang turned 57 in 1901, the age his father was when he died. Every year after that seemed like a gift. He resisted the idea that nobody accomplished anything great after 40. He took comfort in the thought of notable achievements by older men—*Paradise Lost* finished when Milton was 'no chicken'; Tennyson's 'Crossing the Bar', written when he was about 80; Darwin, over 40 when he wrote *Origin of Species*.[46] He wondered how much he still had in him. He saw others younger than himself decline, among them, heartbreakingly, T.W., his brother. The doctor at first feared typhoid, but then T. W. was taken to Holloway sanitorium at Virginia Waters, which specialized in the treatment of the mentally ill.[47] Lang told Emmeline Puller, 'It will be necessary for me to do all I can for him. This is one of the worst cruel sorrows of my life: this malady. However, pray say nothing of it'. Doing what was needed meant paying for his brother's treatment and care and helping T. W.'s wife Ada financially. He gave up the Angling Club, feeling he could no longer afford luxuries, and 'it *was* hardly a necessity'. He spent some days in July alone with Herbert Maxwell at Brigton on Maxwell's estate in the Galloway Forest, 'partly for the purpose of not saying anything, as nothing is bad but words make it worse'.[48] Maxwell, a friend from his Oxford days, shared his literary and historical interests as well as his devotion to fly-fishing. After that quiet time, he went with Nora to Loch Awe, determined to be more resolute: 'I suppose one must grow accustomed to everything—at all events, the game has to be played'. He was pleased to find Mason there, writing another novel. Their hope was that Marie Corelli would not make an appearance that year and spoil things.[49]

Lang was never an uncritical champion of romance. He thought ridiculous the combination of lurid melodrama and high-toned moralizing in Corelli's best-selling romances, as he did those of Hall Caine, another author of sensational best-sellers, and Corelli's male counterpart in the art of self-advertisement. Lang was the likely originator of the *Punch* cartoon of Caine as 'The Boomster', beating on a big drum with pound notes stuck all over his jacket. He told William Archer, 'Well, I think *The Boomster* should be kept in his proper place, with Miss Corelli and Robert Buchanan. Thank heaven I never helped to boom any of that crew: not that I ever wrote to the contrary. "It may be that only silence suiteth best".[50] His silence had resulted in Corelli's mocking dedication of her critique of the literary trade, *The Silver Domino*, 'To ANDREW LANG whose Literary Generosity Towards Me is Past All Praise'. Corelli had followed *The Silver Domino* with a caricature of him in *The Sorrows of Satan* as the unscrupulous critic David McWhig, who charges for reviews. Lang did not mind being satirized but resolutely avoided her, particularly after her brother turned up at his door unannounced one day to ask his verdict on some verses, and Corelli herself wrote to him pleading, 'Oh, *do* be friends'. He burned her letter and told Gosse, 'I quite understand Miss Minnie Mackay's popularity with the intellectual middle classes. She is by Edmund Yates out of Lewis Morris'.[51]

Attempting to overcome his sadness at T. W.'s illness, Lang wrote a novel, rich in comic incident and self-parody—*The Disentanglers*. His hero, Merton, a university type in a Zingari cricket jacket, whose 'most obvious vice' is 'a thirst for general information',[52] founds an agency to save people from unsuitable marriages. His recruits are young, educated men and women searching for a place and purpose in an overcrowded market. Contrary to the focus in Gissing's novels on the disappointments of the educated, 'unclassed' generation of his day, Lang preferred to show youth's cheerful resilience and enterprising spirit. The novel ran in serial form in *Longman's Magazine* through 1902 and was issued in book form for Christmas. Many thought it his best. The *Academy* believed it owed its humorous manner to *Three Men in a Boat*, a book Lang had never read. More perceptively, the *Saturday Review* found its 'whimsical humour, and reckless disregard of probabilities' reminiscent of the type of farcical social comedy staged by George Alexander at the St James's Theatre in the 1890s, a view encouraged perhaps by revivals of Wilde's *The Importance of Being Earnest* and *Lady Windermere's Fan* in London that year.[53]

In real life, Lang's family troubles seemed only to deepen. His patience was severely tested when his brother Bill in Australia published an unflattering, thinly disguised story about him in the Melbourne *Pastoralist*. John Steedman, his father's old legal partner, brought it to his attention when Lang's brother Pat sent the story to Selkirk's local newspaper, asking that it be reprinted there. Lang guessed the story was Bill's revenge for being told not to send his

14-year-old son 'Dandy' to school in England 'unless he was *certain* that he could support him and find a home for him'. Lang gave vent to annoyance in writing to John:

> As I understand it, it was Bill who wrote in the *Pastoralist* Jan 15 the tale of good Colonel Robert who brings his dear boy to London, meets wicked Peter, his brother, at the Oval, is snubbed by wicked Peter (who has no kids) and horrid Helen his wife (who has none either as far as we learn). Robert, with an aching heart goes to Selkirk, where he gives full and public play to his emotions ... What am I to do? I can't overlook this; I can't pretend to think other than Steedman thinks and his language is very fierce and powerful.[54]

He intended never to let Nora know: 'If she did, I think the paraffin would be in the fire'.[55]

He had seen a recent example of the harm that fiction could inflict. He asked Clement Shorter to help the family of the late William Carus Wilson, the founder of the Clergy Daughters' School at Cowan Bridge, who had been savagely depicted half a century earlier by Charlotte Brontë in *Jane Eyre* as the cruel and autocratic Mr Brocklehurst. The Wilson family had suffered as a result. Lang wrote:

> You perhaps knew that the great grandson of that being who founded the school where the two Brontës were so happy, is paralysed, indigent, and a type of writer. I have sent him some money, and if pity for the family of a person so popular as the man from Lowood animates you, and you can get him any typing. He can't read *my* hand of course. I can give you his address.[56]

He had a soft spot for struggling writers and always tried to find them some work or put them in touch with someone who might help. He said despairingly to Gilbert Murray, who promised to help a South Wales man living in Oxford, 'The difficulty of finding billets for literary people is almost insurmountable, unless they are good at writing short stories. They seem so helpless, except in the way of asking to be helped'.[57]

Nora was in Bristol in the early months of the year. Hannah Kelly, who had been her mother's maid and practically a mother to Nora when she was a girl, had died, and Nora took on the heart-breaking task of settling her affairs and 'shredding up the accumulation' of a lifetime.[58] She also took turns at the bedside of her black Barbadian nurse, 'Elyth Burnham, now a frail 80-year-old. Lang was therefore alone when he received word from Holloway Sanitorium

Figure 10.1 Lang, about 1902, by Walter L. Colls.
From the frontispiece of Lang's *Poetical Works*, volume III.

that T. W. had reached 'the third and last stage of his malady'.[59] T.W. died on 30 May. Lang arranged that only a handful of people attended the funeral, as T.W. would have wished—Ada, his widow, and her sister, and one or two close friends. Their cousin Eppie brought flowers to the country churchyard. That evening, Lang wrote to John's wife, Jean, in Australia: 'The grave is too near the gate, but I hope, with Eppie's help, who lives near, to have the grass and flowers as he would wish. It may be foolish to care, but I do'.[60] He also wrote that night to Rider Haggard, the one friend he felt he could confide in:

> I think I ought to tell you that I have just lost my little brother, he was always little, and ten years younger than I. When he was only a child, he was a celebrated cricketer, worthy of Tweed, and later of Oxford, and for Gloucestershire. But he had no belief in his own talents and left the University for business—in which I have no belief. For nine months, his brain had given way, and he is fortunate in his escape. I daresay no two brothers ever passed their lives so entirely and absolutely in amity as we. I tell you because you are a good fellow if ever there was one, and so was he.[61]

He was in Oxford that October at the beginning of the new academic year and gave three silver cups, with T.W.'s name engraved on them, to Balliol College.[62]

A review of the American edition of *James VI and the Gowrie Mystery* in the New York *Catholic World* in February 1903 hesitated to call it Lang's latest book, suspecting that 'in the three months since its publication something in literature, a new fairy book, a Christmas legend, or a study on the philosophy of religion has most probably been added to the works of Andrew Lang'.[63] The review was not far wrong. The second volume of Lang's *History of Scotland* was already in the book shops, and he was about to publish *Social Origins*, an account of the origins of totemism in early kinship groups or phratries, in a single volume with *Primal Law*, his recently deceased cousin J. J. Atkinson's thirty-year-long study of tribal customs and marriage laws in New Caledonia.

Lang's book not only challenged Frazer's theory that totemism had its origin in magic and superstition; it struck at the heart of those like Emile Durkheim, a founding figure of the new science of sociology, who insisted that 'a totem was not only a name; it is first and above all a religious principle'.[64] Lang's main objection to Durkheim and the moral school was that they derived much of their evidence from Australian Aboriginal practices which they took to be the vestige of primitive institutions, but which were in fact 'very remote from "the beginning"'.[65] Lang aimed, on the contrary, to 'show the process of the birth of society' from 'a long past of forbidden unions', *before* the prohibitions preventing marriages of 'too near flesh' evolved into conscious morality.[66]

Lang surmised that totems may have been at first simply names, often irreverent nicknames, given to kinship groups by their neighbours. The elements of nature worship, superstitions, and taboos arose when human imagination invented myths and stories to explain the origin of the name. In this Lang took direction not only from his cousin's treatise, but from Herbert Spencer's suggestion that totemism may have originated in the custom of naming individuals after animals or natural objects, and the subsequent confounding of revered ancestors with the metaphorical name. Where he differed was in the idea of the clan name being imposed on the group 'from without' and in his attention to man's mythmaking habit. Totemism, he surmised, was 'not an element in the origin of religion, but a field later invaded by religion'. He enlivened his technical arguments with amusing examples of group sobriquets from outside, such as the rude '*blason populaire*' of rival Cornish villages. In explaining sexual avoidance, Lang conceived that exogamy, the custom of marrying outside, may have existed within each small, anonymous group for reasons of sexual jealousy, superstition, or indifference to 'persons familiar from infancy', before the acceptance of the totem name by the group. Exogamy would have been reinforced subsequently with the evolution of totem superstitions and taboos.[67] He tentatively concluded:

> Certain primitive conditions of life led to the evolution of certain rules, independent of any theory about the noxiousness or immorality of marriages of near kin; and then reflection on those primal rules helped to beget moral ideas, and improvements on the rules themselves. In the original restrictions, morality, in our sense, was only implicitly or potentially present, though now it has arisen into explicit consciousness.[68]

Though weighed down with work, he took time to read the proofs of Garnet Wolseley's autobiography, *The Story of a Soldier's Life*. When first approached for his help on the book, he agreed on one condition:

> You must allow me to make my own terms, which are, in the popular tongue, *nuppence*. It is the Rule of a lifetime, when the authors concerned are personally known to me, and I have written leagues of "copy" on these conditions. If I am of any use, then, if you wish it very much you may give me—a Jacobite relic, or a tortoise shell snuff box.[69]

He had read the typescript and suggested revisions and cuts for publishing. He advised that the account of the Ashanti campaign needed shortening. 'West African pickles are all very well', he wrote. 'What I and the public want is the Indian Mutiny'.[70] He advised against sending the manuscript to Longmans, not knowing how that might 'turn out', and who, in any case, were not 'high bidders'. The book went to Constable 'without auction'.[71] The parcels of proofs kept arriving at the houses and hotels where Lang stayed in Scotland that summer and early autumn. He enjoyed reading of war amid tranquil scenery. He reported to the Wolseleys from Loch Awe, 'We have had some lovely days here—it is deadly slow, except for the face of nature. That is good enough.'[72] Possibly at Lang's request, neither Garnet Wolseley's 'Preface' nor dedication made any mention of Lang's significant contribution.

Lang and Nora were in Oxford in October 1903 to see Tylor. They stayed at the Randolph Hotel, about which Lang said, 'To millionaires wholly indifferent to cookery, also to fastidious salamanders, I can recommend the Randolph, brass bands and all.'[73] They spent an enjoyable Sunday with Tylor and his wife.[74] Tylor had 'not been well', and Tylor's wife Anna had not allowed him to read Lang's *The Making of Religion* or his *Magic and Religion*, for fear of its effect on him.[75] The subject of these books was precisely what Lang wanted to discuss with Tylor, who had always insisted that the higher elements in the religion of primitive peoples were borrowings from Christian missionaries. Lang had evidence to persuade him otherwise. He had received a report in German from Carl Strehlow, a Lutheran missionary among the Aborigines of central Australia, who pointed to errors in Baldwin Spencer and James Gillen's fieldwork, on account of their limited knowledge of native languages and use of interpreters.[76] Strehlow, who knew three native languages, claimed there did indeed exist among the Arunta people a concept of a 'high god' or 'supreme being'. Lang had already sent a copy of the report to Baldwin Spencer in Australia and was waiting a reply when he visited Tylor in Oxford.[77]

Lang received Spencer's derogatory, ill-tempered response to the report in mid-January. It informed him that Strehlow's claim for an Arunta 'high god' was 'rubbish', and simply a wishful conflation of Christian assumptions and indigenous native traditions. Lang informed Tylor of developments:

> Today comes a long tirade of Spencer against Strehlow. Is it proper to send it to you? If you think so, I will add, typed, my reply, which, at all events, I may send, and from it you will gather what Spencer said. It comes to this, Strehlow was a beast of a missionary, not admitted to ceremonies, and would not go if he got a ticket ... Spencer thinks Strehlow wants to discredit him, whereas he only answered enquiries ... Temper and bias have set in like a flood.[78]

This was true. Scholarly vanity reared its head. Controversy was to intensify when Lang published *The Secret of the Totem*. This united Howitt, Frazer, Spencer, and Gillen, and their allies in anthropological circles in regarding Lang as 'the common enemy'. Howitt published a complaint in *Folklore* that

Lang had misunderstood and misrepresented his views of a 'tribal All-Father' among the Aborigines of south-east Australia.[79] Lang issued a formal apology in the *Academy* for any 'inadvertent misrepresentation' of Howitt's meaning.[80] But Spencer goaded Howitt 'not to stay his hand' against 'the common enemy', and that it was his 'sacred ethnographic duty to punch, pound and pulverise Lang until he hasn't a whole bone in his body'.[81] Howitt rejected Lang's apology for 'inadvertent misrepresentation', on the grounds that the wording concealed the fact that Lang had mutilated and misquoted passages from his book.[82] Howitt also ordered the printing of 500 copies of his *Folklore* article to be distributed with the help of Frazer and his associates to anthropological societies around the world.

Lang felt no personal hostility to those he criticized. He valued Howitt's *Native Tribes* as 'one of the classics of Anthropology',[83] and praised Spencer and Gillen's studies in the field as 'masterpieces of method'.[84] What frustrated him was Spencer's refusal to explain or even to mention his coauthor Gillen's early report of an Aboriginal belief in 'a great being of the heavens', which Lang had used as evidence for 'high gods' in *The Making of Religion*. If people 'disclaim their published words', he protested to Tylor, 'How can we trust anybody's report?'[85] He argued too, as he had in his criticisms of *The Golden Bough*, that privileging systems over facts was perilous to truth in the social sciences, and that self-correction in the face of contradictory evidence was essential if anthropology was to be accepted as a serious field of scientific enquiry. To be a science, anthropology, he insisted, must 'not blink at facts … She really must give as much prominence to the evidence which contradicts as to that which supports her theory'.[86] His war on that front was not over.

Just days after Lang's visit to Tylor in Oxford in November 1903 came news that George Brodrick, the Warden of Merton College, had died. Although Lang did not know it at the time, he was spoken of as Brodrick's possible successor.[87] Francis Bradley, who disliked Lang, allegedly led a motion to defeat the proposal. Insiders claimed this dislike went back to their undergraduate days when Bradley got a Second in finals and felt patronized by Lang. Harold Joachim, Bradley's disciple at Merton, considered Lang's once reported remark of Bradley condescending, 'Oh, has he gone to Philosophy? I'm glad to hear he's been doing well'.[88] In fact, the suggestion of indifference may have been directed against Bradley's Hegelian metaphysics rather than against Bradley himself.

Honours came in another form in 1904. A hint that something was afoot was William Courtney's tribute to him in the *English Illustrated Magazine*, containing a list of publications by and about him that ran to four pages.[89] He learned soon after that he was to be made an honorary Doctor of Letters of Oxford. He humorously down-played it, saying, 'Lord, I am having an unlooked-for honour thrust on me, though not that of gilded spurs which the papers periodically inflict. Goodness knows I never asked anybody for it, but this wondrous thing is not to be mentioned to mortal. In fact, it is desperately humdrum.'[90] The annual celebration of Encaenia, when honorary degrees were presented, fell on 22 June. Among other honorands that day was his old adversary from across the ocean in the realism versus romance war, W. D. Howells. Lang looked forward to meeting him in person. He got in touch with Horace Howard Furness, an American Shakespeare scholar and a friend of Howells, predicting in comic style the likely outcome of meeting his rival face to face:

Your M. Howells and I are to be dubbed Doctors of Oxford, there will be a fight, if we meet, i'fegs. My weapon is a small sword. I suppose he does not fear the white arm? Parry in circle, riposte in seconde—no more Howells! 'I die,' he said, 'in harness, let my dirgie be sung by the monks of Dryburgh.' So he fell the great Apostle of realism, a converted man, the saints have him in their keeping.[91]

When the meeting took place, they buried the hatchet, and 'in the short space of their conversation', they discovered they both liked the tragi-comic blend of realism and romance in the novels of Leonard Merrick.[92]

Another unexpected honour was his election as Ford Lecturer in English History at Oxford for 1904–5. The annual series of six lectures was normally given in Hilary Term. Lang took the unusual step of delivering all his lectures over a two-week period in Michaelmas, at the beginning of the academic year. He stayed at the warden's house at Merton College. The fellows had elected Thomas Bowman as the new warden, the college's former Dean and Principal of Postmasters. Lang chose as the subject of his Ford Lectures 'Anglo-Scottish Relations'. They were to form the basis of a new life of John Knox, which he planned to publish in 1905, supposed at that time to be the 400th anniversary of Knox's birth. He had already indicated his dissatisfaction with Hume Brown's biography of Knox in volume two of his *History of Scotland*. He intended to go further in challenging the accuracy of Knox's *History of the Reformation in Scotland* and the view, promoted by Scottish historians, of Knox as saintly reformer. He saw sentimentality on both sides of the religious divide—Mary Queen of Scots revered as 'saintly being' by Catholics; the Knox party admitting 'scarcely a blemish' on their hero. Lang wrote, 'That

Knox was a great man; a disinterested man; in regard for the poor a truly Christian man; as a shepherd of Calvinistic souls a man fervent and considerate; of pure life; in friendship loyal; by jealousy untainted; in private character, genial and amiable, I am entirely convinced. In public and political life, he was much less admirable'. He argued that although Knox did much to advance permanent political union between Scotland and England, his resistance to religious union and his founding of a separate Church of Scotland fuelled religious intolerance and sowed the seeds of violence and needless bloodshed. His Knox was a lawbreaker and inciter of mob hatred and violence, and a false historian whose less admirable traits included his brutal utterances against women. This last point did not go unremarked on the book's appearance in the summer of 1905. That year the suffragettes adopted the motto 'Deeds not Words' and staged their first large demonstration in Hyde Park. The *Review of Reviews*, in an early notice of Lang's *John Knox and the Reformation*, labelled Knox the 'first vehement anti-woman's righter'.[93]

The latest volume of Lang's *History of Scotland* had already made him a target of abuse in Scotland, showing, as it did, that Presbyterian Covenanters were as guilty of terrible atrocities as any blamed on Royalist forces during the seventeenth-century religious wars. Accusations of bias and 'irresponsible animus' against Puritans and Presbyterians continued to plague him.[94] Thomas Drummond Wanliss, a Scottish Home Ruler and pamphleteer, castigated him for belittling his country and pandering to 'the lowest form of Oxford bigotry'.[95] Lang's response, 'My History Vindicated', pointed out that his purpose was to record fairly 'the actual course of events' in the light of 'public records and increased knowledge', and that his position on Scottish history in the period 1559–1689 was not approval of royal policy, but Scotland as 'a conflict of two intolerable forms of tyranny, royal and presbyterian.[96] His biography of Knox only fuelled the flames. Wanliss hit back with an even more abusive pamphlet, smearing him as 'The Muckrake in Scottish History' and 'Historiographer of the Scottish Gutter'.[97] Lang thought it 'good old actionable libel, at least if injurious falsehoods are actionable', although he had no intention of putting it to the test.[98] He lamented privately to Anna Hills, 'I continue to be persecuted by ignorant and mendacious Knoxites: how they do lie, to be sure! It riles Radicals most, I'm sure I don't know why. Probably Radicals have fewer legends, and don't like the legends they have to be proved mythical.[99] He allowed his feelings to spill out in his causerie in *Longman's* for August 1905: 'What the friends of freedom of conscience desired in Scotland was not merely leave to go to sermon, but to beat and bully persons who preferred to go to Mass'.[100]

That month, he wrote his 'At the Sign of the Ship' causerie for the October issue of *Longman's*, knowing it would be his last. The magazine was to cease publication. He had long known the end was coming. The magazine's selling point from the beginning was that it offered high-class fiction for sixpence, but many new rivals on the market offered the same, with the additional attraction of illustrations and photographs. In the August number, he exclaimed about the *Pall Mall Gazette*, one of their keenest rivals, 'How that magazine can be vended at sixpence, pictures and all, as it is, makes the despair of economists'.[101] His financial situation preoccupied him a great deal that year. His brother John, now 52, had returned from Australia and married their cousin, Jean Lang Blaikie, and the two hoped to make a living from writing. Lang advised them to avoid ambitious and time-consuming projects: 'If you reflect that I get £20.30 as the profits of 1000 pages of Scotch history ... —what I would make in a couple of hours or so by an article'.[102] He warned them of the poor returns for those who followed the writer's trade rather than a more financially profitable profession: 'In a long life, I have only been able to howk a livelihood by the pen point'.[103] He pressed home the message:

> If Nora died tomorrow, and I were unemployed, my finances would be, after all these thirty-five years, where they were when I was twenty-four. I have not made friends with Mammon of any sort and am of little use to other anti-mammonites.[104]

The cheques he received periodically from Haggard as his share of royalties of *The World's Desire*, small though they were, only highlighted the risible sum he had earned for 2,000 pages of Scottish history, and with it, 'abuse from every gutter snipe Presbyterian preacher thrown in'. He said to Haggard, 'Well, *vous l'avez voulu* ... nobody to blame but myself'.[105] He was pleased when John eventually found a niche in the literary trade with the Edinburgh publisher Edwin Jack, editing their 'Children's Hero Series'.

For some, the discontinuation of *Longman's* was 'cause for real sorrow'.[106] Others were happy to see Lang's predominance as a critic and reviewer suffer an eclipse. Even *Blackwood's*, to which he contributed regularly, had long grumbled about his influence on public taste, declaring it was 'not well to have a dictator of letters' whose personal prejudices and off-the cuff opinions could settle a book's fate.[107] Henry James had expressed a similar dissatisfaction privately in a letter to Stevenson, condemning Lang's use of 'his beautiful thin facility to write everything down to the lowest level of Philistine twaddle— the view of the old lady round the corner or the clever person at the dinner party'.[108] James regarded popular culture and the press as vulgar and of little merit. He had reason to be resentful of Lang, who failed to treat his work with the seriousness he had come to feel was his due. For Lang, who believed in the collective function of art in human evolution, the assumption that 'serious' or 'high' forms of art were intrinsically superior to popular or 'low' kinds was wayward and largely nonsense. He was wary, for instance, of efforts to establish a British Academy, suspecting that such a body would 'not exist in the interests of what the public calls literature, but in the interests of learning, research, science, style, and such trifles'.[109] He feared cultural divisions would only widen. He regretted the trend towards unnecessary obscurity of style among academics and exclaimed, 'Why not write like a man of this world?'[110] In his own books and articles, even on difficult subjects, he tried always to write with a clarity of style that everyone who cared for reading could understand. In a survey on the reading habits of the British Public he carried out in collaboration with 'X, A Working Man', he concluded that 'X's' description of working-class reading habits applied to every level of society: 'To be wearied at the day's end, and read nothing that demands more concentrated attention than an illustrated magazine, is only human nature'.[111] He felt keenly the loss of the 'Ship'. Having people, from every walk of life, wake up eager to read his regular columns in newspapers and periodicals, was not, to his mind, a worthless life.

11

The Last Cast

'The Last Cast', Lang's poem about autumn and ageing, resists Macbeth's plain-tive, 'My way of life/ Is fall'n into the sere, the yellow leaf' and affirms that life's hopeful dreams and ambitions survive into old age:

> Just one cast more! how many a year
>> Beside how many a pool and stream,
> Beneath the falling leaves and sere,
>> I've sighed, reeled up, and dreamed my dream![1]

The loss of his column in *Longman's* in October 1905 made him cast his net wider. A month after *Longman's* folded, he launched a new causerie under the flag, 'At the Sign of St Paul's' in Clement Shorter's *Illustrated London News*. He adopted a more personal tone, to engage the interest of the casual reader of a light entertainment paper. He also followed his own advice and accepted com-missions that paid the bills but took up little time—prefaces and introductions to works by others; a short life of *Sir Walter Scott*; *The Story of Joan of Arc* for John's 'Children's Hero Series'; and, reluctantly, a *History of English Literature* for Charles Longman, who was convinced there was money to be made from the expanding market in English studies. Lang told Mrs Hills, 'Why the young should be bored with horrid Early English books which they will never see, and which no human being can read with pleasure, I do not know. However, I pick out the very few plums in these half-cooked puddings'.[2] Another commis-sion, a biography of Sir George Mackenzie, undertaken at the request of his descendants, proved an equally uphill task. The Mackenzies clearly thought him the ideal choice of biographer of Charles II's Lord Advocate of Scotland, who had vigorously opposed 'Knoxian ideas and clerical pretentions', but Lang was resolved not to let 'sympathy with the Dr Jekyll' blind him to 'the Mr. Hyde' in Mackenzie, who kept his official and actual self in separate compartments.[3] Lang felt 'watched, corrected, harassed' by the family, who disliked the line he was taking[4]—that their distinguished ancestor had allowed the law to serve ruthless authority. He had no hesitation in turning down some requests. He could scarcely believe when a 'Yankee publisher' invited him to write a life of Oscar Wilde, telling Gosse, 'What a man that must be. I replied as became me'.[5]

Andrew Lang. John Sloan, Oxford University Press. © John Sloan (2023). DOI: 10.1093/oso/9780192866875.003.0011

The spirit of Wilde and the Decadent movement lingered on in literature and popular culture. A sensational best-selling novel, Guy Thorne's *When It Was Dark: A Story of a Great Conspiracy*, drew inspiration from Wilde's agnostic parables of Christ.[6] Thorne's success prompted Lang's satirical parody *When It Was Light: A Reply to When It Was Dark* 'By a Well-Known Author'. It marked his return to the ragging spirit of *Much Darker Days* in earlier years. In Thorne's *When It Was Dark*, an archaeological discovery of an inscription by Joseph of Arimathea disproving the Resurrection leads to social and moral anarchy in the world. In Lang's version, the matter-of-fact villagers of his fictional Broadmarsh in rural Norfolk simply disregard the sensational discovery as nonsense. Thorne (real name Ranger Gull) admired Marie Corelli, and his novel, like Corelli's pulpit fiction, provided readers with a morality tale, while simultaneously satisfying the taste for sin and sensationalism. Lang had already fired a satirical dart in 1902 at Corelli's moralizing novel, *Temporal Power*:

> ... each excellent king
> May have reason to sing
> To the praise of Miss Marie Corelli.[7]

In *When It Was Light*, he sent up the vogue among clergymen of drawing on popular fiction for their sermons. The vicar of his Broadmarsh lauds the moral lesson of Marie Corelli's anti-Decadent *Wormwood: A Drama of Paris*:

> 'Absinthe! 'Tis an abomination I have never even seen. But, of course, I have heard of it. And I have read the marvellous and striking romance of our great prose poetess, Marie Corelli, the female Carlyle of our day, entitled *Worm-wood*. Never do I remember having read a more powerful indictment of the terrible vice. Absinthe is indeed a drug, which as Miss Corelli fitly points out, absolves the soul.'[8]

Writing potboilers helped Lang fund his more serious writings. He authored four more in quick succession over the next few years. Three were ironic 'theological romances'—*The Sins of the Smart Set*, making fun of ambitious evangelical preachers in the Church of England; *The Fool Hath Said*, puncturing the attempted reconciliation of Christianity and science by the 'new Theology'; and *The Rector and the Rubric*, giving a comic turn to the war between High Church Ritualists and Low Church advocates of simple liturgy—a conflict which had faced Mandell Creighton as Bishop of London. *Mantrap Manor*, the last of his yellowbacks, was a burlesque crime shocker, in which a plucky English hero escapes the diabolical death-traps laid for him by the novel's devious villain, an American millionaire. Lang reflected ruefully on the fate of popular fiction in his humorous 'Ballade of Literary Fame':

> Suns beat on them; tempests downpour,
> On the chest without cover or locks,
> Where they lie by the bookseller's door—
> They are *all* in the Fourpenny Box![9]

There is a sense of closure, of saying his last on long-contested issues in many fields from this time on. He returned first to the Homeric Question, marshalling his arguments to prove that the epics were not the work of many hands over centuries, but single-author compositions depicting the life of a single, brief, late-Bronze Age feudal culture. He had already devoted a chapter on Homer and archaeology in his *Homer and the Epic*. *Homer and His Age* went much further in comparing Homer's descriptions of battle armour, burial rites, and domestic life with the evidence of recent archaeological discoveries. He challenged the idea that later poets carefully adhered to the customs, dress, and weapons of the past. He pointed out that only writers in modern times showed this 'archaeological refinement': poets in earlier times did not 'archaise'.[10] He took the existence of later forms of grammar and vocabulary in his stride, since only four, or at the most five books of the *Iliad* contained examples of lateness, and 'all the Books would be equally modified' if refashioned by later contributors.[11] He also questioned a common assumption that the *Odyssey* was a work of a milder, more civilized age, listing as examples of barbarism, 'the hanging of Penelope's maid and the abominable torture of Melanthius'.[12] The *Academy* praised the book as a 'fine piece of reconstructive criticism' which showed the value of close reading.[13] But voices from the enemy camp continued to accuse him of neglecting 'science' in favour of mere 'literary appreciation'.[14] He decided that *Homer and His Age* would not be his last word after all.

In the spring of 1907, he brought out the fourth and final volume of his *History of Scotland*. He ended his history with the defeat of the Stuart cause at Culloden. Nine years earlier, he had concluded *The Companions of Pickle* with a benign image of the descendants of the clans as more fortunate than 'their fathers in the old days that were not really golden'.[15] The close of his *History of Scotland* conveys a more sombre doubt about the policies of those whose zeal for profit and improvement resulted in the Clearances and in the passing away of a traditional culture and way of life:

> Within thirty years from 1745, the economic conditions of the Highland estates altered, values were many times multiplied, and the old tribal relations of the patriarch and his children having ceased to exist, some clans migrated, happily to themselves, to America; others waited to be evicted and see their places filled with sheep, grouse, and deer.[16]

Lang's view of the history, like that of most men of his generation, was informed by an evolutionary belief in the progress of civilization. Yet study and reflection had also led him to question more profoundly than many of his contemporaries the prevailing myth that our prehistoric ancestors, and so-called primitive or savage man, were intellectually inferior and less complex than ourselves. He observed, for instance, that Charles Darwin had found his first view of the Fuegian people of Tierra del Fuego as the lowest, least civilized of humans 'to be nonsense', as 'they learned English rapidly', and Darwin 'never could speak German'. Lang concluded that the Fuegian people had 'as good brains as me'.[17] Anthropology, in this respect, had also altered his sense of his country's past. Responding with irony to Edward Clodd's evolutionary assumptions, he declared, 'You believe in progress, do you? I'd rather believe in wraiths. There is only a kind of pendulum. The Highlands were infinitely happier before 1745, than they will be till savagery returns—and infinitely better'.[18]

There was some dissatisfaction with his history among reviewers. They accused him of treating Jacobitism too much as a 'story',[19] and of neglecting Scotland's progress as a modern, wealth-producing nation following Union with England.[20] Lang left it to others 'to tell the story of ... the very gradual harmonising of Scotland and England'.[21] There are, in fact, hints in his history of a sense of national loss at Scotland's surrender of her legislative independence. Commenting on the mood in Scotland after the defeat of the first Jacobite uprising of 1715, he wrote, 'The majority of Scots, at this time, while relieved of Popery and the Pretender, writhed under a sense of being citizens of a conquered country—their laws trampled on; their counsels rejected; their friends ruined and exiled'.[22] He gave fuller voice to that feeling in his contribution to *The Union of 1707*, a collection of essays by different hands, to coincide with the 200th anniversary of the Union of the Crowns. He argued that religion and the need to avoid further wars, not economic considerations, 'made Union inevitable': 'Nobody in Scotland thought the Union a delightful marriage of the kingdoms, but beneath all their hostile sentiments men felt that the Union was the least evil of the choices before them'.[23]

Lang as a historian eventually lost out to Hume Brown in popularity and influence. Hume Brown's tale of Scotland in partnership with England, 'making the United Kingdom great and powerful', better satisfied the mood of the nation in the late nineteenth and early twentieth centuries.[24] The present writer, at school on Deeside in the early sixties, remembers Hume Brown's *A Short History of Scotland* as the standard work on the subject in the lower forms. Not until the late 1960s and early 1970s was Hume Brown eventually superseded by histories of modern Scotland which questioned the cultural and economic benefits of Union and Empire,[25] an issue now again at the centre of political life in the United Kingdom in a way that Lang and Hume Brown could never have envisaged.

Lang and Nora chose Banchory on the Royal Route (now Royal Deeside) that summer. They stayed at Tor-na-Coille, a converted country house which still sits today on a hillside of pine trees. They spoke little to the other guests, made up mainly of family members of those being treated for tuberculosis at Nordrach Sanitorium, newly built on the edge of the village, the first such sanitorium in Scotland. Their hopes for peace and relaxation received a blow with the arrival of alarming news from Clifton. Nora's unmarried sister Annie had long been plagued with 'horrible delusions'.[26] There had been unpleasant scenes.[27] At times Lang wished Clifton 'were at the bottom of the sea'.[28] He loved Annie, but he suspected her hysteria was 'really a deep-rooted affectation' and suggested that hypnotism might be her only chance of a normal life.[29] The distress was also a sad reminder of T. W., who had suffered mentally. Nora's mother, who had died when Nora was 13, had been afflicted by the same 'terrible misfortune'.[30] An added distress was news that his brother Pat had suffered a stroke.[31] Pat had inherited estates at Lara and Titanga on his father-in-law's death and seemed until then the one member of the family Lang thought the most settled and fortunate in life. Helen, now resident in Menton and almost entirely dependent on a small quarterly allowance, was often agitated about money or social status. Lang lost patience when she started to fret that their mother's old nurse, Miss Sibbald, a distant kinswoman, may have been of mixed descent. He wrote to John in exasperation:

> Nobody in this country cares, and what Nell has to fuss about, or why all the fusses I can't imagine. Miss Sibbald might descend from an Octoroon herself, but how does that affect a much older generation? For my part I would not

care if my grandmother had been a member of an Australian tribe, the whole thing is too silly.[32]

Bill, with his fondness for the track, never had enough money. He still practised as a doctor at Corowa and wrote a regular monthly column on horse-racing. He continued, too, to write fiction. Lang thought his novel, *The Thunder of the Hooves*, an improvement on his early efforts, although the sentimental use of family history grated on him. Particularly uncomfortable was the account of the death of the hero's mother, and the role of 'old Nancy, the faithful domestic who had been his nurse':

> When Mrs Elliott was dying after an operation, she had asked Nancy, with her last breath, to remain always and look after her little son. So she remained ... a mother, a friend, a monitor, and yet a faithful servant to her dear son.

On being asked to comment on an early draft, Lang complained to John, 'The rot about the old sinner and "my mother" would sicken a Frenchman.'[33]

At Oxford, in October 1907, he gave a lecture in honour of Tylor's 75th birthday. He paid tribute to Tylor's energy and example as Keeper of the University Museum, and for his part in the establishment of a School of Anthropology in the university. But in the Oxford manner of saying frankly what one thinks to friends, he expressed disappointment at Tylor's avoidance of controversy, particularly in the field of Australian ethnography, and criticized the university for having done little for anthropology compared to 'how much Cambridge had done and is doing'. There was, he told his audience, no incentive for Oxford undergraduates to take up the new science: 'There's no money in it'.[34] Robert Marett, who was tipped to succeed Tylor, walked back with him to Merton after dinner that evening. On their arrival at Merton Lodge, Lang remarked, 'If I could have made a living out of it, I might have been a great anthropologist', before disappearing into the lodge-door that the porter had just opened.[35]

In response to Lang's criticisms, Marett, with the help of Gilbert Murray, immediately set about planning a series of lectures by specialists on the subject of 'Anthropology and the Classics'. Lang, at Murray's suggestion, was invited to speak on 'Homer and Anthropology'. He took up the offer eagerly: 'Marett told me your suggestion which would suit me excellently, if fate permit me to lecture'. Murray's *The Rise of the Greek Epic*, just out, made clear his adherence to the separatist theory of the epics as 'traditional' books, expanded, like the Pentateuch, by succeeding generations, with the gradual expurgation of the ugly and disgusting elements of savage story. Lang had come to very different conclusions about the absence of savage survivals in Homer's epics: they were, in his view, works of a prehistoric age of loosely feudal values, written for an aristocratic audience with a taste for purity and noble ideals. This, not bowdlerization, was the reason one did not find harlots in Homer: 'Homer was like Scott, he could not draw that sort of lady'.[36] He relished the prospect of crossing swords with Murray again.

In the early months of 1908, he again took up the cause of Joan of Arc, when Anatole France published a two-volume *Life of Jeanne d'Arc* which portrayed her as a 'perpetually hallucinated' victim of hysteria, manipulated by string-pulling clerics. The biography was especially contentious as the Congregation of Rites in Rome was reaching the end of its examination of the case for her beatification. Lang's counterblast, *The Maid of France*, written in the space of three or four months, corrected Anatole France's numerous errors of fact, and argued from the historical evidence that the mystery of Joan of Arc was not to be explained away by modern-day scepticism or mockery. He told the French scholar J.J. Jusserand, 'She was not what a vain Anatole France supposes. He did not verify his references'.[37] There was consensus among both French and English critics that he had greater knowledge than his French counterpart of fifteenth-century French texts, a fact acknowledged by Anatole France in the Preface to his revised English edition of his book, in which he thanked Lang for helping him to correct errors. Lang said that writing on Joan of Arc took 'the taste of Mackenzie out of my mouth'.[38]

He completed the book in August at a 'windswept and waterlogged' Banchory.[39] From there they went as guests of Lord Strathmore to spend a week at Glamis Castle, to be followed by a visit to Ella Christie, the intrepid Victorian lady-traveller, who had created a Japanese-style garden on her estate at Cowden in Perthshire. Lang had known her and her sister Alice (now Mrs King Stewart) when they were small girls, living a few doors down from the Sellars' family home in Edinburgh.[40] Nora wrote to Ella from Glamis to ask if they could bring forward their visit to Cowden, as her husband had a 'very bad cold' and 'a medieval castle is hardly the place for him', especially so since he was 'not fit for a party of 24—of whom 18 are lively young people', with the girls 'waltzing together at 10 a.m.'.[41] Lang's letter to Anna Hills a week later suggests that it may have been Nora who wanted to escape Glamis:

We have just returned from Glamis, where we had lovely weather with a cricket team in the house, and 'to everyman a damsel or two', very pretty damsels. The ghosts lay low ... The little girl offered us a lovely Persian kitten, but Nora can't bear having one, as they die, sooner or later. I'd risk it.[42]

The 'little girl' who offered the kitten was Elizabeth Bowes-Lyon, Lord Strath-more's youngest daughter, later wife of George VI, and grandmother of the present King. That Christmas, Nora dedicated *The Book of Princes and Princesses* to her—the first of the coloured fairy books to have Nora's name on the cover. The book gave new direction to the series in its choice of 'true stories', with tales of the childhood of real figures from history. In his Preface for the book, Lang humorously reminded his young readers of the advantages of being born to ordinary parents, so being spared the 'many uncomfortable risks of all poor royal children'.[43]

Lang finished preparing his Oxford lecture on 'Homer and Anthropology' at Carnoch House, Glencoe, on 23 September. He wrote from there to Murray, 'I have left you out of the memorial ... Don't leave me out if you can deal me any shrewd blows'.[44] Murray took him at his word. In his opening lecture in October, Murray began by saying that Andrew Lang seemed 'not quite to have understood' his *Rise of the Greek Epic*, and that the 'uglier and un-cleaner elements' of 'primitive pre-Hellenic habits of thought' were gradually removed from the *Iliad* and the *Odyssey* and not from other saga material because the two poems were selected at some early time for public recitation. Lang, with canny diplomacy for his Oxford lecture, chose as the target of attack not Murray, but A. V. Verrall, a Cambridge classicist, whose theory that the Homeric epics were shaped by learned Athenians from a 'nebulous mass of old poets' and bowdlerized for educational purposes, bore some similarity to Murray's theory.[45] The lectures attracted large audiences, Lang and Murray's known rivalry giving zest to the series. The *Athenaeum* described Lang as having managed 'to strike fire out of a subject which on his own showing somewhat resembles the snakes of Ireland'.[46]

There was further cause for sadness in the early months of 1909. They received news in April of Pat's death, not through family channels, but from Pat's business partners, the wool merchants Sanderson and Murray of Galashiels. It was a 'horrid shock'.[47] Lang had imagined Pat to be recovered and enjoying life 'in a quiet way' since his stroke eighteen months ago. He confided to Anna Hills:

Both he and I are older than we had any hereditary right to be. It was a great distress to me because he had been better and, though not himself, had a good deal of simple pleasure in evidence. But nobody could endure another shock without sinking below a level at which existence is not worth having, and from that he has escaped. I do not wish it otherwise in my own case.[48]

A month later Anna Hills was dead. He struggled for words in answering Jack's letter: 'I need not tell you how shocked and grieved we are by this unlooked-for calamity, and how much we feel for you all. We have lost the kindest of friends, and of all to whom she was kind none owed more to her than myself'.[49]

Lang's criticism of the poor funding of anthropology at Oxford continued to have an effect. Marett and his Oxford colleagues joined their Cambridge counterparts in helping to raise funds for a Cambridge-led expedition to Western Australia. The aim was to study the social organization and religious beliefs of remote Aboriginal tribes. The planned expedition, to be led by Alfred Radcliffe-Brown, a young Cambridge scholar, was a response in part to the findings of Daisy Bates, an Irish-born journalist turned welfare-worker among the Aborigines. Her paper on the marriage laws and customs of the West Australian Aborigines, containing details about female puberty, menstruation, and sexual habits, attracted widespread interest.[50] She was writing a book on the subject for the Western Australian government, and, through anthropological contacts, began sending the typescript chapter by chapter to Lang for comment. She was invited to join the expedition, though it was soon evident that she and Radcliffe-Brown would not get on—she, despite her humble origins, being snobbishly Tory; he, a Cambridge man, socialist in sympathy. Lang had a letter from her describing Radcliffe-Brown as 'no gentleman, I'm sure'.[51] Lang's marginal comments on her book ranged from mildly critical, 'You skip without a break to a new subject', to a blunt, 'Bosh—omit!'[52] He thought the manuscript too disjointed and repetitive for publication in its present form, but he encouraged her to revise it, and sent the chapter on totemism to Radcliffe-Brown before the expedition set out, for him to use in his report. He promised the rest would follow, saying, 'Scissors are needed for that vast and wandering work'.[53] Radcliffe-Brown showed her Lang's letter, and she wrote Lang an angry letter. He apologized to her 'that anything I have said in a letter to Mr. Brown annoyed you ... I shall never again write to Mr. Brown'. But he added, '*He* would be gratified by what *you* wrote about *him*'.[54]

Lang had reached a standoff in his disputes with Frazer on the origins of religion. Under Clodd's Presidency, the Rational Press Association, publisher of scientific reprints mainly by agnostic or atheistic authors, reissued a series of his essays on *The Origins of Religion*. It was a source of amusement in Frazer's circle to see Lang published by the freethinking Rational Press Association, given his criticisms of Frazer for being anti-religious.[55] In fact, in 'Theories of the Origin of Religion', written especially for the collection, Lang made clear that he was not in the camp of the irreligious: 'I am a rationalist about the rationalism of most of my masters and teachers, and deserve to be an outcast from the church anthropological of Mr. Tylor, Mr. Huxley, Mr. Herbert Spencer, Sir Alfred Lyell, and Mr. Grant Allen. But I have summarized the facts on which my opinion is based, and, for the rest, have gone where the *logos* led me'.[56]

The situation heated up again in 1910 when Frazer published his encyclopaedic four-volume study, *Totemism and Exogamy*. Frazer had abandoned his two previously held theories: the first, that totemism originated in the ritual preservation of a person's soul in the totem plant or animal during initiation; the second, that it was associated with the tribal organization of the food supply. Lang thought he detected a glaring fallacy in Frazer's new 'conceptual theory'. The ruling idea of Frazer's 'conceptual theory' was that totemism was originally a non-hereditary, non-exogamous identification of the individual with the spirit of an animal or living thing at birth by primitive people ignorant of the male role in procreation. The problem was he also conjectured that in primitive tribes with male descent, the exogamous division was made to prevent copulation of fathers with daughters as too consanguine, thus recognizing fatherhood, and the male's part in procreation. Lang exclaimed, 'What price Cambridge logic'.[57] Lang remained clear in his mind about the primacy of hereditary, exogamous totemism, in relation to which Frazer's individual totemism was 'very late', and 'belief in spiritual impregnation ... a comparatively tardy fruit of philosophy'.[58] Through Clodd, he tried to alert Frazer to fallacies in his new theory after reading Frazer's statements ahead of the book's publication.[59] Frazer's response was to tell Clodd not to show him any more of Lang's letters, prompting Lang's sardonic comment, 'It is a useful thing for a scientific Johnny to be thin-skinned, and to shut up like an oyster instead of answering objections'.[60]

Lang received some support in his objections. Clodd told Frazer frankly he thought Andrew Lang's theory of hereditary, exogamous totemism was 'more satisfactory than others'.[61] Gilbert Murray, reviewing *Totemism and Exogamy*, wished Frazer 'had dealt more fully' with some of Andrew Lang's criticisms.[62] Murray's praise for Frazer's 'candour and modesty' in abandoning his earlier theories of totemism reads like a tactful way of suggesting that Frazer might have to consign his new theory of individualistic 'conceptual totemism' to the same fate. He pointed out that 'the separation-out of the individual, so as to possess qualities and beliefs of his own' came 'much later than the tribe' and was 'one of the regular processes of civilisation'.

Having concluded that the future of the subject no longer rested on his disputes with Frazer, Lang looked to a new, enterprising adversary in a young, Russian-born American, Alexander Goldenweiser. Goldenweiser objected to all their theories—Lang's, Frazer's, Durkheims's—for reducing the varieties of totemism in different parts of the world at different times to a single social or psychological origin, whether that be practical exogamy, the soubriquet hypothesis, or superstitious or religious descent. He commented drily, 'I am sure that Lang, who is such an adept at following the *logos*, could without much effort construct a theory of the totem with any one of these elements to start with'.[63] Taking direction from Franz Boas, his teacher, Goldenweiser adopted a relativistic approach to totems as a richly varied tendency of social groups 'to become associated with objects and symbols of emotional value'. Lang had always acknowledged the problems of a general theory of totemism—the mistake in assuming the same social evolution everywhere, and the complication of there being a rich diversity of personal, sexual, tribal, as well as hereditary totems.[64] But in *Method in the Study of Totemism*, and in his 'discussion and correspondence' following its publication, he argued that the onus fell on Goldenweiser to explain the 'amazing resemblances' of totemic organization around the world, rather than on himself to account for differences.[65] The book was Lang's last published word on the subject in his lifetime. He worked privately on a book that would bring up to date all recent facts and theories, but he felt there was no longer a public for it, and when the book was finished, he stored the manuscript away among his papers, with a message attached to be read after his death.

For a man born in an age of coach travel and slow trains, technology was rapidly changing everyday life in surprising ways. The death of Edward VII in May 1910 felt like the end of an era. The new King George V, an aircraft enthusiast, augured a new world. The *Illustrated London News*, for which Lang still wrote his 'At the Sign of St Paul's' column, now featured photographs of aeroplanes and Zeppelin airships. Lang had not the slightest desire to go up in one. Their friend Ellie Christie had a motor car, but it had taken a great deal of persuasion to get him into it.[66] He preferred the old lamps and candles to the electric light they had installed at Marloes Road, even though he admitted grudgingly that electric light was 'cooler and less dusty'.[67] He refused to have a telephone.

Technological themes were also finding their way into literature. The flying machine he had introduced in *The Mark of Cain* was nothing to the technological extravagances of H. G. Wells' scientific romances. Lang felt out of sympathy with the brashness of the new breed of literary man. Frank Harris' *The Man Shakespeare and His Tragic Life-Story* appalled him. He told Gosse, 'Great cheek and madness must be near allied ... For blind and naked ignorance [Harris] runs in G. B. Shaw pretty close'.[68] His distaste for Gosse's own habit of self-advertisement had led to a cooling in their friendship. Gosse did not send him a copy of his autobiography, *Father and Son*, prompting Lang to ask Matthews, 'Have you read "Father and Son"? I only saw it lying about at a tea party'.[69] Lang tried to resist Gosse's efforts to conscript him to a new 'Academic Committee of English Letters' under the aegis of the Royal Society of Literature: 'You are very kind, but please tell me why much better men than me are left out? Won't they come in? I don't like to stand where one of them should be'. Eventually he gave in: 'All right, I am at your disposal. But nobody has told me what it is all about, and where the use of it comes in. As to some of the names, the mystery is more than Eleusinian'.[70]

He accepted more readily an invitation from Herbert Warren, President of Magdalen College, to a dinner in honour of Theodore Roosevelt, who was to give the 1910 Romanes Lecture on 7 June. Roosevelt had asked especially that Lang be invited. Lang travelled to Oxford at the end of May to spend a few days with Robert Bridges at Chilswell, outside Oxford, on the edge of Boar's Hill, an out-of-way spot even today. He told Murray, whom he had arranged to meet in Oxford before the Romanes Lecture, 'It is almost impossible to leave this place, the communications being difficult'.[71] Both he and Murray were planning a return to Homer territory. Oxford University Press had given Murray the go-ahead for a new edition of *The Rise of the Greek Epic*. Charles Longman preferred Lang 'to say his last say' in a new book. Lang did too: there was 'so much new to say'.[72]

He succeeded eventually in arranging for a carriage to take him back to Oxford in time for Roosevelt's lecture on 'Biological analogies in History' at the Sheldonian Theatre. Though Roosevelt did not mention him by name, there was a tacit tribute to him in Roosevelt's observation that 'the anthropologist and historian of to-day' have shown how terms such as Aryan, Teuton, and Celt, once held 'ethnologically sacred', mean 'almost nothing', and 'how artificial most great nationalities are'.[73] Lang sat next to Roosevelt at dinner and found the ex-President 'brilliantly clever and amusing in private'.[74] Warren recalled that Lang was 'in very good form'.[75] Lang stayed on in Oxford to act as external examiner of an anthropological thesis on 'The Fairy Folk of Celtic Counties', submitted by Walter Evans Wentz, who later went on to become a Tibetan scholar. The internal examiner was the Welsh scholar, Sir John Rhys, the Principal of Jesus College, who, forty years earlier, as plain John Rees, had been a fellow with Lang at Merton College. After the *viva* exam, Lang stayed overnight in college. He reported afterwards to Murray that between writing up his examiner's report at midnight and 'having a lordly bedroom *over the kitchen*' he passed 'a strange night'.[76]

He and Nora had an enjoyable and restful time with Ella Christie at Cowden that summer. From Cowden they went as guests of Lord Lorne to Inveraray Castle, where they were surrounded by 'a lot of pretty and clever girls and young men'.[77] Nora lay awake coughing all night. Lang had a cold. He wrote to Ella Christie from the library:

> I *ought* to be seeing the short, kilted phantasm who carries books, for I am alone in the library, in the dim and misty light of two tapers, but I don't think he will show up. What clever young people the new generation here are, it is quite surprising to an aged literary gent. They can read *Tono Bungay* and *Joseph Vance*. But I still prefer Miss Austen.[78]

The World of Homer, his final bow, came out that autumn. Fresh archaeological evidence, particularly the striking discovery of Cretan seals showing Minoan warriors wearing full body armour, considerably strengthened his case against the claim that references to the corslet were unconsciously interpolated into the ancient lays and sagas by later poets. He took heart from the growing support for his unitary view of the epics. The American classicist and Biblical scholar John Adams Scott applauded his achievement in turning the tide of Homeric scholarship. Scott observed that when Lang wrote his first book, he was 'well-nigh alone in his belief in the unity of Homeric authorship, but times have changed' and 'what was then only heresy may now be considered orthodox belief'.[79] Murray conceded that 'on points of pure archaeology', his 'famous and inveterate foe, Mr. Andrew Lang' had shown convincingly that 'phase after phase' of Homer's world had almost nothing in it that corresponded with what was known of the post-Mycenaean period from roughly the tenth to the eighth century BC.[80] But he interpreted the facts differently. Lang believed the epics to be single-author poems of a very brief, local, pure 'Achaean' age of around 1,000 BC; Murray insisted that the unity of the poems was the achievement of rhapsodes (literally 'singers of stitched lays') and adaptors around the time of Pisistratus in the sixth and fifth century BC. Lang, who was looking into the Shakespeare Question, teased Murray that he was like one of those who believed that Francis Bacon was the author of Shakespeare's plays: 'I am attending to Baconians; it is very like the Homeric Question. Bacon is Pisastratus'.[81] Homer, in Lang's unshaken view, was a poet as 'alone, aloof, sublime' as Shakespeare.

In January 1911, Lang joined Conan Doyle, Haggard, Clement Shorter, and others in a campaign to raise money for Dickens' descendants. The proposed Copyright Act that year was to extend the period of copyright to fifty years after an author's death. But as Dickens had died in 1870, his descendants, including nine granddaughters in very poor circumstances, would not benefit from the change. The idea, initiated by the *Strand* magazine, was to issue a penny Dickens Stamp in 1912, the centenary of Dickens' birth, for people to stick in their books, like bookplates. All the money collected would go to the descendants. Lang was tireless in writing to newspaper editors to promote the scheme.[82]

That same month, he received touching proof of Murray's friendship when Murray raised the flag on his behalf for the Oxford Professorship of Poetry, which came up for election that year. Lang felt uneasy about it:

> It is really most kind of you to take the trouble about me and the Poetry chair. This is the third or fourth time of asking, and they were all too late. I do hate being the object of canvassing, and these are not haunts for you to go ... A man who hath in one week been made President of the S.P.R. and a member of the Swedish Academy of Science has more than his share of glory.[83]

Herbert Warren of Magdalen College had already declared his candidature. The response from Merton College to Murray's proposal was initially lukewarm. Murray heard back that the warden, Thomas Bowman, 'would nominate if Warren were the sole alternative—but won't go beyond that. Most of us, I fancy, would go as far as that.'[84] Within days, however, Murray received backers from Merton and beyond, including William Courthope, a previous holder of the post, and Robert Bridges, who was confident that Strachan-Davidson, the Master of Balliol, would join in supporting Lang.[85] Bowman declared he would add his name to the list on condition that Lang 'has specifically agreed to stand'.[86] Lang hedged:

> I am in a strait. If there is no Latin prose to be written by the Professor of Poetry, I would like the job, and fire off lectures on the lines of comparative literature: a subject always trotting into my head. But if there is only an off chance of getting the chair, I would detest your wasting your time over the thing. So please do as you think best.[87]

His proposal to 'fire off lectures' on comparative literature, if elected, was typical of a readiness he had always shown to extend and challenge disciplinary boundaries and encourage intercultural understanding. In Oxford at that time comparative literature was regarded as a non-subject and remained so until very recent times. Lang sent Murray an anxious telegram at 10.45 the following morning from St Andrews. It reached Murray's home in Woodstock Road, Oxford, less than an hour later: 'If I have not been nominated, please let my name remain outside. Am writing, Lang'. Lang explained his reasons in the letter that followed:

> When I woke today my conscience pressed it on me that my voice is very unfit for oratory and is apt to desert me. This seems more than a strong reason for giving you no more trouble. I need not say how very highly I value your kindness to a Homeric heretic like me. I have sent a telegram.[88]

Charles Longman was disappointed. He planned to issue a single volume Pocket Library edition of *Ballads in Blue China* and *Rhymes à la Mode*, with some poems from *Grass of Parnassus*.[89] He told Lang regretfully, 'I was up at Oxford last weekend, and from what I heard I believe you could have been Professor of Poetry if you would have stated, easily enough'.[90]

Lang had already agreed to become President of the SPR. On being invited by Oliver Lodge, he joked, 'Can't you get a man with a reputation to lose?'[91] When he learned just days later he was to be made a member of the Swedish Academy of Letters, he wrote to tell Lodge that he had a 'small, recently acquired reputation' to protect after all.[92] In accepting the Presidency of the SPR, he hoped to persuade the members to extend their psychical research to the field of cultural anthropology. In his Presidential Address, he laid stress on the 'historical, folk-lore and anthropological side of the subject' and how the 'same sort of beliefs and delusions' that the society investigated had been 'current for hundreds of years' and were 'world-wide'.[93]

The beginning of his presidency coincided with the controversial publication of a book, *An Adventure*, by 'Elizabeth Morison' and 'Charlotte Lamont', who claimed to have seen the ghosts of Marie Antoinette and members of her court on a visit to the Petit Trianon in the grounds of Versailles ten years earlier. It was no secret in Oxford that 'Elizabeth Morison' was, in fact, Charlotte Moberley, Principal of St Hugh's Hall for women, and 'Charlotte Lamont', Eleanor Jourdain, her vice-principal. The SPR had discounted their report at the time as unworthy of investigation. Their book set out to discredit the society's original verdict. Their publisher sent a copy of the book to the SPR, and the society's sceptical investigator, Alice Johnson, agreed reluctantly to re-examine the case. Lang found himself dragged into the quarrel when Charlotte Moberly objected to 'extremely disagreeable' interviews with Alice Johnson, and to a review of their book in the society's *Proceedings*, which dismissed their reported paranormal experience as most likely an illusion brought on by heat and fatigue and embellished unconsciously over time by pseudo-reminiscences.[94]

Lang, forced to arbitrate, largely agreed with Alice Johnson's report:

> Whether they had *no* déjeûner, or whether they had a pint of white wine, it was a sleepy afternoon, and my own capacity for getting lost in a house or a wood makes me feel that *they* got lost, and, later on other occasions saw everything smaller and clearer and different from those sleepy August views ... once lost, everything is glamour.[95]

Even so, he was intrigued by its similarities to other historic cases of retrocognition and arranged a meeting to 'go over the ground' with them again.[96] Crucially, he discovered that the women's original accounts, written independently not long after the incident, corresponded in all essentials with their later published account, and appeared not to have been added to by later research. He knew, however, that sceptics would argue that the women must have known, but had forgotten they ever knew, many of the curious period details. He prepared a private report for the SPR and sent the women a typed copy, 'which, of course', he wrote, 'is not for publication, but merely to tease Miss Johnson'.[97] He succeeded in winning the women's trust. Charlotte Moberly thanked him for his 'kindness in writing and in letting us see what you have written. It is a shock to think that there are people who think us so dreadfully dishonest'.[98] He reassured her, 'I do not think that the S.P.R. lady thinks you more wicked than the rest of mankind when they try to remember anything of this sort or indeed of any sort. She generally thinks all the stories which I send to her on the same grounds are the illusiveness of memory'.[99] Alice Johnson refused to change her mind. She firmly rejected the 'supposed apparition' of the Trianon case on the grounds that the so-called 'ghosts' had not behaved 'in some way that a real person could not'.[100] Lang advised Charlotte Moberly that, if he were her and wanted to appeal against the SPR findings, he would merely send copies of their first written accounts of the incident; but he warned, 'Perhaps it may not be worthwhile to do anything'.[101]

Scepticism did not damage either the sales or popularity of *An Adventure*, which went through many editions and spawned numerous theories. Explanations, in recent times, have ranged from the psycho-sexual theory of repressed lesbian feelings between the women as the trigger of their shared fantasy,[102] to a historical focus on the religious atmosphere of Anglican Oxford at that time, and the blurring of orthodox Christian faith and occult beliefs.[103] One unexplored fact is the curious correspondence between *An Adventure* and the Oxford Newdigate prize poem on 'Marie Antoinette' written and recited by Charlotte Moberly's brother Robert at the Sheldonian Theatre in Oxford in June 1867, when she was 21, and he a year older. Notably, it was Robert who, on hearing his sister's account, suggested that the women may have seen the Queen on 10 August 1792, the day armed revolutionaries stormed the Tuileries Palace, and, indeed, there are parallels between Robert Moberly's recreation in his youthful poem of the Queen's sense of doom on the eve of the Reign of Terror, her 'innocent breast/Big with a strange foreboding and unrest',[104] and the women's belief in their paranormal, retrocognitive participation in the Queen's feelings of being 'shut in and oppressed' on that fateful day. As for Lang, his hope of converting the SPR to the historical and anthropological side of the subject, was disappointed. Psychical research, he concluded with regret, 'had no use for savages who could not be cross-examined at 20 Hanover, or by emissaries from that scientific centre'.[105]

In the summer of 1911, he began to ail both physically and mentally. Herbert Warren saw him at the Varsity Match at Lord's Cricket Ground in July, look-ing 'very much aged and blind'.[106] He had effectively lost the use of one eye; his other eye distorted things. It was the same affliction which had troubled his father in the year before his death. That summer, the hottest on record, the major ports and railways were brought to a halt. In Liverpool, on 13 August, which became known as 'Bloody Sunday', police and soldiers broke up a mass demonstration of striking transport workers that left over 350 injured. Just a week later, six men died during violent clashes between railways workers and troops in South Wales. Charles Longman was alarmed by Lang's 'strange depression' at the newspaper reports of strikes and social unrest—something which normally did not unsettle his natural equanimity. To take his mind off things, Longman suggested they bring out a fifth edition of *The Mystery of Mary Stuart*. Lang resisted. He had begun to doubt his original conclusions and suspected that Mary Stuart may have written the incriminating letters after all. He told Hay Fleming, 'I might let it stand with a long appendix and intro-duction, but that would be tiresome work for £0.0.0 ... So, I have suggested to my pals the publishers, to let it drop'.[107] Haggard, on Longman's prompt-ing, asked Lang to collaborate with him on a sequel to *She*. Haggard put it to him, '*The World's Desire* about which you were rather melancholy, has stood the test of time fairly well and many people still like it'. Lang again declined: '*She* I think is not easily raised again unless she drops her veil for some prehis-toric admirer. The W. D. took in despite my ill-omened name; I brought you worse luck than you would have had alone'.[108] At Tor-na-Coille that August, the sweltering heat drove him to frenzy, and he was in and out of bed all night, which kept Nora awake.[109]

Instead of taking a much-needed rest, he arranged to give a series of six lectures at Glasgow University in October and November on 'The Making of Scotland Presbyterian'. They would be his final, long-postponed answer to those in Scotland who had accused him of publishing lies about John Knox and the Reformation. He intended to dispute the cherished myth of the Scottish Covenanters as heroic precursors of constitutional liberty and democratic values in Great Britain as a whole and to show that, far from the wealth of the Old Church being used by the Reformers for the education and relief of the poor, in many places education was 'despoiled' and the 'poor oppressed'.[110] He was in St Andrews for the St Andrews University Quincentenary Festival in September. He attended a procession round the town headed by the band of the Scots Guards to a service in the Church of Holy Trinity on the morning of Wednesday 13 September, earning a rebuke from Herbert Maxwell for wearing a 'suit of mustard coloured tweed, over which he had donned a shabby gown of black bombazine and a red hood all awry'.[111] He contributed his reminiscences of his student days, 'Religio Loci', to *Votiva Tabella*, a memorial volume of the Quincentenary, which concluded with his poem, 'Almae Matres'.[112]

A month later, on Monday 23 October, he wrote to Ella Christie, 'Tomorrow I am to begin lecturing at Glasgow, at 8.30, and so on for Three Tuesdays and Three Fridays ... Well, I have writ the lectures, and the balance sheet of the Covenant shows an appalling deficit'.[113] He began his first lecture by saying he did not feel at all certain that the Reformation had any particular effect on the national character of Scotland, and that Scotland's 'hardy, thrifty, venturesome, enquiring, and extremely independent people' had been formed *before*, not *by* the Reformation.[114] He meant to go on to show that the high ideals of the Book of Discipline were rejected by the politicians, and that education was 'despoiled' and the poor oppressed. There was a large group of Presbyterian clergymen at his first lecture, but they did not come back. Ella Christie, who attended the second lecture, remembered his wonderful 'living pictures' of John Knox's mother-in-law, and of Mary of Guise under attack from 'the Presbyterian divines'.[115] He had planned to stay between lectures with Mrs Alice King Stewart at Murdostoun Castle just outside Glasgow, but bad weather and 'a face swollen like a turnip' forced him to abandon the idea.[116] By the end, the lectures had left him 'a wreck'.[117]

That winter at St Andrews, he was in poor health and rarely went out, with Nora 'not much to boast about either'.[118] He completed his *History of English Literature from Beowulf to Swinburne*. Writing it had not lessened his feeling that readers were 'born to be so' and did not need to be 'allured'. One surprising 'plum' in Early English Poetry had been Layamon's *Brut*, whose similes were 'as good as Homer's'.[119] In his roll call of the leading Victorian novelists, he paid tribute to Robert Louis Stevenson as 'a man of genius' and a 'master of romance' whose place in literature he considered to be in little doubt. To his mind, Stevenson had 'practically revived in England the historical novel'.[120] His recently completed Introduction to the Swanston edition of *The Works of Robert Louis Stevenson* had taken his thoughts back to the letter from Stevenson before his death, 'full of apprehension' about living on, a burden to others. His own mood had taken the same turn. He wrote candidly to his sister-in-law Jean, who was recovering from a near fatal illness:

> 'You have grit,' as the Yankees also say. When you were so ill, I did not think so much of you—for to be quit of this life is far better—but of poor old John. I have been with him when we were very young, and our mother had a horrible operation, and I knew what he felt. I did, if we might speak of such things, help him a little bit ... So many things come upon this worn pen.[121]

One morning in January he saw his family's legendary death-omen. He told readers of his column in the *Illustrated London News*: 'A black cat, obviously hallucinatory, ran across my study at 10 a.m.'.[122] Medically, a black shape appearing and seeming to move and disappear across the room is often a symptom of macular degeneration. He gave his last public talk in St Andrews on 12 February—a lecture on Joan of Arc to the University Society.[123] He tried again without success to step away from any involvement in the Academic Committee of the Royal Society of Literature, but Gosse refused to take no for an answer. Lang submitted, 'Just as you please. I shall sit tight. But I am quite sure that a new man of genius, like Mr. Wells, would give much more prestige than an aged pedant. What is an Academic Society, without Wellses and the rest of the crowd?'[124] He went on Thursday 11 April to see an eye specialist and was told there was something wrong with 'the yellow spot' of his left eye. He told Hay Fleming about his eye problem: 'They have done their dang!' His wonder was that his 'careful reading eye' had lasted so long. He was 68. In the same letter to Hay Fleming, he said of their disputes, 'I hope there has never been an unkind thought on my side, nor an unsportsmanlike criticism on yours ... And I owe you unbounded gratitude in making me, as I went on, try to keep up a certain level of accuracy'.[125] Two days after his visit to the eye specialist, he made a coda to his will, giving Nora greater power to direct the investment funds of his estate after his death into companies in any foreign country.

A distressed Nora took Marie Belloc, a popular novelist, aside at the Sesame Club in Westminster and confided that her husband was convinced some 'awful calamities were about to befall Europe' and was trying to persuade her that they should leave London and St Andrews and move to America.[126] Irrational, deep-seated anxieties are evident in his letters to John. He feared the government would be powerless to stop a revolution and felt that 'the middle classes should have made a volunteer army, long ago': 'It is clear to me that we should be out of this place ... But I can't do what I want to do—there is a hideous humour in my position, and I wish I were in my resting grave.'[127]

They shut up Marloes Road on Tuesday 15 July 1912 and left for Banchory, resting between trains at the Caledonian Hotel in Edinburgh. Nora's name had already featured on the covers of the Christmas storybooks, *The Book of Princes and Princesses* and *The Red Book of Heroes*, as sole author. At Tor-na-Coille, she worked on *The Book of Saints and Heroes*. He prepared *Shakespeare, Bacon, and the Great Unknown*, a defence of Shakespeare's authorship of the plays, for the typist. He also had fun helping Nora put together for publication a collection of her essays, *Men, Women and Minxes*, which included her satirical portrait of the married literary man—unmistakably himself—as he appeared in the eyes of his wife.[128] Her list of common trials of being a writer's wife included being asked to read her husband's works in progress because her judgement was 'a criterion of that of the average public' and being ignored at writers' gatherings. To the original *Longman's* article, Nora, with the Christmas storybooks evidently in mind, added the fresh complaint for the book version that if 'her name, and not his appears on the title-page of the book, it is he, and *not* she, who will obtain all the credit and all the praise.'[129]

On the morning of Saturday 19 July, about 8 o'clock, he had a terrible pain. He thought at first it was indigestion. Shortly after, he collapsed. The local doctor was sent for, and after examining him, went to fetch his senior partner for a second opinion. They decided a specialist had to be consulted. Dr Ashley Mackintosh, a physician at Aberdeen Royal Infirmary, hurried from the city to Lang's bedside.[130] He diagnosed acute angina and judged the condition critical. Lang lost consciousness at 4.30 that afternoon. He appeared to rally in the evening, and the doctors thought they saw an improvement. Nora's account of what happened after that is chillingly brief: 'At 11.50, just as I had undressed, he gave a sigh and that is all.'[131] He was pronounced dead at midnight. Nora consoled their grieving family and friends with the thought that 'the end was swift and painless', and he 'had not the least idea he was dying.'[132] Yet she told Marie Belloc many years later that when he had regained consciousness that day and they were alone together, he 'tried to make her promise she would leave the old world and settle in America'.[133]

Nora made the arrangements for his body to be taken to the Episcopal Church in St Andrews on Wednesday. The funeral service would be held at 2 o'clock the next day. She had secretly bought a grave plot at St Andrews eighteen months before, knowing he wanted to be buried there—the last plot, she was told, in the Cathedral precinct.[134] He had wanted to be buried in the church-yard in the village of Caddon-foot near Selkirk, 'like Scott within the sound of the Tweed', but this was not allowed, as he was not a parishioner.[135] Nora wrote to her dressmaker in London, asking for a black dress to be posted if possible on Tuesday night.[136] She could not face being in St Andrews on Wednesday when he was taken to the church and arranged to stay the night at Cowden with Ella Christie, and for her to drive her on Thursday.

Her sister Elizabeth was in St Andrews on Tuesday in time to see Lang laid out for burial. She wrote emotionally afterwards to John's wife, Jean, 'I thought as I looked on his beautiful face, so entirely as it was in life that he seemed to be still living out the great enigma. His face was full of built up thought just as in life—only one missed the dear brown eyes—& there was no pallor, not even when we left him on Tuesday, covered with flowers. I am so sorry for John— for I felt as if he had a *right* to be there—and I know he would have liked it. There was of course nothing that he could do as Nora had made the minutest arrangements'.[137]

Nora and Ella Christie left Cowen at 11 on the morning of the funeral and stopped outside St Andrews for lunch. Nora drank a whisky and water. They arrived at the church a few minutes before two. John Lang was chief pallbearer. Elizabeth sat by Nora's side during the service. From the church, the hearse in a slow-moving motorcade moved towards the cemetery through the main streets of the town, followed by a great procession of mourners—relatives, friends, town councillors, and representatives of the university. The burial plot was at the north-eastern corner of the graveyard, adjoining the Cathedral burying ground. A few steps from the grave, through a walled gate, the ground sloped down towards the sea. The cemetery was crowded. There were people at the top of St Rule's Tower, looking down in silence as Andrew Lang's coffin, bearing on the lid a wreath of red roses from the Maxwell-Scotts of Abbots-ford, was lowered into the earth. Elizabeth was displeased that Nora did not speak to anyone at the funeral and 'rushed away' immediately afterwards.[138]

There were many obituaries in the London weeklies when Nora arrived back at Marloes Road on Sunday 27 July. The obituary in the *Saturday Review* quoted from a sermon by Benjamin Jowett, 'We do not wish that the moment our backs are turned, and the door closed upon us, our character or fortune or behaviour should at once become the subject of discussion'[139]—a recognition of Lang's wish to be spared the 'life and letters plague'. His diversity challenged attempts to sum up his influence and importance. Edward Clodd suggested that 'a syndicate of assessors' was needed to do 'bare justice' to his 'marvellous versatility'. Among obituarists, the most informed stuck to their own area of expertise—Clodd evaluating Lang's contribution to the sciences of folklore and comparative mythology; Hume Brown praising his writings on Knox and Scottish History; Robert Marett, paying personal tribute to his role, with Tylor, in establishing anthropology within the 'broad penumbra' of Literae Humaniores at Oxford.[140]

Nora faced the task of sorting through his manuscripts 'of every kind without dates or names'.[141] It did not help that she damaged her eye the day after her return to London. Among his papers, she came upon the manuscript of his unpublished book on 'Totemism and Exogamy'. The note with it stated that he did not expect to publish the book, but that the chapter on his theory of totemic exogamy might perhaps be detachable, and, if so, *Folklore* magazine might allow space for it. Nora wrote to Alexander Milne, Secretary of the Folklore Society, who agreed the chapter ought to be published, provided Hartland and J. G. Frazer approved.[142] The essay, acknowledging indebtedness to Darwin and J. J. Atkinson, reconstructed in Lang's most lucid and convincing manner the likely social origins of exogamy in the brutal custom of ancestral jealous hostility, and its gradual modification by advancing man.[143] Hartland gave his consent, wholeheartedly. Frazer's response has not survived. A hint of what it may have been can be guessed from a letter from Hartland to Frazer, expressing dismay that Frazer should think that Lang had made an open insinuation of his honesty in reviews of *The Golden Bough*.[144] Robert Ackerman, Frazer's biographer, regards as 'gracious' Frazer's tribute to Lang after his death, given his previous dislike,[145] but Frazer's tribute to Lang as a poet and man of letters clearly served to counter any claim for Lang as his serious rival in the field of cultural anthropology. Commenting on the obituary notice of Lang in the *Athenaeum*, which he did not think 'very generous or sympathetic', Frazer said, 'It hardly, I think, noticed his poetry which always seems to me to possess the true poetical ring ... His light humorous prose was also exquisite in its way ... it would have been better for his reputation and for the world if he had given us more of pure literature'.[146]

Lang, in life, joked that for the peace of the living and the reputation of the dead, everyone should join the 'L.B.S.'—the Letter Burners' Society.[147] He told friends he destroyed their letters as soon as read and urged them to do the same with his. But shortly before his death he admitted to Haggard, 'I have a few sealed up, but dare not look at them'.[148] Nora claimed that her wrists ached for weeks after tearing up his correspondence and personal papers.[149] Her niece, Thyra Blanche Alleyne, helped her in the task, but begged to keep Jowett's testimonial, which described Lang as 'greatly regarded' as a literary man and 'likely to become more so'.[150] Nora sent small items of memorabilia to his closest friends. Herbert Maxwell was moved by her gift of a gold ring and even more by her words, 'There are few people in the world my husband cared for more than you'. He deeply regretted that Lang had set his face so determinately against an official biography.[151]

Andrew Lang left an estate of the value of £12,498. His will made provision for a life annuity of £50 to be paid to his sister Helen in Menton. He also put £2,000 upon trust to his brother John and his issue, and £6,000 upon trust to his nephew, Craig Sellar Lang, his late brother Alexander Craig's only child. His books, auctioned at Sotheby's in December, brought a return of £1,793.17.6. The last of the Christmas storybooks—*The Strange Story Book*—appeared the following Christmas, with Lang's name as editor on the cover. In her farewell 'Preface', Nora paid warm tribute to him as the originator and guiding spirit of the series through its twenty-five years of existence.

Nora moved to a flat at 57 Cheniston Gardens, just a street from their old house in Marloes Road. She had literary ambitions of her own and evidently meant to pursue them. Her collection of essays, *Men, Woman and Minxes*, the last thing she and Lang worked on, came out in the autumn following his death. A year later, her sole labours on *The Strange Story Book* brought the series to a close. She continued to write for children, adapting from Dumas' the *Vicomte de Bragelonne* the exciting incident involving General Monk in the plot to restore Charles II to the English throne.[152] There are critics today who believe her literary labours behind the scenes on her husband's behalf have been marginalized, and that Nora was much more than simply his able assistant.[153] In contrast, Nora's sister Elizabeth, on Lang's passing, voiced a more sceptical view of Nora's abilities as a writer for herself. She said, rather unfairly perhaps, although she had a decided advantage in being a close relative who observed first-hand Nora's and Lang's relationship, 'I often think she does not realise how very much she owed to him. It will come in time no doubt. She will plunge into writing, I rather suspect, but she is not a spontaneous writer & that must suffer badly without Andrew's inspiring presence'.[154] The truth is that Nora's most significant and genuinely lasting literary work after Lang's death was undertaken in securing his memory. She introduced the new edition of *The Maid of France* following the canonization of Joan of

Arc by the Catholic Church in 1920 and edited *The Poetical Works of Andrew Lang*, handsomely printed and bound in four volumes. She also lived to see the founding of the annual lecture in his honour at St Andrews University, which aimed to keep alive his many-sided achievements as a classical scholar, poet, historian, and anthropologist. There were betrayals. Gosse, just months after Lang's death, described Lang as a 'slightly inhuman' person whose 'sympathy could not be counted on beyond a point which was very easily reached', and likened him to an 'angora cat' whose 'gentleness and soft purr ... invite caresses which are suddenly met with outspread paw and claws awake'. A decade later, when it was clear that Lang's writings were still read and valued, Gosse, who did not like to be out of step with whatever might reflect well on himself, wrote a more appreciative essay on Lang's literary achievement.[155]

Nora resolutely resisted those who urged her to write her memoirs. She told relatives:

> No, I'm not going to write my memoirs though I am always being asked to. I know too well what is said of people who do. You are found to be dull unless you ride roughshod over the survivor's feelings, so all the fun has to be left out. And you can't write of the things that really made or marred your life. At least *I* couldn't.[156]

She taught herself Russian in order to correspond with Russian soldiers in hospitals and camps during the Great War.[157] She died, aged 82, in 1933, almost twenty-one years to the day after her husband's death. Her funeral was held at St James's Church, Piccadilly, at 3 o' clock on Wednesday 12 July. Her coffin was taken from there by train to St Andrews, and on a grey Friday at midday, with rain falling, she was buried beside Andrew Lang in the Cathedral precincts.

Epilogue

Of the many tributes paid to Andrew Lang's achievements in the human sciences after his death, perhaps the warmest was made by the young American anthropologist, Alexander Goldenweiser, the last of Lang's friendly adversaries, who said:

> To expound Lang and leave out controversy is not unlike playing Hamlet without the Prince of Denmark ... Lang's literary productivity was proverbial and his achievement in this respect must be regarded as little short of amazing. Articles, essays and even books signed by his name continued to appear for a year after his death. He shone on, like one of those distant stars whose brilliance continues to delight our eye, while its material source may long since have been reduced to dust.[1]

Lang's reputation was not snuffed out, as many others were, in the Great War, nor in the cultural dazzle and din of the 1920s. The annual Andrew Lang Memorial Lectures commenced at St Andrews University in 1927. The first lecturer, George Gordon, was Merton Professor of English Literature, and, like Lang, a Scot who had completed his studies at Oxford. Astutely, he recognized the importance of Lang's decision to leave Oxford and the quasi-official barriers between subjects. 'It was his destiny in life', Gordon observed, 'while never out of touch with Universities, to break the fences between specialists, and to establish understandings, whether cordial or not ... between all branches and departments of the humanities'. He suspected there was 'something Scottish' about this and regretted that the embargo against an official biography meant that Lang was 'still imperfectly understood'.[2]

The annual lectures, ranging widely in subject matter from the Homeric Question to poetry, to folklore, history, and anthropology, kept before the eyes of the academic community Lang's remarkable many-sided achievements. Lang's legacy as a writer and thinker positively encouraged disagreement and debate. Herbert Grierson, confronting with fresh facts Lang's biography of Lockhart, said of Lang that he could not imagine a man 'who would have less desired insincere, or even sincere encomia being allowed to disturb the lecturer's quest for truth'.[3] Although the lectures were suspended on the outbreak of war in 1939, they resumed in 1947 and continued to attract distinguished academic speakers.

Andrew Lang. John Sloan, Oxford University Press. © John Sloan (2023). DOI: 10.1093/oso/9780192866875.003.0012

The decline in Lang's reputation really dates from the late 1950s. Lang, an outspoken critic of 'restricted specialism' (his phrase),[4] fell out of favour at a time when the rapid expansion of the university sector encouraged increased specialization in the humanities. The Andrew Lang lectures dried up, and when reconvened in the 1960s, ceased to focus exclusively on Lang's work. Lang, however, proved difficult to write off entirely. The frequent charge against him of being a 'dilettante' among professionals seemed at odds with his incisive contribution to many fields. Equally, attempts to disregard him as an unabashed populist did not square with his rigorous methods nor with his criticism of those who wrote down to people. Lang objected to the popular notion of 'the man in the street'—the average person as distinct from the expert. He told his fellow classicist, Gilbert Murray, to 'shake off the superstition' that 'the man in the street' formed a *couche sociale*, an actual social group.[5] From boyhood, he saw that there were people in every walk of life and in every level of society, who either had or hadn't an appreciation of literature. He wrote for those who had. As a writer, his address was scholarly but accessible, his instincts democratic.

Lang's wider intellectual significance and worth began gradually to be rediscovered in the 1980s. Andrew Duff-Cooper, while a postgraduate at Oxford, undertook an edition of Lang's unpublished 1912 manuscript on 'Totemism', at the suggestion of his research supervisor, Rodney Needham, Professor of Social Anthropology. This was published in 1994 with the title *Andrew Lang on Totemism*. Duff-Cooper believed that anthropologists could still learn from Lang's example. He singled out for special notice Lang's endeavour to keep his own view of the world in check and insistence that 'social forces should, first-of-all at least, be understood on their own terms'. 'It is remarkable', Duff-Cooper wrote, 'how little evaluative language we find in his work … all his writing contrasts sharply with the stance adopted to savage life by many of his contemporaries'.[6] In another development, Robert Crawford, and later Julia Sparks, drew attention to Lang's key role in the coming together and continuing interaction of literary and scientific writing in the last decades of the Victorian age.[7] Lang's call for folklore studies to combine with other closely related subject disciplines was also taken up by researchers, most notably in the field of children's studies and fairy tales. Tolkien may have disagreed with Lang's views on fairy-stories, but, as Ruth Berman was the first to point out,[8] Lang helped shape Tolkien's taste, and the taste of a whole generation, in fairy tale and fantasy—an influence which remains vibrant to this day. Andrew Teverson's recent scholarly edition of Lang's selected children's fictions, folk tales, and fairy tales, highlights Lang's significant influence on children's literature and fantasy to the present time.[9]

The demand for academics to share their findings with a broader audience, together with the perceived value of interdisciplinary study, gave momentum to Lang's work being treated seriously. An important development in Lang studies has resulted from the opposition between two rival camps in the field of Scottish historiography over Lang's value as a historian. Catriona Macdonald, in a radically new reading of Lang, takes sides with those who cast doubt on the supposed death in nineteenth-century Scotland itself of the romantic, antiquarian nationalism fostered by Walter Scott, which continued to be influential throughout Europe. By reaffirming the place of romance in 'serious' Scottish history, and by placing religious conflict, rather than the development of constitutional government, centre-stage in the history of Scotland from the Reformation, Lang, she argues, was historically sensitive to wider 'intellectual' and 'popular perceptions' outside the grand narrative of Anglo-British identity.[10] This reading not only questions the presumption of Scottish inferiority and difference from the rest of Europe; it challenges, too, the influential hypothesis among Scottish scholars of an eroded democratic intellect—an imagined weakening by anglicization in the nineteenth century of the generalist, intrinsically egalitarian Scottish tradition of learning which encouraged connection with the principles and attitudes of the people. Lang's legacy has also been felt in the study of internet learning and cultural production. Nathan Hensley argues that Lang is to be valued not as a writer of scholarly masterpieces, but as a 'connective figure', a mediator between 'apparently separate fields of knowledge and previously unconnected ideas', who provides a model for attempts in our democratized, network-making age, to develop new, more collaborative, anti-specialist ways of sharing, developing and evaluating facts and information.[11]

Lang remains as challenging a figure today as he was in his lifetime. In life, many who met him found him perplexing, distant, even supercilious. Lang's standoffish manner unnerved the young Scottish poet John Davidson on their first meeting in the offices of the *Daily News* in the 1890s, although Davidson soon found himself revising his opinion and rather liking Lang's cultural polish and Scottish reserve.[12] The journalist Charles Boyd, Lang's colleague for thirty years on the staff of the *Saturday Review*, recalled that to youth Lang 'could be alarming', although he remembered with affection Lang's 'dark unfathomable gaze—rather beautiful than auspicious', and Lang's many concealed acts of kindness 'for other people'.[13] Lang was no different from many people in having two different, even contradictory sides to his nature—in his case, fiercely combative and confrontational in debate, with great ambition for his work, and, on the other hand, the most modest of men, humble about his achievements, and entirely free of malice or vanity. That contradiction is resolved perhaps in his conviction that the work itself was the important thing, not fame or self-promotion. Among his older contemporaries, he admired Alfred Russel Wallace, who discovered independently the theory of evolution by natural selection, but unselfishly let Darwin take the credit, believing Darwin better positioned to gain acceptance for the theory. To Lang, Wallace's selfless action was an example of 'beautiful conduct' in the world of learning.[14] 'Nothing matters but the work done', Lang wrote, 'and that depends on a man's temperament and genius. To these he accommodates his "aesthetic principles", if he keeps such things, and does just what God gave him the power of doing'.[15] Lang was a remarkable man, whose work, it is hoped, will continue to be more widely read and understood, and his unparalleled place in nineteenth-century culture and learning remembered.

Notes

Chapter 1

1. *The Langs of Selkirk*, compiled by Patrick Sellar Lang of Titanga, Victoria, Australia (Melbourne, 1910). St Andrews. See also Thomas Craig-Brown, *The History of Selkirkshire, or Chronicles of Ettrick Forest*, 2 Vols. (Edinburgh, 1886).

2. For an account of these events, see Eric Richards, *Patrick Sellar and the Highland Clearances: Homicide, Eviction, and the Price of Progress* (Edinburgh, 1999). For a defence of Patrick Sellar, see Thomas Sellar, *The Sutherland Evictions of 1814* (London, 1883).

3. Donald E. Meek, ed., *Tuath is Tighearna; Tenants and Landlords: An Anthology of Gaelic Poetry of Social and Political Protest from the Clearances to the Land Agitation 1800–1890* (Edinburgh, 1995), pp. 55–6; see also T. M. Devine, *The Scottish Clearances: A History of the Dispossessed 1600–1900* (London, 2018), pp. 296–7.

4. Dorothy Richardson, *The Curse on Patrick Sellar* (Stockbridge, 1999), p. 38.

5. To E. W. B. Nicholson, 19 October [1897]. Bodleian.

6. *Southern Reporter* (2 May 1929); newspaper clipping in *The Langs of Selkirk*. St Andrews.

7. 'Adventures Among Books', *Adventures Among Books* (London, 1905), p. 5.

8. *The Poetical Works of Andrew Lang*, ed. Mrs. Lang, Vol. 1 (London 1923), p. 136; hereafter referenced as *Poetical Works*.

9. 'Adventures Among Books', pp. 9–10

10. Lines written in a copy of *Books and Bookmen* (1887), quoted Roger Lancelyn Green, 'Andrew Lang: "The Greatest Bookman of His Age"', *Indiana University Bookman* (April 1965), p. 14.

11. 'Introduction', *The Works of Robert Louis Stevenson*, Swanston Edition, Vol. 1 (London, 1911), p. xi.

12. 'At the Sign of the Ship', *Longman's Magazine*, July 1896, p. 1; Lang's regular monthly column in Longman's Magazine, hereafter referenced simply as 'At the Sign of the Ship'.

13. Sir John Lang Macpherson Fayrer, private letter of 11 September 1985; quoted in Philippa Bayliss, 'Andrew Lang and the Study of Religion in the Victorian Era with special reference to his High God Theory', PhD Dissertation, University of Aberdeen (1987), p. 14. Sir John Fayrer (1944–2017) was the son of Sir Joseph Herbert Spens Fayrer, 3rd Bt. (1899–1976) and Lady Helen Diana Scott Lang Fayrer (1910–61), the daughter of Andrew Lang's brother John (1849–1917).

14. Richards, *Patrick Sellar and the Highland Clearances*, p. 332.

15. William B. Herapath, *The Handbook for Visitors to the Bristol and Clifton Hotwell* (Bristol, 1911), pp. 46–7; see also A. B. Granville, *The Spas of England and Principal Bathing-Places*, Vol. 3 (London, 1841), pp. 345–60.

16. 'The Watering-Places of England', *Illustrated London News* (17 August 1850), p. 149; *Illustrated London News* hereafter referenced as *ILN*.

17. 'Adventures Among Books', pp. 6–7.

18. Jane Plenderleath Sellar to Helen Brown, 16 September 1850. St Andrews.

19. Elizabeth D. Cross, *An Old Story, and Other Poems* (London, 1868). Tibby Cross was the older sister of John Walter Cross, later George Eliot's husband. She married William Henry Hall (originally Bullock) and died in childbirth, aged 33. The Cross family were banking partners and relatives by marriage of Alexander Dennistoun, Lang's uncle Thomas Sellar's employer.

20. 'Adventures Among Books', p. 26.

21. Benjamin Jowett to Francis Palgrave, 21 August 1849. Balliol.

22. Benjamin Jowett to William Young Sellar, 24 October 1851. Balliol.

23. Eleanor Mary Sellar, *Recollections and Impressions* (Edinburgh, 1907), p. 38.

24. Robert Robertson, 'Alexander Scott 1853-1947', *Obituary Notices of Fellows of the Royal Society*, 6 (November 1948), p. 253.

25. See Sarah Williams, *Religious Belief and Popular Culture in Southwark 1880–1939* (Oxford, 1999).

26. Mrs Leonora Lang to Mr and Mrs Munro, 20 December 1927. NLS.

27. 'Adventures Among Books', pp. 4–5.

28. To Thomas Craig-Brown, 3 October 1900. Hawick.

29. Roger Lancelyn Green, *Andrew Lang: A Critical Biography* (Leicester, 1946), p. 12.

30. 'Introduction', *Pickwick*, Gadshill Edition (London, 1898), p. x.

31. To Mrs Puller, 26 March [1898?]. Hertford. Lang refers to this in 'Rashin Coatie—Nicht, Nought, Nothing; Scotch Tales', *Revue Celtique*, 3 (1876–8), pp. 365–78. A version of this family legend is also narrated in *The Langs of Selkirk*, p. 66.

32. 'Cinderella and the Diffusion of Tales', *Folklore*, 4 (December 1893), pp. 413–32.

33. 'At the Sign of the Ship', December 1895, p. 207.

34. Sellar, *Recollections and Impressions*, p. 97.

35. Richardson, *The Curse on Patrick Sellar*, p. 77.

36. 'At the Sign of Ship', May 1899, p. 93.

37. Donald McLeod, *Gloomy Memories of the Highlands* (1841), reprinted in Alexander Mackenzie, *The History of the Highland Clearances* (Stirling and Inverness, 1883). Among those who entered the debate was Karl Marx ('The Duchess of Sutherland and Slavery', *The People's Paper* (45) (March 1853)), who accused the duchess of hypocrisy for campaigning against the slave trade, when her own wealth came from the expropriation of crofters' rights.

38. Harriet Beecher Stowe, *Sunny Memories of Foreign Lands*, Vol. 1 (London, 1854), pp. 301–13.

39. 'Adventures Among Books', p. 18.

40. Thomas Lang (1816–1884) and William Lang (1823–1877) emigrated in 1839. They were joined two years later by Gideon Scott Lang (1819–1880), author of *Land and Labour in Australia* (Melbourne, 1845) and *The Aborigines of Australia* (Melbourne, 1865).

41. 'Books About Red Men', *Letters on Literature* (London, 1889), p. 182.
42. Lang, 'William Young Sellar', in William Young Sellar, *The Roman Poets of the Augustan Age: Horace and the Elegiac Poets* (Oxford, 1891), p. xxii.
43. William Anderson, *Selkirk Cricket Club Centenary 1851–1951* (Galashiels, 1954), p. 1.
44. 'Adventures Among Books', p. 11.
45. Jane Plenderleath Lang to Agnes Sellar, Viewfield, Selkirk [no date]. St Andrews. Lang's mother wrote, 'I have been away on long travels again. I took Andrew to Edinburgh to spend a few days at Mrs. Lang's. I did all that I had to do'.
46. 'Adventures Among Books', p. 11.
47. 'Adventures Among Books', p. 4.
48. 'Some Japanese Bogie Books', *Books and Bookmen* (New York, 1886), p. 134; see also 'Adventures Among Books', p. 12.
49. 'At the Sign of the Ship', May 1899, p. 92.
50. Sir D'Arcy Wentworth Thompson, 'Andrew and Pat', *Scots Magazine*, 41 (May 1944), p. 86.
51. *Prince Prigio* (Bristol, 1889), p. 143.
52. 'Adventures Among Books', p. 13
53. 'The Boy', *Adventures Among Books*, pp. 298–9.
54. 'At the Sign of the Ship', December 1893, p. 191.
55. 'At the Sign of the Ship', July 1891, p. 315.
56. 'Adventures Among Books', p. 16.
57. Magnus Magnussen, *The Clacken and the Slate: The Story of Edinburgh Academy 1824–1974* (London, 1974), pp. 190–2.
58. 'Homer and the Study of Greek', *Essays in Little* (London, 1891), p. 82.
59. 'At the Sign of St Paul's', *ILN* (25 November 1905), p. 786.
60. James Ballantine, ed., *Chronicle of the Hundredth Birthday of Robert Burns* (Edinburgh and London, 1859).
61. George Anderson and John Findlay, eds., *The Burns Centenary Poems: A Collection of Fifty of the Best* (Glasgow, 1857). The winning poem was written by 'Isa Craig' (Isabella Craig Knox).
62. 'At the Sign of the Ship', March 1901, p. 473.
63. Quoted Green, *Lang* (1946), p. 18.
64. 'Enchanted Cigarettes', *Adventures Among Books*, pp. 256–7.
65. 'At the Sign of the Ship', May 1898, p. 92.
66. James Payn, *The Backwater of Life: Or Essays of a Literary Veteran* (London, 1899), p. xxviii.
67. 'Rab's Friend', *Adventures Among Books*, p. 61.
68. Sellar, *Recollections and Impressions*, pp. 127–8; p. 159.
69. To RLS, Sunday [1882], Marysa Demoor, ed., *Dear Stevenson: Letters from Andrew Lang to Robert Louis Stevenson with Five Letters from Stevenson to Lang* (Leuven, 1990), p. 51; hereafter referenced as *Dear Stevenson*.
70. 'Adventures Among Books', p. 14.

Chapter 2

1. 'Religio Loci', *Andrew Lang at St Andrews, A Centenary Anthology*, ed. J. B. Salmond (St Andrews, 1944), p. 26.
2. John Campbell Shairp and others, *Life and Letters of James David Forbes*, (London, 1873) pp. 401–2; see also Arthur Thomson, *Ferrier of St Andrews: An Academic Tragedy* (Edinburgh, 1985), pp. 113–4.
3. 'Old St Leonard's Days', *Andrew Lang at St Andrews*, p. 36.
4. 'Adventures Among Books', p. 24.
5. 'Recitation', *Kate Kennedy Annual*, 1872 ([St Andrews], 1872–9). Bodleian.
6. 'Old St Leonard's Days', p. 36.
7. *Life and Letters of James David Forbes*, p. 411.
8. 'Our Bogey Books', *College Echoes*, 5 (11 January 1894), pp. 81–2.
9. J. M. Anderson, 'Library Notes and Documents', *Library Bulletin of the University of St Andrews*, 5 (October 1912), pp. 220–1.
10. 'At the Sign of the Ship', May 1905, p. 91.
11. 'Suggestions for Improvement of Degree Examinations', *College Echoes*, 4 (20 October 1892), p. 3.
12. Lang, *Alfred Tennyson* (Edinburgh, 1901), p. 81.
13. 'Clevedon Church: In Memoriam H. B.', *Poetical Works*, Vol. 1, pp. 141–2.
14. To C. M. Falconer, 6 December 1889; quoted 'Religio Loci', p. 14.
15. Allan Menzies, *College Echoes*, 24 (October 1912); quoted Green (1946), p. 22.
16. 'Old St Leonard's Days', p. 40.
17. Allan Menzies, *College Echoes*, 17 (12 June 1906), p. 118.
18. 'Adventures Among Books', p. 26.
19. *St Leonard's Magazine* (1863), p. 44. St Andrews.
20. 'Nugae Catulline', *Poetical Works*, Vol. 2, p. 198.
21. 'From 'A Scottish Workshop', *ILN* (21 March 1896), p. 363; see also 'At the Sign of St Paul's', *ILN* (13 January 1906), p. 54.
22. 'Sir Launcelot', *St Andrews University Magazine* (March 1863), pp. 139–40; see also *Andrew Lang at St Andrews*, p. 46.
23. 'Flos Regum', *St Andrews University Magazine* (March 1863), p. 108.
24. 'Old St Leonard's Days', p. 40.
25. Anderson, 'Library Notes and Documents', p. 222.
26. *A History of Scotland from the Roman Occupation*, Vol. 1 (London, 1900), pp. 163–76.
27. Duke of Argyll, *Passages from the Past* (New York, 1908), p. 79; also handwritten notes in *Kate Kennedy Annual* (1872–9). Bodleian.
28. 'Old St Leonard's Days', p. 36.
29. 'Old St Leonard's Days', p. 37.
30. 'Old St Leonard's Days', p. 39.
31. *A History of Scotland from the Roman Occupation*, Vol. 4 (London, 1907), p. 401.
32. Lindsay Paterson, 'George Davie and the Democratic Intellect', in Gordon Graham, ed., *Scottish Philosophy in the Nineteenth and Twentieth Centuries* (Oxford, 2015). Oxford Scholarship Online.

33. 'Old St Leonard's Days', p. 39.

34. 'Adventures Among Books', p. 28.

35. Thomson, *Ferrier of St Andrews*, pp. 115–7.

36. Sellar, *Recollections and Impressions*, p. 160.

37. Thomson, *Ferrier of St Andrews*, p. 124.

38. W. Innes Addison, *The Snell Exhibitions: From the University of Glasgow to Balliol College, Oxford* (Glasgow, 1901).

39. 'Reminiscences of Balliol College', *English Illustrated Magazine*, 11 (November 1893), p. 126.

40. 'St Andrews', *Harper's Monthly*, 80 (January 1890), p. 304.

41. 'Glasgow in 1864', *The Book of the Jubilee: In Commemoration of the Ninth Jubilee of the University of Glasgow 1451–1901* (Glasgow, 1901), p. 27.

42. Sellar, *Recollections and Impressions*, p. 129.

43. 'On the Interpretation of Scripture', *Essays and Reviews* (London, 1860), pp. 330–433.

44. 'The Influence of Mr. Jowett', *ILN* (10 August 1895), p. 175.

45. 'The Master of Balliol', *ILN* (14 October 1893), p. 479.

46. Long Hop, 'The Lay of the Bookselling Elder', *St Leonard's Magazine* (28 November 1863). St Andrews.

47. 'The Master of Balliol', p. 479.

48. In *Cock Lane and Common Sense* (London, 1894), p. 340, Lang writes, '"There are no gods, or only *dei otiosi*, careless, indifferent deities. There is nothing conscious that survives death, no soul that can exist apart from the fleshly body." Such were the doctrines of Epicurus and Lucretius'.

49. 'Dei Otiosi', *St Andrews University Magazine* (November 1863); see also *Andrew Lang at St Andrews*, p. 11, and 'Poems, Songs and Verses, Hitherto Uncollected, transcribed by C. M. Falconer'. St Andrews.

50. 'Glasgow in 1864', pp. 26–9.

51. 'At the Sign of the Ship', November 1898, p. 93.

52. 'Glesky', *St Leonard's Magazine* (28 November 1863). St Andrews.

53. 'Glasgow in 1864', p. 28.

54. *St Leonard's Magazine* (29 January 1864). St Andrews.

55. 'A Prospective Farewell', *St Leonard's Magazine* (5 March 1864). St Andrews.

56. 'Glasgow in 1864', p. 29.

57. *The Loretto Register 1825–1925* (Edinburgh, 1927).

58. *Loretto Register 1825–1925*.

59. Quoted Geoffrey Faber, *Jowett: A Portrait with Background* (London, 1957), pp. 170–1.

60. *Loretto's 100 Years 1827–1927* (London, 1928), p. 31.

61. 'School Song', Appendix, *Loretto's 100 Years*.

62. *Loretto's 100 Years*, p. 41.

63. Magnusson, *Clacken and Slate*, pp. 250–1.

64. 'The Art of Mark Twain', *ILN* (14 February 1891), p. 222.

65. Robert Jameson MacKenzie, *Almond of Loretto* (London, 1906), pp. 38–9.

Chapter 3

1. 'Reminiscences of Balliol College', *English Illustrated Magazine*, 11 (November 1893), pp. 122–7.
2. 'Religio Loci', p. 25.
3. *St Andrews* (London, 1893), p. 300.
4. 'Freshman's Year', *College Echoes*, 1 (7 November 1889), p. 2, and *Poetical Works*, Vol. 1, pp. 6–7.
5. 'The Master of Balliol', p. 479.
6. *Oxford: Brief Historical and Descriptive Notes* (London, 2nd ed., 1882) p. 7.
7. 'The Master of Balliol', p. 479.
8. Sebastian Lecourt, *Cultivating Belief: Victorian Anthropology, Liberal Aesthetics and Secular Imagination* (Oxford, 2018), p. 164.
9. 'At the Sign of the Ship', September 1895, p. 539.
10. Quoted Linda Dowling, *Hellenism and Homosexuality in Victorian Oxford* (Ithaca, 1994), p. 76.
11. 'The Master of Balliol', p. 479.
12. Adolphus George Charles Liddell, *Notes from the Life of an Ordinary Mortal* (London, 1911), pp. 69–70.
13. 'At the Sign of the Ship', July 1901, p. 281.
14. 'At the Sign of the Ship', July 1902, p. 282.
15. 'On the Study of the Evidences of Christianity', *Essays and Reviews*, pp. 94–144.
16. 'The Influence of Mr. Jowett', *ILN* (10 August 1895}, p. 175.
17. To Rich—[Ralph Richardson (1845–1933)?], Monday [1865 or 1866]. NLS.
18. 'Memoir of William Young Sellar', in W. Y. Sellar, *The Roman Poets of the Augustan Age: Horace and the Elegiac Poets* (Oxford, 1892), p. xxxvi.
19. 'Adventures Among Books', pp. 28–9; see also 'The Master of Balliol', p. 479.
20. For the culture of 'tutor worship', see Dowling, *Hellenism and Homosexuality in Victorian Oxford*, pp. 33–5.
21. 'Adventures Among Books', pp. 29–31.
22. 'At the Sign of the Ship', May 1902, pp. 94–5.
23. Evelyn Abbott and Lewis Campbell, *Life and Letters of Benjamin Jowett*, Vol. 1 (London, 1897), p. 328.
24. 'Adventures Among Books', p. 32; 'At the Sign of the Ship', December 1889, p. 191.
25. *Oxford Undergraduate's Journal* (6 March 1867), p. 125.
26. *Oxford Undergraduate's Journal* (24 October 1866), p. 77.
27. The poem was reprinted, with the first line for title 'Oh, what should I do there' (After J. C. Shairp), in *Poetical Works*, Vol. 1, p. 10.
28. *St Leonard's Magazine* (1867). St Andrews.
29. *Oxford Undergraduate's Journal* (27 June 1867), p. 178.
30. John Jones, *Balliol College: A History* (Oxford, 2nd ed. revised, 2005), pp. 208–9.
31. *Oxford Undergraduate's Journal* (7 February 1867), p. 111.
32. 'Reminiscences of Balliol College', p. 123.
33. 'Reminiscences of Balliol College', p. 124.
34. 'At the Sign of the Ship', October 1892, p. 651.

35. Robert Robertson, 'University Theatre at Oxford', *Educational Theatre Journal*, 8 (October 1956), pp. 194–206.

36. Michael Pimbury, *A Short History of the Oxford University Dramatic Society* (Oxford, 1955), p. 6.

37. Stuart Mason, *Bibliography of Oscar Wilde* (London, 1914), p. 6.

38. *The Oxford Spectator* (30 November 1867), p. 16.

39. Quoted 'Preface', *In College Gardens: Old Rhymes Written in 1871*, ed. Roger Lancelyn Green (Poulton, 1972).

40. *Reminiscences of Lord Kilbracken* (London, 1931), pp. 61–2.

41. 'The Poems of William Morris', *Westminster Review*, 34 (October 1868), pp. 302–12.

42. *The Oxford Spectator* (2 June 1868), p. 127.

43. 'Rabelais and the Renaissance', *Fraser's Magazine* (March 1870), pp. 363–72.

44. Lecourt, *Cultivating Belief*.

45. 'Mr. Stevenson's New Novel', *ILN* (16 September 1893), p. 350.

46. 'The Influence of Mr. Jowett', p. 175.

47. 'The Master of Balliol', p. 479.

48. 'Rabelais and the Renaissance', p. 367-8.

49. *Oxford: Brief Historical and Descriptive Notes*, p. 54.

50. 'Rabelais and the Renaissance', p. 372.

51. Clement K. Shorter, 'Reminiscences of Andrew Lang', *The Bookman's Journal and Print Collector*, 5 (December 1921), p. 74; reprinted as 'On an Expensive Volume of Verse', *Poetical Works*, Vol. 3, p. 218.

52. Lang, *Alfred Tennyson* (Edinburgh, 1901), p. 42.

53. 'Hesperothen', *Poetical Works*, Vol. 1, pp. 91–105.

54. 'Adventures Among Books', p. 31; see also 'At the Sign of the Ship', December 1888, p. 281.

55. 'The Influence of Mr. Jowett', p. 175.

56. 'Reminiscences of Balliol College', p. 126.

57. *Life, Letters and Diaries of Sir Stafford Northcote*, Vol. 1 (Edinburgh, 1890), p. 31.

58. To Miss A. L. Sellar, Saturday, 1868. St Andrews.

Chapter 4

1. 'Words of Comfort', *ILN* (5 October 1895), p. 427.

2. *The Life and Letters of John Gibson Lockhart*, Vol. 1 (London, 1897), p. 67

3. Bernard W. Henderson, *Merton College* (London, 1899), p. 168.

4. Louise Creighton, *The Life and Letters of Mandell Creighton*, Vol. 1 (London, 1904), p. 50.

5. 'An American at Oxford', *ILN* (7 October 1893), p. 454, and 'At the Sign of St Paul's', *ILN* (22 December 1906), p. 930.

6. Dorothy Richardson Jones, *King of Critics: George Saintsbury 1845–1933* (Ann Arbor, 1992), p. 20.

7. G. H. Martin and J. R. L. Highfield, *A History of Merton College, Oxford* (Oxford, 1997), p. 308.

8. *Life and Letters of Mandell Creighton*, Vol. 1, p. 21.

9. 'At the Sign of the Ship', March 1901, p. 472.

10. *Life and Letters of Mandell Creighton*, p. 45.

11. *Life and Letters of Mandell Creighton*, p. 47; see also John Sutherland, *Mrs Humphry Ward Eminent Victorian, Pre-Eminent Edwardian* (Oxford, 1990), p. 52.

12. 'At the Sign of the Ship', March 1887, p. 533.

13. To Jean Lang, 28 March 1912. St Andrews.

14. To RLS, 11 May [1887], *Dear Stevenson*, p. 108.

15. 'Twilight on Tweed', *Poetical Works*, Vol. 1, pp. 32-3.

16. *Reminiscences of Lord Kilbracken*, pp. 59–60.

17. William Tuckwell, *Reminiscences of Oxford* (London, 1900), p. 143.

18. Henderson, *Merton College*, p. 182.

19. *Modern Mythology* (London, 1897), pp. 3–6.

20. J. F. McLennan, 'The Worship of Animals and Plants: Part 1, Totems and Totemism', *Fortnightly Review*, 12 (October 1869), pp. 407–27; 'Part 2, Totem-gods Among the Ancients', *Fortnightly Review*, 13 (February 1870), pp. 562–82.

21. 'Adventures Among Books', p. 36.

22. 'Adventures Among Books', p. 37.

23. Sellar, *Recollections and Impressions*, pp. 225–7.

24. 'Two Homes', *Poetical Works*, Vol. 2, p. 9.

25. *Oxford Spectator* (12 December 1867), p. 47.

26. 'Giordano Bruno', *Macmillan's Magazine*, 23 (February 1871), p. 303.

27. 'On an Expensive Volume of Verse', *Poetical Works*, Vol. 3, p. 218.

28. James Thayne Covert, *A Victorian Marriage: Mandell and Louise Creighton* (London, 2000), p. 1.

29. *Life and Letters of Mandell Creighton*, Vol. 1, p. 77.

30. John Richard Green to Olga von Glehn, 19 February and 10 March 1871, *Letters of John Richard Green,1837–1883*, ed. Leslie Stephen (London, 1901), p. 286; p. 289.

31. Mandell Creighton to Louise von Glehn, 20 September 1871, in *Life and Letters of Mandell Creighton*, p. 82.

32. 'Théophile Gautier', *Dark Blue*, 1 (March 1871), pp. 26–33.

33. 'Three Poets of French Bohemia', *Dark Blue*, 1 (May 1871), pp. 284–93.

34. *Oxford Undergraduate's Journal* (9 March 1871), p. 988.

35. *Oxford Undergraduate's Journal* (11 May 1871), p. 1043.

36. 'Spent Golden Hair', *Oxford Undergraduate's Journal* (18 May 1871), p. 1055. For Lang's translation of Villon, see *Dark Blue*, 1 (May 1871), p. 385.

37. *Oxford Undergraduate's Journal* (13 June 1866), p. 65.

38. *Oxford Undergraduate's Journal* (8 June 1871), p. 1102; reprinted in *In College Gardens: Old Rhymes Written in 1871* (Poulton, 1972).

39. Sellar, *Recollections and Impressions*, p. 230.

40. To RLS, 5 June [1886], *Dear Stevenson*, p. 98.

41. Sellar, *Recollections and Impressions*, p. 229.

42. Veronica Burbridge, 'Sympathy, Synthesis and Synergy: Patrick Geddes and the Edinburgh Social Union', in Walter Stephen, ed., *Learning from the Lasses: Women of the Patrick Geddes Circle* (Edinburgh, 2014), pp. 81–2.

43. A. G. Reekie, 'Lang the Elusive', *Scots Review*, 2 (1850), p. 153; p. 159; see also Roger Lancelyn Green, 'The Mystery of Andrew Lang', *Blackwood's*, 306 (December 1969), p. 527.

44. Green, 'Preface', *In College Gardens*.

45. Robert Buchanan (pseudonym 'Thomas Maitland'), 'The Fleshly School of Poetry', Contemporary Review, 18 (August 1871), pp. 334–50.

46. *North British Review*, 52 (July 1870), pp. 598–9. Lang's authorship is identified by Robert Crawford in 'Pater's *Renaissance*, Andrew Lang, and Anthropological Romanticism', *English Literary History*, 53 (Winter 1986), p. 860.

47. 'At the Sign of St Paul's', *ILN* (24 November 1906), p. 748. For his translation of Baudelaire's poem, see 'More Strong than Time', *Poetical Works*, Vol. 2, pp. 175–6

48. *The Miscellany Magazine*, 6 (January 1872), pp. 1-7; pp. 62-5; pp. 71-76; and 8 (April 1874), pp. 97-9. Bodleian.

49. 'At the Sign of the Ship', December 1887, p. 237.

50. Crawford, 'Pater's *Renaissance*, Andrew Lang, and Anthropological Romanticism', p. 865.

51. 'Edward Burnett Tylor', *Anthropological Essays Presented to Edward Burnett Tylor on his 75th Birthday*, ed. W. H. R. Rivers, et al. (Oxford, 1907), pp. 1-15.

52. 'Kalevala: or the Finnish National Epic', *Fraser's Magazine*, 5 (June 1872), pp. 667–77.

53. 'The Chanson de Roland', *Westminster Review*, 44 (July 1873), pp. 32–44.

54. 'Adventures Among Books', p. 37.

55. *Life and Letters of Mandell Creighton*, p. 89.

56. Professor W. H. Garrod to Roger Lancelyn Green; quoted Green, *Andrew Lang* (1946), p. 37.

57. Louise Creighton, *Memoir of a Victorian Woman*, ed. James Thayne Covert (Bloomington, 1994), p. 48.

58. Covert, *A Victorian Marriage*, p. 89.

59. 'Adventures Among Books', p. 34.

60. *Poetical Works*, Vol. 1, pp. 11–3.

61. Green, 'The Mystery of Andrew Lang', p. 527.

62. Pater to John Chapman, 27 November [1872], *Letters of Walter Pater*, ed. Lawrence Evans (Oxford, 1970).

63. Théophile de Valcourt, *Sketch of Cannes and its Climate* (London, 1872), p. 17; see also F. M. S., *Visitors' Guide to Cannes and Its Vicinity* (London, 1878).

64. 'At the Sign of St Paul's', 7 July 1906, p. 14.

65. To Robin Benson [7 April 1878]. NLS.

66. 'Mythology and Fairy Tales', *Fortnightly Review*, 13 (May 1873), pp. 618–31.

67. 'At the Sign of the Ship', February 1899, p. 376.

68. De Valcourt, *Sketch of Cannes*, p. 21.

69. Green, *Andrew Lang* (1946), p. 36.

70. To Edmund Gosse, 22 November [1911]. Brotherton.

71. *Oxford: Brief Historical and Descriptive Notes*, p. 29.

72. 'Recollections of Robert Louis Stevenson', *Adventures Among Books*, pp. 42–4.

73. RLS to his mother [13 February 1874], *The Letters of Robert Louis Stevenson*, Vol. 1, ed. Bradford A. Booth and Ernest Mehew (Newhaven and London, 1994), p. 483; hereafter referenced as *RLS Letters*.

74. RLS to Colvin [17 March 1874], and to his mother [23 March 1874], *RLS Letters*, Vol. 1, pp. 492–3; p. 497.

75. 'Recollections of Robert Louis Stevenson', p. 42.

76. Edmund Gosse, 'Robert Louis Stevenson', *Critical Kit-Kats* (London, 1913), p. 277. In Stevenson's *Kidnapped* (Ch. 16), the hero David Balfour sees an emigrant ship setting off from Loch Aline.

77. 'Recollections of Robert Louis Stevenson', pp. 42–4.

78. Lang to RLS Thursday [end of 1874?], Dear Stevenson, p. 36. For an account of this incident, see Michael Matthew Kaylor, *Secreted Desires: The Major Uranians* (Brno, 2006), p. 81.

79. Leonora Lang to William Munro, 28 November 1928. NLS.

80. Mrs A. Lang, 'Sir F. Leighton: His Life and Work', *The Art Annual for 1884*.

81. Ella Christie and Alice King Stewart, *A Long Look at Life, by Two Victorians* (London, 1940), pp. 170–1.

82. *The Mark of Cain* (London, 1886), pp. 54–5.

83. 'At the Sign of the Ship', January 1895, p. 328.

84. Sellar, *Recollections and Impressions*, p. 32.

85. 'Sketches of Italy and Greece', *Academy*, 5 (9 May 1874), p. 505.

86. To RLS, Thursday [June 1874], *Dear Stevenson*, p. 34.

87. To RLS, Thursday [June 1874], *Dear Stevenson*, p. 33.

88. Quoted Roger Lancelyn Green, *Andrew Lang* (London, 1962), p. 28.

89. To RLS, Sunday [August 1874], *Dear Stevenson*, p. 35.

90. Sellar, *Recollections and Impressions*, p. 261.

91. 'The Loves of Pulvis and Umbra, by Pulvis', *Miscellany Magazine*, 8 (October 1874), pp. 2–6. Bodleian.

92. 'On the Poems of Pulvis' (Reply), *Miscellany Magazine*, 8 (January 1875), p. 5. Bodleian.

93. To RLS, Monday [1875], *Dear Stevenson*, p. 41.

94. 'Rococo', *Poetical Works*, Vol. 3, p. 160.

95. Louise Creighton to her mother [4 October 1874], *A Victorian Family, As Seen through the Letters of Louise Creighton, 1872–1880* (London, 1998), p. 57.

96. Creighton, *A Victorian Family* p. 62.

97. 'Recollections of Robert Louis Stevenson', p. 44.

98. *Oxford: Brief Historical and Descriptive Notes* (1882, 2nd edition), p. 51.

99. 'Homer and Recent Criticism', *Fortnightly Review*, 23 (April 1875), pp. 275–89.

100. 'A Slipshod Story', *Miscellany Magazine*, 8 (April 1874), pp. 73–80.

101. To RLS [Monday, early January 1875], *Dear Stevenson*, pp. 40–1.

102. Quoted Green, *Andrew Lang* (1946), p. 38.

103. To RLS [Sunday 7 March 1875], *Dear Stevenson*, p. 37.

104. Green and others give the date as Saturday 17 April 1875, but in a letter to RLS in March, Lang states, 'My nuptials are 13 April'. This 13 April is supported by their marriage certificate.

105. *Oxford: Brief Historical and Descriptive Notes*, p. 30.

Chapter 5

1. 'Adventures Among Books', p. 15.
2. 'The Poets of French Bohemia', p. 281.
3. Sir Henry Lucy, *The Diary of a Journalist*, Vol. 3 (London, 1923), pp. 99–100.
4. Richard Whiteing, *My Harvest* (London, 1915), p. 273.
5. Jones, *King of Critics*, p. 63.
6. Saintsbury, 'Andrew Lang in the Seventies and After', in *The Eighteen-Seventies: Essays by Fellows of the Royal Society of Literature*, ed. Harley Granville-Barker (Cambridge, 1929), p. 90.
7. *Life and Letters of Mandell Creighton*, p. 250.
8. Covert, *A Victorian Marriage*, pp. 127–8.
9. Louise Creighton to her mother, 11 August 1872, *A Victorian Family*, pp. 32–3.
10. Elizabeth Grieve to Jean Lang, 3 August 1912. St Andrews.
11. Manuscript poem, 'The Wreck of the Diana: A Poem Composed in a Dream, 16 September 1875'. St Andrews.
12. To Hartley Coleridge, 20 April 1876. Harry Ransom Centre, University of Texas at Austin.
13. Stevenson, 'Forest Notes', *Cornhill Magazine*, 33 (May 1876), pp. 545-61.
14. Lang to RLS, Thursday [May 1876], *Dear Stevenson*, p. 42.
15. Janet E. Courtney, *The Making of an Editor: W. L. Courtney, 1850–1928* (London, 1930), p. 46.
16. *Aristotle's Politics* (London, 1877), pp. 10–2; pp. 90–105.
17. *Saturday Review*, 43 (3 March 1877), p. 266.
18. Henry James to his mother, 24 December 1876 and 31 January 1877; to Thomas Sergeant Perry, 12 January 1877, *The Complete Letters of Henry James, 1876–1878*, Vol. 1, ed. P. A. Walker and G. W. Zacharias (Lincoln and London, 2013), p. 14; p. 42; p. 38; hereafter referenced as *James Letters*.
19. Henry James to Thomas Sergeant Perry, 28 February 1877; 18 April 1877, *James Letters*, p. 74; p. 99.
20. Henry James to Perry, 17 January 1880, *James Letters, 1878–1880*, Vol. 2, (2015) p. 100. James's article appeared in the *North Atlantic Review*, 130 (January 1880), pp. 51–68.
21. Henry James to Lady Wolseley, 6 December 1886, *James Letters, 1884-1886*, Vol. 2, ed. M. Anesko and G. W. Zacharias (2021), p. 251.
22. To RLS [8 February 1877], *Dear Stevenson*, p. 43.
23. 'On Viol and Flute', *Academy*, 5 (31 January 1874), pp. 53–71.
24. Gosse, 'A Plea for Certain Forms of Exotic Poetry', *Cornhill Magazine*, 35 (May 1877), p. 71.
25. 'Proverbs in Porcelain', *Pall Mall Gazette* (6 June 1877), p. 12.
26. To Austin Dobson [18 July 1887]. London.
27. Gosse to Dobson, 24 July 1877; quoted Evan Charteris, *Life and Letters of Edmund Gosse* (London, 1931), p. 101.
28. William Davenport Adams, *Latter-Day Lyrics* (London, 1878), p. 345.
29. Hopkins to Robert Bridges, 13 May 1878, *The Letters of Gerard Manley Hopkins to Robert Bridges*, ed. Claude Colleer Abbott (London, 1935), pp. 49–50.

30. Hopkins to Bridges, 18 August 1888, *Letters of Hopkins to Robert Bridges*, pp. 279–80.

31. 'Drawing-Room Verse', *Saturday Review*, 45 (23 March 1878), pp. 365–6.

32. To Dobson [26 March 1878]. London.

33. RLS to Charles Baxter [June or July 1877], *RLS Letters*, Vol. 2, p. 214.

34. Lang to Dobson, 'The Nemesis of Art' (Handwritten enclosure), 'Tuesday' [1877 or 1878]. London.

35. 'The Nemesis of Art', 'At the Sign of the Ship', December 1900, pp. 188–9. Mrs Lang included the revised version of the double sonnet in Lang's *Poetical Works*, Vol. 3, pp. 85–6.

36. 'Théodore de Banville', *New Quarterly Magazine*, 10 (October 1878), pp. 559-78; reprinted in *Essays in Little* (London, 1891), pp. 51-76.

37. To Dobson [December 1877 or early 1878]. London. Lang's letter to Dobson, 'Tuesday' [1887 or 1888], mentions Henley's arrival in London, which took place in October 1887.

38. John Connell, *W. E. Henley* (London, 1949), p. 82.

39. 'Bishop Callaway's Appeal', *Academy*, 12 (17 November 1877), p. 470.

40. 'Bishop Callaway's Stories', *Academy*, 12 (1 December 1877), p 515.

41. William Thoms, 'A Folk-Lore Society', *Academy*, 12 (8 December 1877), p. 533.

42. 'The Folk-Lore of France', *Folk-Lore Record*, 1 (1878), p. 109.

43. Henley to RLS, 5 February 1879, *The Letters of William Ernest Henley to Robert Louis Stevenson*, ed. Damian Atkinson (High Wycombe, 2008), p. 57; hereafter referenced as *Henley to Stevenson*.

44. To RLS, Wednesday [March 1879], *Dear Stevenson*, p. 44.

45. Henley to RLS, early March 1879, *Henley to Stevenson*, p. 62.

46. To Henley, March 1879. Beinecke.

47. To RLS, Tuesday [1879], *Dear Stevenson*, p. 46.

48. To Gosse, 13 March 1879. Brotherton.

49. To Gosse, 'Madrigal of Robert Buchanan'. Brotherton.

50. To Gosse, Thursday [1879]. Brotherton.

51. 'Notes on Books', *Cosmopolis*, 9 (January 1898), p. 64.

52. 'Preface', *Odyssey of Homer*, trans. S.H. Butcher and Andrew Lang (London, 1879), p. v.

53. 'Preface', *Odyssey of Homer*, p. vii.

54. *London: The Conservative Weekly* (15 February 1879).

55. 'At the Sign of the Ship', January 1896, p. 315.

56. To RLS, Saturday [1879], *Dear Stevenson*, p. 45.

57. To Dobson, Thursday [1879]. London.

58. 'Ballade of Theocritus', *Poetical Works*, Vol. 1, p. 193.

59. To Patrick Sellar Lang, 18 May 1879. St Andrews.

60. To John Fergusson McLennan, 6 November [1879]. Columbia.

61. Henry James to his father, 11 October 1879, *James Letters 1878–1880*, Vol. 2, p. 19.

62. 'Mr. Max Müller and Fetishism', *Mind: A Quarterly Review of Psychology and Philosophy*, 4 (October 1879), pp. 453–69.

63. To MacLennan, 6 November [1879]. Columbia. Lang's final revised version of the poem, with three additional stanzas by Tylor, was retitled 'Double Ballade of Primitive Man', *Poetical Works*, Vol. 1, pp. 221–3.

64. Edward Clodd, 'George Meredith: Some Recollections', *Fortnightly Review*, 86 (July 1909), p. 29.

65. Mrs Lang to Mr E. V. Lucas, 18 October 1928. St Andrews.

66. *Spectator*, 53 (3 July 1880), p. 849.

67. 'Ballade of Blue China', *Poetical Works*, Vol. 1, pp. 197–8.

68. *Punch*, 79 (October 1880), p. 194.

69. Dobson, 'Dizain', *XXII Ballades in Blue China* (London, 1880), p. 57.

70. 'Ballade of Sleep', *Poetical Works*, Vol. 1, pp. 187–8.

71. Henry James to Thomas Sergeant Perry, 22 February 1880, *James Letters 1878–1880*, Vol. 2, p. 132.

72. To Gosse, 17 April 1880. Brotherton.

73. James, 'Italy Revisited', *Atlantic Monthly*, April–May 1878; reprinted in *Italian Hours* (London, 1909), pp. 107–35.

74. 'San Terenzo', *Poetical Works*, Vol. 2, p. 10.

75. 'The Romance of the First Radical: A Prehistoric Apologue', *Fraser's Magazine* (September 1880), pp. 289–300; revised for *In the Wrong Paradise* (London, 1887).

76. *Prometheus Unbound*, Act IV, II. 378–84.

77. See, for example, Marianne Sommer, 'The Romantic Cave: The Scientific and Poetic Quests for Subterranean Spaces in Britain', *Earth Sciences History*, 22 (2003), pp. 172–208.

78. Ralph O'Connor, *The Earth on Show: Fossils and the Poetics of Popular of Popular Science, 1802–1856* (Oxford, 2008), p. 446.

79. Julia Sparks, 'At the Intersection of Victorian Science and Fiction: Andrew Lang's 'Romance of the First Radical', *English Literature in Transition*, 42 (1999), pp. 124–42. Leigh Wilson goes further to claim of 'Romance of the First Radical' that 'fact and fantasy are so tightly bound together that they cannot be separated', in *Journal of Literature* and *Science*, 6 (2013), pp. 29–43.

80. To Gosse, 17 April 1880. Brotherton.

81. Francis Hueffer, 'Modern Troubadours', *Macmillan's Magazine*, 43 (1 November 1880), p. 45.

82. Mrs Lang to Mr E. V. Lucas, 18 October 1928. St Andrews.

83. 'At the Sign of the Ship', March 1897, p. 482.

84. *Life and Letters of Edmund Clarence Stedman*, ed. Laura Stedman and George M. Gould, Vol. 2 (New York, 1910), p. 28.

85. Edmund Clarence Stedman, 'Some London Poets', *Harper's*, 64 (1 May 1882), pp. 880–1.

86. Brander Matthews, *These Many Years* (New York, 1917), p. 263.

87. To Matthews, Sunday [1881], p. 30, *Friends across the Ocean: Andrew Lang's American Correspondents 1881–1912*, ed. Marysa Demoor (Gent, 1989), p. 30; hereafter referenced as *Friends*.

88. 'The Plumber and the Publisher: A Ballad of the Trade', *Recreations of the Rabelais Club 1882–1885*, pp. 8–9.

89. To Matthews, 27 April [1882], *Friends*, p. 38.
90. To RLS Sunday [1882], *Dear Stevenson*, p. 53.
91. Mrs Lang to Mr Lucas, 18 October 1928. St Andrews. James moved to De Vere Gardens in 1886.
92. Henley to RLS, 1 November 1881, *The Selected Letters of W. E. Henley*, ed. Damian Atkinson (Aldershot, 2000), pp. 90–1.
93. To Matthews, 26 December [1881], *Friends*, p. 33.
94. 'Idylls of the Dado. I: The Private View', *Pall Mall Gazette* (4 January 1882), p. 4.
95. 'Idylls of the Dado. 2: The Disappointing Deep', *Pall Mall Gazette* (7 January 1882), p. 4. Richard Ellmann references 'The Disappointing Deep' in *Oscar Wilde* (London, 1887), p. 151, apparently unaware that Lang was the author.
96. To Matthews, 1 February [1882], *Friends*, p. 34.
97. RLS to Henley [20 October 1881], *RLS Letters*, Vol. 3, p. 241.
98. To RLS, 17 December [1883], *Dear Stevenson*, p. 62.
99. Alfred Russel Wallace, *Land Nationalisation: Its Necessity and Aims* (London, 1882).
100. John Stuart Blackie, *Altavona: Fact and Fiction from My Life in the Highlands* (Edinburgh, 1882), p. 281; p. 291.
101. Stuart Wallace, *John Stuart Blackie: Scottish Scholar and Patriot* (Edinburgh, 2006), p. 287.
102. Wallace, *Blackie*, p. 287.
103. *Athenaeum* (1 July 1882), p. 11.
104. *Saturday Review*, 54 (3 June 1882), pp. 701–2.
105. Peter Bushell, 'Hall Grove, Bagshot, Surrey: A History'. Online.
106. To Matthews, 30 November 1881, *Friends*, p. 32.
107. To Dobson, 17 April [1882]. London.
108. To Matthews, 25 July [1882], *Friends*, p. 39.
109. To Dobson, [1882]. London.
110. To Matthews, 22 April 1882, *Friends*, p. 37.

Chapter 6

1. Lang to RLS, Sunday [1882], *Dear Stevenson*, p. 51; see also Roger Lancelyn Green, 'Dear Andrew and Dear Louis', *Scribner's Magazine*, 43 (9 August 1945), pp. 375–81.
2. Lang to RLS, 3 February [1882], *Dear Stevenson*, p. 48.
3. Lang to Gosse, [21 October 1882]. Brotherton.
4. Lang to Gosse, Thursday 15 December 1882. Brotherton.
5. 'Mr. Morris's Poems', *Adventures Among Books*, pp. 100–1.
6. *Poetical Works*, Vol. 4, p. 68.
7. W. L. Courtney, 'Poets of Today', *Fortnightly Review*, 34 (November 1883), pp. 713–27. Other reviews expressing similar reservation, are: *Harper's*, 66, March 1883, pp. 638–40, and *Century Illustrated Magazine*, 24 (October 1883), p. 955
8. *Poetical Works*, Vol. 4, p. 99.
9. *Poetical Works*, Vol. 4, p. 104.
10. Lang to Symonds, 5 January [1883]. Bristol.

11. Gosse, *Portraits and Sketches* (London, 1912) p. 204.

12. To Symonds, 5 January [1883]. Bristol.

13. To RLS, 7 March 1875, *Dear Stevenson*, p. 37.

14. To Matthews, 28 October 1882, *Friends*, p. 41.

15. 'Introduction', *Custom and Myth* (London, 1884), p. 9.

16. To RLS, December 1882, *Dear Stevenson*, p. 61.

17. Lang to Matthews, 11 February 1883, *Friends*, p. 43–4. Eliza Cook was a poet, Chartist, and believer in self-improvement through education.

18. To Gosse, 22 January 1883. Brotherton.

19. To Matthews, 27 April [1882], *Friends*, p. 38.

20. 'Almae Matres', *Poetical Works*, Vol. 1, pp. 3–5.

21. To RLS, [Sunday 1882], *Dear Stevenson*, p. 54.

22. *Oxford Magazine*, 7 February 1883; reprinted in *Echoes from the Oxford Magazine* (London, 1890), p. 63. Arthur Quiller-Couch wrote to Lang's bibliographer, C. M. Falconer, saying he believed J. W. Mackail wrote 'The Ballade of Andrew Lang'. Roger Lancelyn Green's added a pencil note to the letter, 'It was D. S. MacColl'. A. T. Quiller-Couch to C. M. Falconer, 30 May 1898. St Andrews.

23. To Matthews, 11 April [1883], *Friends*, pp. 46–7.

24. To RLS, 3 June [1884], *Dear Stevenson*, p. 70.

25. To Gosse, 22 March [1880]. Brotherton.

26. To Matthews, 3 October [1882], *Friends*, p. 40.

27. To Matthews, 17 October [1883], *Friends*, p. 47.

28. 'The Dreadful Trade', *Scots Observer*, 1 (16 February 1889), pp. 365–7.

29. To RLS, 11 November 1883; quoted *RLS Letters*, Vol. 4, p. 205.

30. To RLS, 22 June [1884] and Sunday [1885], *Dear Stevenson*, pp. 70–1; p. 84

31. To Bridges, Sunday [1883]. Bodleian.

32. 'Mano: A Poetical History', *Saturday Review*, 56 (8 September 1883), pp. 313–4.

33. Bridges to Richard Watson Dixon, 15 September [1883]. Bodleian.

34. Myth, *Ritual and Religion*, Vol. 1 (London, 1887), p. 154.

35. To Matthews, 17 October [1883], *Friends*, p. 47.

36. James to Lady Wolseley, 8 December 1883, *James Letters*, 1883–1884, ed. Michael Anesco, Greg Zacharias, Katie Summer, Vol. 1 (Lincoln and London, 2018), pp. 274–5.

37. 'The Palace of Bric-à-Brac', *Century Illustrated Magazine*, 28 (May 1884), p. 57, and *Rhymes à La Mode* (London, 1885), pp. 97–9. Mrs Lang omitted the poem from his *Poetical Works*.

38. Gosse, 'Some Recollections of Lord Wolseley', *Aspects and Impressions* (London, 1922), p. 277.

39. To Matthews, 4 April [1884], *Friends*, p. 53.

40. To Matthews, 3 March [1884], *Friends*, p. 52.

41. *Custom and Myth*, p. 2.

42. *Custom and Myth*, p. 154.

43. *Custom and Myth*, p. 63.

44. *Custom and Myth*, p. 216.

45. Teverson, Warwick, and Wilson, eds., 'Introduction', *Selected Writings of Andrew Lang* (Edinburgh, 2015), p. 34.

46. *Custom and Myth*, p. 203, pp. 214–20. De Brosses' actual words, with reference to African tribal fetish-worship, are: '*Quoique quelques-uns d'entre eux qui ont quelque foible idee d'un Être Supérieur ne les regardent pas égaux à lui*' ('Some of those who have a faint idea of a Higher Being do not regard them [i.e. their fetishes] as equal to him'). *Culte des Dieux Fétiches* (1760), p. 20.

47. *Poetical Works*, Vol. 2, p. 22.

48. *The Odyssey of Homer*, p. 32.

49. To George Bell, 19 December 1884. Reading.

50. To RLS, 8 May [1884], *Dear Stevenson*, p. 27.

51. Mrs Lang, *Dissolving Views,* Vol. 1 (London and New York, 1884), p. 32.

52. *Dissolving Views*, Vol. 1, pp. 134–5.

53. *Dissolving Views*, Vol. 2, pp. 30–1.

54. *Spectator*, 57, 12 July 1884, pp. 919–20.

55. To Gosse, 13 May [1884]. Brotherton.

56. 'Ballade of Neglected Merit', *Poetical Works*, Vol 1, pp. 207–8.

57. Henley to RLS, 3 February 1880, *Henley Letters*, p. 79; see also 'The Sign of the Ship', February 1893.

58. *The Theatre* (1 March 1884), p. 149.

59. Mrs Lang to Mr Lucas, 18 October 1928. St Andrews.

60. To RLS, 24 April [1884], *Dear Stevenson*, p. 65.

61. 'Ballade of Middle Age', *Poetical Works*, Vol. 1, pp. 199–200

62. 'Desiderium, In Memoriam S. F. A.', *Poetical Works*, Vol. 1, pp. 154–5.

63. To Gosse, 3 September [1884]. Brotherton.

64. Lady Wolseley to Lord Wolseley, 20 November 1884, *The Letters of Lord and Lady Wolseley 1870–1911*, ed. Sir George Arthur (London and New York, 1922), p. 146.

65. To Tylor, 6 January [1885]. Pitt Rivers.

66. To Gosse, 8 September 1884. Brotherton. To Symonds, 7 December 1884. Bristol.

67. To Matthews, 8 November [1884], and 9 December [1884], *Friends*, pp. 54–5; p. 57.

68. Walter Herries Pollock, Note to 'XXVIII, Viperum Malum', *A New Friendship's Garland.*

69. To Matthews, 11 February [1885], *Friends*, p. 60.

70. To RLS, 14 December [1884]; and 30 December [1884], *Dear Stevenson*, p. 34; p. 76.

71. 'Quite the Wrong Man', *Punch*, 88 (11 April 1885), p. 173; p. 180. The serial continued with O'Dwyer escaping another adventure in 'The Fenians' Den', *Punch*, 88 (18 April 1885), p. 192.

72. To Symonds, 7 December [1884]. Bristol.

73. To Gosse, 22 December [1884]. Brotherton.

74. *Magazine of Art*, 8 (January 1885), pp. 390–1.

75. *Punch*, 88 (3 January 1885), p. 2.

76. 'Beauty and the Beast', *Longman's Christmas Number* (December 1884) p. 22.

77. 'Beauty and the Beast', *Punch*, 88 (28 March 1885), p. 150.

78. To Lady Wolseley, 28 January [1885]. Hove.

79. 'The White Pacha', *Poetical Works*, Vol. 1, pp. 80–1.

80. To Matthews, 11 February [1885], *Friends*, p. 59

81. To Lady Wolseley, 30 April [1885]. Hove.

82. To RLS, Wednesday and Sunday [1885], *Dear Stevenson*, p. 79; p. 85. See also RLS to Symonds, 30 February 1885, *RLS Letters*, Vol. 5, pp. 80–1.

83. 'Νήνεμος Αἰών', *Poetical Works*, Vol. 3, p. 57.

84. To Matthews [1885], *Friends*, p. 61.

85. To RLS, 11 March [1885], *Dear Stevenson*, p. 83.

86. Grant Allen, 'That Very Mab', *Longman's Magazine* (November 1885), pp. 83–7.

87. Quoted Haggard, *The Days of My Life*, Vol. 1 (London, 1926), p. 227.

88. Quoted, *The Days of My Life*, Vol. 1., p. 227.

89. To Mrs Puller, 13 November 1900. Hertford.

90. Quoted Morton Cohen, *Rudyard Kipling to Rider Haggard* (London, 1965), p. 123.

91. Haggard, *The Witch's Head*, Vol. 2 (London, 1884), Ch. 8.

92. 'At the Sign of the Ship', February 1888, p. 459.

93. 'The End of Phæacia', first appeared in *Time* (London), 14 (January, February, March 1886), pp. 46–60; 168–81; pp. 280–91; 'My Friend the Beachcomber', in *Longman's Magazine* (August 1885), pp. 417–23; and 'A Cheap Nigger', in *Cornhill Magazine*, 52 (August 1885), pp. 154–73. All three stories were reprinted in *In the Wrong Paradise* (London, 1886).

94. To RLS, 17 April [1885], *Dear Stevenson*, p. 87.

95. *The Mark of Cain* (Bristol, 1886), p. 3; pp. 27–8; p. 70.

96. *Academy*, 26 (29 May 1886), pp. 377–8.

97. To Mrs Ritchie, 22 May [1886]. Eton.

98. To Gosse, 15 October [1885]. Brotherton.

99. *Academy*, 27 (9 May 1885), p. 331, and (13 June 1885), p. 422.

100. *Academy*, 27 (20 June 1885), pp. 438–9.

101. To Gosse, 14 November [1885]. Brotherton.

102. Quoted Marysa Demoor, 'Andrew Lang versus W. D. Howells: A Late-Victorian Duel', *Journal of American Studies*, 21 (December 1987), p. 417.

103. Abraham Hayward, 'Varieties of History and Art', *Biographical and Critical Essays: New Series*, Vol. 2 (London, 1873), pp. 1–2.

Chapter 7

1. To Matthews, 2 May [1886], *Friends*, p. 73.

2. Typed note for Anderson Sale Catalogue, November 1914. St Andrews.

3. RLS to Lang [May 1886], *RLS Letters*, Vol. 5, p. 253.

4. To Matthews, 24 January 1886, *Friends*, p. 70.

5. To RLS, 5 June [1886], *Dear Stevenson*, p. 98.

6. To Gosse [4 June 1886]. Brotherton.

7. 'To Percy Bysshe Shelley', *Letters to Dead Authors* (London, 1886), pp. 173–83.

8. Quoted from *A Book of Sybils* (London, 1883), p. 198, in *Letters to Dead Authors*, p. 85.

9. *Letters to Dead Authors*, p. 2.

10. To Mrs Ritchie, 22 May [1886]. Eton.

11. 'Letters to Dead Authors', *Spectator*, 50 (1 May 1886), p. 584.

12. RLS to Lang, 10 March [1886], *RLS Letters*, Vol. 5, pp. 226–8; reprinted with slight changes in *Underwoods*.

13. Benjamin Jowett, 'Testimonial for A. Lang', 26 June 1886. M421, Balliol.

14. Hayward, 'Varieties of History and Art', pp. 1–2.

15. 'At the Sign of the Ship', January 1888, p. 351.

16. To Gosse, 4 September [1885]. Brotherton.

17. To Gosse, 22 March 1880. Brotherton.

18. *Letters to Dead Authors*, p. 207.

19. 'At the Sign of the Ship', November 1886, pp. 107–9.

20. To Gosse, 29 December [1885]. Brotherton.

21. To Symonds, July [1886]. Bristol.

22. To RLS, 25 July [1886], *Dear Stevenson*, p. 99.

23. To RLS, 12 November [1882], *Dear Stevenson*, p. 59.

24. To Gosse, 7 January [1886]. Brotherton.

25. To Symonds, 10 August [1886]. Bristol.

26. To Matthews, 28 September 1886, *Friends*, p. 75.

27. To Lady Wolseley, 28 September [1886]. Hove.

28. Churton Collins, *Quarterly Review*, 163 (October 1886), pp. 289–329.

29. 'At the Sign of the Ship', May 1901, p. 95.

30. To Symonds, 15 July [1886]. Bristol.

31. To Matthews, 18 February [1890], *Friends*, p. 104.

32. Gosse, 'The *Quarterly Review* and Mr. Gosse', *Athenaeum* (23 October 1886), pp. 534–5.

33. *Pall Mall Gazette* (23 October 1886), p. 3.

34. 'At the Sign of the Ship', December 1886, pp. 216–20.

35. *Pall Mall Gazette* (29 November 1886), p. 5.

36. To RLS, 3 December [1886], *Dear Stevenson*, p. 103.

37. To Matthews, 23 November [1886], *Friends*, p. 76.

38. 'Literary Quarrels', *Saturday Review*, 48 (15 November 1879), pp. 594–5.

39. William Dean Howells, 'Henry James Jr.', *Century Illustrated Magazine*, 25 (November 1882), pp. 25–9.

40. To Matthews, 1 January [1883], *Friends*, p. 42.

41. 'The Restoration of Romance', 'At the Sign of the Ship', March 1887, pp. 554–5; reprinted in *Poetical Works*, Vol. 3, pp. 196–8.

42. 'Ballade of Railway Novels', 'At the Sign of the Ship', July 1884, p. 296; reprinted in *Poetical Works*, Vol. 1, pp. 126–7.

43. To Matthews, 22 May [1887], *Friends*, p. 83.

44. 'Realism and Romance', *Contemporary Review*, 52 (November 1887), pp. 683–93.

45. W. H. Pollock, note to 'VI, A Friend Sketched', *A New Friendship's Garland*.

46. 'The Avengers of Romance', *ILN* (30 April 1892), p. 539.

47. 'Realism and Romance', p. 689.

48. 'At the Sign of the Ship', June 1891, p. 217.

49. 'Romanticism and Realism', *Saturday Review*, 78 (8 December 1894), 615–6.

50. 'Realism and Romance', p. 685.

51. To Rhoda Broughton, 9 July [1898]. Cheshire.

52. 'At the Sign of the Ship', February 1891, p. 445; June 1899, p. 186.

53. Obituary, *Oxford Magazine* (11 June 1920).

54. To Lady Wolseley, 23 November [1886]. Hove.

55. To Rhoda Broughton, 10 December 1886. Cheshire.

56. To Rhoda Broughton, 14 December 1886. Cheshire.

57. To Rhoda Broughton, 29 January [1887]. Cheshire; see also *Poetical Works*, Vol. 1, pp. 121–2.

58. To Lady Wolseley, 26 December 1996. Hove.

59. Jowett to Mrs Lang, 16 January 1887. St Andrews.

60. 'Cupid and Psyche' (Review), *Saturday Review*, 63 (11 June 1887), pp. 845–6.

61. To Matthews, 7 January and 21 January [1887], *Friends*, pp. 77–8.

62. *Academy*, 69 (9 May 1896), p. 385; 'At the Sign of St Paul's', *ILN* (26 February 1910), p. 304.

63. To Lady Wolseley, 10 July [1887]. Hove.

64. To Matthews, 13 July [1887], *Friends*, p. 86.

65. To RLS, 12 March [1886], *Dear Stevenson*, p. 94.

66. Benjamin Jowett to Mrs Eleanor Sellar, 12 May 1887. Balliol.

67. 'Ah Fortune, thy wheel'. St Andrews.

68. To Matthews, 17 September [1887], *Friends*, p. 88.

69. *Poetical Works*, Vol. 1, pp. 34–5.

70. To Matthews, 25 July [1887], *Friends*, p. 87.

71. To RLS, 10 November [1887], *Dear Stevenson*, p. 110.

72. *Poetical Works*, Vol. 1, pp. 34–5.

73. To Matthews, 5 October [1887], *Friends*, p. 89.

74. 'At the Sign of the Ship', June 1887, pp. 223–4.

75. Evelyn Abbott and Lewis Campbell, *The Life and Letters of Benjamin Jowett* Vol. 2 (London, 1897), p. 289.

76. Jowett to Miss C. M. Symonds, 2 January 1888, *Life and Letters of Jowett*, Vol. 2, p. 335.

77. Eleanor Sellar recalls that on a visit to Balliol, William Young Sellar was given the manuscript to read by Jowett. *Recollections and Impressions*, p. 327. The manuscript is now in NLS, Acc. 13025.

78. 'The Influence of Mr. Jowett', *ILN* (10 August 1895), p. 210.

79. *La Mythologie*, trans. Léon Parmenter, with a Preface by Charles Michel (Paris, 1886).

80. *Myth Ritual and Religion*, Vol. 1 (London, 1887), pp. 62–3. Lang's reference is to his uncle, Gideon Scott Lang's *The Aborigines of Australia*.

81. *Myth, Ritual and Religion*, pp. 164–7.

82. 'Preface', *Myth, Ritual and Religion*, p. vii.

83. *St James's Gazette*, 15 (3 December 1887), pp. 6–7.

84. *New Englander and Yale Review*, 12 (January 1888), p. 44.

85. *Unitarian Review*, 29 (February 1888), pp. 186–8.

86. To Matthews, 21 November [1887], *Friends*, p. 91.

87. *Myth, Ritual and Religion*, 2nd edition, Vol. 1 (London, 1899), p. 339.

88. To Lady Wolseley, 9 February [1888]. Hove.

89. *Pictures at Play, or Dialogues of the Galleries* (London, 1888).

90. 'Mr. Henley's Book of Verses', *Saturday Review*, 65 (23 June 1888), p. 724.

91. Henley to Charles Whibley, 12 November 1888, in Connell, *Henley*, p. 135.
92. 'At the Sign of the Ship', September 1890, p. 56.
93. Courtney, *The Making of An Editor*, p. 35.
94. 'Theological Romances', *Contemporary Review*, 53 (1 January 1888), p. 814.
95. Quoted Haggard, *The Days of My Life*, Vol. 1, p. 282.
96. To Matthews, 13 April [1888], *Friends*, p. 97.
97. 'The Gifford Lectures', *Scots Observer*, 1 (19 January 1889), pp. 233–4.
98. 'At the Sign of the Ship', May 1888, p. 105.
99. To Rhoda Broughton, 21 March [1888]. Cheshire.
100. To Rhoda Broughton, 16 April [1888]. Cheshire.
101. 'At the Sign of the Ship', June 1888, p. 217.
102. Mrs Humphry Ward, *A Writer's Recollections*, Vol. 2 (London, 1918), p. 84.
103. To RLS, 28 September [1888], *Dear Stevenson*, p. 114.
104. *The Gold of Fairnilee*, Ch. 10.
105. To Matthews, Dec 12 [1887], *Friends*, p. 94.
106. Green, *Andrew Lang* (1946), p. 82.
107. Pennell, 'Andrew Lang as a Lecturer', *The Critic*, 10 (December 1888), p. 329.
108. To Gosse, 3 December [1888]. Brotherton.
109. To Unknown Correspondent, 18 May 1888. St Andrews.
110. To RLS, 20 April [1889], *Dear Stevenson*, p. 115.
111. For an account of the novel's construction, see Green, *Andrew Lang* (1946), pp. 125–9. Lang's letters to Haggard are deposited at Lockwood Memorial Library, University of Buffalo, N.Y., with copies at St Andrews.
112. To Matthews, 26 October [1887], *Friends*, p. 90.
113. 'The Gifford Lectures', *Scots Observer*, 1 (19 January 1889), p. 233.

Chapter 8

1. M. Leicester Addis, 'St Andrews and Andrew Lang', *Frank Leslie's Popular Monthly*, 39 (January 1895), pp. 1–12.
2. Quoted Andrew Boyd Kennedy Hutchison, *Twenty-Five Years of St Andrews, September 1865 to September 1890* (London, 1892), p. 324.
3. *Scots Observer*, 1 (19 January 1889), p. 234.
4. *The Making of Religion* (London, 3rd edition, 1909), p. 46.
5. Quoted in *The Making of Religion*, p. 59.
6. *The Making of Religion*, p. 39.
7. *The Making of Religion*, p. 202.
8. To Sir James Donaldson, 10 January [1890]. St Andrews.
9. To Craig-Brown, 11 May [1889]. Hawick.
10. To Craig-Brown, 1 and 5 June [1889]. Hawick.
11. *Scots Observer*, 2 (29 June 1889), pp. 148–9.
12. To Gilbert Murray, 1 August [1889]. Bodleian.
13. Quoted Sharin F. Schroeder, 'Lasting Ephemera: Margaret Oliphant and Andrew Lang on Lives and Letters', *Victorian Periodical Review*, 50 (Summer 2017), p. 341.

14. To G. R. Thomson, 3 August 1888; quoted Linda K. Hughes, *Graham R.: Rosamund Marriott Thomson, Woman of Letters* (Athens, 2005), pp. 70–1.
15. To Murray, 1 August [1889]. Bodleian.
16. To Murray, 10 July [1889]. Bodleian.
17. To Lady Wolseley, undated [1889]. Hove.
18. 'At the Sign of the Ship', January 1888, pp. 347–8.
19. 'At the Sign of the Ship', May 1896, pp. 101–110.
20. *Life, Letters and Diaries of Sir Stafford Northcote*, Vol. 1, p. 6; p. 26; p. 43.
21. 'Rudyard Kipling: Biographical and Critical Sketch', in Rudyard Kipling, *The Courting of Dinah Shadd and Other Stories* (New York, 1890), pp. vii–xii.
22. 'At the Sign of the Ship', October 1886, pp. 675–7.
23. 'Mr Kipling's Stories', *Saturday Review*, 68 (10 August 1889), p. 165. He followed this up with two further notices: 'An Indian Story-teller', *Daily News* (2 November 1889), p. 4; and 'Anglo-Indian', *Daily News* (15 March 1890), pp. 4–5.
24. Kipling to Lang, 26 October 1889, in Thomas Pinney, ed., *The Letters of Rudyard Kipling, Vol. 1, 1872–1889* (London, 1990), pp. 351–2.
25. Mrs Thackeray Ritchie to Mrs Gerald Ritchie [1889], quoted Hester, Thackeray Ritchie, ed., *Thackeray and His Daughter* (New York, 1924), p. 226. For a record of the press reports on the Countess de la Torre's appearances in the police courts, see Sarah Hartwell, 'The Case of the Countess de la Torre—a Nineteenth Century Cat Hoarder' (2014). Online, messybeast.com.
26. Green, *Andrew Lang* (1946), pp. 81–2.
27. Sanjay Sircar, 'The Generic Decorum of the Burlesque *Kunstmärchen*: E. Nesbit's The Magician's Heart', *Folklore*, 110 (1999), pp. 75–91.
28. J. R. R. Tolkien, 'On Fairy-Stories', in C. S. Lewis et al., *Essays Presented to Charles Williams* (Oxford, 1947), p. 45.
29. Green, *Andrew Lang* (1946), p. 105.
30. 'At the Sign of the Ship', March 1898, p. 469.
31. *Academy*, 8 (15 July 1875), p. 57.
32. 'Introduction: Literary Fairy Tales', *Little Johannes*, trans. From the Dutch of Frederik van Eeden (London, 1895), p. xvi; p. xii.
33. 'Literary Fairy Tales', p. xvii.
34. 'How to Fail in Literature', (London, 1890). The lecture contained passages from his earlier 'The Dreadful Trade', *Scots Observer*, 1 (16 February 1889), pp. 356–7.
35. To Lady Wolseley, 29 November [1889]. Hove.
36. *Scots Observer*, 3 (7 December 1889), pp. 63–4.
37. *Scots Observer*, 2 (24 August 1889), pp. 375–6.
38. *Athenaeum* (28 September 1889), p. 420. See Henley to Whibley, 2 October, 5 November, and 10 December 1889, *The Letters of William Earnest Henley to Charles Whibley 1888–1903*, ed. Damian Atkinson (Lewiston, 2013), p. 49; p. 61; pp. 71–2; hereafter referenced as *Henley to Whibley*.
39. To Matthews, 18 November 1889, *Friends*, p. 102.
40. To Gosse, 2 November [1888]. Brotherton.
41. 'Semitic Religion', *Speaker*, 1 (4 January 1890), pp. 21–2.
42. To Sir James Donaldson, February [1890]. St Andrews.

43. *College Echoes*, 19 (27 March 1890), p. 155.
44. To Matthews, 7 April [1890], *Friends*, p. 105.
45. To Sir James Donaldson, April [1890]. St Andrews.
46. 'Lines on Mr. Andrew Lang's "Gifford lectures" on Natural Theology', *Temple Bar*, 89 (1 May 1890), p. 172.
47. A. H. Miller, 'An English Rendering of the Foregoing', *Evening Telegraph* (26 May 1890); reprinted in *A New Friendship's Garland*.
48. To Jean Lang, 17 July 1890. St Andrews.
49. 'At the Sign of the Ship', September 1890, p. 575.
50. Lewis Campbell, 'Professor Sellar, LLD', *Classical Review*, 4 (November 1890), pp. 438–40.
51. 'Memoir of William Young Sellar', p. xxii.
52. To Matthews, 14 December [1888], *Friends*, p. 99.
53. To RLS, 16 December [1890], *Dear Stevenson*, p. 120.
54. 'The Origin of the Aryans', *National Observer*, 3 (22 March 1890), pp. 500-1. For correspondence on the subject, see *National Observer*, 3 (19 March and 5, 19, 26 April 1890).
55. Henley to Whibley, 1 and 4 April 1890, *Henley to Whibley*, p. 106; p. 108.
56. Henley, 'Culture and Anarchy', *National Observer* (13 December 1890), pp. 99–100.
57. To Matthews, 16 September [1890], *Friends*, p. 106.
58. To Gosse, 1 January [1891]. Brotherton.
59. To Dobson, 14 January [1891]. London.
60. To Gosse, 4 January [1891]. Brotherton.
61. *Saturday Review*, 70 (1 November 1890), pp. 505–6.
62. Lord to Lady Wolseley, 11 November 1890, *The Letters of Lord and Lady Wolseley, 1870–1911*, (London, 1922), pp. 371–3.
63. To Lord Wolseley, 15 November [1890]. Hove.
64. To Matthews, 16 September [1890], *Friends*, p. 106.
65. *College Echoes*, 3 (3 December 1891), p. 134.
66. To Matthews, 25 May [1892], *Friends*, p. 117.
67. *College Echoes*, 3 (3 March 1892), p.134.
68. *College Echoes*, 8 (8 January 1891), pp. 59–60.
69. To Gosse, 9 November [1892]. Brotherton.
70. To William Henry Helm, 19 February [n. y.]. St Andrews.
71. Philippa Levine, *The Amateur and the Professional: Antiquarians, Historians and Archaeologists in Victorian England 1838–1886* (Cambridge, 1986), pp. 142–3.
72. *College Echoes*, 4 (26 March 1891), p. 158.
73. *Author* (1 July 1891), pp. 43–4; reprinted in *Gissing: Critical Heritage*, eds. Pierre Coustillas and Colin Partridge (London and Boston, 1972), pp. 183–4.
74. *Poetical Works*, Vol. 1, pp. 18–9.
75. *College Echoes*, 4 (2 March 1893), p. 158; 5 (8 February 1894), p. 125.
76. *Angling Sketches* (London, 1891), p. 8; p. 95.
77. To Mrs Maxwell-Scott, 9 October 1891. NLS.
78. To Mrs Maxwell-Scott, 9 October 1891. NLS.
79. Stevenson to Colvin, 3 January 1892, *RLS Letters*, Vol. 7, p. 220.

80. *New Review*, 6 (February 1892), pp. 247–9.
81. Hardy to Clodd, 4 February 1892, *The Collected Letters of Thomas Hardy, Vol. 1: 1840–1892*, eds. Richard Little Purdy and Michael Millgate (Oxford, 1978), p. 257.
82. Hardy, *Tess* (5th edition, 1892); extract quoted *ILN* (1 October 1892), p. 435.
83. 'At the Sign of the Ship', November 1892, pp. 100–106.
84. To RLS, 28 November [1892], *Dear Stevenson*, p. 141.
85. RLS to Sidney Colvin, 19 May 1892, and RLS to J. M. Barrie, 20 June 1892, *RLS Letters*, Vol. 7, p. 284; p. 315.
86. 'Was Jehovah a Fetish Stone?', *Contemporary Review* 57 (March 1890), pp. 356–65.
87. To RLS, 7 October [1890], *Dear Stevenson*, p. 117.
88. To Oliver Lodge, 27 February [1890]. SPR, Cambridge.
89. To Clodd, 6 June 1900. Brotherton.
90. To RLS, 8 November 1890, *Dear Stevenson*, p. 118.
91. Levine, *The Amateur and the Professional*, p. 34.
92. Walter Leaf, *A Companion to the Iliad for English Readers* (London, 1892).
93. *Homer and the Epic* (London, 1893), pp. 296–7.
94. 'At the Sign of the Ship', September 1892, pp. 543–5.
95. 'The Master of Balliol', p. 479.
96. To Matthews, 12 December [1892], *Friends*, p. 119
97. Platt, *Classical Review*, 7 (July 1893), pp. 318–22.
98. *Poetical Works*, Vol. 1, pp. 147–8.
99. To W. T. Stead, 29 July [1893]. St Andrews.
100. 'Comparative Psychical Research', *Contemporary Review*, 64 (September 1893), pp. 372–87.
101. See Marjorie Wheeler-Barclay, *The Science of Religion in Britain 1860–1915* (Charlottesville, 2010), p. 128.
102. 'Preface', *The Making of Religion* (London, 2nd edition, 1900), p. viii.
103. Clodd, 'Presidential Address', *Folklore*, 6 (March 1895), p. 81.
104. To Clodd, 18 July [n. y.]. Brotherton.
105. To Clodd, 17 October [1908]. Brotherton.
106. Clodd, 'In Memoriam: Andrew Lang', *Folklore* (23 September 1912), p. 361. Fontenelle's *De L'Origine des Fables* ends, '*Tous les hommes se ressemblent si fort, qu'il n'y a point du Peuple don't sotises ne nous dois faire trembler*' ('All men are so alike that there are no people whose stupidities do not make us tremble'), *Oeuvres*, Vol. 3 (Paris, 1758), p. 295.
107. Wheeler-Barclay, *Science of Religion in Britain*, pp. 127–8.
108. Wilson, '"These the Facts Are": Andrew Lang, Facts and Fantasy', pp. 29–44.
109. 'Preface', *Cock Lane and Common Sense* (London, 1896), pp. xix–xx.
110. 'The Master of Balliol', p. 479.
111. To Mrs Hills, 10 November [1893]. St Andrews.
112. John Jones, 'A Contested Mastership: The Election of Jowett's Successor', *Balliol College Annual Register* (1977), pp. 49–56
113. William Wallace, *Academy*, 45 (3 February 1894), p. 96; see also *Spectator*, 72 (28 April 1894), pp. 555–6.

114. *Fife Herald*, 27 December 1893; 'Mr. Lang on the Reformers and Covenanters', *British Weekly*, 15 (1 March 1894), p. 302.

115. Salmond, 'Introduction', *Andrew Lang and St Andrews*, p. 19.

116. Lang, 'The Scotch Reformation', *British Weekly*, 15 (8 March 1894), p. 318; Fleming, 'Mr. Andrew Lang on the Scotch Reformation and Covenanters', *British Weekly*, 15 (15 March 1894), pp. 329-30.

117. 'Irish Fairies', *ILN* (23 December 1893), p. 802.

118. To Lady Wolseley, 20 November [1893]. Hove.

119. To Mrs Alice Stewart, 27 June [n. y.]. NLS.

120. To Lady Wolseley, 31 May [1894]. Hove.

121. To RLS, 3 March [1894], *Dear Stevenson*, pp. 143–4.

122. To Mrs Puller, 26 March [1898]. Hertford.

123. To Mrs Ritchie, 6 January [1892]. Eton. In her 'Introduction' (p. x), Anne Ritchie quotes Lang's account, in *Perrault's Popular Tales* (1888), of the coming of the fairy tale genre to the Court of Versailles.

124. To Mrs Ritchie, 4 May [1892]. Eton.

125. To Mrs Ritchie, 4 March [1894]. Eton.

126. To RLS, 16 August [1894]; 21 September [1894], *Dear Stevenson*, pp. 146–7.

127. To Oliver Lodge, 25 and 26 October [1894]. SPR, Cambridge. See also Lang's letter, 'Eusapian Mysteries', *Speaker*, 12 (16 November 1895), pp. 525–6.

128. RLS to Lang, *c*.4 November 1894, quoted *Daily News* (18 December 1894), p. 5, and *RLS Letters*, Vol. 8, p. 388.

129. To Mrs Hills, 17 December [1894]. St Andrews.

130. *Spectator*, 73 (22 December 1894), pp. 881–2.

131. To Mrs Hills, 24 December [1894]. St Andrews.

132. 'At the Sign of the Ship', February 1895, pp. 432–9.

133. To Matthews, 14 January and 27 March 1891, *Friends*, pp. 109–10; p. 113.

134. *Poetical Works*, Vol. 4, pp. 230–1.

Chapter 9

1. To Mrs Hills, 24 December [1894]. St Andrews.

2. *Whirlwind*, 1 (12 July 1890), p. 38.

3. To RLS, 3 March [1894], *Dear Stevenson*, p. 144.

4. 'Preface', *The Strange Story Book* (1913).

5. To Lodge, 5 February [1895]. SPR, Cambridge.

6. To Lodge, 4 January [1895]. SPR, Cambridge.

7. 'At the Sign of the Ship', June 1894.

8. To Gosse, 20 July [1894]. Brotherton.

9. To Matthews, 30 November [1890], *Friends*, p. 109.

10. 'The Sign of the Ship', December 1896, p. 195.

11. Wilde, 'Andrew Lang's "Grass of Parnassus"', *Pall Mall Gazette* (2 January 1889), p. 3, in *The Complete Works of Oscar Wilde*, Vol. 7, eds. John Stokes and Mark W. Turner (Oxford, 2013), pp. 151–2. Wilde first dubbed Lang the 'Divine Amateur' in 'English

Poetesses', *The Queen* (8 December 1888), pp. 742–3, in *The Complete Works of Oscar Wilde*, Vol. 7, p. 124. For an account of Wilde's use of Lang in 'The Decay of Lying', see Horst Schroeder, review of *The Complete Works of Oscar Wilde*, Vol. 4, *Wildean*, 37 (July 2010), p. 22.

12. 'At the Sign of the Ship', August 1889, p. 448.

13. 'At the Sign of the Ship', February 1896, p. 231.

14. *Proceedings of the Society for Psychical Research*, 11 (July 1895), pp. 198–212; reprinted in *The Valet's Tragedy, and Other Stories* (London, 1903), pp. 1–28.

15. 'Eusapian Mysteries', *Speaker*, 12 (16 November 1895), pp. 525–6.

16. *Daily Chronicle* (29 October 1895); reported in the *Speaker*, 12 (2 November 1895), pp. 467–8.

17. To Lodge, 18 December [1895]. SPR, Cambridge.

18. 'Eusapian Mysteries', *Speaker*, 12 (16 November 1895).

19. 'Charles Dickens', *Letters to Dead Authors*, p. 13.

20. Ada Levenson, *Letters to the Sphinx from Oscar Wilde: with Reminiscences of the Author* (London, 1930) pp. 39–40; also quoted Richard Ellmann, *Oscar Wilde* (London, 1987), p. 441.

21. William Robertson Nicholl, *Bookman*, 9 (March 1896), p. 191.

22. *Athenaeum* (15 February 1896), p. 212.

23. *Saturday Review*, 81 (22 February 1896), pp. 208–9.

24. Introduction to J. A. Farrer, *Literary Forgeries* (London, 1907), p. xv. See also, letter to Charles Longman, 20 January [1898]. Reading.

25. To John Lang, 10 February 1896. St Andrews.

26. To John Lang, 24 May 1896. St Andrews.

27. Jones, *King of Critics*, pp. 200–1.

28. 'At the Sign of the Ship', June 1895, pp. 214–5.

29. To Gosse, 28 March [1896]. Brotherton.

30. To Mrs Hills, 16 June [1894]. St Andrews.

31. *The Collected Letters of George Gissing*, Vol. 6, eds. Paul F. Matthiesen, Arthur C. Young, and Pierre Coustillas (Athens, 1995), p. 142.

32. Wheeler-Barclay, *The Science of Religion in Britain*, pp. 113–4.

33. 'Emile Zola', *Fortnightly Review*, 37 (April 1882), p. 445.

34. 'At the Sign of the Ship', September 1889, pp. 553–4. For Lang's comments on bank holiday excess, see letter to Graham Thomson, 3 August 1888, quoted in Hughes, *Graham R.*, pp. 70–1; and to Lady Wolseley, 22 July 1889. Hove.

35. Gissing's Diary, 3 July 1896; quoted *Collected Letters of George Gissing*, Vol. 6, p. 146.

36. 'At the Sign of the Ship', September 1898, p. 468.

37. For example, Pierre Coustillas, *The Heroic Life of George Gissing*, Vol. 2 (London, 2002), p. 286.

38. 'Introduction', *The Pickwick Papers*, Gadshill Edition, pp. ix–xi.

39. Colvin, *Memories and Notes of Persons and Places* (London, 1921), pp. 117–8.

40. Lodge, *Past Years: An Autobiography* (London, 1931), p. 220.

41. To Twain, 10 June 1897, quoted D. H. Fear, 'Mark Twain Day by Day: An Annotated Chronology of the Life of Samuel Langhorne Clemens', 3 (2011). Online.

42. To Matthews, 4 September [1898], *Friends*, p. 108

43. Two letters to Colvin, 23 December [1895]. NLS.
44. To Mrs Puller, 25 March 1896. Hertford.
45. To Matthews, 5 December [1895], *Friends*, p. 129.
46. See Sharin Schroeder, 'Lasting Ephemera: Margaret Oliphant and Andrew Lang on Lives and Letters', *Victorian Periodical Record*, 50 (Summer 2017), pp. 336–65.
47. Mrs Ritchie to Lang [December 1895]. Eton.
48. To Mrs Ritchie, 26 December [1895]. Eton. Lang quotes Anne Ritchie's reminiscence in *The Life and Letters of John Gibson Lockhart*, Vol. 2 (London, 1897), pp. 328–9.
49. To Mrs Puller, 25 March 1896. Hertford.
50. *Blackwood's*, 160 (November 1896), pp. 607–25.
51. *Calcutta Review*, 105 (July 1897), pp. 3–5.
52. Nicholl, 'Life and Letters of John Gibson Lockhart', *Bookman*, 63 (December 1896), pp. 67–8.
53. To Gosse, 25 April [1896]. St Andrews.
54. To Mrs Puller, 14 April [1896]. Hertford.
55. To Herbert Maxwell, 15 April [1896]. NLS.
56. To RLS 23 June [1892], *Dear Stevenson*, p. 133. To Mrs Hills, 12 November [1894]. St Andrews.
57. 'Three Portraits of Prince Charles', *Poetical Works*, Vol. 1, pp. 59–61.
58. *Pickle the Spy* (London, 1897), p. 12.
59. To Mrs Hills, 12 November [1894]. St Andrews.
60. To Mrs Puller, 27 June 1896. Hertford.
61. To Mrs Puller, 22 August 1896. Hertford.
62. To Mrs Puller, 3 October 1896. Hertford.
63. To Mrs Puller, 8 October 1896. Hertford.
64. *Athenaeum* (30 January 1897), pp. 141–2.
65. *Spectator*, 78 (13 February 1897), pp. 243–4.
66. 'The Highland Character', *Spectator*, 78 (20 February 1897), p. 270.
67. To Sidney Lee, 29 October [no year]. Bodleian.
68. To Sir Sidney Lee, 29 May [1897?]. Bodleian.
69. To Sir Sidney Lee, 24 February [1897?]. Bodleian.
70. To Gosse, 15 March 1897. Bodleian.
71. To Gosse, 20 March 1897. Bodleian.
72. To Murray, 21 March 1897. Bodleian.
73. To Murray, 30 October 1899. Bodleian.
74. To Matthews, 5 April 1897, *Friends*, p. 134.
75. To William Alexander Craigie, 10 April [1897]. Hawick.
76. 'Introduction', *The Highlands of Scotland in 1750* (Edinburgh, 1898), p. xlii.
77. Duke of Argyll, *Scotland as It Was and as It Is* (Edinburgh, 1887), p. 247.
78. To Lady Wolseley, 26 December [1897]. Hove.
79. *The Companions of Pickle, Being a Sequel to Pickle the Spy* (London, 1898), p. 285.
80. *Companions of Pickle*, pp. 278–9.
81. *Companions of Pickle*, p. 264; pp. 277–8
82. *Companions of Pickle*, p. 255.
83. *Companions of Pickle*, p. 285.

84. To E. W. B. Nicholson, 19 October [1897]. Bodleian.
85. 'Irish Fairies', *ILN* (23 December 1893), p. 802.
86. 'The Celtic Renaissance', *Blackwood's*, 161 (February 1897), pp. 181–91.
87. Yeats, 'The Celtic Element in Literature', *Cosmopolis*, 10 (June 1898), pp. 675–86.
88. Letter from Julian Sturgis to Eva Gore-Booth, 7 May 1898; quoted Sonja Tiernan, *Eva Gore-Booth: An Image of Such Politics* (Manchester, 2012), p. 50.
89. To Mrs Puller, 30 July [1900]. Hertford.
90. *Literature*, 3 (30 July 1898), p. 93.
91. William Patrick Ryan, 'Andrew in Killarney', *The Sun* (5 September 1898).
92. To the Editor, *Spectator*, 81 (27 August and 3 September 1898), p. 275; p. 307.
93. For the material Lang collected, see 'A Creeful of Stories', *Blackwood's*, 164 (December 1898), pp. 792–880.
94. To Clodd, 9 October [1911]. Brotherton. The book in question was Clodd's *Tom Tit Tot: An Essay on Savage Philosophy on Folk-Tale* (London, 1898).
95. *The Collected Letters of W. B. Yeats, Volume Two: 1896–1900*, eds. Warwick Gould, John Kelly, and Deidre Toomey (Oxford, 1997), pp. 280–1, dates the letters between Lang and Yeats as October 1898, previously misdated 1899.
96. 'A Creeful of Celtic Stories', pp. 729–800.
97. *The Disentanglers* (London, 1902), p. 237.
98. Robertson, 'Mr Lang on the Origin of Religion', and Lang, 'A Reply', *Fortnightly Review*, 64, (November 1898), pp. 726–44.
99. Tyrell, *The Month*, 92 (September 1898), pp. 225–40.
100. To Clodd, 11 October [1898]. Brotherton.
101. To Tylor, 10 October 1898. Pitt Rivers.
102. Alfred Howitt, 'Some Australian Beliefs', *Journal of the Anthropological Institute of Great Britain and Ireland*, 13 (1884), pp. 185–95.
103. Edwin Hartland, 'The "High Gods" of Australia', *Folklore*, 9 (December 1898), pp. 290–329.
104. Hartland, 'Australian Gods: Rejoinder', *Folklore*, 10 (March 1899), p. 57.
105. B. Meredith Longstaff, 'Preface', *Indiana University Bookman*, (April 1965), p. 5.
106. John Kendrick Bangs, 'XII, An Open Letter', *A New Friendship's Garland; from Chap-Book* (Chicago, 1897).
107. Hatchards' 'Books of To-day and To-morrow' (14 January 1899).
108. *Lives of the 'Lustrous*, eds. Sidney Stephen and Leslie Lee (London, 1901).
109. To Gosse, 14 February [1899]. Brotherton.
110. Roger Lancelyn Green, *A.E.W. Mason* (London, 1952), p. 73.
111. To Mrs Puller, 8 July [1898]. Hertford.
112. *Athenaeum* (3 February 1900), p. xl.
113. *Blackwood's*, 166 (August 1899), pp. 266–74.
114. Lang, *A History of Scotland from the Roman Occupation*, Vol. 1 (Edinburgh and London, 1890), p. viii.
115. To Herbert Maxwell, 13 March [1899]. NLS.
116. Peter Hume Brown, *History of Scotland*, Vol. 1 (Cambridge, 1899), p. 28.
117. Lang, *A History of Scotland*, Vol. 1, pp. 36–7.
118. *A History of Scotland*, Vol. 1, p. 85.

119. *A History of Scotland*, Vol. 1, p. 175.
120. To Herbert Maxwell, 12 January [1900]. NLS.
121. To Lady Wolseley, 28 June [1900]. Hove.
122. To Lady Wolseley, 24 December [1900]. Hove.
123. *Blackwood's*, 167 (May 1900), pp. 599–614.
124. 'Preface', *A History of Scotland*, Vol. 1 (1900, 2nd edition), p. xiii; p. xi.

Chapter 10

1. 'At the Sign of the Ship', October 1900, pp. 191–2.
2. Georgina Müller, *The Life and Letters of the Right Honourable Friedrich Max Müller*, Vol. 2 (London, 1902), pp. 452–3.
3. To Mrs Hills, 14 May 1899. St Andrews.
4. To Matthews, 29 January [1901], *Friends*, p. 144.
5. To Frazer, 21 July [n. y.]. Trinity.
6. *Athenaeum* (31 July 1897), pp. 151–2.
7. 'Preface', *The Homeric Hymns* (London, 1899), p. x.
8. 'Mr. Frazer's Theory of Totemism', *Fortnightly Review*, 65 (June 1899), pp. 1012–25. Lang was responding to Frazer's 'The Origin of Totemism', *Fortnightly Review*, 65 (April 1899), pp. 647–65, and (May 1899), pp. 835–52.
9. 'Mr. Frazer's Theory of Totemism', pp. 1017–8.
10. To Matthews, 26 March [1901], *Friends*, p. 145.
11. Quoted Robert Ackerman, *J. G. Frazer: His Life and Work* (Cambridge, 1997), p. 171.
12. To Tylor, 5 February 1901. Pitt Rivers.
13. 'Mr. Frazer's Theory of the Crucifixion', *Fortnightly Review*, 69 (April 1901), pp. 650–62.
14. Clodd, Diary, 17 April 1901; quoted Ackerman, *Frazer: His Life and Work*, p. 173.
15. Frazer to Edwin Sidney Hartland, 2 April 1901. Trinity.
16. To Tylor, 12 June [1901]. Pitt Rivers.
17. Magic and Religion (London, 1901), p. v.
18. See *Magic and Religion*, p. 212, for Lang's comment on Frazer's interpretation of Virgil (*Aeneid*, VI, 208) in *The Golden Bough*, Vol. 3, p. 449. *The Golden Bough* was to find an equally dismissive critic in the later twentieth century in Edmund Leach. See Mary Beard, 'Frazer, Leach, and Virgil: The Popularity (and Unpopularity) of *The Golden Bough*', *Comparative Studies in Society and History*, 34 (April 1992), pp. 203–24.
19. *Saturday Review*, 92 (26 October 1901), p. 530.
20. Frazer to Hartland, 22 September 1901; quoted Ackerman, *Frazer: His Life and Work*, p. 174.
21. Frazer to Fison, 14 July 1901; quoted Robert Ackerman, *Selected Letters of Sir J. G. Frazer* (Oxford, 2005), p. 195.
22. *The Making of Scottish Presbyterianism* (Glasgow, 1911).
23. *A History of Scotland*, Vol. 2 (1902), pp. 85–6.
24. *American Historical Review*, 8 (July 1903), pp. 752–6.
25. Hay Fleming to W. A. Craigie, 21 February 1902. St Andrews.

26. Hay Fleming, 'Knox in the Hands of the Philistines', *British Weekly*, 33 (19 and 26 February 1903), pp. 493–4; pp. 517–8.

27. Hay Fleming, 'Mr. Lang and the Scotch Reformers and Covenanters', *British Weekly*, 15 (15 March 1894), 329-30.

28. William Croft Dickinson, *Andrew Lang: John Knox and Scottish Presbyterianism* (Edinburgh, 1952) p. 29.

29. Neil Forsyth, 'Presbyterian Historians and the Invention of British History', *Scottish Church History*, 34 (2004), pp. 91–110.

30. Catriona M. M. Macdonald, 'Andrew Lang and Scottish Historiography, Taking on Tradition', *Scottish Historical Review*, 94 (October 2015), pp. 207–36.

31. To Lodge, 17 January [1911]. SPR, Cambridge.

32. *The Mystery of Mary Stuart* (London, 1901), p. viii.

33. To Matthews, 15 April [1902?], *Friends*, p. 147.

34. *James VI and the Gowrie Mystery*, (London, 1902), pp. 1–2.

35. 'Andrew Lang's The Mysteries of History', *Sewanee Review*, 16 (1908), pp. 458–65.

36. To Lodge, 9 February [1904]. SPR, Cambridge.

37. 'At the Sign of the Ship', February 1900, pp. 377–8.

38. To Gosse, 27 May 1896. Brotherton.

39. 'At the Sign of the Ship', October 1899, p. 571.

40. 'R.L.S.', *Pall Mall Magazine*, 25 (December 1902), pp. 505–14.

41. *As You Like It*, Act 2, Scene 4.

42. To Gosse, 10 December [1901]. Brotherton.

43. To Matthews, 28 December [1901], *Friends*, p. 146.

44. Violet Hunt, 'Walks with Andrew Lang', *T. P.'s Weekly*, 11 (23 March 1929), p. 658.

45. To Gosse, 20 November [1911]. Brotherton.

46. 'At the Sign of the Ship', April 1905, pp. 563–5.

47. To Jean Lang, 15 January 1901. St Andrews.

48. To Mrs Puller, 13 July [1901]. Hertford.

49. To Mrs Puller, 24 July [1901]. Hertford.

50. To William Archer, 6 September [1891]. BL. The quotation is from Tennyson's 'To J. S.', a poem to Tennyson's friend James Spedding on the death of Spedding's brother, Edward.

51. To Gosse, 26 February [1895]. Brotherton.

52. *The Disentanglers*, p. 2.

53. *Contemporary Review*, 83 (January 1903), p. 143; *Academy*, 63 (6 December 1902), p. 609; *Saturday Review*, 94 (27 December 1902), pp. 814–5.

54. To John Lang, 16 March 1902. St Andrews.

55. To John Lang, 11 March 1902. St Andrews.

56. To Clement Shorter, 7 January [1902]. St Andrews.

57. To Gilbert Murray, 3 May [n. y.]. Bodleian.

58. To Mrs Hills, 14 February [1902]. St Andrews.

59. To John Lang, 15 March 1902. St Andrews.

60. To Jean Lang, 2 June 1902. St Andrews.

61. To Haggard, 2 June 1902; quoted *The Days of My Life*, p. 80.

62. To John Lang, 27 October 1902. St Andrews.

63. *Catholic World*, 76 (February 1903), p. 690.
64. Durkheim, *L'Année Sociologique*, 5 (1902), pp. 82–121.
65. *Social Origins* (London, 1903), p.3.
66. *Social Origins*, p. 42.
67. *Social Origins*, p. 34.
68. *Social Origins*, p. 40.
69. To Lady Wolseley, 20 October [1902]. Hove.
70. To Lady Wolseley, 31 December [1902]; 21 and 26 January [1903]. Hove.
71. To Lady Wolseley, 13 August [1903]. Hove.
72. To Lady Wolseley, 20 October [1902]. Hove.
73. To Gilbert Murray, 5 June [n. y.]. Bodleian.
74. To Tylor, 2 November [1903]. Pitt Rivers.
75. To Henry Sidgwick, 9 September [n. y.]. Trinity.
76. To Tylor, 19 October [1903]. Pitt Rivers.
77. To Tylor, 28 October [1903]. Pitt Rivers.
78. To Tylor, 13 January 1904. Pitt Rivers.
79. Howitt, 'The Native Tribes of South-East Australia', *Folklore*, 17 (24 June 1906), pp. 174–89.
80. *Academy* (14 July 1906), pp. 42–3.
81. Spencer to Howitt, 27 August and 1 September 1906, quoted Mary Howitt Walker, *Come Wind, Come Weather: A Biography of Alfred Howitt* (Melbourne, 1971), p. 245. See also, Spencer to Frazer, 7 September [1906]. Pitt Rivers.
82. *Academy* (6 October 1906), p. 334.
83. *Man* (1908), pp. 85–8, quoted Walker, *Come Wind, Come Weather*, p. 250.
84. 'The Aborigines of Australia', *Quarterly Review*, 23 (October 1905), pp. 445.
85. To Tylor, 13 January [1904]. Pitt Rivers.
86. *Magic and Religion*, p. 4.
87. To John Lang, 11 June [1905]. St Andrews.
88. Bertrand Russell to Alys Russell, 22 October 1895, in *Selected Letters of Bertrand Russell, Vol. 1: The Private Years* (London, 1992), p. 68.
89. Courtney, 'Andrew Lang', *English Illustrated Magazine*, 30 (March 1904), pp. 682–90.
90. To John Lang, 24 May 1904. St Andrews.
91. To Horace Howard Furness, 10 June 1904. University of Pennsylvania; quoted Marysa Demoor, 'Andrew Lang versus W. D. Howells: A Late Victorian Duel', *Journal of American Studies*, 21 (December 1987), pp. 416–22.
92. To Furness, 7 August [1904]; quoted 'Andrew Lang versus W. D. Howells', p. 420.
93. *Review of Reviews* (February 1905), p. 170.
94. A. Taylor Innes, *Speaker*, n.s. 12 (5 August 1905), pp. 440–2. See also Hay Fleming, 'Mr Lang's *History of Scotland*', *Bookman*, 18 (May 1890), pp. 53–5. For Lang's reply, see *Speaker*, n.s. 12 (26 August 1905), pp.503–4.
95. Thomas Drummond Wanliss, *Scotland and Presbyterianism Vindicated* (Edinburgh, 1905), p. 60.
96. *Blackwood's*, 177 (October 1905), 477–95.
97. Wanliss, *The Muckrake in Scottish History* (Edinburgh, 1906).
98. To Robert Rait, 19 June 1906. NLS.

99. To Mrs Hills, 23 August [1905]. St Andrews.
100. 'At the Sign of the Ship', August 1905, p. 376.
101. 'At the Sign of the Ship', August 1905, p. 376.
102. To John Lang, 19 March 1905. St Andrews.
103. To John Lang, 11 June 1905. St Andrews.
104. To John Lang, 21 June 1905. St Andrews.
105. To Haggard, 19 December [n. y.]. Norfolk.
106. *Academy* (30 September 1905), p. 1004.
107. *Blackwood's*, 164 (November 1898), p. 595.
108. James to RLS, 31 July [1888], *The Letters of Henry James*, Vol. 1, ed. Percy Lubbock (New York, 1920), p. 136.
109. 'At the Sign of the Ship', January 1898, pp. 274–5.
110. To Clodd, 25 January [1909]. Brotherton.
111. Andrew Lang and "X", A Working Man, 'The Reading Public', *Cornhill Magazine*, 11 (December 1901), pp. 783–95.

Chapter 11

1. *Poetical Works*, Vol. 2, p. 82.
2. To Mrs Hills, 27 December [1908]. St Andrews.
3. 'Preface', *Sir George Mackenzie, King's Advocate, of Rosehaugh* (London, 1909), p. vii.
4. Marysa Demoor, 'Andrew Lang's Biographies; A Late Victorian Stance', in *The Art of Biography; An Analysis of Two Contrasting Views* (Gent, 1986), p. 9.
5. To Gosse, 11 May [1905]. Brotherton.
6. See Jennifer Stevens, *The Historical Jesus and the Literary Imagination, 1860–1920* (Liverpool, 2010).
7. 'Ode on the Distant Prospect of a New Novel', *Poetical Works*, Vol. 1, pp. 123–4.
8. *When It Was Light, a Reply to When It Was Dark*, by a well-known author (London, 1905), p. 177.
9. *Poetical Works*, Vol. 1, pp. 183–4.
10. *Homer and His Age* (London, 1906), p. 3.
11. *Homer and His Age*, pp. 245–6.
12. *Homer and His Age*, pp. 252–3.
13. *Academy* (29 June 1907), pp. 624–5.
14. See *Bookman*, 31 (January 1907), pp. 15–16; *Athenaeum* (13 June 1907), pp. 38–9.
15. *Companions of Pickle*, p. 285.
16. *A History of Scotland*, Vol. 4, p. 522.
17. To Clodd, 14 February 1909. Brotherton. Lang's view of Darwin's naivete in overlooking linguistic sophistication may have been indebted to Müller's essay 'The Savage', *Nineteenth Century*, 17 (January 1885), pp. 109–32.
18. To Clodd, 18 May [n. y.]. Brotherton.
19. *Athenaeum* (4 May 1907), pp. 531–2.
20. *Academy* (27 April 1907), pp. 405–6.
21. *A History of Scotland*, Vol. 4, p. 522.

22. *A History of Scotland*, Vol. 4, p. 324.

23. 'The Romantic Plot Against the Union', *The Union of 1707*, p. 27; pp. 75–6.

24. Hume Brown, *A Short History of Scotland*, p. 557.

25. T. M. Devine and Jenny Wormald, 'Introduction: The Study of Modern Scottish History', *The Handbook of Modern Scottish History* (Oxford, 2012), p. 18.

26. To John Lang, 19 June 1903. St Andrews.

27. To Gosse, [August or September 1907]. Brotherton.

28. To Mrs Hill, 14 February 1903. St Andrews.

29. To John Lang, 19 June 1903. St Andrews.

30. To Herbert Maxwell, 9 May [1907]. NLS.

31. To Mrs Hills, 26 April 1909. St Andrews.

32. To John Lang, 8 August 1907. St Andrews.

33. To John Lang, 25 June 1905. St Andrews.

34. 'Edward Burnett Tylor', *Anthropological Essays Presented to Edward Burnett Tylor in Honour of His 75th Birthday* (Oxford, 1907), pp. 1–15; see also 'The Invention of Museum Archaeology 1850–1920'. Online, prm.ox.ac.uk.

35. Robert Ranulph Marett, *A Jerseyman at Oxford* (London, 1941), pp. 168–9.

36. To Murray, 10 February [1908]. Bodleian.

37. Quoted Jusserand, *What Me Befell* (London, 1933), p. 165.

38. To Hepburn Millar, 23 May [1908]. NLS.

39. To William Henry Helm 4 August 1908. St Andrews.

40. Stewart, *'Alicella': A Memoir of Alice King Stewart and Ella Christie*, p. 98; p. 117.

41. Ella Christie and Alice King Stewart, *A Long Look at Life, by Two Victorians* (London, 1940), p. 165.

42. To Mrs Hills, 23 August 1908. St Andrews.

43. *The Book of Princes and Princesses* (London, 1908), p. xii.

44. To Murray, 23 September [1908]. Bodleian.

45. 'Homer and Anthropology', in *Anthropology and the Classics*, ed. R.R. Marett (Oxford, 1908), pp. 44–65.

46. *Athenaeum* (21 November 1908), p. 650.

47. To John Lang, 15 April 1909. St Andrews.

48. To Mrs Hills, 6 April [1909]. St Andrews.

49. To Jack Walter Hills, 21 May 1909. St Andrews.

50. 'Marriage Laws and Some Customs of the Western Australian Aborigines', *Victoria Geographical Journal*, 23 (1905), pp. 36–60, was read at a meeting of the Glasgow Obstetrical and Gynaecological Society by the President on 19 December 1906, and reprinted in *Glasgow Medical Journal*, 67 (1907), pp. 357–73.

51. Quoted Isobel White, 'Mrs Bates and Mr Brown: An Examination of Rodney Needham's Allegations', *Oceania*, 51 (March 1981), p. 195.

52. Quoted White, 'Mrs Bates and Mr Brown', p. 204.

53. Quoted White, 'Mrs Bates and Mr Brown', p. 201.

54. Quoted White, 'Mrs Bates and Mr Brown', p. 202.

55. James Hope Moulton to Frazer, 7 October 1913. Trinity.

56. *The Origins of Religion, and other essays* (London, 1908), p. 127.

57. To Clodd, 30 June [1910]. Brotherton.

58. *Anthropos*, 5 (September 1910), pp. 1092–1108.
59. To Clodd, 9 July 1909 and 15 June 1910. Brotherton.
60. To Clodd, 27 June 1910. Brotherton.
61. Clodd to Frazer, 12 March 1911. Trinity.
62. Murray, 'Totems', *Saturday Review*, 110 (16 July 1910), pp. 74–5.
63. A. A. Goldenweiser, 'Totemism: and Analytic Study', *Journal of American Folklore*, 23 (1910), p. 280.
64. See *Social Origins*, pp. 2–3, and *The Origins of Religion*, p. 110.
65. Lang, *Methods in the Study of Totemism* (Glasgow, 1911); for their 'Discussion and Correspondence', see *American Anthropologist*, 14 (April 1912), pp. 268–82.
66. 'Preface', *The Strange Story Book* (London, 1913), p. vii.
67. To Mrs Hills, 14 May 1899. St Andrews.
68. To Gosse, 28 November [1909]. Brotherton.
69. To Matthews, 23 February [1907], *Friends*, p. 150.
70. To Gosse, 13 and 14 April [1910]. Brotherton.
71. To Murray, 1 June [1910]. Bodleian.
72. To Murray, 26 May and 18 October [1910]. Bodleian.
73. Theodore Roosevelt, *Biological Analogies in History, Romanes Lecture* (Oxford, 1910), pp. 20–1.
74. Mrs Alice Stewart to Ella Christie, [June 1910]. NLS.
75. Laurie Magnus, *Herbert Warren of Magdalen* (London, 1932), p. 169.
76. To Murray, 10 June [1910]. Bodleian.
77. Nora Lang to Ella Christie, [September 1910]. NLS.
78. To Ella Christie, 6 September [1910]. NLS.
79. *Classical Weekly*, 4 (October 1910), pp. 109–11.
80. 'Preface', *The Rise of the Greek Epic* (2nd edition, 1911), pp. 6–7.
81. To Murray, 7 May [n. y.]. Bodleian.
82. 'Andrew Lang and the Dickens Stamp, 1910'. MS 37477. St Andrews.
83. To Murray, 24 January [1911]. Bodleian.
84. H. W. Garrod to Murray, 23 January [1911]. Bodleian.
85. Bridges to Murray, 26 January [1911]. Bodleian.
86. Garrod to Murray, [1911]. Bodleian.
87. To Murray, 26 January [1911]. Bodleian.
88. To Murray, 27 January [1911]. Bodleian.
89. Longman to Lang, 27 February 1911. Reading.
90. Longman to Lang, 1 March 1911. Reading.
91. To Lodge, 12 January [1911]. SPR, Cambridge.
92. To Lodge, 17 January [1911]. SPR, Cambridge.
93. Reported in the *Athenaeum* (26 August 1911), p. 246.
94. Eleanor Sidgwick, *Proceedings of the SPR*, Supplement, 63 (June 1911), pp. 353–60.
95. To Alice Johnson, 16 May [1911]. SPR, Cambridge.
96. To Charlotte Moberly, 4 July [1911]. Bodleian.
97. To Charlotte Moberly, 16 July [1911]. Bodleian.
98. Moberly to Lang, 18 July [1911]. Bodleian.
99. To Charlotte Moberly, 20 July [1911]. Bodleian.

100. Alice Johnson to Lang, 27 July [1911]. SPR, Cambridge.
101. To Charlotte Moberly, 6 August [1911]. Bodleian.
102. For a discussion of this, see Terry Castle, 'Contagious Folly; An Adventure and Its Sceptics', *Critical Inquiry*, 17 (1991), pp. 741–72.
103. Laura Schwartz, 'Enchanted Modernity, Anglicanism and the Occult in early 20th-Century Oxford: Charlotte Moberly, Eleanor Jourdain and their 'Adventure' Revisited', *Cultural and Social History*, 14 (2017) pp. 301–19.
104. Robert C. Moberly, *Marie Antoinette: A Prize Poem Recited in the Theatre, Oxford, 26 June 1867* (Oxford, 1867).
105. 'Last Words on Totemism, Marriage and Religion', *Folklore*, 23 (September 1912), pp. 377.
106. Quoted Green, *Andrew Lang* (1946), p. 204.
107. To Hay Fleming, 3 October [1911] and 11 April 1912. St Andrews.
108. To Haggard, 10 November 1911, quoted Haggard, *The Days of My Life*, Vol. 2, p. 75.
109. Nora Lang to Ella Christie, 4 August [1911]. NLS.
110. 'The Making of Scotland Presbyterian' (Glasgow, 1911).
111. Maxwell, *Evening Memories* (London, 1932), pp. 307–8.
112. *Votiva Tabella: A Memorial Volume* (St Andrews, 1911), pp. 401–13; pp. 417–8.
113. To Ella Christie, 23 October [1911]. NLS.
114. *Scotsman* (25 October 1911); quoted MacDonald, 'Andrew Lang and Scottish Historiography', p. 220.
115. Ella Christie, 'I Remember Andrew Lang', BBC Broadcast, 4 January 1937. Transcript, NLS.
116. To Mrs Alice Stewart, 7 November [1911]. NLS.
117. To Ella Christie, 9 November [1911]. NLS.
118. To John Lang, 1 November 1911. St Andrews.
119. *History of English Literature* (London, 1912), pp. 48–51. See also, letter to Murray, 27 December [1908]. Bodleian.
120. 'Literature', in Alfred Russell Wallace, et al., *The Progress of the Century* (New York and London, 1901), p. 408.
121. To Jean Lang, 28 March 1912. St Andrews.
122. 'At the Sign of St Paul's', *ILN* (27 January 1912).
123. Salmond, 'Introduction', *Andrew Lang at St Andrews*, p. 10.
124. To Gosse, 1 March [1912]. BL.
125. To Hay Fleming, 11 April 1912. St Andrews.
126. Marie Belloc Lowndes, *The Merry Wives of Westminster* (London, 1946), p. 21.
127. To John Lang, 29 March and 8 April 1912. St Andrews.
128. 'Prefatory Note', Mrs Lang, *Men, Women and Minxes* (London, 1912), p. ix.
129. *Men, Women and Minxes*, pp. 108–9.
130. *Aberdeen Press and Journal* (22 July 1912).
131. Mrs Lang to Ella Christie, 23 July 1912. NLS.
132. Mrs Lang to Mrs Alice Stewart, 23 July 1912. NLS.
133. Lowndes, *Merry Wives of Westminster*, p. 22.
134. Mrs Lang to Austin Dobson, 19 August 1912. London.
135. *Angling Sketches* (London, 1891), p. 130.

136. Mrs Lang to Ella Christie, 22 July 1912. NLS.

137. Mrs Elizabeth Grieve to Mrs Jean Lang, 3 August 1912. St Andrews.

138. Mrs Elizabeth Grieve to Mrs Jean Lang, 3 August 1912. St Andrews.

139. Charles Boyd, 'Andrew Lang', *Saturday Review*, 114 (27 July 1912), pp. 106–7.

140. Clodd, 'In Memoriam Andrew Lang', Folklore, 23 (September 1912), pp. 358–67; Hume Brown, *Proceedings of the British Academy*, Vol. 5 (1822–1912), pp. 552–8; Marett, 'Andrew Lang: Folklorist and Critic', *Folklore*, 23 (September 1912), pp. 363–4.

141. Nora Lang to Austin Dobson, 19 August [1912]. London.

142. Milne to Frazer, 13 January [1913]. Trinity.

143. 'Mr Andrew Lang's Theory of the Origins of Exogamy and Totemism', *Folklore*, 24 (July 1913), pp. 155–86.

144. Hartland to Frazer, 15 January 1913. Trinity.

145. Ackerman, *Selected Letters of Sir J. G. Frazer* (Oxford, 2005), p. 317.

146. Frazer to Marett, 14 August 1912. Trinity.

147. *ILN* (7 February 1891), p. 187.

148. *The Days of My Life*, p. 74.

149. Green, *Andrew Lang* (1946), p. ix.

150. Thyra Alleyne to A. D. Lindsay, 24 February 1944. Balliol.

151. Maxwell, *Evening Memories* (London, 1932), pp. 218–9.

152. Mrs Andrew Lang, 'Little General Monk', *The Storytellers' Magazine*, 4 (June 1916), pp. 340–9; (concluded), 4 (July 1916), pp. 432–8.

153. See, Andrea Day, '"Almost Wholly the Work of Mrs. Lang": Nora Lang, Literary Labour, and the Fairy Books', *Women's Writing*, 26 (2019), pp. 400–20.

154. Mrs Elizabeth Grieve to Mrs Jean Lang, 3 August [1912]. St Andrews.

155. 'Some Personal Impressions', *Bookman* (September 1912), p. 258, reprinted in *Portraits and Sketches* (London, 1912), p. 207; also Andrew Lang, *Silhouettes* (London, 1925), pp. 163–70.

156. Mrs Lang to William Munro, 16 October 1926. NLS.

157. Mrs Andrew Lang, 'Obituary Notice', *The Times* (London, 12 July 1933).

Epilogue

1. Goldenweiser, 'The Views of Andrew Lang and J. G. Frazer and Émile Durkheim on Totems', *Anthropos*, 10/11 (September 1915/1916), p. 948.

2. Gordon, 'Andrew Lang' (London, 1928); reprinted in *Concerning Andrew Lang, Lectures 1927–1937* (London, 1949).

3. Grierson, 'Lang, Lockhart and Biography', Andrew Lang Lecture, 6 December 1933; in *Concerning Andrew Lang.*

4. 'Preface', *The Making of Religion*, p. viii.

5. To Gilbert Murray, 27 October 1899. Bodleian. See also 'At the Sign of the Ship', January 1900, pp. 279–80.

6. Duff-Cooper, 'Andrew Lang: Aspects of his Work in Relation to Current Social Anthropology', *Folklore*, 97 (1986), pp. 186–201. Duff-Cooper's B.Litt. thesis ('Andrew Lang on Totemism'. University of Oxford. Faculty of Anthropology and Geography,

1978) was published with the title, *Andrew Lang on Totemism: the 1912 text on Totemism* (Canterbury: Centre for Social Anthropology and Computing, University of Kent at Canterbury, 1994).

7. Crawford, 'Pater's *Renaissance*, Andrew Lang, and Anthropological Romanticism'; Sparks, 'At the Intersection of Victorian Science and Fiction'.
8. Berman, 'Tolkien as a Child of the Green Fairy Book'.
9. Teverson, *The Selected Children's Fiction, Folk Tales and Fairy Tales of Andrew Lang* (Edinburgh, 2021).
10. Macdonald, 'Andrew Lang and Scottish Historiography: Taking on Tradition', p. 209.
11. Hensley, 'Network, Discipline, Method: Andrew Lang in and after the 1880s'.
12. John Davidson to John Lane, 3 May 1894. NLS.
13. Boyd, 'Andrew Lang', *Saturday Review*, 114 (27 July 1912), pp. 107–8.
14. Lang, 'From a Scottish Workshop', ILN (6 June 1896), p. 727.
15. Lang, 'Charles Dickens', *The Gadshill Edition of The Works of Charles Dickens*, Vol. 24 (1898), p. xxxiii.

Select Bibliography

Andrew Lang's Major Writings

Ballads and Lyrics of Old France, and Other Poems (London: Longmans, Green, and Co., 1872).

Oxford: Brief Historical and Descriptive Notes (London: Seeley, 1880; 2nd ed., 1882).

XXII Ballades in Blue China (London: Kegan Paul, 1880; enlarged ed., *XXII and X Ballades in Blue China*, 1881; new enlarged ed., *XXXII Ballades in Blue China* (London: Kegan Paul, Trench, 1888)).

The Library (London: Macmillan, 1881).

Helen of Troy (London: George Bell and Sons, 1882).

Ballades and Verses Vain (New York: Scribner's, 1884).

Custom and Myth (London: Longmans, Green, and Co., 1884; new ed., 1898).

'Household Tales; Their Origin, Diffusion, and Relations to the Higher Myths', Introduction to Mrs Margaret Hunt, *Grimm's Household Tales*, 2 Vols. (London: George Bell and Sons, 1884), pp. ix-lxxv.

The Princess Nobody: A Tale of Fairyland (London: Longmans, Green, and Co., 1884).

Rhymes à La Mode (London: Kegan Paul, Trench, 1884).

Books and Bookmen (New York: George J. Coombes, 1886; English ed., (London: Longmans, Green, and Co., 1887; with new introduction, 1912)).

In the Wrong Paradise, and Other Stories (London: Kegan Paul, Trench, 1886).

Letters to Dead Authors (London: Longmans, Green, and Co., 1886; new enlarged ed., *New and Old Letters to Dead Authors*, 1907).

The Mark of Cain (Bristol: Arrowsmith, 1886).

Myth Ritual and Religion, 2 Vols. (London: Longmans, Green, and Co., 1887; 2nd ed., 1899).

The Gold of Fairnilee (Bristol: J. W. Arrowsmith, 1888).

Grass of Parnassus, Rhymes Old and New (London: Longmans, Green, and Co., 1888; enlarged ed., *Grass of Parnassus: First and Last Rhymes*, 1892).

'Introduction' to *Perrault's Popular Tales* (Oxford: Clarendon Press, 1888).

The Blue Fairy Book (London: Longmans, Green, and Co., 1889).

Prince Prigio (Bristol: J. W. Arrowsmith, 1889).

Letters on Literature (London: Longmans, Green, 1889; new ed., 1892).

Lost Leaders (London: Kegan Paul, Trench, 1889).

Old Friends: Essays in Epistolary Parody (London: Longmans, Green, and Co., 1890).

The Red Fairy Book (London: Longmans, Green, and Co., 1890).

Life, Letters and Diaries of Sir Stafford Northcote, 2 Vols. (Edinburgh: William Blackwood, 1890).

Essays in Little (London: Henry and Co., 1891).

The Green Fairy Book (London: Longmans, Green, and Co., 1892).

St Andrews (London: Longmans, Green, and Co.,1893).

'Introduction' by Andrew Lang to Robert Kirk, *The Secret Commonwealth of Elves, Fauns and Fairies* (London: David Nutt, 1893), pp. ix–lxv.

Homer and the Epic (London: Longmans, Green, and Co., 1893).

Prince Ricardo of Pantouflia, Being the Adventures of Prince Prigio's Son (Bristol: J. W. Arrowsmith, 1893).

Ban and Arrière Ban: A Rally of Fugitive Rhymes (London: Longmans, Green, and Co., 1894).

Cock Lane and Common-Sense (London: Longmans, Green, and Co., 1894; new ed., 1896).

The Yellow Fairy Book (London: Longmans, Green, and Co., 1894).

A Monk of Fife, Being the Chronicle Written by Norman Leslie of Pitcullo, Now First Done into English out of the French (London: Longmans, Green, and Co., 1896).

The Book of Dreams and Ghosts (London: Longmans, Green, and Co., 1897).

Life and Letters of John Gibson Lockhart, 2 Vols. (London: John C. Nimmo and New York: Charles Scribner's Sons, 1897).

Pickle the Spy: Or, the Incognito of Prince Charles (London: Longmans, Green, and Co., 1897).

The Pink Fairy Book (London: Longmans, Green, and Co., 1897).

The Companions of Pickle: Being a Sequel to Pickle the Spy (London: Longmans, Green, and Co., 1898).

The Making of Religion (London: Longmans, Green, and Co., 1898; new ed., 1900).

The Grey Fairy Book (London: Longmans, Green, and Co., 1900)

The History of Scotland from the Roman Occupation, 4 Vols. (Edinburgh: William Blackwood, 1900–1907).

Prince Charles Edward (London: Groupil, 1900); new. ed. *Princes Charles Edward: The Young Chevalier* (London: Longmans, Green, and Co., 1903).

Alfred Tennyson (Edinburgh: William Blackwood and Sons, 1901).

Magic and Religion (London: Longmans, Green, and Co., 1901).

The Mystery of Mary Stuart (London: Longmans, Green, and Co., 1901).

The Violet Fairy Book (London: Longmans, Green, and Co., 1901).

The Disentanglers (London: Longmans, Green, and Co., 1902).

James VI and the Gowrie Mystery (London: Longmans, Green, and Co., 1902).

The Crimson Fairy Book (London: Longmans, Green, and Co., 1903).

Social Origins, with *Primal Law*, by J. J. Atkinson (London: Longmans, Green, and Co., 1903).

The Valet's Tragedy and Other Studies (London, Longmans, Green, and Co., 1903).

The Brown Fairy Book (London: Longmans, Green, and Co., 1904).

Historical Mysteries (London: Smith, Elder, & Co., 1904).

Adventures Among Books (London: Longmans, Green, and Co., 1905).

The Clyde Mystery: A Study in Forgeries and Folklore (Glasgow: J. MacLehose, 1905).

John Knox and the Reformation (London: Longmans, Green, and Co., 1905).

New Collected Rhymes (London: Longmans, Green, and Co., 1905).

The Puzzle of Dickens's Last Plot (London: Chapman and Hall, 1905).

The Secret of the Totem (London: Longmans, Green, and Co., 1905).

Homer and His Age (London: Longmans, Green, and Co., 1906).

Sir Walter Scott (New York, Charles Scribner's Sons, 1906).

The Orange Fairy Book (London: Longmans, Green, and Co., 1906).

Portraits and Jewels of Mary Stuart (Glasgow: J. Maclehose, 1906).

The Olive Fairy Book (London: Longmans, Green, and Co., 1907).

The Maid of France: Being the Story of the Life and Death of Jeanne d'Arc (London: Longmans, Green, and Co.,1908; new ed., 1913).

The Origins of Religion, and Other Essays (London: Watts & Co., 1908).

Sir George Mackenzie, King's Advocate, of Rosehaugh (London: Longmans, Green, 1909).

The Lilac Fairy Book (London: Longmans, Green, and Co., 1910).

Sir Walter Scott and the Border Minstrelsy (London: Longmans, Green, and Co., 1910).

The World of Homer (London: Longmans, Green, and Co., 1910).

Method in the Study of Totemism (Glasgow: R. Maclehose & Co., 1911).

A History of English Literature from 'Beowulf' to Swinburne (London: Longmans, Green, and Co., 1912).

Shakespeare, *Bacon, and the Great Unknown* (London: Longmans, Green, and Co., 1912).

The Poetical Works of Andrew Lang, ed. Mrs Lang, 4 Vols. (London: Longmans, Green, and Co., 1923).

In College Garden: Old Rhymes Written in 1871, ed. Roger Lancelyn Green (Poulton: Privately Printed, 1972).

Co-Authored Books, Editions, Translations

Aristotle's Politics, books i, iii, iv (vii). The Text of Bekker, with translation by W.E Bolland, together with intro. essays by A. Lang (London, Longmans, Green, and Co., 1877); reissued as *The Politics of Aristotle: Introductory Essays* (London: Longmans, Green, and Co., 1886).

Odyssey of Homer, with S. H. Butcher (London: Macmillan, 1879).

Theocritus, Bion and Moschus, Rendered into English Prose (London: Macmillan, 1880).

The Iliad of Homer, with Walter Leaf and Ernest Myers (London: Macmillan, 1883).

That Very Mab, anonymous, with May Kendall (London: Longmans, Green, and Co., 1885).

Aucassin and Nicolete (London: David Nutt, 1887).

He, anonymous with W. H. Pollock (London: Longmans, Green, and Co., 1887).

The Dead Leman, and Other Tales from the French, with 'Paul Sylvester' (Pauline Schletter) (New York: Scribner & Welford, 1889).

The World's Desire, with H. Rider Haggard (London: Longmans, Green, and Co., 1890).

Border Edition of the Waverley Novels by Sir Walter Scott (London: John C. Nimmo, 1892–1894).

Gadshill Edition of the Works of Charles Dickens (London: Chapman & Hall, and New York: C. Scribner's Sons, 1897–1899).

Homeric Hymns, A New Prose Translation and Essays, Literary and Mythological (London: George Allen, 1899).

Parson Kelly, with A. E. W. Mason (London: Longmans, Green, and Co., 1899).

The King over the Water, with Alice Shield (London: Longmans, Green, and Co., 1907).

Highways and Byways of the Borders, with John Lang (London: Macmillan, 1913)

Books and Articles About Andrew Lang

For critical editions of Lang's writings, see Andrew Teverson, Alexandra Warwick, and Leigh Wilson, eds., *The Edinburgh Critical Edition of The Selected Writings of Andrew Lang*, 2 vols. (Edinburgh: Edinburgh University Press, 2015) and Tom Hubbard and

Celeste Ray, eds., *The Selected Writings of Andrew Lang*, 3 Vols. (London: Routledge, 2016). For editions of Lang's letters, see Marysa Demoor, *Friends Over the Ocean: Andrew Lang's American Correspondents 1881-1912* (Gent: Rijksversiteit te Gent, 1989), and *'Dear Stevenson': Letters from Andrew Lang to Robert Louis Stevenson, with five letters from Stevenson to Lang* (Leuven: Peeters, 1990). For an overview of Lang criticism, see Andrew Teverson, 'Andrew Lang', Oxford Bibliographies Online.

Addis, M. Leicester, 'St Andrews and Andrew Lang', *Frank Leslie's Popular Monthly*, 39 (January 1895), pp. 1–12.

Anderson, J. M., 'Library Notes and Documents', *Library Bulletin of the University of St Andrews*, 5 (48) (October 1912), pp. 220–1.

Berman, Ruth, 'Tolkien as a Child of the Green Fairy Book', *Mythlore: A Journal of J.R.R. Tolkien, C.S. Lewis, Charles Williams and Mythopoeic Literature*, 26 (99/100) (2007), pp. 127–35.

Christie, Ella, 'I Remember Andrew Lang', BBC Broadcast, 4 January 1937. Transcript, NLS.

Crawford, Robert, 'Pater's *Renaissance*, Andrew Lang, and Anthropological Romanticism', *English Literary History*, 53 (4) (Winter 1986), pp. 849–79.

Day, Andrea, 'Almost Wholly the Work of Mrs. Lang: Nora Lang, Literary Labour, and the Fairy Books', *Women's Writing: The Elizabethan to the Victorian Period*, 26 (4) (2019), pp. 400–20.

Demoor, Marysa, 'Andrew Lang on Gissing: A Late Victorian Point of View', *Gissing Newsletter*, 20 (2) (April 1984), pp. 20–30.

Demoor, Marysa, *The Art of Biography: An Analysis of Two Contrasting Views* (Gent, 1986).

Demoor, Marysa, 'Andrew Lang's Letters to E. Gosse: The Record of a Fruitful Collaboration as Poets, Critics, and Biographers', *Review of English Studies*, 38 (152) (1987), pp. 492–509.

Demoor, Marysa, 'Andrew Lang's Letters to H. Rider Haggard: The Record of a Harmonious Friendship', *Études Anglaises*, 40 (3) (January 1987), pp. 313–22.

Demoor, Marysa, 'Andrew Lang Versus W. D. Howells: A Late Victorian Duel', *Journal of American Studies* (December 1987), pp. 416–22.

Demoor, Marysa, 'Andrew Lang's "Causeries" 1874–1912', *Victorian Periodicals Review*, 21, (1) (Spring 1988), pp. 15–22.

Dickinson, William Croft, *Andrew Lang, John Knox and Scottish Presbyterianism* (Edinburgh: Thomas Nelson and Sons, 1952).

Donaldson, William, 'Andrew Lang: A World We Have Lost', *Studies in Scottish Literature*, 43 (1) (2017), pp. 155–65.

Dorson, Richard M., 'The Great Team of English Folklorists', *Journal of American Folklore*, 64 (1951), pp. 1–10.

Dorson, Richard M., 'Andrew Lang's Folklore Interests as Revealed in "At the Sign of the Ship"', *Western Folklore*, 11 (1952), pp. 1–19.

Dorson, Richard M., *The British Folklorists: A History* (London: Routledge & Kegan Paul, 1968; 'Andrew Lang', pp. 206–20.

Duff-Cooper, Andrew, 'Andrew Lang: Aspects of His Work in Relation to Current Social Anthropology', *Folklore*, 97 (2) (1986), pp. 186–205.

Duff-Cooper, Andrew, *Andrew Lang on Totemism: The 1912 Text of Totemism* (The University of Kent at Canterbury: Centre for Social Anthropology and Computing, 1994).

Falconer, Charles M., *A New Friendship's Garland* (Dundee, 1899).

Gosse, Edmund, *Portraits and Sketches* (London: Heinemann, 1912), 'Andrew Lang 1844–1912', pp. 197–211.

Gosse, Edmund, *Silhouettes* (London: Heinemann, 1925), 'Andrew Lang', pp. 161–70.

Green, Roger Lancelyn, 'Andrew Lang: Poet and Romantic 1844–1912', *Journal of English Association*, 5 (26) (Summer 1944), pp. 37–44.

Green, Roger Lancelyn, *Andrew Lang: A Critical Biography, with a Short-title Bibliography of the Works* (Leicester: Edmund Ward, 1946).

Green, Roger Lancelyn, *Andrew Lang* (London: Hogarth, 1962).

Green, Roger Lancelyn, 'Andrew Lang: The Greatest Bookman of His Age', *Indiana University Bookman*, 7 (April 1965).

Green, Roger Lancelyn, 'The Mystery of Andrew Lang', *Blackwood's Magazine*, 306 (December 1969), pp. 522–38.

Harris, Christopher, '"English Parnassianism" and the Place of France in the English Canon', *Working with English: Medieval and Modern Language, Literature and Drama* (2006), pp. 37–46.

Hensley, Nathan K., 'Network: Andrew Lang and the Distributed Agencies of Literary Production', *Victorian Periodicals Review*, 48 (3) (2015), pp. 359–82.

Hensley, Nathan K., 'Network, History, Method: Andrew Lang in and after the 1880s', in Penny Fielding and Andrew Taylor, eds., *Nineteenth-Century Literature in Transition: The 1880s* (Cambridge: Cambridge University Press, 2019), pp. 117–38.

Hensley, Nathan and Molly Clark Hillard, eds. 'Special Issue. The Andrew Lang Effect: Network, Disciple, Method', *Romanticism and Victorianism on the Net*, 64 (October 2013).

Hines, Sara, 'Collecting the Empire: Andrew Lang's Fairy Books (1889–1910), *Marvels and Tales*, 24 (1) (2010), pp. 39–56.

Hunt, Violet, 'Walks with Andrew Lang: A Girl Student's Truancy', *T. P.'s Weekly*, 9 (23 March 1929), pp. 658-9.

Hutchinson, Andrew Boyd Kennedy, *Twenty-Five Years of St Andrews, September 1865 to September 1890* (London: Longmans, Green, and Co., 1892).

Hutchinson, Horace G., *Portraits of the Eighties* (London: T.F. Unwin, 1920); 'Andrew Lang', pp. 208–17.

Lang, Patrick Sellar, *The Langs of Selkirk* (Melbourne, 1910). Diana Fayrer's copy at St Andrews University, with handwritten annotations; later enlarged edition, with career notes and portraits (1910–1992), at Hawick.

Lecourt, Sebastian, *Cultivating Belief: Victorian Anthropology, Liberal Aesthetics and the Secular Imagination* (Oxford: Oxford University Press, 2018); Ch. 5, 'Natural Supernaturalism: Andrew Lang, World Literature, and the Limits of Eclecticism', pp. 161–95.

Leighton, Mary Elizabeth, 'Andrew Lang and the 1885 Merton Professorship of English Language and Literature at Oxford', *Notes and Queries*, 53 (3) (September 2006), pp. 336-8.

Lodge, Sara, '*He and She*: The 1880s, Camp Aesthetics and the Literary Magazine', in Fielding and Taylor, eds., *Nineteenth-Century Literature in Transition: The 1880s*, pp. 178–99.

Macdonald, Catriona M.M., 'Andrew Lang and Scottish Historiography: Taking on Tradition', *Scottish Historical Review*, 94 (2) (2015), pp. 207–36.

Mauser, Oscar, 'Andrew Lang and *Longman's Magazine* 1882–1905', *University of Texas Studies in English*, 34 (1955), pp. 152–78.

Michalski, Robert, 'Towards a Popular Culture: Andrew Lang's Anthropological and Literary Criticism', *Journal of American Culture*, 18 (3) (Fall 1995), pp. 13-7.

Montenyohl, Eric L., 'Andrew Lang's Contributions to English Folk Narrative Scholarship: A Re-evaluation', *Western Folklore*, 47 (4) (October 1988), pp. 269–84.

Orel, Harold, 'Andrew Lang', in *Victorian Literary Critics* (London: Macmillan, 1984), pp. 124–50.

Pennell, Elizabeth Robins, 'Andrew Lang as a Lecturer', *Critic* (December 1888), p. 329.

Raia, Courtenay, *The New Prometheans: Faith, Science, and the Supernatural Mind in the Victorian Fin de Siècle* (Chicago: University of Chicago Press, 2019); Ch. 6, 'Uncanny Cavemen: Andrew Lang, Psycho-Folklore and the Romance of Ancient Man', pp. 226–302.

Reekie, A. G. 'Lang the Elusive', *Scots Review*, 2 (8) (1850), p. 153; p. 159.

Reid, Julia, '"King Romance" in *Longman's Magazine*: Andrew Lang and Literary Populism', *Victorian Periodical Review*, 44 (4) (1 December 2011), pp. 354–76.

Saintsbury, George, 'Andrew Lang in the Seventies and After', *The Eighteen Seventies*, ed. H. Granville-Barker (Cambridge: Cambridge University Press, 1929).

Salmond, J. B., ed., *Andrew Lang at St Andrews: A Centenary Anthology* (St Andrews: St Andrews University Press, 1944).

Schroeder, Sharin, 'Lasting Ephemera: Margaret Oliphant and Andrew Lang on Lives and Letters', *Victorian Periodicals Review*, 50 (2) (2017), pp. 336–65.

Sherbo, Arthur, 'On the Ethics of Reprinting: Thomas Mosher vs. Andrew Lang, *The New England Quarterly*, 64 (1) (March 1991), pp. 100–12.

Shorter, Clement K., 'Reminiscences of Andrew Lang', *The Bookman's Journal and Print Collector*, 5 (3) (December 1921), pp. 73–5.

Smol, Anna, 'The "Savage" and the "Civilized": Andrew Lang's Representation of the Child and the Translation of Folklore', *Children's Literature Association Quarterly*, 21 (4) (Winter 1996), pp. 177–83.

Sparks, Julie, 'At the Intersection of Victorian Science and Fiction: Andrew Lang's 'Romance of the First Radical', *English Literature in Transition*, 42 (2) (1999), pp. 124–42.

Stephen, Sidney and Leslie Lee, *Lives of the 'Lustrous: A Dictionary of Irrational Biography* (London, 1901).

Sumpter, Caroline, 'Devulgarizing Dickens: Andrew Lang, Homer and the Rise of Psycho-Folklore', *ELH*, 87 (3) (Fall 2020), pp. 733–79.

Susina, Jan, '"Like the Fragments of Coloured Glass in a Kaleidoscope": Andrew Lang Mixes Up Richard Doyle's "In Fairyland"', *Marvels and Tales*, 17 (1) (2003), pp. 100–19.

Teverson, Andrew, *The Selected Children's Fiction, Folk Tales and Fairy Tales of Andrew Lang* (Edinburgh: Edinburgh University Press, 2021).

Thompson, Sir D'Arcy Wentworth, 'Andrew and Pat', *Scots Magazine*, 41 (May 1944), pp. 83–6.

Tolkien, J. R. R., 'On Fairy-Stories', in Verlyn Flieger and Douglas A. Andersen, eds., *Tolkien on Fairy-Stories* (London: HarperCollins, 2008).

Warner, Marina, *Once Upon a Time: A Short History of Fairy Tale* (New York: OUP, 2014).

Webster, A. Blyth and J. B. Salmond, eds., *Concerning Andrew Lang: Being the Andrew Lang Lectures Delivered before the University of St Andrews 1927–1937* (Oxford: Clarendon Press, 1949).

Wheeler-Barclay, Marjorie, 'Andrew Lang, The Antipositivist Critique', in *The Science of Religion in Britain 1860–1915* (Charlottesville: University of Virginia, 2010), pp. 104–39.

Wilson, Leigh, 'These the Facts Are': Andrew Lang, Facts and Fantasy', *Journal of Literature and Science*, 6 (2) (2013), pp. 29–41.

Weintraub, Joseph, 'Andrew Lang: Critic of Romance', *English Literature in Transition*, 18 (1) (January 1975), pp. 5–15.

Index

Abbey, Edwin Austin 93
Aborigines 9, 64, 123, 176, 193, 195–6,
 206, 209
Academy 55, 58, 100, 108–9, 190, 196, 203
Ackerman. Robert 222
Adams, William Davenport
 Latter-Day Lyrics 66–7
Adlington, William
 Cupid and Psyche 120
Aeschylus
 Agamemnon 78–9
Aesthetic movement 35, 41, 73–4, 79,
 82–3, 159
Agrippa, Cornelius 16
Alexander, George 190
Allen, Grant 105, 148, 176, 210
 Woman Who Did, The 159
Alleyne, Annabel ('Annie',
 sister-in-law) 205
Alleyne, Charles Thomas 57
Alleyne, Foster McGeachy
 (brother-in-law) 34, 52, 61,
 64
Alleyne, Rev. John Foster 61
Alleyne, Mrs Margaret Frances 57, 205
Alleyne, Percy (brother-in-law) 57, 99
Alleyne, Sarah Frances ('Fanny',
 sister-in-law) 52, 57, 61, 99
Alleyne, Thyra Blanche (niece) 223
Almond, Henry Hutchinson 25–6
Anderson, Mary 101
Andrieu, Jules 58, 61
Ansell, Mary (Mrs J.M. Barrie) 154
Anstey, Fred
 Tinted Venus, The 67
anthropology 43–4, 50–51, 55, 60, 63–4,
 105–6, 131, 148, 152, 176, 179,
 182–5, 193–6, 204, 206, 208–12,
 215, 217, 222, 226
Appleton, Charles **55**
Appleton and Company, Daniel 101

Arabian Nights 5
archaeology 76–8, 148, 153, 179, 203, 213
Archer, William 190
Ardtornish 8, 13, 49, 56
Argyll, George Douglas Campbell, Duke of
 Scotland as It Was and as It Is 172
Aristophanes
 Clouds, The 97
Aristotle 22
 Politics 32, 44, 58, 63–4
Arkoll, Cecil 163
Arnold, Mary, see Ward, Mrs Humphry
Arnold, Matthew 28–9, 33, 36, 47, 70, 113,
 127, 173–4
Arnold, Tom 47
Arnold, William 50
Art Annual 57
Arunta people 183, 195–6
Athenaeum 67, 84, 127, 162, 169, 208, 222
Atkinson, James Jasper 25, 106, 148, 193,
 222
 Primal Law 193
Atlantic Monthly 76
Austen, Jane 111, 118–19, 213
Austin, Alfred 67
Ayrole, J.B
 La Vraie Jeanne d'Arc 158

Bacon, Francis 213
Bàillidh, Domhnall 2
Balfour, Graham 188
'Ballade of Andrew Lang' 91
Balliol College 6, 22, 25–35, 39, 46, 49, 66,
 79, 84, 91, 119–20, 145, 153, 193,
 214
Bangs, John Kendrick 177
Banville, Théodore de 76, 79
Barrie, J. M. 154
 Peter Pan 128
Basano 126
Bates, Daisy 209

Baudelaire, Charles 159
Beaton, Mrs
   Book of Household Management 193
Beerbohm, Max 159
Behn, Aphra 141
Beilby, George 25–6
Belgravia 65
Bell, George 85, 96
Bell, Hugh and Florence 112
Belloc, Marie, see Lowndes, Marie Belloc
Bennett, James 55
Benson, Frank 79
Benson, Robert Henry ('Robin') 65
Berman, Ruth 226
Bernhardt, Sarah 158
Besant, Walter 81
Bins, Paul 55
Bismarck 44
Bjornson, Bjornstjerne 70
Black, William
   Princess of Thule, The 54
Blackie, John Stuart 91
   Altavona 84
Blackstone Prize 24
Blackwood, William 171
Blackwood's Magazine 132, 166–7, 175,
      178, 180–1, 199
Blake, William 92
Boas, Franz 211
Boer War 180–1
Bolland, William 58
Bookman, The 162
Borderland 151
Boswell, James 186–7
Bowen, Charles 55
Bowes-Lyon, Claude, Earl of
      Strathmore 208
Bowes-Lyon, Elizabeth (Queen
      Mother) 208
Bowman, Thomas 197, 214
Boyd, Charles 227
Bracegirdle, Anne 141
Bradley, A. C. 50, 108, 132
Bradley, F. H. 51, 196
Bradley, George Granville 50
Bradley, Margaret Louisa ('Daisy', Mrs
      George Henry Woods) 50
Bradley, Miriam 50
Braxfield, Lord 156

Bridges, Robert 92, 99, 212, 214
   Prometheus: The Firegiver 92
British Academy 200
British Weekly 153
Brodie, Sir Benjamin 47
Brodrick, George Charles 40, 196
Charlotte Brontë
   Jane Eyre 191
Brosses, Charles de
   Du culte des dieux fétiches 95
Broughton, Rhoda 119, 126–7
   Belinda 126
   Joan 119
   Nancy 119
Brown, Helen 5
Brown, Henry 16–17, 90
Brown, Peter Hume 179, 205, 222
Brown, Robert Glasgow 65
Browning, Robert 19, 33, 54, 79, 86, 154
   Men and Women 5
   Ring and the Book, The 162
Bruno, Giordano 46, 48
Buchanan, Robert ('Thomas
      Maitland') 49, 70
Buffalo Bill's Wild West Show 117
Burnand, F. C. 101
Burne, Charlotte 69
Burne-Jones, Edward 169
Burnham, Elizabeth ('Elyth') 191
Burns, Robert 12
Butcher, Samuel Henry 70, 91, 174–5
Byron, Lord 50, 112
   Don Juan 10

Caine, Hall 190
Caird, Edward 140, 143, 153
Callaway, Bishop Henry 68
Calcutta Review 168
Campbell, Lord Archibald 18, 121, 124,
      169
Campbell, Elspeth 169
Campbell, Janey Sevilla 121
Campbell, John, Marquess of Lorne 18,
      213
Campbell, Lewis 72, 124, 141
Canning, George
   Rovers, The 124
Carlyle, Thomas 30, 133
Carroll, Lewis, see Dodgson, Charles

Cassell and Company 82, 106
Catholic World 193
Catullus 19
Celtic Magazine 83
Celts 113, 153–4, 172–5
Century Illustrated Magazine 90, 97, 139
Chambers' Journal 12
Chanson de Roland, La 51, 53
Chapman, George 70
Chapman, John 53
Charles II 201, 223
Charles III 208
Christie, Ella 207, 213, 218, 221
Christian World 114
Clemens, Mrs Olivia 165
Clemens, Susy 165
Clifton Association for Higher Education
    of Women 52
Clifton College 52
Clifton, Robert 40
Clodd, Edward 69, 147, 152, 175–6, 184,
    204, 209–10, 222
Coleridge, Hartley 63
College Echoes 139–40, 143–4
Collins, John Churton 54, 108, 114–15
Collins, Wilkie 13
Colvin, Sidney 55, 58, 61, 165, 167
comparative mythology 43, 50–1, 54–5,
    60, 93–4, 122–3
Connington, John 42
Constable, publishers 194
Contemporary Review 70, 117, 151
Conway, Hugh
    Called Back 87, 101
    Dark Days 100–1
Cooke, Eliza 90
Cooke, George Alfred 156
Coombes, George J. 105
Copleston, Reginald 51
Corelli, Marie (Mary Mackay) 189–90,
    202
    Silver Domino, The 190
    Sorrows of Satan, The 190
    Temporal Powers 202
    Wormwood: A Drama of Paris 202
Cornhill Magazine 66, 69
Cosmopolis 164
Courthope, William 65, 214
Courtney, William 57–8, 125–6, 196

Cox, Sir George
    Mythology of the Aryan Nations, The 96
Cox, Robert 16, 20
Craig, Margaret (great-aunt) 7
Craig-Brown, Thomas 132
Crawford, Robert 226
Creighton, Mrs Louise 46–7, 51–2, 59, 63,
    99, 182
Creighton, Mandell 40–1, 45–7, 51–2, 59,
    62–3, 99, 182
Craik, Dinah Maria Mulock
    Alice Learmont 127–8
Crofters Holding (Scotland) Act 113
Cromwell, Oliver 172
Cross, Elizabeth ('Tibby') 5, 19
Cross, John Walter 65
Culloden 7, 172, 204
Cumberland, Duke of 7

Daily News 61–2, 65, 91, 98, 110, 162, 180,
    227
Dark Blue, The 47–8
Darnley, Lord 183, 186–7
Darwin, Charles 130, 133, 204, 222, 228
    Origin of Species, The 23, 189
Darwin, Francis 133
D'Aulnoy, Madame 137, 154
Davidson, John 163, 227
Decadent movement 141, 159, 202
Defoe, Daniel
    Robinson Crusoe 180
Desmond, Fred 98
Dickens, Charles 12, 86, 108, 114–15,
    164–5, 169, 213–14
    Bleak House 114
    David Copperfield 142
    Gadshill Edition 164–5
    Hard Times 6
    Little Dorrit 165
    Old Curiosity Shop, The 162
    Pickwick Papers 114, 165, 169
Dickinson, William Croft 186
Dictionary of National Biography
    (*DNB*) 169–73, 177
Disraeli, Benjamin 56, 65–6
Dixon, Richard Watson
    Mano 92
Dobson, Austin 66–8, 75, 78–9, 85–6, 90,
    101, 163

Dobson, Austin (*Continued*)
  Proverbs in Porcelain 66
Dobson, Mrs Mary 67
Dodgson, Charles ('Lewis Carroll') 119
  Alice in Wonderland 136
Donaldson, James 140
Donne, John 159
Douglas, David 84
Dowden, Edward 108
Doyle, Sir Arthur Conan 34, 213
  'Lot No. 249' 34
Doyle, Sir Francis 34, 64
Doyle, Richard ('Dicky')
  In Fairyland 100, 127
Duckworth, Stella (Mrs Stella Hills) 169,
  174
Duff-Cooper, Andrew 226
Dumas, Alexander 127, 223
Durkheim, Émile 193, 211

Eccentric Flamingos, The 30–1
Edinburgh Academy 9–13, 15, 55
Edward I 20, 179
Edward VII 211
Eliot, George 51, 86
  Middlemarch 89, 126
Elton, Sir Edmund and Lady Agnes 17
Encyclopaedia Britannica 58, 71, 123, 189
'Enfants Perdus, Les' 31
English Illustrated Magazine 196
'English Worthies' 101–2, 114
Epicurus 23
Essays and Reviews 23, 30
Esson, William 40
Eusebius 43
Evening Telegraph 140
Ewing, Julia Horatia
  Jan of the Windmill 136
Eyre, Edward John 30, 40
exogamy 43, 64, 96, 209–11, 222
Ezekiel 72

fairy tales 4, 6–7, 44, 50, 54, 95–6, 100,
  127–8, 134–7, 154, 226–7
Falconer, Charles MacGregor
  New Friendship's Garland, A 176–7
Fenian bombing campaign 91, 105
Ferrier, Professor James Frederick 21–2,
  29, 56

Ferrier, Walter 56
Fielding, Henry
  Tom Jones 150
Figaro (Paris) 177
Fison, Lorimer 185
Flandre, M. de 25
Fleming, David Hay 153, 185–6, 217, 219
Folklore (originally *Folk-Lore Record*) 69,
  76, 196, 222
Folklore Society 68–9, 137, 148–9, 150–1,
  176, 222
Fontenelle, Bernard de
  De l'origine des fables 43, 152
Forbes, James David 15–16, 21
Ford, Henry Justice 135, 137–8
Ford Lectures 197–8
Forsyth, James and Maria Magdalena 49
Fortnightly Review 58, 60
France, Anatole
  Life of Jeanne d'Arc, The 207
Fraser-Mackintosh, Charles 172
Fraser's Magazine 17, 105
Frazer, J.G. 176, 182–5, 193, 195–6
  Golden Bough, The 182–5, 196, 209–11,
  222
  Totemism and Exogamy 210
Frederick of Baden, Grand Duke 44
Freeman, A. E. 108–9
Freund, John Christian 47
Froude, James Anthony 133, 178
Fuegians 204
Fuguet, Émile 187
Furness, Horace Howard 197
Furniss, Harry 125

Gautier, Théophile 33, 47–8
Gell, Philip 82
George V 212
George VI 208
Gibbon, Edward
  *Decline and Fall of the Roman Empire,
  The* 44
Gifford Lectures 124–9, 130–2, 139–40,
  153, 174
Gilbert, W. S. 93
Gilbert and Sullivan
  Patience, or Bunthorne's Bride 82
  Pirates of Penzance, The 72
Gillen, Frank 195

Gissing, George 164–5
  Charles Dickens; A Critical Study 164–5
  Nether World, The 164
  New Grub Street 144–5
Gladstone, William 56, 66, 91, 104, 110, 125, 129
Glasgow, University of 6, 22–6, 132
Globe, The 69
Godley, Arthur (Lord Kilbracken) 35
Goldenweiser, Alexander 210–11, 225
Goldsmith, Oliver
  She Stoops to Conquer 145
Gomme, Laurence 137
Good Words 12, 24
Gordon, General Charles George 104
Gordon, George, 225
Gore-Booth, Eva
  Poems 174
Gore-Booth, Sir Henry 174
Gosse, Edmund 66–7, 69–70, 76, 78–9, 81, 87–91, 97, 99–102, 108–10, 113–15, 128, 139, 142, 144, 163–4, 170–1, 188–9, 211–12, 219, 224
  From Shakespeare to Pope 113
  New Poems 70, 87–8
  On Viol and Flute 66
  Studies in the Literature of Modern Europe 69–70
  Walter Raleigh 114
Gosse, Mrs Ellen 67
Grant, Sir Alexander 84
Gray, Nancy 42, 206
Green, Mrs Charlotte, née Symonds 52, 64, 99, 120
Green, John Richard 47
Green, Roger Lancelyn 52, 136
Green, Thomas Hill 30, 32, 52, 64
Greenwood, Frederick 111
Grierson, Herbert 225
Grieve, Charles 63
Grieve, Mrs Elizabeth Willing, née Alleyne (sister-in-law) 63, 221, 223
Grimm's Fairy Tales 95

Haddon, Alfred 184
Haggard, H. Rider 106–7, 114, 126, 177, 193, 199, 213, 217, 223
  Colonel Quaritch, V.C. 129
  King Solomon's Mines 106

She 118, 217
Witch's Head, The 106–7
World's Desire, The (with Andrew Lang) 129, 134, 141, 217
Haggard, John 106
Hallam, Arthur 18
Hamilton, Constance 49
Hamilton, Sir William 21
Hammond, George 40
Hardy, Thomas
  Tess of the D'Urbervilles 147–8, 162
Harper (publishers) 126
Harper's Magazine 79, 93, 106, 109, 112, 132, 139, 154
Harris, Frank
  Man Shakespeare, The 211
Harte, Bret 134
Hartland, Edwin 176, 184, 222
Hegel 39, 196
Heinemann 170
Helen of Troy 85–6, 87–9, 118
Helm, William 144
Henderson, Alexander 130
Henley, Joseph 68
Henley, William 68–9, 82–3, 92, 96, 98, 114, 121–2, 125, 129, 137–8, 141–2, 163, 176, 188–9
  Book of Verse, A 125, 138
  Deacon Brodie (with R.L. Stevenson) 98
  Pictures at Play (with Andrew Lang) 125
Hensley, Nathan 227
Hessels, John Henry 100
Highland Clearances 1–2, 8–9, 83–5, 113, 168–73, 203–4
Highlands of Scotland in 1750, The 171–2
Hill, Frank 62, 110
Hills, Mrs Anna 145, 156, 164, 168, 201, 207–9
Hills, Herbert 145
Hills, Jack 145, 169, 174, 209
Hodgson, Richard 155, 160
Hodson, James Stephen 12
Hole, William 56
Holl, Frank 125
Homer 12, 44, 58, 60, 70–1, 85, 88, 91–5, 100, 149–50, 153, 171, 203, 206, 208, 213
Homeric Question 149–50, 171, 203, 206, 208, 213, 225

Hopkins, Gerard Manley 35, 66, 92
Howells, William Dean 109, 115–18, 165, 197
Howitt, Alfred 176, 185, 195
  Native Tribes of South-East Australia, The 196
Hueffer, Francis 78
Hughes, Thomas
  Tom Brown's Schooldays 9
Hugo, Victor 50
Hume, David
  'Miracles' 130–1
Hunt, Leigh 166–7
Hunt, Margaret 95, 132
Hunt, Violet 132
Huxley, T.H. 210

Iddesleigh, Lady 140
Illustrated London News 147, 182, 201, 211, 219
Image, Selwyn 50, 160–1
Index Expurgatorius 175–6
Innes, Cosmo
  Scotland in the Middle Ages 178
International Folklore Congress 148
International Review 69
Irish Home Rule 110
Irish Literary Revival 153, 174

Jack, Edwin 199
Jacobite history 122, 155, 157, 168–9, 171, 174, 177, 203–4
Jacobs, Joseph 69
James I and VI 185–7, 193
James, Henry 65, 71–2, 76, 81, 92–3, 101, 108, 115, 119, 134, 199–200
  Portrait of a Lady, The 92
James, William
  Will to Believe, The 131
Jenkin, Mrs Anne 79
Jenkin, Fleeming 78
Jerome, Jerome K.
  Three Men in a Boat 190
Joachim, Harold 196
Joan of Arc 158, 160–2, 164–5, 184, 207, 219, 224
Johnson, Alice 215–16
Johnson, Arthur and Bertha 52
Johnson, Lionel 163

Johnson Samuel 163
Jonson, Ben 101–2, 144
  Bartholomew Fair 114
Jourdain, Eleanor
  An Adventure (with Charlotte Moberly) 215–17
Journal of Philosophy 72
Jowett, Benjamin 6, 23, 25, 29–30, 32, 34–5, 37–8, 40–1, 52, 57, 79, 108, 111, 119, 121–4, 150, 152, 221
  Essays and Reviews 23, 30
Jusserand, J. J. 207

Kate Kennedy 21
Keats, John 98, 166–7
Kelly, Hannah 97, 191
Kendall, May 102
  That Very Mab (with Andrew Lang) 105, 132, 135
Kid, Paul Jones & Co. 81
Kipling, Rudyard 134, 142, 144, 157
  Departmental Ditties 134
  Light that Failed, The 157
Kirk, Robert
  Secret Commonwealth, The 151
Knox, John 153, 185–6, 197–8, 201, 218, 222
  History of the Reformation in Scotland, The 185, 197

Ladies' Association for the Advancement of Women's Education 45
Lamb, Charles
  Beauty and the Beast 120
Land Nationalisation Society 83
Lang, Mrs Ada (sister-in-law) 189, 193
Lang, Alexander Craig ('Craig', brother) 31, 42, 162–3, 223
Lang, Andrew (grandfather) 1, 7, 9
Lang, Andrew
  Books
    Angling Sketches 145
    Aucassin and Nicolete, translation 120
    Ballades and Lyrics of Old France 49–50, 52, 56, 66
    Ballads and Verses Vain 90
    Ballades in Blue China 72–6, 79, 81, 215
    Ban and Arrière Ban 122, 157

Blue Fairy Book, The 134–5, 137
*Book of Princes and Princesses,
   The* 208
Books and Bookmen 105, 115
Border Ballads 127
Brown Fairy Book, The 137–8
Cock Lane and Common Sense 151–2,
   155
Companions of Pickle, The 172–4, 204
Custom and Myth 93–5, 99
Disentanglers, The 175, 190
Fool Hath Said, The 202
Gold of Fairnilee, The 127–8, 136
Grass of Parnassus 127, 215
Green Fairy Book, The 135, 154
Grey Fairy Book, The 137
He (with Walter Pollock) 117
Helen of Troy 85–9, 118
*Highlands of Scotland in 1750,
   The* 171–2
Historical Mysteries 187
*History of English Literature from
   Beowulf to Swinburne* 210, 218–19
*History of Scotland from the Roman
   Occupation, A* 178–81, 185–6, 193,
   198, 203
Homer and His Age 203
Homer and the Epic 149–50, 203
Homeric Hymns, translation with
   essays 171, 175, 183
Iliad, prose translation (with Leaf and
   Myers) 91
In the Wrong Paradise 112, 119
James VI and the Gowrie Mystery 187,
   193
John Knox and the Reformation 197–8
Letters to Dead Authors 111–12, 118
Library, The 78–80
*Life and Letters of John Gibson
   Lockhart* 165–8
*Life, Letters, and Diaries of Sir Stafford
   Northcote* 129, 133–4, 140–1
Magic and Religion 184, 195
Maid of France, The 207, 224
Making of Religion, The 131, 174–6,
   185, 195–6
Mantrap Manor 202–3
Mark of Cain, The 57, 108, 110, 211
Method in the Study of Totemism 211

Modern Mythology 182–3
Monk of Fife, A 160–2, 165
Much Darker Days 101, 108, 202
Mystery of Mary Stuart, The 186–7,
   217
Myth, Ritual and Religion 89, 110,
   120, 123–4, 175–6
Odyssey, prose translation (with S.H.
   Butcher) 42, 65, 70–1
*Old Friends: Essays in Epistolary
   Parody* 126
Origins of Religion, The 209–10
Parson Kelly (with E.A.W.
   Mason) 177–8
Pickle the Spy 155, 168–9, 172
Pictures at Play (with W.E.
   Henley) 125
Poetical Works 224
Politics of Aristotle, The 44, 63–4
Prince Prigio 11, 134, 136–7
Princess Nobody, The 100
Rector and the Rubric, The 202
Red Fairy Book 135
Rhymes à la Mode 99, 102, 215
Secrets of the Totem, The 195–6
*Shakespeare, Bacon and the Great
   Unknown* 213, 220
Sins of the Smart Set 202
*Sir George MacKenzie of
   Rosehaugh* 201, 207
Sir Walter Scott 201
Social Origins 193–4
St Andrews 153
Story of Joan of Arc, The 201
Strange Story Book, The 223
That Very Mab (with May
   Kendall) 105
Theocritus, Bion, Moschus, prose
   translation 71, 78
Valet's Tragedy, The 187
When It Was Light 202
World of Homer, The 213
World's Desire, The (with Rider
   Haggard) 129, 134, 141, 217
Essays and Short Stories
   'Apparitions' 58
   'Avengers of Romance, The' 118
   'Ballads' 58

Lang, Andrew (*Continued*)
    'Bull-Roarer; A Study of Mysteries,
       The' 94
    'Chanson de Roland, La' 51, 53
    'Charm of the Stuarts, The' 175
    'Cheap Nigger, A' 107
    'Comedies of Shakespeare, The' 139
    'Comparative Psychical Research' 151
    'Creeful of Stories, A' 175
    'Cupid, Psyche and the Sun-Frog' 94
    'Edinboro Old Town' 90–1
    'Edward Burnett Tylor' 206
    'End of Phaeacia, The' 107
    'Flos Regum' 20
    'Folklore of France, The' 69
    'Giordano Bruno' 46
    'History as She Ought to be
       Wrote' 178
    'Homer and Recent Criticism' 60
    'Homer and Anthropology' 206–8
    'Household Tales: Their Origin,
       Diffusion, and Relation to the
       Higher Myths' 95–6
    'How to Fail in Literature' 137
    'In the Debatable Land' 50
    'In the Wrong Paradise' 105–6
    'Kalevala, or the Finnish National
       Epic' 51
    'Lady of White Heather, A' 50
    'Literary Fairy Tales' 137
    'Literary Quarrels' 115
    'Loves of Pulvis and Umbra, The' 59
    'Making of Scottish Presbyterianism,
       The' 218
    'Moly and Mandragora' 94
    'My Friend the Beachcomber' 107
    'My History Vindicated' 198
    'Mythology' 123
    'Mythology and Fairy Tales' 54
    'Patrick Sellar', *DNB* entry 169–70,
       173
    'Poppy's Heart' 50
    'Quite the Wrong Man' 101
    'Reading Public, The' (with 'X, A
       Working Man') 200
    'Realism and Romance' 117–18
    'Rabelais and the Renaissance' 38
    'Religio Loci' 218
    'Restoration of Romance, The' 115
    'Romance of the First Radical,
       The' 77–8, 105
    'Romantic Plot Against the Union,
       The' 204–5
    'Savage Art' 82
    'Scottish Nursery Tales' 20
    'Slipshod Story, A' 60
    'Spiritualism Medieval and
       Modern' 20
    'Théophile Gautier' 47
    'Theories of the Origin of
       Religion' 209–10
    'Three Poets of French Bohemia' 47–8
    'Totemism and Exogamy' 222
    'Voices of Jeanne d'Arc, The' 160
    'Was Jehovah a Fetish Stone?' 148
    'William Young Sellar, Memoir
       of' 141
  Poems
    'Ah, Fortune, thy wheel' 121
    'Almae Matres' 90–1, 218
    'Ballade of a Bookworm' 4
    'Ballade of Blue China' 73–4
    'Ballade of Literary Fame' 203
    'Ballade of Middle Age' 98–9
    'Ballade of Neglected Merit' 97–8
    'Ballade of Primitive Man' 72–3
    'Ballade of Railway Novels' 115–16
    'Ballade of Sleep' 75–6
    'Ballade of Theocritus' 71
    'Ballant o' Ballantrae' 121–2
    'Beauty and the Beast' 100–3
    'Clevedon Church' 18, 90
    'Dear Louis of the awful cheek!' 121
    'Dei Otiosi' 23
    'Desiderium, In Memoriam S.F.A.' 99
    'Doris's Books' 119
    'End of Term, The' 145
    'Freshman's Year' 27–8
    'Good-by' 52
    'Here's a contest; here's a treat' 100
    'Hesperothen' 37–8
    'Idylls of the Dado' 82–3
    'In College Gardens' 48
    'Last Cast, The' 201
    'Lay of the Bookselling Elder, The' 23
    'Letter from Bird-of-Freedom
       Sawin' 19
    'Log-Rolliad, The' 143–4

'Love and Wisdom' 52
'Madrigal of Thomas Buchanan' 70
'Natural Theology' 96
'Nemesis of Art, The' 67–8
'Nugae Catulline' 19
'Νηνεμος Αἰών' 104–5
'Ode to Mr Saintsbury' 163
'On an Expensive Volume of Verse' 46
'Palace of Bric-à-Brac, The' 93
'Plumber and the Publisher, The' 81
'Poet's Apology, A' 157
'Prospective Farewell, A' 24
'Rococo' 59
'San Terenzo' 77
'Since I have set my lips to your full cups' 50
'Singing Rose, The' 52
'Sir Lancelot' 19
'Sirens' Music Heard Again, The' (later retitled 'They Hear the Music for a Second Time') 37–8
'Spent Golden Hair' 48
'Summer Ending' 52
'Three Portraits of Prince Charles' 168
'To Lord Byron' 112
'To Robert Louis Stevenson' 151
'Twilight on Tweed' 42
'Two Homes' 45
'White Pasha, The' 104
'Why They Don't Stand for the Poetry Chair' 33
Lang, Craig Sellar (nephew) 223
Lang, Mrs Eva (sister-in-law) 162–3
Lang, Gideon Scott 9, 123
    Aborigines of Australia, The 64
Lang, Helen ('Nell', sister) 39, 42, 98, 205, 223
Lang, Jane, née Sellar (mother) 2, 5–6, 38, 41–2, 56
Lang, Mrs Jean Blaikie (sister-in-law) 193–4, 199, 219, 221
Lang, John (brother) 31, 42, 163, 199, 201, 220–1, 223
Lang, John of Overwells (father) 1, 6, 10, 38, 41–2, 56
Lang, Mrs Leonora Blanche, née Alleyne ('Nora', wife) 56–8, 61, 73, 75,
78–9, 81, 93, 98–9, 104, 112–13, 119, 120–2, 124, 126, 129, 135–6, 139, 145–6, 153–5, 159, 174, 180, 189, 191, 195, 199, 205, 207–8, 213, 218–24
    Book of Princes and Princesses, The 220
    Book of Saints and Heroes, The 220
    'Country Conversations' 123
    Dissolving Views 57, 96–7
    Geography for Beginners, A 63
    History of Russia, A by Alfred Rambaud, translation 67
    Men, Women and Minxes 220, 223
    Red Book of Heroes, The 220
    'Sir F. Leighton: His Life and Work' 57
    Strange Story Book, The 223
    'Versatilio' 57
Lang, Margaret, née Suter (grandmother) 1, 9
Lang, Patrick Sellar ('Pat', brother) 42, 71, 190, 205, 208
Lang, Thomas William ('T.W.', brother) 31, 42, 52, 61, 86, 163, 189–90, 192–3, 205
Lang, William Henry (brother) 42, 52, 98, 190–1, 206
    Thunder of the Hooves, The 206
Lapsley, Gailland Thomas 185
Latimer, Hugh 27
Layamon's Brut 219
Le Gallienne, Richard 157
Leaf, Walter 91, 149–50
Lecourt, Sebastian 36
Lee, Sir Sidney 169–70, 177
Leighton, Sir Frederick 57, 79
Leo XIII, Pope 158
Lewes, George Henry 51
Lewis, C. S.
    Chronicles of Narnia 128
Liddell, Augustus 29
Liddon, Canon Henry 104
Lingard, John
    History of England 38
Lives of the 'Lustrous 177
Lissadell 174–5
Locker-Lampton, Frederick 79, 112
Lockhart, John Gibson 145, 165–8, 225
    'Cockney School of Poetry, The' 166–7

Lodge, Sir Oliver 148, 155–6, 159–60, 165, 187, 215
London Magazine 65–6, 68–9, 71, 87
London, University of 110, 111–12
Longfellow, Henry 86
Longman, Ada Mary 53
Longman, Charles 49, 84, 87, 100, 109, 119, 174, 194, 201, 212, 215, 217
Longman, Frederick 49, 52–3
Longman, Sybil Augusta 52–3, 132
Longman's Magazine 87, 100, 105, 109–12, 115, 122, 147, 150, 157, 175, 177, 190, 198–201, 220
Loretto School 25–6
Lothian, Lord 132
Louis Napoleon 44–5
Lovelace, Richard 18
Lowell, James Russell 120
    Biglow Papers, The 19
Lowndes, Marie Belloc 220
Lubbock, Sir John 124
Lucy, Henry 62
Lyell, Alfred 210

MacAlpine, Kenneth 179
Macaulay, Thomas Babington 178
MacCunn, Mrs Florence, née Sellar (cousin) 49, 57, 63, 120–1
MacCunn, John 120
Macdonald, Catriona M. M. 186, 227
Macdonnell, Alistair Ruadh (Young Glengarry) 155, 168–9
MacGregor, James Mohr 155
MacGregor, Rob Roy 155
Mackenzie, Alexander 83
MacKenzie, Sir George 201, 207
MacKintosh, Dr Ashley 220
McLennan, Donald 72
McLennan, John Ferguson 43, 64, 72, 76–7
MacLeod, Donald
    Gloomy Memories of the Highlands 8, 83–4
Macleod, Dr Norman 24
Macmillan, Frederick 85, 177
Macmillan's Magazine 17, 46, 54, 63, 78
McWilliam, Nelly 7
Magazine of Art 69, 72
Maitland of Lethington 186

Malborough, John Churchill, Duke of 93, 142–3
Mallock, W. H. 50, 59
    New Republic, The 65
'Man in the Iron Mask, The' 54
Manchester Guardian 69
Malory, Sir Thomas
    Morte d'Arthur 19–20
Marett, Robert 206, 209, 222
Marie Antoinette 32, 215–17
Marlowe, Christopher
    Doctor Faustus 17
Marshall, Calder 12
Marsham, Robert Bulloch 40
Mary of Guise 218
Marzials, Theo 78
Maskelyne, John Nevil 156, 158
Mason, E.A.W. 177–8, 189
    Four Feathers, The 178
    Parson Kelly (with Andrew Lang) 177–8
Masson, David Orme 55
Matthews, Brander 79, 81–3, 85, 90–1, 93, 102, 105, 109–10, 115, 120–2, 126, 146, 150, 182, 187–9
    Marjory's Lovers 98
Maurice, Colonel John Frederick 93
Maurier, George du 74
    'Maudle' cartoons 82
Maxwell, Sir Herbert 189, 218, 223
Maxwell-Scott, Mrs Mary Monica 145, 221
Meadows, Kenny 7
Menzies, Allan 19
Meredith, George 73
Meredith, Mrs Marie 73
Mérimée, Prosper
    Venus d'Ille, The 67
Merrick, Leonard 197
Merton College 38–43, 46–7, 51, 53–4, 57–62, 108–9, 126, 197, 206, 212, 214
Middlemore, John 76
Milne, Alexander 222
Milton, John
    Paradise Lost 189
Mind 72
Miscellany Magazine 50, 59, 60
Moberly, Charlotte
    An Adventure (with Eleanor Jourdain) 215–17

Moberly, Robert 217
Molière 71, 81, 89
Month, The 176
Morgan, William De
    Joseph Vance 213
Morning Post 144
Morris, Jane 134
Morris, Lewis 190
Morris, William 35, 38, 59, 88, 134
Morvich 2, 7, 8, 173
Mull 49
Müller, Mrs Georgina 182
Müller, Max 43, 50–1, 54, 72–3, 94, 96,
    123, 125–6, 130–1, 182–3
    Chips from a German Workshop 163
    Essays on the Science of Language 43
    *Lectures on the Origin and Growth of
        Religion* 72–3
    Life and Letters 182
    Oxford Essays 96
Murger, Henri 47
    Scènes de la Vie de Bohème 48, 62
Murray, Gilbert 133, 191, 206–7, 210,
    213–15, 226
    Gobi and Shamo 133
    *History of Ancient Greek
        Literature* 170–1, 208
    Rise of the Greek Epic, The 206–8, 212
Musset, Alfred de 33
Myers, Ernest 64, 91
Myers, Mrs Eveleen 91
Myers, Frederick 12, 64, 158, 165

Napier, Arthur Sampson 109
National Observer, see *Scots Observer*
National Society for Aid to the Sick and
    Wounded 45
Needham, Rodney 226
Nerval, Gérard de 47–8
Nesbit, Edith
    Five Children and It 128
Newdigate Prize 32, 82, 217
Nichol, John 132
Nicholl, William Robertson 162, 168
Nicholson, Edward 173
Nordau, Max
    Degeneration 159
Northcote, Sir Stafford 129, 133–4, 140,
    142–3

Notes and Queries 68
Nutt, Alfred 69

O'Connor, Ralph 77–9
O'Shaughnessy, Arthur 76, 78
Oliphant, Margaret 110, 167–8
    Autobiography and Letters 188
Once a Week 38
Orleans, Charles of 49
Ortman, Fernand 164
Oxford Magazine, The 91
Oxford Spectator, The 35, 45, 51
Oxford Undergraduate's Journal 33–4, 48
Oxford University Dramatic Society 79

Paget, F. E
    Hope of the Katzekopfs, The 136
Palgrave, Francis 10
Pall Mall Gazette 69, 92, 115, 199
Palladino, Eusapia 155–6, 158–60
Parker, Langloh 176
Parnell, Charles Stewart 91, 159
Parsons, Alfred 93
Pastoralist, The 190
Pater, Hester and Clara 51
Pater, Walter 35–6, 51, 59, 188
    Marius the Epicurean 89
    *Studies in the History of the
        Renaissance* 54, 59, 64–5,
        120
Paul, Charles Kegan 81, 85
Payn, James 12–13
Payne, John 78, 88
Pennell, Elizabeth Robins 128
Perrault, Charles
    Popular Tales 120
Pisistratus 95, 213
Pitcairn, Robert
    Ancient Criminal Trials of Scotland 7
Pitt Rivers, Augustus 148
Pitt Rivers Museum 148
Platner, Samuel Ball 123
Plato 22, 38, 63
Platt, Arthur 150
Poe, Edgar Allan 10, 107
Pollock, Walter 101, 117
Pope, Alexander 70
Powell, Professor Baden 30

psychical research 131, 150–2, 158, 160, 215–17
'puddex' 26
Puller, Mrs Emmeline Giles, née Longman 167, 189
Punch 17, 74, 82, 101–2, 162

Quarterly Magazine 17, 65
Queen Victoria 117, 182

Rabelais, François 35–8, 46
  Gargantua and Pantagruel 36–8
Rabelais Club 76, 81
Radclifffe-Brown, Alfred 209
Raeburn, John 156
Raleigh, Walter 163
Raleigh, Sir Walter 102, 114
Rambaud, Alfred
  History of Russia, A 67
Ramsay, Professor William 6
Rational Press Association 209
realism versus romance 108, 115–20, 197
Reformation, the 153, 179–81, 185–6, 197–8, 218, 227
religion, the origin of 64, 72, 94–5, 123–4, 130–1, 139, 148, 175–6, 183, 185, 195–6, 209–11
Renan, Ernest 173–4
Review of Reviews 198
Revis, Miss Theresa ('Tizzy') 134
Rhoades, Henry 16
Rhymers' Club 163
Rhys, Sir John 212
Richardson, Samuel
  Sir Charles Grandison 122–3
Richmond, William Blake 102–3, 125, 134
Ridley, Nicholas 27
Ritchie, Anne Thackeray 111, 134, 154–5, 157
Ritchie, Richmond 154
Rizzio, David 186
Roberts, Frederick ('Bobs') 180
Robertson, John 180
Robertson, John Mackinnon 176
Romanes Lecture 212
Roosevelt, Theodore 212
Rossetti, Dante Gabriel 49–50, 59, 66, 86
Royal Society of Literature 212, 219
Ruskin, John 46

Russell, Lord Arthur 93
Ruthven, Alexander 187
Ruthven, John, Earl of Gowrie 187
Ryan, William Patrick 175

St Andrews, University of 13–22, 27, 30, 56, 124–6, 130, 140–1, 143–5, 218, 224
  Andrew Lang Lectures 224–6
  Quincentenary 218
St Andrews University Magazine 20
St James's Gazette 111, 121–3, 126
St Leonard's Hall 15
St Leonard's Magazine 18–19, 21, 24, 30, 33–4
Saint-Beuve, Charles 65, 112
Saintsbury, George 62–3, 66, 108, 163
Sala, Augustus 98
Sand, George 65
Sanderson and Murray 208
Sappho 89
Sardou, Victorien
  Les Pattes de Mouches 99
Saturday Review 55, 58, 62, 64–5, 69, 84–5, 92, 101, 142, 162, 184, 190, 221, 227
Savile Club 55, 58, 83, 92, 152, 176
Schliemann, Heinrich 149
Scots Observer 129–30, 132, 137–9, 141–2
Scott, Alexander 6
Scott, Gideon (great-great uncle) 1
Scott, John Adams 213
Scott, Rev. Robert 28–9, 34
Scott, Sir Walter 1, 3, 10, 157, 165, 207, 221, 227
  Border Edition 145–7
  Bride of Lammermoor, The 10
  Ivanhoe 150
  Waverley 160–1
Scottish Historical Society 178
Scribner, Charles 85, 90
Scribner's Magazine 122, 137
Sellar, Adele Leonide (cousin) 39
Sellar, Agnes, née MacPherson (aunt) 9
Sellar, Alexander Craig (uncle) 43, 55, 85
Sellar, Ann, née Craig (grandmother) 2, 7–8
Sellar, Constance Helen ('Eppie', cousin) 49, 192–3

Sellar, Eleanor Mary, née Denniston (aunt) 6, 19, 48–9, 55, 65
Sellar, Eleanor Charlotte ('Nellie', cousin) 49
Sellar, Florence (cousin), see MacCunn, Mrs Florence
Sellar, May Violet (cousin) 121
Sellar, Patrick (grandfather) 1–3, 8–9, 83–5, 141, 169–71
Sellar, Patrick ('Arthur', cousin) 85
Sellar, Patrick Plendeleath (uncle) 2
Sellar, Thomas (great-grandfather) 1
Sellar, Thomas (uncle) 2, 5–6, 39, 60–1
    Sutherland Evictions of 1814, The 84, 170
Sellar, William Young (uncle) 2, 5–6, 13, 22, 32, 39, 44, 48–9, 55, 57–8, 63, 84, 120–1, 141
    Roman Poets of the Augustan Age, The 141
Sesame Club 220
Shairp, John Campbell 15, 33, 65
    Kilmahoe: A Highland Pastoral with Other Poems 33
Shakespeare 5, 7, 12, 213, 220
    As You Like It 121, 188
    Henry VI, Part 2 158
    King Lear 147
    Macbeth 201
    The Winter's Tale 101
Shaw, G. B. 211
Shelley, Mary
    Frankenstein 78
Shelley, Percy Bysshe 40, 109, 111
    Prometheus Unbound 76–7
    Queen Mab 105
Sheridan, Richard Brinsley
    The Rivals 145–6
Sherlock Holmes 187
Shield, Alice 132
'Shooting Stars, The' 34, 52
Shorter, Clement 163, 191, 201, 213
Shorthouse, Joseph Henry
    John Inglesant 127
Sidney, Lady Dorothy 48
Sidney, Sir Philip 46
Simpson, Violet 169
sircar, Sanjay 136
Sitwell, Mrs Frances 56, 58–9, 61, 137

Skene, William Forbes
    Celtic Scotland: A History of Ancient Alba 178
Slavery Abolition Act of 1833 57
Smith, Adam 180
Smith, Mrs Gertrude 49
Smith, William Robertson 72
    History of the Semites 139
Snell Exhibitions 22–5, 124, 140
Society for Psychical Research (SPR) 131, 150–2, 155, 165, 214–17
Socrates 22
Solomon, Simeon 56
Sparks, Julia 78, 226
Spectator, The 97, 105, 111, 115, 156–7, 169
Spencer, Baldwin 195–6
Spencer, Herbert 194, 210
Spenser, Edmund
    Faerie Queene, The 90
Stanhope Prize 144
Stanley, Sir Henry Morton 140
Star, The 163
Starr, Frederick 176
Stead, W. T. 115, 151, 164
Stedman, Edmund Clarence 79, 81
Steedman, John 190–1
Stephen, Julia 169
Stephen, Leslie 169, 177
Stephen, Vanessa and Virginia 169
Stevenson, Mrs Fanny 81
Stevenson, Robert Louis 3, 13, 41, 55–6, 58–9, 61, 63, 68–9, 81, 83, 87, 89, 96, 101, 104–7, 110–11, 127, 129, 147–8, 151, 156–8, 160, 176, 199, 219
    Ballads 142
    Black Arrow, The 118
    Catriona (in America, David Balfour) 147, 155
    Child's Garden of Verses, A 92, 105
    Deacon Brodie (with W.E. Henley) 98
    Dynamiter, The (with Fanny Stevenson) 105
    Master of Ballantrae, The 121–2
    New Arabian Nights 87, 101
    'Ordered South' 56
    'Pirate and the Apothecary, The' 92
    Treasure Island 92, 106
    Underwoods 121

Stevenson, Robert Louis (*Continued*)
   Weir Of Hermiston 148, 156
   'Young Chevalier, The' 147–8, 155
Stewart, Mrs Alice King 154, 207
Stewart, Lord John Roy 7
Stewart, James, 1st Earl of Moray 185
Stillman, Marie 134
Stirling, John Hutchison 130
Stowe, Harriet Beecher
   Sunny Memories of Foreign Lands 8–9
   Uncle Tom's Cabin 8–9
Strachan, Alexander 70
Strachan-Davidson, James Leigh 153, 214
Strand, The 214
Strehlow, Carl 195
Stuart, Charles Edward ('Bonnie Prince
   Charlie') 7, 147, 155, 168–9
Stuart, House of 4, 132, 175
Stuart, Mary, Queen of Scots 185–7, 197,
   217
Sturgis, Julian 174
Sun, The 175
Suter, Thomas (great-grandfather) 1
Sutherland Clearances, see Highland
   Clearances
Sutherland, Duke and Duchess of 1, 7, 85
Swedish Academy of Sciences 214–15
Sweet, Henry 100, 109
Swift, Jonathan
   'Gulliver in Lilliput' 135
Swinburne, Algernon 32–3, 54
   Atalanta in Calydon 32
   Poems and Ballads 33, 66
Symonds, Charlotte, see Green, Mrs
   Charlotte
Symonds, John Addington 29, 52, 57, 76,
   89, 100, 113–14, 126
   Ben Jonson 102, 114
   Renaissance in Italy, The 60
   Shelley 102
   Sketches of Italy and Greece 58
   Studies of the Greek Poets 64–5

Tait, Peter Guthrie 156, 158–9
Temple Bar 17, 19, 140
Tennant, Dorothy 140
Tennyson, Alfred Lord 8, 33, 79, 86
   'Crossing the Bar' 189
   In Memoriam 17
   'Ulysses' 37–8

Teverson, Andrew 226–7
Thackeray, William M. 86, 108, 111, 115,
   125, 147, 154
   Pendennis 13–14, 17, 62
   Rose and the Ring, The 136–7
Thales 22
Theatre, The 98
Theocritus 71, 76, 78
Thomas, Moy 98
Thompson, D'Arcy Wentworth 11
Thompson, Francis 163
Thoms, William 68
Thomson, Rosamund ('Graham R.')
   *Selections from the Greek
   Anthology* 132–3
'Thorne, Guy' (Ranger Gull)
   When It Was Dark 202
Thyraeus, Petrus 17
Times, The 91
Toft, Albert 125
Tolkien, J.R.R. 136, 226–7
Tone, Wolf 174
totemism 72, 193–4, 209–11, 222, 226
Trollope, Anthony 13
Trotter, John ('Old Trot') 9
Twain, Mark 165
   Huckleberry Finn 107, 165
   Tom Sawyer 92, 165
Tylor, Alfred 50
Tylor, Mrs Anna 195
Tylor, Edward Burnett 50, 56, 73, 94–5,
   106, 123–4, 130, 135, 176, 182–3,
   195–6, 206, 210, 222
   Primitive Culture 50, 130
Tylor, Janet Mary 50
Tyrell, George 176
Tyrwhitt, Richard St John 65

Unitarian Review 124

Vanity Fair 82
Verrall, A.V. 208
Villon, François 47–50
Virgil 97, 184
Von Göler, Herr 44
Votiva Tabella 218

Wallace, Alfred Russel 83–4, 228
Wallace, Sir William 20, 58
Waller, Edmund 48

Wanliss, Thomas Drummond 198
Ward, Mrs Humphry 36, 51–2, 112, 126–7, 183
  Milly and Olly 63
  Miss Bretherton 101
  Robert Elsmere 36, 126, 144
Ward, Thomas Humphry 47, 51–2, 63, 112, 126
Warren, Herbert 212, 214, 217
Watt, A. P. 155
Watts, George Frederick 122
Wellington, Duke of 13
Wells, H.G. 211, 219
  Tono Bungay 213
Wentz, Waller Evans 212
Wesdrop, Aeneas Ranald 155
Westminster Review 53
Weyer, Johann 17
Wheeler-Barclay, Marjorie 152
'Where is Rose' 87, 101
Whibley, Charles 125, 141
Whishaw, Alexander (uncle) 5–6
Whishaw, Helen, née Sellar (aunt) 5–6
Whiteing, Richard 62
Wilamowitz-Muellendorff, Ulrich von 171
Wilde, Oscar 82–3, 142, 144, 159–60, 163, 201–2
  'Decay of Lying, The' 159–60
  Happy Prince and Other Tales, The 134
  Importance of Being Earnest, The 190

Lady Windermere's Fan 190
Picture of Dorian Gray, The 42
Poems 82
'Portrait of Mr. W.H., The' 34, 160
Wilkins, Henry Musgrave 51
Wilson, John ('Christopher North') 166–8
Wilson, Lee 152
Wilson, William Carus 191
Winkworth, Mrs Stephen 78
Wolf, Friedrich 149–50
Wolseley, Frances 139
Wolseley, General Garnet 72, 93, 103–4, 139, 142–3, 153–4, 180
  Story of a Soldier's Life, The 194–5
Wolseley, Lady Louisa 72, 93, 99, 104, 119–20, 125, 139, 142, 154, 172, 180, 195
Wordsworth, Bishop Charles 124
Woods, George Henry **51**
Woollcombe, Rev. Mr 28
World, The 82
Wright, Winnie 135

Yates, Edmund 19, 82, 190
Yeats, W.B. 153–4, 173–4
  Celtic Twilight, The 153, 173–5
Yellow Book, The 159

Zellar, Eduard
  History of Greek Philosophy 57
Zola, Émile 164